NATIONAL GRANGE

Family Cookbook
From Country Kitchens

A Collection of Family Tested Recipes from Rural America

© Favorite Recipes® Press/Nashville EMS MCMLXXIX
P.O. Box 77, Nashville, Tennessee 37202
Library of Congress Cataloging in Publication Data
Main Entry Under Title:

National Grange family cookbook from country kitchens.

    Includes Index.
    1. Cookery. I. Patrons of Husbandry. National
Grange. II. Title: Family Cookbook from Country Kitchens.
TX 715.N328 1979   641.5   79-22823
ISBN 0-87197-128-3

Dear Patrons and Friends:

Several years ago when we published the National Grange Bicentennial Year Cookbook, we thought that would be our one and only venture into the cookbook business. However, much to our delight, we discovered that lots of people are hungry for and appreciate recipes from "scratch." We received hundreds of wonderful letters about our first book and many asking if we would ever publish another one.

Fortunately, with over a quarter of a million women in the Grange we have a wealth of culinary talent. Most of our Grange women, born and raised in rural America, still believe country cooking is healthier and more economical. We are happy once again to share with you a selection of recipes from their personal files which encourages the use of American agricultural products. You will find that rarely will you have to make a special trip to the store-most of the ingredients you already have on your shelves or in your refrigerator.

In addition to the hundreds of family-tested recipes in each of the main sections, there are also recipes for men from men and recipes for young folks from our young Grange members. As a special treat there is a VIP section with interesting recipes from some of our friends in the nation's capitol. Finally, there is a section of recipes for diabetics which I'm sure many of you will find extremely helpful.

We are indeed grateful to our publishers, the fine folks at Favorite Recipes Press in Nashville, Tennessee, for their months of labor, counsel and encouragement. And, of course, to our Grange women who make all of this possible.

Happy eating.

Fraternally and sincerely,

Jenny Grobusky

Mrs. Jenny Grobusky

BOARD OF ADVISORS

Cookbook Committee

Coordinator
Mrs. Judy Taylor Massabny
Director of Information and Public Relations

Editorial Director
Mrs. Robert (Mary) Proctor
Wife, National Secretary

Consultants

Mrs. John (Dorothy) Scott
Wife, National Master

Mrs. Lorena D. Stigers

Mrs. George (Jenny) Grobusky
Director of Women's Activities

J. C. Stigers

Contents

Our sincere appreciation to all who submitted the hundreds of recipes for inclusion in the cookbook. We regret we were unable to incorporate all of the recipes due to similarity and lack of space.

Family Recipes
From Friends On Capitol Hill

The families of America's leaders living in Washington, D.C. have always been renowned for their ability to prepare food beautifully for any occasion, whether entertaining a world dignitary, dining with good friends, or enjoying a relaxed meal with family members. This renown carries with it a rich background of cooking skills that no truly good cook can do without.

Because many of our nation's regional cuisines are represented in Washington, D.C., it has become a showcase of America's finest family foods. Like all Americans, our national officials are proud of the cooking traditions they bring to Washington from the home states they represent. And, like all Grange members, these officials know that it is our great American agriculture that assures the quality and variety inherent in America's cooking.

This special category of recipes from our leaders on Capitol Hill emphasizes that family cooking in the United States is the best cooking of all!

PLAINS-SPECIAL CHEESE RING

1 lb. grated sharp cheese
1 c. finely chopped nuts
1 c. mayonnaise
1 sm. onion, finely grated

Pepper to taste
Dash of cayenne pepper
Strawberry preserves (opt).

Combine all ingredients except preserves; mix well. Place in lightly greased 5 or 6-cup ring mold. Refrigerate for several hours until firm or overnight. Invert on serving plate to serve. Fill center with strawberry preserves. Serve with plain crackers.

Mrs. Jimmy Carter
Wife of President of United States

CHOCOLATE UPSIDE-DOWN CAKE

1¼ c. sugar
1 c. flour
2 tsp. baking powder
½ tsp. salt
2 tbsp. butter, melted

2 sq. baking chocolate, melted
½ c. milk
1 tsp. vanilla extract
½ c. (firmly packed) brown sugar
1 tbsp. cocoa

Sift ¾ cup sugar and next 3 ingredients together into mixing bowl. Add butter and chocolate to dry ingredients; mix well. Add milk and vanilla; mix well. Place batter in 8-inch square pan. Combine ½ cup sugar with brown sugar and cocoa. Sprinkle over batter in baking pan. Pour ¾ cup boiling water over all. Bake at 350 degrees for 45 minutes. Invert on serving plate. Serve warm or cold.

Mrs. Walter F. Mondale
Wife of Vice President of United States

SHRIMP WITH HOT MEDITERRANEAN SAUCE

1 lb. shrimp
2 c. Bechamel sauce
Gruyere cheese, grated
2 tbsp. catsup

½ tsp. chili sauce or 2 or 3 drops of Tabasco sauce
Jack cheese, grated
Bread crumbs

Cook shrimp in small amount of boiling water until just pink. Cool with cold water. Peel and devein. Combine Bechamel sauce with ¼ cup Gruyere cheese, catsup and chili sauce; mix well. Reheat shrimp in small amount of boiling water; drain. Combine enough Gruyere cheese with Jack cheese to coat shrimp. Coat shrimp with sauce mixture. Sprinkle with cheese mixture. Sprinkle with bread crumbs. Place on baking sheet. Broil for 5 to 10 minutes. Serve hot. Yield: 4 servings.

Mrs. Cyrus R. Vance
Wife of Secretary of State

OLD-FASHIONED TURKEY DRESSING

1 loaf bread or 1 sm. package preseasoned
   bread crumbs
3 c. diced celery
½ c. celery leaves
½ c. butter or margarine

½ c. whole blanched almonds
½ tsp. salt
½ tsp. pepper
½ tsp. poultry seasoning
3 eggs, beaten

Toast bread slices; crush into crumbs. Brown celery and celery leaves in butter until lightly brown. Combine all dry ingredients. Add celery and celery leaves; mix well. Blend in eggs; mix well. Place in baking dish. Bake at 300 degrees until brown. Dressing may be stuffed into turkey and baked according to turkey recipe.

Mrs. Warren E. Burger
Wife of Chief Justice of United States Supreme Court

BOB'S FAVORITE GREEN BEANS

Fresh green beans, cut into bite-sized pieces

Milk
Salt and pepper to taste

Cook beans with enough water to cover until tender. Drain. Cover with milk. Season with salt and pepper. Heat until milk is scalded. Serve in soup bowls.

Mrs. Bob Bergland
Wife of Secretary of Agriculture

INDIAN FRY BREAD

3 c. flour
3 tbsp. baking powder

2 tbsp. salt
Lard for frying

Combine flour, baking powder and salt. Add enough warm water to make soft dough; mix well. Knead until dough is soft but not sticky. Tear off one small piece at a time. Stretch and pat dough until thin. Drop into frypan in sizzling hot lard. Brown on both sides. Serve hot.

Barry Goldwater
Senator from Arizona

VALENTINE SANDWICH COOKIES

1½ c. butter or margarine, softened
¾ c. sugar
3 c. flour
1 tsp. cloves
1 tsp. cinnamon

Strawberry jam
Confectioners' sugar
Vanilla extract
Milk
Red food coloring

Cream butter and sugar together. Add flour and spices; mix well. Chill for 1 hour. Roll out dough on floured board. Cut dough with heart-shaped cookie cutter. Place on baking sheet. Bake at 400 degrees for 6 to 8 minutes. Cool. Spread 1 dozen cookies with thin layer of strawberry jam. Top with remaining cookies. Combine enough confectioners' sugar, vanilla and milk to make a thin frosting. Tint with red food coloring. Frost top of cookie sandwiches. Super rich cookies! Yield: 12 cookies.

Mrs. William L. Armstrong
Wife of Senator from Colorado

CARAMEL-PECAN-OATMEAL MUFFINS

⅓ c. (firmly packed) brown sugar
2 tbsp. butter, softened
Pecan halves
1 c. sifted flour
¼ c. sugar
3 tsp. baking powder

½ tsp. salt
¼ c. shortening or butter
1 c. oats
1 egg, beaten
1 c. milk

Combine brown sugar and butter; cream until smooth. Pat mixture evenly into greased muffin cups. Arrange pecan halves in each. Sift next 4 ingredients together in a bowl. Cut in shortening. Blend in oats thoroughly. Stir in egg and milk until just blended. Fill muffin cups ⅔ full. Bake at 425 degrees for 20 minutes or until lightly browned. Remove from pan immediately.

Mrs. Gary Hart
Wife of Senator from Colorado

ITALIAN MEAT SAUCE

Olive oil
1 to 2 lb. sausage or ground pork
4 cloves of garlic, minced
1 sm. can tomato paste
4 to 5 29-oz. cans crushed tomatoes

Salt and pepper to taste
Oregano, bay leaves, basil, thyme and fresh
  parsley to taste
1 to 2 lb. ground meat

Pour enough olive oil in 6 to 8-quart saucepan to measure ¼ to ½-inch oil. Brown sausage. Remove sausage, reserving oil in saucepan. Add minced garlic. Saute but do not brown. Add tomato paste. Cook until almost black over medium heat, stirring constantly. Add crushed tomatoes; mix well. Bring just to a boil. Add seasonings; mix well. Simmer, covered, for 2 to 3 hours. Brown ground meat in separate frypan. Add sausage and ground meat to saucepan. Simmer for 1 hour longer.

Mrs. Lowell P. Weicker, Jr.
Wife of Senator from Connecticut

LAMB CURRY

2 tsp. oil
2 tbsp. curry powder
4 lb. boneless lean lamb, cut into 1½ in.
  cubes
1 sm. whole clove, crushed
1 tsp. salt
2 tbsp. flour

1 lg. onion, diced
1 sm. tart apple, sliced
Grated rind of 1 sm. orange
6 sm. sweet pickles, sliced
½ c. Idaho purple plum chutney
1½ c. tomatoes
2 c. lamb bone stock

Heat oil and curry powder in frypan. Brown lamb cubes in hot oil mixture. Mix crushed clove with salt. Add to lamb with remaining ingredients; mix well. Cook, covered, over low heat for about 2 hours or until lamb is tender, stirring occasionally. Add additional liquid if necessary. This dish improves with standing for flavors to blend. May be frozen.

Mrs. Frank Church
Wife of Senator from Idaho

CRAB QUICHE

1 c. shredded Swiss cheese
1 unbaked pie shell
1 7½-oz. can crab meat, drained and flaked
2 green onions with tops, sliced
3 eggs, beaten
1 c. light cream

½ tsp. salt
½ tsp. grated lemon rind
¼ tsp. dry mustard
Dash of mace
¼ c. sliced almonds

Sprinkle cheese evenly over bottom of pie shell. Top with crab meat. Sprinkle with onions. Combine eggs, cream, salt, lemon rind, mustard and mace. Pour over crab meat. Top with almonds. Bake at 325 degrees for 45 minutes. Yield: 6-8 servings.

Mrs. James A. McClure
Wife of Senator from Idaho

SUMMER SQUASH CASSEROLE

2 lb. yellow summer squash, sliced
¼ c. chopped onion
1 can cream of chicken soup
1 c. sour cream

1 c. shredded carrot
1 8-oz. package herb-seasoned stuffing mix
½ c. butter or margarine

Cook squash and onion in boiling salted water in saucepan for 5 minutes; drain. Combine soup and sour cream. Stir in shredded carrot. Fold in squash and onion. Combine stuffing mix and butter. Spread half the stuffing mixture in bottom of 12 × 7½ × 2-inch baking dish. Spoon in vegetable mixture. Sprinkle remaining stuffing over vegetables. Bake in 350-degree oven for 25 to 30 minutes or until heated through. Yield: 6-8 servings.

Birch Bayh
Senator from Indiana

CURRIED CHICKEN SALAD

1½ c. cooked rice
2 tbsp. salad oil
1 tbsp. vinegar
1 tsp. salt
¾ tsp. curry powder

2 c. cubed chicken
1 c. chopped celery
¼ c. chopped green pepper
10 oz. cooked peas
¾ c. mayonnaise

Combine rice, salad oil, vinegar, salt and curry powder. Chill overnight. Combine chicken, celery, green pepper, peas and mayonnaise. Combine with rice mixture. Chill for several hours. Serve on lettuce. Yield: 8 servings.

Nancy Landon Kassebaum
Senator from Kansas

NEW ORLEANS PRALINES

Sugar
¾ c. milk
Pinch of soda

1 tsp. vanilla extract
⅓ stick butter
2 c. pecans

Caramelize 1 heaping tablespoon sugar in small iron skillet, stirring until sugar turns tan-colored. Place 2 cups sugar and milk in saucepan. Bring to a boil; add soda. Bring mixture to a boil. Add liquid caramelized sugar. Cook for 7 minutes or to soft-ball stage. Add vanilla, butter and pecans. Remove from stove. Beat until mixture begins to harden around the edges. Drop from tablespoon onto waxed paper.

Mrs. J. Bennett Johnston
Wife of Senator from Louisiana

CRAB MEAT IMPERIAL

Mayonnaise
1 green pepper, diced
2 pimentos, diced
1 tbsp. English mustard
1 tsp. salt

½ tsp. white pepper
2 eggs, beaten
3 lb. crab meat
Paprika to taste

Combine 1 cup mayonnaise with next 6 ingredients. Stir in crab meat. Mix lightly so lumps are not broken. Divide mixture into 8 crab shells or ramekins. Top with thin coating of additional mayonnaise. Sprinkle with paprika. Bake in 350-degree oven for 15 minutes. Yield: 8 servings.

Mrs. Russell B. Long
Wife of Senator from Louisiana

GERMAN APPLE TORTE

2 c. flour
Salt
½ tsp. baking powder
2 sticks butter, softened
1 egg yolk
½ c. sugar

5 or 6 sweet apples, peeled and quartered
Lemon juice (opt.)
1 c. (firmly-packed) brown sugar
1 tsp. cinnamon
Confectioners' sugar

Sift 1 cup flour, dash of salt and baking powder together into bowl. Add 1 stick butter, egg yolk, and ¼ cup sugar. Stir until mixture forms firm dough. Chill for several hours or overnight. Grease and flour springform pan. Press dough into pan, easing to within ½ to 1 inch of rim. Prick with fork. Make about 4 knife slashes on top of each apple piece. Arrange in circular pattern on crust. Sprinkle apples with ¼ cup sugar. Sprinkling lemon juice over fruit will prevent discoloration. Mix 1 cup flour, brown sugar, 1 stick butter, ½ teaspoon salt and cinnamon. Crumble over filling. Bake at 375 degrees for 1 hour. Sprinkle with confectioners' sugar. Serve with whipped cream or ice cream, if desired. Other fruits may be substituted for apples.

Mrs. Rudy Boschwitz
Wife of Senator from Minnesota

CURRIED LAMB

2 tbsp. margarine
2 lg. onions, sliced
2 tbsp. flour
½ tsp. sugar
½ tsp. salt

2 tbsp. curry powder
1 tbsp. parsley
2 c. consomme
3 to 4 c. cooked lamb
1 sm. can mushrooms

Melt margarine in deep saucepan. Add onions. Cook slowly until golden. Stir in flour, sugar, salt, curry powder and parsley. Add consomme. Cook, stirring constantly, until thickened. Add lamb and mushrooms. Heat but do not bring to a boil. Cooked chicken, turkey or pork may be substituted for lamb. This is an excellent recipe for leftovers. Yield: 6 servings.

Thomas F. Eagleton
Senator from Missouri

CZECH LIVER-DUMPLING SOUP

½ lb. calf or chicken liver
1 sm. onion, chopped
½ clove of garlic (opt.)
1 egg, beaten
¾ c. cracker crumbs
1 tsp. parsley flakes

½ tsp. marjoram
½ tsp. salt
Dash of pepper
Flour
Chicken or beef broth

Grind liver, onion and garlic together. Add next 6 ingredients; mix well. Add flour, a small amount at a time, until mixture is thick enough to drop easily. Drop by teaspoon into hot broth. Simmer, covered, for 15 minutes.

Mrs. J. James Exon
Wife of Senator from Nebraska

SENATOR WILLIAMS' FAVORITE CHOCOLATE CAKE

2 c. flour
2 c. sugar
1 tsp. baking powder
1 c. cocoa
½ tsp. salt
2 tsp. soda
½ c. cooking oil

2 eggs, beaten
1 c. coffee, strong and black
1½ c. milk
2 tsp. vanilla extract
4 c. confectioners' sugar
¼ c. butter or margarine
½ c. peanut butter

Combine flour, sugar, baking powder, ¾ cup cocoa, salt and soda. Mix oil, eggs, coffee, 1 cup milk and 1 teaspoon vanilla in separate bowl. Combine mixtures; mix well. Pour into 3 greased 9-inch layer cake pans. Bake at 350 degrees for 25 to 30 minutes. Cool cake layers. Mix ¼ cup cocoa and confectioners' sugar. Cream half the cocoa mixture with butter until smooth. Blend in 1 teaspoon vanilla and ¼ cup milk; mix well. Add remaining milk. Beat to desired spreading consistency, adding additional milk, if necessary. Add peanut butter. Whip until mixture is smooth. Frost cooled cake.

Mrs. Harrison Williams
Wife of Senator from New Jersey

BEEF TACOS

12 corn tortillas
1 lb. ground beef
2 med. potatoes, diced
1 sm. onion, chopped

1 tomato, chopped
Shredded lettuce
2 c. grated sharp cheese
Taco sauce or salsa

Heat enough shortening in frypan to measure 1 inch shortening. Fry tortillas over medium heat until side is slightly crisp. Turn tortilla; fold in half. Fry until crisp. Fry ground beef and potatoes until thoroughly cooked. Place meat mixture in tortilla shells. Arrange on serving plate. Layer with chopped onion, fresh tomato, shredded lettuce and grated cheese. Serve with side dish of taco sauce. Yield: 6 servings.

Mrs. Pete V. Domenici
Wife of Senator from New Mexico

MARION'S RUSSIAN SALAD

½ jar mayonnaise
1 lg. carton sour cream
2 tbsp. minced onion
Juice of 1 lemon
1 tsp. horseradish
3 tbsp. red vinegar

Pepper to taste
2 fresh cauliflower, broken in flowerets
3 pkg. frozen corn niblets
3 pkg. frozen peas and carrots
3 pkg. frozen lima beans
4 to 6 cucumbers, diced

Combine mayonnaise and sour cream. Add onion, lemon juice, horseradish and red vinegar; mix well. Season with pepper. Reserve enough cauliflowerets for garnish. Marinate remaining cauliflowerets in sour cream mixture. Prepare frozen vegetables according to package directions. Cool. Combine marinated cauliflowerets, diced cucumbers and cooked vegetables; mix well. Garnish with reserved cauliflowerets and cucumber slices.

Mrs. Jacob Javits
Wife of Senator from New York

ANNIE GLENN'S BAKED FRUIT

1 lg. can peach halves
1 sm. can pineapple slices
1 lg. can pear halves
Several maraschino cherries with stems

⅓ c. butter
¾ c. (firmly packed) light brown sugar
2 to 4 tsp. curry powder

Drain fruit well. Dry on paper towels. Arrange in 1½-quart casserole. Melt butter. Add brown sugar and curry powder. Spoon over fruit. Bake, uncovered, at 350 degrees for 1 hour. Yield: 4 servings.

Mrs. John Glenn
Wife of Senator from Ohio

MAGGIE CAKE

5 eggs, separated
1 c. butter
2½ c. sugar
1 c. buttermilk
5 tsp. coffee
3 c. flour

1 tsp. baking powder
1 tsp. soda
4 tsp. cocoa
1 tsp. salt
2 tsp. vanilla extract

Beat egg yolks in large mixer bowl. Add remaining ingredients except egg whites; mix well. Fold in stiffly beaten egg whites. Pour into 5 greased and floured layer cake pans. Bake at 350 degrees for 15 to 20 minutes. Cool.

Icing

½ c. butter
1 egg
3 tsp. coffee
2 tsp. cocoa
Dash of salt

1 tsp. vanilla extract
1 lb. confectioners' sugar
Cream (opt.)
Oklahoma pecans

Place first 6 ingredients in mixer bowl. Add sugar gradually until of spreading consistency. Add small amount of cream, if necessary. Spread between layers and on top of cake. Decorate with pecans.

Mrs. David. L. Boren
Wife of Senator from Oklahoma

CURRIED CHICKEN SALAD

1 c. Curry Paste
1 c. mayonnaise
Juice of 3 oranges
Juice of 1 lemon
1 lg. apple, peeled and chopped
⅕ c. currants

⅕ c. raisins
⅕ c. sultanas
1 sm. package slivered almonds
½ c. shredded nonsweetened coconut (opt).
4 c. cooked chopped chicken breasts

Combine first 4 ingredients in large bowl. Blend well. Add remaining ingredients; mix well. Chill before serving.

Curry Paste

1 c. finely chopped onions
Minced parsley to taste

Curry powder to taste
1 tbsp. tomato puree

Saute onions and parsley until tender in top of double boiler. Add curry powder. Cook for 15 minutes, stirring to prevent burning. Place over hot water. Add tomato puree. Simmer gently for 5 minutes. Blend to a smooth paste.

Mrs. H. John Heinz III
Wife of Senator from Pennsylvania

FRUIT CRUNCH

6 c. peeled and diced apples, peaches and
  cherries
1 c. flour
1¼ c. sugar
1 tsp. baking powder

½ tsp. salt
1 egg, beaten
½ c. butter, melted
Cinnamon and nutmeg to taste

Place fruit in greased 9-inch square baking dish. Combine dry ingredients; mix well. Add egg; mix well. Sprinkle mixture over fruit. Pour melted butter over all. Sprinkle with cinnamon and nutmeg. Bake at 350 degrees for 50 to 60 minutes or until golden brown. Serve warm or at room temperature with sour cream or ice cream. Yield: 8 servings.

Mrs. Ernest F. Hollings
Wife of Senator from South Carolina

SAUSAGE CASSEROLE

1 lb. sausage
2 c. sliced onions
2 tbsp. margarine
¼ c. flour
2 c. beef bouillon

½ tsp. salt
¼ tsp. oregano
¼ tsp. thyme
1 c. partially cooked rice
Mushrooms to taste

Cook sausage, stirring constantly, until lightly brown. Drain grease. Add onions; mix well. Melt margarine in separate frypan. Add flour; mix well. Add bouillon. Cook, stirring constantly until smooth and thick. Season with salt and spices. Add sauce to sausage mixture; mix well. Place rice in casserole. Pour sausage mixture over rice. Sprinkle with mushrooms. Bake at 350 degrees for 30 minutes. Yield: 8 servings.

Mrs. Strom Thurmond
Wife of Senator from South Carolina

DAKOTA PHEASANT

½ c. butter
1 pheasant, cut up
Flour

Salt and pepper to taste
1 c. cream
½ c. sour cream

Melt butter in frypan. Roll pheasant pieces in flour, salt and pepper. Fry until golden brown. Remove pieces from pan; place in casserole. Add cream and sour cream to drippings; heat. Pour over pheasant in casserole; cover. Bake at 350 degrees for 1 hour and 30 minutes. Yield: 4 servings.

Mrs. Antone Pressler
Mother of Senator from South Dakota

CARROT-PINEAPPLE CAKE

1 c. oil
1½ c. sugar
4 eggs, beaten
2 c. grated carrots
1 c. well drained crushed pineapple
1 c. chopped walnuts
2 c. sifted flour

1½ tsp. soda
2 tsp. baking powder
1½ tsp. salt
½ lb. confectioners' sugar
¼ c. butter or margarine, softened
½ tsp. vanilla extract
1 3-oz. package cream cheese, softened

Combine oil and sugar in mixing bowl. Add eggs; mix well. Add carrots, pineapple and walnuts. Sift dry ingredients together. Add to carrot mixture; mix well. Pour into greased and floured 9 × 13 inch baking pan. Bake at 350 degrees for 35 to 40 minutes. Cool cake. Combine confectioners' sugar, butter, vanilla and cream cheese. Beat well. Spread on cooled cake.

Mrs. Jake Garn
Wife of Senator from Utah

HOT CRAB CANAPE PIE

1 lb. lump back fin crab meat
1 tbsp. horseradish
½ bottle of capers, drained
1½ tsp. Accent

1 tsp. grated lemon rind
Dash of Tabasco sauce
2 c. mayonnaise
¾ c. grated sharp cheese

Combine all ingredients except cheese. Spread in 10-inch Pyrex pie plate. Cover top with cheese. Bake in 350-degree oven for 20 to 25 minutes or until mixture bubbles. Place under broiler to lightly brown cheese. Serve with toast rounds or crackers. Yield: 12 servings.

Mrs. Warren G. Magnuson
Wife of Senator from Washington

SHRIMP CURRY

1¼ c. minced onions
¾ c. butter
1 c. less 1 tbsp. flour
8 tsp. curry powder
3¼ tsp. salt
½ tsp. ginger
1¼ tsp. sugar

3¼ c. chicken broth
5 c. milk
Garlic to taste
Worcestershire sauce to taste
Tabasco sauce to taste
5 lb. small cooked shrimp

Saute onions in butter in Dutch oven. Blend in flour. Remove from heat. Add curry powder, salt, ginger and sugar. Return to heat. Add broth and milk slowly; mix well. Season to taste with garlic, Worcestershire sauce and Tabasco sauce. Add shrimp; heat thoroughly. Serve over rice with desired condiments, such as chopped peanuts, pineapple chunks, chutney, avocado slices, grated fresh coconut, bacon bits and chopped green onions. Yield: 10 servings.

Mrs. Beryl Anthony, Jr.
Wife of U. S. Representative from Arkansas

MAMA NELL'S FAVORITE POUND CAKE

3 c. cake flour
3 c. sugar
½ c. Crisco
2 sticks margarine, softened

5 eggs, beaten
½ c. 7-Up or Mountain Dew
2 tbsp. vanilla extract

Combine all ingredients; mix well. Pour into greased bundt pan. Bake at 300 degrees for 1 hour and 30 minutes or until cake tests done. Yield: 10-12 servings.

Mrs. Dawson Mathis
Wife of U. S. Representative from Georgia

BARBECUE TERIYAKI CHICKEN

1 in. fresh gingerroot, crushed
½ c. soy sauce
½ c. sugar

1 tbsp. Sherry
¼ c. catsup
2 lb. chicken wings or thighs

Mix all ingredients except chicken wings in saucepan. Bring to boiling point. Add chicken wings. Simmer for approximately 25 to 30 minutes. Remove chicken wings. Broil until brown, basting with remaining sauce. Yield: 3-4 servings.

Mrs. Daniel K. Akaka
Wife of U. S. Representative from Hawaii

HIGH SCHOOL BOYS CHILI

¼ lb. bacon
1 lg. green pepper, chopped
1 med. onion, chopped
1 lb. hamburger
1 No. 2 can tomatoes

1 tsp. sugar (opt.)
Salt and pepper to taste
Chili powder to taste (opt.)
1 can red kidney beans

Fry bacon in skillet; remove. Drain excess grease from skillet, reserving small amount. Add green pepper and onion to skillet. Saute until nearly done. Add hamburger; brown lightly. Add tomatoes, sugar, bacon, salt, pepper and chili powder; cover. Simmer for 10 minutes. Add kidney beans. Simmer until heated through. Pour mixture over toasted half slices of white bread or serve over cooked rice. Yield: 6 servings.

Mrs. Charles Whitley
Wife of U. S. Representative from North Carolina

Appetizers, Soups and Beverages

Appetizers, soups and beverages are the foods that receive too little attention in family menu planning. What an oversight! These are the very foods that add interest to cooking and zest to mealtime.

Appetizers serve many purposes! Before dinner, they not only preview the taste treats to come, but also take the hungry edge off diners' appetites so they can relax, eat slowly, and truly enjoy the meal. Appetizers are also a thrifty way to prepare nourishing snacks for family and friends.

Soups are equally as versatile. They can be a light, clear and refreshing first-course appetizer, or a piping-hot main dish, savory and rich with meat, vegetables, and pasta or potatoes. And, for nutritious and thrifty meal planning, soups just cannot be beat! For generations, many cooks have kept the "stock pot" bubbling on the back of the stove, always adding bits of meat or vegetables. Then, at any time, there was a delicious meal, ready to be served—even to company!

There are delicious ways galore to supplement the use of milk, tea and coffee as daily beverages. Fresh fruit juices are an especially delicious touch for many menus, and a lively addition to iced and hot tea. And, don't overlook milk or fruit punches, either—families just can't resist them!

Appetizers, soups and beverages all spell happiness for the menu planner who wants to please her family. And, success is doubly assured when the following fresh-food recipes from Grange are the feature.

CHEESE STRAWS

¼ c. butter
¼ tsp. Tabasco sauce
¾ c. shredded sharp Cheddar cheese
⅔ c. flour

Cream butter with Tabasco sauce. Add cheese and flour; mix thoroughly. Chill for 1 hour. Place on lightly-floured surface. Roll into 6 × 15-inch rectangle, ⅛-inch thick. Cut into ¾ × 6-inch strips. Place on ungreased baking sheet. Bake at 350 degrees for 10 minutes or until lightly browned. Serve warm. Yield: 20 servings.

Cheryle Lundgren
Potomac Grange, No. 1
Arlington, Virginia

CHEESE SPREAD

1 8-oz. package cream cheese
1 can pimentos, chopped
2 eggs, beaten
½ tsp. each salt and dry mustard
2 tbsp. flour
3 tbsp. sugar
¾ c. milk
¼ c. vinegar

Combine first 7 ingredients in top of double boiler. Cook over gently boiling water. Stir until smooth and thick. Stir in vinegar very slowly to prevent curdling. Cover. Cool. Store in refrigerator. Yield: 2 pints.

Mildred Shaw,
Buffalo Grange, No. 1523
Washington County, Pennsylvania

CHEESE BALL SUPREME

3 8-oz. packages cream cheese, softened
4 oz. sharp Cheddar cheese, softened
1 sm. bunch green onions, chopped fine
1 5-oz. jar dried beef, chopped fine
Chopped nuts

Blend cheeses until smooth. Add onions and beef, mix well. Chill until firm. Shape into balls or log. Roll in nuts or additional finely chopped dried beef.

Chill until firm. Serve at room temperature. Yield: 60 servings.

Mrs. Beverly Stewart
Armstrong Co., Rural Valley Grange, No. 1750
Dayton, Pennsylvania

CHEESE FINGERS

1 recipe unbaked pie pastry
Grated cheese
Salt to taste
Pinch of cayenne pepper

Cut pie pastry into ½ × 2-inch strips. Combine cheese, salt and cayenne. Sprinkle over strips. Fold lengthwise; pinch edges together. Sprinkle with additional cheese. Bake in 450-degree oven until golden brown. Serve hot.

From a Grange Friend

HOT CHEESE-NUT BALLS

2 tsp. flour
⅛ tsp. cayenne pepper
½ tsp. salt
1 c. grated American cheese
1 egg white, slightly beaten
½ c. finely chopped nuts

Mix flour, cayenne pepper, salt and cheese. Fold in egg white until well blended. Form mixture into small balls. Roll in chopped nuts. Fry in 375-degree deep fat until golden brown. Yield: 15 servings.

From a Grange Friend

MEXICAN CHEESE DIP

8 oz. Velveeta cheese
8 oz. Cheddar cheese
1 1-lb. can stewed tomatoes, drained and chopped
1 3-oz. can El Paso green chiles, drained and chopped

Melt cheeses in 2-quart saucepan, stirring constantly. Add tomatoes and chiles; blend well. Serve warm with tortilla chips. May be served in fondue pot. Yield: 2 quarts.

Mary Ellen Wiley
Potomac Grange, No. 1
Arlington, Virginia

ARABIC MEAT PIES (SFEEHA)

¾ c. chopped pine nuts
1 med. onion, chopped
1½ lb. lean ground beef
Juice of 1 lemon
Salt and pepper to taste
Allspice to taste
1 tbsp. (heaping) yogurt
2 loaves thick-sliced bread
½ lb. sweet butter, clarified

Combine pine nuts, onion and ground beef in frypan. Fry until ground beef is just done. Cool slightly. Add lemon juice, salt, pepper and enough allspice to give piquant flavor. Stir in enough yogurt to bind mixture. Cut bread into rounds with biscuit cutter. Butter one side with clarified butter. Place buttered side up, on greased cookie sheet. Spread meat mixture on bread rounds; press lightly into bread. Bake at 350 degrees for 15 minutes or until brown. May be baked until lightly brown, then frozen. Yield: 75 servings.

Teena Mayers, Grange Friend
Arlington, Virginia

AVOCADO HALF-SHELLS WITH STEAK TARTARE

1 lb. twice-ground sirloin or round of beef
¼ c. minced onion
2 tbsp. chopped parsley
¾ tsp. salt
2 lg. California avocados
Lemon juice
4 egg yolks (opt.)
Capers
Worcestershire sauce, Tabasco sauce, cracked pepper, lemon wedges, shredded dill pickle

Mix beef, onion, parsley and salt together in mixing bowl. Halve avocados lengthwise, twisting gently to separate halves. Whack a sharp knife directly into seeds; twist to lift out. Brush half-shells with lemon juice. Fill with beef mixture. Make indentation in centers; add egg yolks. Sprinkle with capers. Serve, or garnish with remaining ingredients.

Photograph for this recipe on page 21.

CHINESE SPRING ROLLS

1 egg
2½ c. flour
Oil for deep frying

Beat egg in mixer bowl. Add flour; mix thoroughly with a fork. Add enough water gradually to form soft, smooth, elastic dough. Place dough on well-floured board. Cover; let rest for 20 minutes. Cut in half for easier handling. Roll out into thin sheets. Cut into 2½-inch squares. Place 1 tablespoon filling in center of each square, spreading lengthwise. Turn opposite ends in and roll up to enclose filling. Seal edges with water. Heat oil in frypan to 375 degrees. Fry rolls until golden brown and crisp. Drain on paper towel. Serve with Chinese mustard. Yield: 4-6 servings.

Spring Roll Filling
½ lb. boneless pork
4 tbsp. vegetable oil
½ tsp. salt
¼ c. green onions, sliced thin
½ c. mushrooms, chopped
½ c. water chestnuts, diced
¼ c. bean sprouts
1 tbsp. cornstarch
2 tbsp. dry Sherry
1 tbsp. soy sauce

Cut pork into ½ × ⅛-inch slices. Heat oil in large skillet. Saute pork for 5 to 10 minutes over low heat until browned. Sprinkle with salt. Remove to pork side dish. Add onions, mushrooms, water chestnuts and bean sprouts to same skillet. Saute 5 minutes over medium heat, stirring frequently. Sprinkle with cornstarch and Sherry. Mix in soy sauce and pork. Mix all ingredients thoroughly. Cool.

From a Grange Friend

CHICKEN LIVER APPETIZERS

6 chicken livers
2 tbsp. prepared mustard
2 tbsp. finely chopped olives
6 slices bacon, cut in halves
¼ c. fine bread crumbs

Rinse chicken livers; cut in half. Combine mustard and olives. Spread on chicken livers to coat. Wrap in bacon; secure with toothpicks. Roll in bread crumbs. Bake in 425-degree oven for 10 to 15 minutes. Yield: 12 appetizers.

From a Grange Friend

DEVILED OYSTERS

Oysters
Juice of 1 lemon
2 tbsp. melted butter
Salt to taste
Pinch of cayenne pepper
Fine cracker or bread crumbs

Pat oysters dry. Mix next 4 ingredients. Dip oysters in butter mixture. Coat in cracker crumbs. Broil until brown. Serve hot.

From a Grange Friend

SWEET AND SOUR CHICKEN WINGS

20 chicken wings
Salt
Cornstarch
Eggs, beaten
½ c. catsup
¾ c. vinegar
2 tbsp. soy sauce
1½ c. sugar
2 tsp. Accent (opt.)

Disjoint chicken wings. Cook in a small amount of water until tender. Reserve 1 cup broth; discard tips. Soak remaining chicken wings in salted water for 3 hours. Drain. Dip in cornstarch, then in eggs. Brown in hot oil. Combine remaining ingredients with reserved chicken broth and a dash of salt. Cook, stirring occasionally, until sugar dissolves. Place chicken wings in baking dish. Pour sauce over chicken wings. Bake in 350-degree oven for 1 hour. Can be frozen. Yield: 40 servings.

Winifred Clark
Quartz Hill Grange, No. 697
Los Angeles, California

ASPARAGUS CANAPES

12 thin slices bread, crusts removed
Mustard
6 thin slices boiled ham, cut in half
12 asparagus tips, cooked
Mayonnaise

Spread bread with mustard. Place ham on bread; trim to fit. Dip asparagus in mayonnaise. Place on edge of bread; roll as for jelly roll. Secure with toothpick. Place on broiler rack. Toast under preheated broiler, turning to brown. Yield: 12 servings.

From a Grange Friend

STUFFED TOMATOES

30 to 36 cherry tomatoes
Salt to taste
2 3-oz. packages cream cheese, softened
½ c. mayonnaise
½ c. chopped salad olives
½ c. chopped pecans
Salad greens

Cut top from tomatoes; remove seeds carefully. Sprinkle tomatoes with salt. Turn upside down to drain. Combine cream cheese and mayonnaise with electric mixer. Add olives and pecans; stir. Fill tomatoes with cheese mixture. Arrange on salad greens. Chill thoroughly before serving. Yield: 30-36 servings.

Roberta H. Steele
Kaylor Grange, No. 1396,
Kittanning, Pennsylvania

PICKLED EGGS

12 hard-boiled eggs
1 can beets, sliced
⅓ c. sugar
¼ c. pickling spices
1 tbsp. salt
⅔ c. vinegar
Onion slices

Bring eggs to a boil. Boil 12 to 15 minutes. Drain. Shake eggs slightly to crack shells. Let stand in cold water until cool. Peel. Mix juice from beets with next 4 ingredients. Add ½ to ¾ cup water. Boil 5 minutes. Place eggs in large bowl. Pour hot mixture over eggs. Add beets and onions. More vinegar and water may be added to cover mixture. Let stand a few hours before serving. Yield: 6 servings.

Essie J. Bertacchi
Quartz Hill Grange, No. 697
Lancaster, California

PUFFS

½ c. milk
¼ c. butter
½ c. sifted all-purpose flour
⅛ tsp. salt
2 eggs, beaten

Place milk and butter in saucepan. Bring to a boil. Add flour and salt. Stir batter until it leaves the side of pan and forms a ball. Remove from heat. Add eggs, one at a time, beating thoroughly after each addition. Place spoonfuls of batter on greased cookie sheet, allowing 2 inches between puffs. Bake at 400 degrees for 30 minutes. Reduce temperature to 350 degrees; bake 5 minutes longer. Puffs are done when tapped puff does not fall. Cool. Cut gash in side of puffs. Fill with favorite filling. Blend crab, chicken, caviar or minced ham with softened cream cheese or mix sandwich spread with 2 drops of Worcestershire sauce. May be frozen unfilled. Yield: 35 puffs.

Mary Richmond
Kahlotus Grange, No. 939
Pasco, Washington

SMOKED WALNUTS

1 tsp. liquid smoke
2 c. walnut halves
2 tsp. oil
Salt to taste

Mix liquid smoke and 4 teaspoons water. Add walnuts. Toss to coat. Spread in shallow pan. Cover; let stand overnight. Add oil to walnuts; toss to coat. Roast at 300 degrees for 25 minutes. Add salt. Store in tight container. May be frozen.

Emma Michalk
Tulare Co., Farmersville Grange, No. 637
Visalia, California

FISH CHOWDER

2 lb. haddock or cod
Salt
1½ in. cube salt pork, diced
1 med. onion, minced
4 c. diced potatoes
1 qt. milk, scalded
1 c. light cream, scalded
⅛ tsp. pepper
6 crackers, split
2 tbsp. butter

Cover haddock with salted cold water. Bring to a boil slowly. Simmer, covered, for 5 minutes. Drain, reserving stock. Remove skin and bones from haddock. Fry salt pork in large kettle; drain cracklings on absorbent paper. Saute onion in pork drippings. Add potatoes and 2 cups boiling water. Boil for 5 minutes. Add fish and stock. Bring to a boil. Simmer 15 minutes. Add milk, cream, 1 tablespoon salt and pepper. Heat thoroughly. Add crackers and butter. Garnish with cracklings. Serve at once. Yield: 6 servings.

From a Grange Friend

MANHATTAN CLAM CHOWDER

2 white onions, minced
½ clove of garlic, minced
¼ c. chopped celery
2 tbsp. minced green pepper
2 tbsp. butter
2 lg. potatoes, diced
2 tsp. salt
1 pt. fresh clams, minced
1½ c. tomato juice
Dash each of sage and cayenne pepper
¼ tsp. thyme

Saute onions, garlic, celery and green pepper in butter in large saucepan for 4 minutes. Add potatoes, 2½ cups boiling water and salt. Boil until potatoes are soft. Bring fresh clams and clam liquor to boiling point. Add tomato juice and seasonings. Blend clam mixture with potato mixture. Bring to a boil. Yield: 4 servings.

From a Grange Friend

NEW ENGLAND CLAM CHOWDER

½ lb. salt pork, chopped
3 sm. onions, minced
3 c. diced potatoes
⅛ tsp. pepper
1 qt. fresh clams, minced
3 c. milk, scalded

Place salt pork and onions in large saucepan. Saute until onions are golden brown. Add 3 cups boiling water, potatoes and pepper. Boil for 15 minutes or until potatoes are soft. Bring fresh clams and clam liquor to boiling point. Add millk. Combine clams with potato mixture. Bring to boiling point. Yield: 6 servings.

From a Grange Friend

TOMATO CORN CHOWDER

6 slices bacon, diced
¼ c. chopped onion
2 c. cubed potatoes
1½ tsp. salt
⅛ tsp. pepper
12-oz. can whole kernel corn, drained
2 c. tomato juice
¼ c. flour
½ c. milk

Place bacon in large saucepan; partially cook. Add onion. Cook until bacon is crisp. Drain off all but 2 tablespoons drippings. Add potatoes, 1 cup water, salt and pepper. Simmer, covered, 20 minutes or

until potatoes are tender. Stir in corn and tomato juice. Combine flour and milk; stir into soup. Bring to a boil. Cook, stirring constantly, until mixture thickens. Garnish with chopped parsley. Yield: 6 servings.

Kholetts Downard, C.W.A.
Lenawee Co., Pomona Grange, No. 15
Adrian, Michigan

MANHATTAN TUNA CHOWDER

2 bacon slices, diced
1 lg. onion, sliced
2 c. cubed, pared potatoes
1 c. diced, pared carrots
½ c. diced celery
2 1-lb. cans tomatoes
1½ tsp. salt
1 tsp. thyme
¼ tsp. pepper
2 7-oz. cans tuna
Chopped parsley

Fry bacon until crisp in 3-quart saucepan. Add onion. Cook until tender but not brown. Add potatoes, carrots, celery, tomatoes, 2 cups water, salt, thyme and pepper. Simmer, uncovered, 30 minutes. Add tuna; simmer 5 minutes longer. Sprinkle with chopped parsley. Yield: 6 servings.

Photograph of this recipe on page 24.

WHITE BEAN SOUP

1 lb. navy beans
½ c. chopped onions
½ c. chopped celery
1 hambone
Salt and pepper to taste

Wash beans. Cover with water. Soak overnight. Add onions, celery, hambone and seasonings. Simmer 3 to 4 hours, stirring often. Keep covered with water. Yield: 10-12 servings.

Julia Roberts
Washington Grange, No. 521
South Charleston, West Virginia

GREEN SPLIT PEA SOUP

1 c. dried peas
1 quarter onion, minced
1 tsp. salt
¼ tsp. white pepper (opt.)
1 tsp. sugar
⅛ tsp. celery salt
⅛ tsp. paprika
2 c. milk
2 tbsp. butter or other shortening
1 tbsp. flour

Soak peas overnight in 4 cups water. Cook slowly in same water in which they were soaked until peas are soft and mixture makes about 2½ cups. Add onion. Add next 6 ingredients. Blend butter and flour to a paste. Add to soup mixture. Cook, stirring constantly, until soup is smooth and as thick as cream. Yield: 6 servings.

Hattie Hammer
Washington Grange, No. 521
St. Albans, West Virginia

MINESTRONE

2 c. dried beans
1 tbsp. salt
4 peppercorns
1 c. chopped celery with leaves
1 c. finely chopped onion
1 garlic clove, minced
½ c. olive oil
2½ c. canned tomatoes
¼ c. chopped parsley
2 c. shredded cabbage
1 zucchini, thinly sliced
2 c. macaroni
Grated Parmesan cheese

Soak beans in 10 cups water overnight. Bring to a boil in same water; reduce heat. Add salt and peppercorns; cover. Simmer for 1 hour. Saute celery, onion and garlic in olive oil for 10 minutes or until onion is lightly browned. Add to beans. Add tomatoes and parsley. Bring to a boil. Reduce heat; cover. Simmer for 1 hour. Add cabbage, zucchini and macaroni. Simmer, uncovered, for 15 minutes, stirring occasionally. Serve with grated Parmesan cheese.

Julia Chavez
Inland Grange, No. 780
Elk, Washington

POOR MAN'S POTATO SOUP

2 c. diced potatoes
2 tbsp. butter
½ c. flour
Milk
1 tsp. salt

Cook potatoes and butter in 3 pints water until soft. Mix flour with small amount of milk to form crumbly mixture. Add to potatoes; stir well. Add 3 cups milk and salt. Simmer, stirring occasionally, until thick. Add additional seasonings, if desired. Yield: 4 servings.

Helen F. Hipp
Metichewan Grange, No. 190
New Milford, Connecticut

SPINACH SOUP

1 chicken, cut up
Salt to taste
1 tsp. Sherry
1½ c. chopped spinach
2 green onions, sliced finely
2 tsp. sesame oil (opt.)

Bring 2 quarts water to a boil in 3-quart saucepan. Add chicken pieces. Bring to a boil; reduce temperature. Simmer for 1 hour and 30 minutes to 2 hours or until tender. Cool. Skim off fat. Remove bones from chicken; shred meat. Bring chicken stock to a boil. Season with salt. Reduce temperature. Add Sherry, spinach, green onions and chicken. Simmer gently for 5 minutes. Add sesame oil just before serving. Yield: 6 servings.

Bill and Mary Lee Steel
Potoma Grange, No. 1
Arlington, Virginia

RANCH-STYLE POTATO SOUP

3 med. potatoes, peeled and quartered
1 sm. onion, cut up
2 eggs
2 c. milk
Celery salt to taste

Cover potatoes and onion with water. Cook until tender. Mash coarsely in remaining water. Break eggs into simmering potatoes; stir in quickly. Add milk. Simmer, stirring frequently, until slightly thickened. Add celery salt. Yield: 2-4 servings.

Harriet Guthrie
Wife of Master of Colorado State Grange
Mountain View Grange, No. 411
Calhan, Colorado

BEEF-VEGETABLE SOUP

2 lb. short ribs
2 tbsp. salt
Pepper to taste
Worcestershire sauce to taste
1 qt. tomato juice
½ c. lima beans
1 c. cut green beans
½ c. corn
2 potatoes, diced
1 onion, chopped
2 carrots, sliced
½ c. peas
⅛ head cabbage, chopped
1 stalk celery, sliced
½ bell pepper, chopped
1 bouillon cube, (opt.)

Cover short ribs with water in heavy 6 to 8-quart stockpot. Add seasonings. Bring to a boil; reduce heat. Simmer, covered, for 1 hour and 30 minutes or until beef is tender. Cool to remove grease. Strain juices; return juice to saucepan. Remove meat from bones; add meat to saucepan. Add remaining ingredients. Bring to a boil; reduce heat. Simmer, covered, for 1 hour or until vegetables are tender. Season to taste. Yield: 12-15 servings.

From a Grange Friend

VEGETABLE SOUP WITH MEAT

¾ c. dried navy beans
1 soupbone
1 onion, diced
1 c. macaroni or noodles
3 med. carrots, diced
1 qt. tomatoes
½ c. diced celery

1½ c. shredded cabbage
Salt and pepper to taste

Place beans and soupbone in large saucepan. Add water to cover. Cook until beans are just tender. Add remaining ingredients. Cook for 20 minutes longer. Add more water if needed.

Arlene Pharis,
Tamarack Grange, No. 1388
Renovo, Pennsylvania

ZUCCHINI SOUP

2 tbsp. margarine
1 med. onion, chopped
2 cans chicken broth
5 sm. zucchini
½ tsp. salt
¼ tsp. pepper
½ to 1 tsp. curry powder

Melt margarine in 4-quart saucepan. Saute onion until wilted. Add chicken broth, zucchini, salt and pepper. Cook until tender. Puree in blender until smooth. Strain if necessary. Stir in curry powder. Serve hot or cold. Yield: 6 servings.

Mrs. Catherine S. Pulling, Master
Skaneateles Grange, No. 458
Skaneateles, New York

TURKEY-RICE SOUP

¾ c. rice
2 qt. turkey broth
1 c. finely chopped carrots
1 c. cooked chopped turkey
Salt and pepper to taste

Place rice and carrots in turkey broth. Cook for 15 to 20 minutes. Add turkey. Season to taste. Heat thoroughly. Yield: 6-8 servings.

Mrs. James M. Aurand
Fort Granville Grange, No. 1902
Lewistown, Pennsylvania

CRANBERRY PUNCH

1 3-oz. package cherry-flavored gelatin
1 6-oz. can frozen lemonade
1 6-oz. can frozen orange-pineapple juice
1 1-qt. bottle of cranberry cocktail drink
1 12-oz. bottle of lemon soda, chilled

Dissolve gelatin in 1 cup boiling water. Add lemonade, orange-pineapple juice, cranberry drink, and 3 cups cold water. Pour mixture into large punch bowl over a molded ice ring or ice cubes. Pour lemon soda in slowly. Yield: 25 servings.

Naomi Lauchnor
Washington Grange, No. 1763
Slatington, Pennsylvania

EMMA'S PUNCH

1-oz. citric acid crystals
2 lb. sugar
Grated rind and juice of 2 oranges
Juice of 4 lemons
1 pt. grape juice

Dissolve citric acid crystals in ¼ cup warm water. Combine with remaining ingredients. Add 1 gallon water; stir. Let stand for several hours. Serve over ice. Yield: 25 servings.

Mrs. Emma E. Foss
Mt. Cutler Grange, No. 152
East Hiram, Maine

FRUIT PUNCH FOR A CROWD

12 lb. sugar
10 1-pt. bottles of ReaLemon, chilled
4 1-qt. cans orange juice, chilled
4 lg. cans pineapple juice, chilled
10 qt. ginger ale, chilled

Boil sugar and 16 quarts water for 5 to 10 minutes. Cool. Add chilled juices; mix well. Add ginger ale and ice cubes just before serving. Yield: 200 servings.

Caroline Cutts
West River Grange, No. 511
Townshend, Vermont

HAY-TIME SWITCHEL

2 c. (firmly packed) light brown sugar
2 c. apple cider vinegar
1 c. light molasses
2 tbsp. ground ginger

Combine all ingredients with 2 quarts water in large container. Stir well. Serve over ice. Yield: 12 servings.

Mrs. Emma E. Foss
Mt. Cutler Grange, No. 152
East Hiram, Maine

JOANN'S MILK PUNCH

½ gal. milk
½ gal. sherbet, softened
2 qt. ginger ale or club soda, chilled

Combine milk and sherbet in large punch bowl. Stir until sherbet begins to melt. Add ginger ale just before serving. Any flavor sherbet may be used. Yield: 48 servings.

Mrs. David Goodlaxson
Rising Sun Grange, No. 718
Waupun, Wisconsin

LUSCIOUS ALOHA PUNCH

1 No. 2 can pineapple juice
1 12-oz. can frozen orange juice
1 12-oz. can frozen lemonade
3 bananas, mashed
2 c. sugar
2 qt. lemon-lime beverage
2 qt. 7-Up
Orange or lime slices

Combine first 5 ingredients in freezer container; mix thoroughly. Freeze until firm. Let stand at room temperature a few minutes before serving. Stir to a slush consistency. Add beverage and 7-Up; mix well. Garnish with fruit slices. Yield: 25 servings.

Mrs. Lela Patterson
Lake Grange
Uniontown, Ohio

RHUBARB PUNCH

1 qt. rhubarb
3 c. sugar
Juice of 6 lemons
1 c. pineapple juice
1 qt. ginger ale, chilled

Cover rhubarb with water in a saucepan. Cook until soft. Strain rhubarb, reserving juice. Add water to rhubarb juice to measure 3 quarts. Combine sugar with 2 cups water. Boil for 10 minutes. Add lemon juice, pineapple juice and rhubarb juice. Cool. Add ginger ale just before serving. Yield: 24 servings.

Dorothy O. Reichart
Gideon Grange, No. 2010
Hanover, Pennsylvania

Salads

Garden-fresh produce served at its very best usually comes to the table as a tantalizing salad. And, think of the variety that salads can add to family meals! Serve a favorite main dish over and over again, and all you'll need for a change of pace each time is a different salad. It will seem like an entirely different meal!

More and more families are discovering the nutritious and penny-wise place that salads have earned in the menu plan. Plus, the bounteous variety of colorful vegetables and fruits available to today's homemaker has made salads a delight to prepare and serve. Take advantage of color, texture and shape as well as flavor when creating a salad, and you'll have a success every time!

But, don't overlook the salad dressing! Homemade dressings are always the tastiest, especially those based on mayonnaise, vinegar and oil, and sour cream. Take care that the dressing serves to enhance the taste and appearance of the salad, and that it doesn't overpower it.

Grange homemakers know what it means to want the best for one's family, especially at mealtime. And that is what the following pages contain—recipes for the best salads and the best salad dressings for the best family anywhere. Your family, of course!

MARIANNE'S CHICKEN SALAD

6 to 8 cooked chicken breasts
1 med. onion, quartered
1 lg. carrot, sliced
1 c. celery, sliced
1 bay leaf
2½ tsp. salt
⅔ c. mayonnaise
¼ c. milk
2 tbsp. cider vinegar
2 tsp. grated onion
⅛ tsp. pepper
1 c. diced green pepper
1 lb. seedless green grapes
1 c. chopped celery
Leaf lettuce
½ c. coarsely broken walnuts

Combine first 5 ingredients and 1 teaspoon salt in large saucepan. Cover with water. Cook until chicken falls from bones. Remove chicken; discard stock. Bone and skin chicken. Cut into bite-sized pieces. Cool for 3 hours or longer. Combine next 5 ingredients and 1½ teaspoons salt in large bowl; mix well. Add chicken, green pepper, grapes and celery. Toss gently. Line large platter with lettuce. Sprinkle with walnuts. Yield: 6-8 servings.

Mrs. O. J. Adams
Unity Grange, No. 2105
Sidney, Ohio

MACARONI SALAD WITH SHRIMP

3 c. elbow macaroni
Vinegar
1 c. mayonnaise
1 sm. white onion, finely chopped
1 6-oz. can shrimp
1 sm. green pepper, finely chopped
4 stalks celery, coarsely chopped

Cook macaroni according to package directions. Stir small amount of vinegar with mayonnaise; mix well. Combine all ingredients in salad bowl; mix well. Chill. Yield: 6-8 servings.

Brenda Seger
Suffield Grange, No. 27
Suffield, Connecticut

MOSTACCIOLI SALAD

8 oz. mostaccioli
¼ c. chopped onion
6 tbsp. sweet relish
¼ c. diced green pepper
2 tbsp. chopped pimento
½ tsp. Accent
½ tsp. garlic salt
¼ tsp. celery salt or seed
Pinch of each sweet basil, thyme and marjoram
⅛ tsp. oregano
½ c. Miracle Whip

Cook mostaccioli according to package directions until tender; drain. Cool slightly. Combine with remaining ingredients in salad bowl. Chill 24 hours before serving. Yield: 6-8 servings.

Janice I. Cross
Richland Grange, No. 2155
Sully, Iowa

RODEO SALAD

2 c. macaroni
1 16-oz. can kidney beans, rinsed, and drained
1 c. sliced celery
2 tbsp. chopped onion
⅓ c. sliced sweet pickles
1 c. shredded cheese
½ c sliced stuffed olives
½ c. shredded carrots
1 tbsp. dry mustard
Salt and peppr to taste
½ to ¾ c. salad dressing

Cook macaroni according to package directions. Combine all ingredients in 3-quart bowl; mix well. Chill. Yield: 8 servings.

Lillian Deist
Meigsville Grange, No. 79
Beverly, Ohio

CLASSIC RICE SALAD

3 c. cooked rice, cooled
¼ c. diced pimentos
½ c. finely chopped onions
4 hard-boiled eggs, chopped
½ c. finely chopped sweet pickles
1 tsp. salt
¼ tsp. pepper
1 tsp. prepared mustard
1 c. mayonnaise

Combine all ingredients; mix well. Chill. Ganish with tomatoes and ripe olives, if desired. One and one-half cups chopped cooked chicken, turkey, beef or pork may be added, if desired. Yield: 8 servings.

Mrs. Mary Baird
Monroe Grange, No. 2160
Middletown, Ohio

APPLE SALAD

1 c. sugar
1 tbsp. heaping flour
¼ c. vinegar
2 eggs, beaten

1 c. milk
1 tbsp. butter
3 c. chopped apples
2 c. diced bananas
1 c. miniature marshmallows
1 c. chopped nuts

Combine sugar and flour. Add vinegar, eggs and milk. Place in double boiler or heavy saucepan. Cook, stirring often, until thickened. Remove from heat; add butter. Let set until cool. Combine remaining ingredients in large bowl. Pour dressing over fruit mixture; mix lightly. Drop apples into weak salt water before chopping to keep from turning dark. Yield: 8-9 servings.

Lucille Crago
Wawka Grange, No. 2356
Ligonier, Indiana

APPLE CIDER SALAD

3¾ c. apple cider
3 tbsp. sugar
3 tbsp. lemon juice
2 env. unflavored gelatin
½ tsp. salt
3½ c. chopped apple
1 c. chopped celery

Place first 5 ingredients in medium saucepan. Cook over low heat until gelatin is dissolved. Chill until mixture is consistency of unbeaten egg white. Stir in apple and celery. Pour into 5 × 13-inch pan or a 6-cup mold. Chill until firm. Yield: 12 servings.

Francine Fortune, C.W.A.
Porterville Grange, No. 718
Porterville, California

BANANA SPLIT SALAD

Salad greens
1 16-oz. carton cottage cheese
1 banana
Lemon juice
Nuts, finely chopped
Honeydew melon
Cantaloupe
Watermelon balls
Green grapes
Bing cherries
Fresh mint
1 8-oz. carton strawberry-flavored yogurt

Arrange salad greens on serving dish. Space three mounds of cottage cheese on greens. Cut banana in half; cut each half lengthwise. Dip in lemon juice. Arrange only banana at each end of serving dish; sprinkle with nuts. Cut 6 thin slices from each melon; arrange around cottage cheese along with watermelon, grapes and cherries. Garnish with mint. Blend yogurt with fork until smooth. Serve separately to spoon over salad. Yield: 3 servings.

Photograph for this recipe on page 31.

CHEESY SALAD

1 6-oz. package Jell-O, any flavor
½ c. mayonnaise
½ c. evaporated milk
1 lb. cottage cheese
1 1-lb. 4-oz. can crushed pineapple, undrained
Juice of 1 orange
Juice of 1 lemon
¼ c. chopped nuts (opt.)
¼ c. chopped celery (opt.)

Dissolve Jell-O in 1 cup boiling water. Cool. Add remaining ingredients; mix well. Pour into 2-quart mold. Chill until firm. Yield: 12 servings.

Mrs. Mary Bremner
Washington Grange, No. 11
New Milford, Connecticut

CRANBERRY SALAD

2 c. cranberries, coarsely ground
½ c. orange peel, coarsely ground
2 c. sugar
2 c. chopped celery
2 c. chopped apples
1 peeled orange, chopped

Combine cranberries and orange peel with 2 cups sugar in large bowl. Chill overnight. Add celery, apples and orange; mix well. Serve on lettuce leaf. Nuts and marshmallows may be added. Top with whipped cream.

Martha Keller
Newark Grange, No. 1004
Heath, Ohio

FROZEN CHEESE AND DATE SALAD

3 3-oz. packages cream cheese, softened
½ c. maple syrup
1 c. heavy cream, whipped
½ c. chopped dates
½ c. crushed pineapple
½ c. nuts
2 c. miniature marshmallows

Combine cream cheese and maple syrup. Fold in whipped cream. Add remaining ingredients. Place in 8 × 8-inch pan. Freeze.

Mrs. Walter Cordrey
Miami Grange No. 2158
DeGraff, Ohio

LAST-MINUTE HOT SALAD

1 pt. pears, quartered
1 pt. peaches, quartered
1 pt. apricots
1 can pineapple tidbits
1 pt. Bing cherries
1 sm. bottle of maraschino cherries
Honey
Nutmeg

Drain all fruit except pineapple. Place in electric skillet. Heat slowly to simmer. Sprinkle nutmeg over fruit. Pour 3 to 4 tablespoons honey slowly over top. Serve hot in individual dishes.

Peggy Peterson Carda
Nebraska State Princess
Weissert Grange, No. 419
Berwyn, Nebraska

RHUBARB-STRAWBERRY MOLD

1 c. chopped rhubarb
1 6-oz. package strawberry gelatin
1 lb. package frozen strawberries in syrup, partially thawed
1 tbsp. lemon juice
¼ tsp. almond extract

Cook rhubarb in 2 cups water over medium heat until tender. Dissolve gelatin in hot rhubarb liquid. Add strawberries; stir until well blended. Add lemon juice and almond extract; mix well. Spoon into six 1-cup molds. Chill until set. May be served with whipped cream. Yield: 5 servings.

Jean L. Mohler
Stark Co., Marlboro Grange, No. 1401
Hartville, Delaware

GARDEN SALAD

1 c. sugar
½ c. oil
¼ to ½ c. white vinegar
1 c. sm. peas
1 c. French-style green beans
1 sm. jar pimentos
½ c. chopped onion
1 green pepper, chopped
3 stalks celery, chopped

Combine first 3 ingredients in saucepan. Bring to a boil. Remove from heat; cool. Combine vegetables in serving dish. Add dressing; stir. Chill for several hours.

Lois Leibold
Norton Grange, No. 2566
Norton, Ohio

FOUR-BEAN SALAD

2 c. green beans, drained
2 c. yellow wax beans, drained
2 c. red kidney beans, drained
2 c. limas, drained
1 med. green pepper, thinly sliced in rings
1 med. onion, thinly sliced in rings
Romaine lettuce
½ c. sugar
½ c. salad oil
½ tsp. dry mustard
½ tsp. crumbled tarragon leaves
1 tbsp. snipped fresh parsley
½ tsp. basil leaves
½ c. wine vinegar
1 tsp. salt

Mix first 6 ingredients in large lettuce-lined bowl. Combine remaining ingredients well. Drizzle over entire surface of vegetables. Cover. Marinate for several hours or overnight. Stir once or twice. Stir and drain before serving. Accent may be added, if desired. Yield: 12 servings.

Maybert Crane
Mt. Prospect Grange, No. 1995
Matamoras, Pennsylvania

CABBAGE SALAD

1 gal. shredded cabbage
1 green pepper, chopped
2 carrots, shredded
1 tbsp. salt
1 c. vinegar
2 c. sugar
1 tsp. celery seed

Combine cabbage, green pepper, carrots and salt in large bowl. Pour ½ cup boiling water over cabbage mixture. Let stand for 1 hour. Mix vinegar and sugar in saucepan. Boil for 1 minute. Cool. Squeeze water out of cabbage with hands. Mix with vinegar syrup and celery seed. Chill for 1 hour before serving. May be frozen. Yield: 25 servings.

Mrs. Louis Yunker
Perry Grange, No. 1163
Leicester, New York

CONVENIENT SLAW

1 med. head cabbage, shredded
½ c. chopped green pepper
1 sm. onion, chopped
1 c. vinegar
1 c. sugar
1 tsp. celery seed
1 tsp. mustard seed

Combine cabbage with green pepper and onion. Pour boiling water over cabbage mixture. Set aside for 1 hour; drain. Heat remaining ingredients in a saucepan. Pour over vegetables slowly. Refrigerate covered. Yield: 1 quart.

Mary Huck
Wife of Kansas State Exec. Com. Mem.
Kansas City, Kansas

DORIS' COLESLAW

½ c. sugar
½ c. vinegar
1 tsp. celery seed
½ tsp. powdered garlic
½ tsp. pepper
1 tsp. Accent
1 c. mayonnaise
Grated carrots (opt.)
Pineapple chunks (opt.)
2 med. heads cabbage, shredded

Mix sugar and vinegar until syrupy. Add seasonings and mayonnaise. Add carrots, pineapple and cabbage. Chill. May be stored covered, in refrigerator for 2 or 3 days.

Doris Moater
Miranda Grange, No. 690
Miranda, California

GLADYS' COLESLAW

1 lg. head cabbage, shredded
1 med. onion, chopped
1 med. green pepper, coarsely chopped
2 c. sugar
3 tsp. celery seed
1 tsp. mustard seed
¾ tsp. salt
½ c. vinegar

Combine first 3 ingredients in 3-quart bowl; mix well. Combine remaining ingredients. Pour over cabbage mixture; stir well. Chill, covered, in refrigerator for at least 24 hours. May be refrigerated, covered, for up to 1 week. Yield: 12 servings.

Mrs. Gladys A. Day
Greene Co., Harvey's Grange, No. 1444
West Finley, Pennsylvania

NINE-DAY SLAW

1 med. cabbage, shredded
2 stalks celery, diced
2 med. onions, diced
1 green pepper, diced
1 c. sugar
1 c. salad oil
1 c. cider vinegar
2 tbsp. salt
1 sm. jar pimentos, chopped

Combine first 4 ingredients in large bowl; set aside. Place remaining ingredients in saucepan. Bring to a boil, stirring constantly. Remove from heat; pour over cabbage mixture. Cool. Cover; store in refrigerator overnight. Stays fresh and crisp for 9 days. Yield: 12-14 servings.

Mrs. Edrie Dodson
Leon Valley Grange, No. 1581
San Antonio, Texas

SURPRISE SLAW IN CABBAGE BOWL

1 lg. firm cabbage
2 med. beets
¼ c. scallions, chopped
1 c. sour cream
3 tbsp. wine vinegar
2 tbsp. minced parsley
2 tsp. minced capers

1 tsp. salt
1 tsp. sugar
¼ tsp. tarragon
¼ tsp. pepper

Slice off top ¼ of cabbage; chop. Hollow out cabbage to make a bowl. Set aside. Chop remaining cabbage. Peel and shred beets. Pat dry on absorbent paper. Add scallions to chopped cabbage. Chill beets and cabbage separately. Blend sour cream with next 7 ingredients. Combine cabbage with well-drained beets 10 minutes before serving. Toss with sour cream dressing. Heap into cabbage bowl.

From a Grange Friend

SWITCHED SLAW

¾ c. salad oil
¼ c. wine vinegar
1 tsp. salt
½ tsp. dried leaf basil
¼ tsp. dry mustard
¼ to ½ tsp. Tabasco pepper sauce
1 tsp. grated onion
4 c. shredded red cabbage
3 Cape Granny Smith apples, cubed

Combine first 7 ingredients in large bowl; mix well. Stir in cabbage and apples; cover. Chill several hours or overnight. Yield: 6-8 servings.

Photograph for this recipe on page 36.

TWENTY-FOUR HOUR COLESLAW

1 med. head cabbage, shredded
1 green pepper, diced or grated
1 sm. onion, chopped
6 stuffed olives, sliced
Sugar
1 c. white vinegar
1 tsp. salt
1 tsp. celery seed
1 tsp. prepared mustard
⅛ tsp. pepper
½ c. salad oil

Combine first 4 ingredients in large bowl. Sprinkle generously with sugar to almost cover cabbage. Blend remaining ingredients in saucepan. Bring to a boil; boil for 3 minutes. Pour over cabbage mixture while hot. Place in refrigerator, covered, for 24 hours. This slaw will stay fresh as long as it lasts.

Eunice Trible
Papillion Grange, No. 401
Papillion, Nebraska

WARM SLAW

1 3-lb. head cabbage, shredded
Salt
1 tsp. cooking oil
2 eggs, beaten
½ c. sugar
¼ c. vinegar
1 tbsp. flour

Cook cabbage with 1½ teaspoons salt, oil and 1 cup water in skillet until tender. Drain. Combine remaining ingredients and ¼ teaspoon salt with ½ cup water in bowl. Mix until light in color. Add to cabbage. Bring to boiling point, stirring constantly. Yield: 6 servings.

Mrs. Fred A. Towsey
Turbett Grange, No. 781
Port Royal, Pennsylvania

COLESLAW FOR FREEZING

1 tsp. salt
1 med. cabbage, shredded
1 carrot, grated
1 green pepper, chopped
1 c. vinegar
1 tsp. mustard seed
1 tsp. celery seed
2 c. sugar

Mix salt with cabbage. Let stand 1 hour. Squeeze out all moisture. Add carrot and green pepper. Add a small amount of onion, if desired. Combine remaining ingredients with ¼ cup water. Bring to a boil; boil for 1 minute. Cool to lukewarm. Pour over slaw mixture. Pour into freezer containers; cover. Freeze. This thaws in just a few minutes for serving. Leftover slaw can be refrozen easily. Yield: 6-8 servings.

Dorothy Wildermuth
Osco Grange, No. 1782
Osco, Illinois

FROZEN COLESLAW

4 c. sugar
2 c. white vinegar
5 lb. shredded cabbage
2 tbsp. salt
1 bunch of celery, chopped
1 lb. carrots, shredded
1 tbsp. celery seed
1 tbsp. mustard seed

Mix sugar and vinegar with 1 cup water in large bowl. Stir until sugar dissolves. Add cabbage and salt; mix well. Set aside for 1 hour. Press out liquid. Add remaining ingredients. Mix well. Place in freezer containers. Chopped green peppers may be added, if desired.

Mazie Cooper
Slippery Rock Grange, No. 1441
Slippery Rock, Pennsylvania

CARROT RELISH CUPS

1 3-oz. package orange Jell-O
¼ c. sugar
1 8-oz. package cream cheese, softened
½ c. orange juice
½ tsp. grated lemon peel
2 tbsp. lemon juice
1 c. shredded carrots
1 c. chopped unpared apples

Dissolve Jell-O and sugar in 1½ cups boiling water. Add cream cheese; beat until smooth. Stir in orange juice, lemon peel and lemon juice. Chill until partially set. Add carrots and apples. Place in molds. Chill until firm. Unmold. Garnish with carrot curls and orange sections. Yield: 6-8 servings.

Mrs. Brayton Lyke, C.W.A.
Steuben Co., Pomona Grange
Avoca, New York

ELIZABETH'S CARROT SALAD

2 bunches carrots, sliced ¼-in. thick
2 med. onions, sliced and separated into rings
1 med. green pepper, cut into thin strips
1 can tomato soup
¾ c. vinegar
⅔ c. sugar
½ c. cooking oil
1 tsp. Worcestershire sauce
1 tsp. prepared mustard
¼ tbsp. salt

Cook carrots in saucepan in small amount of boiling salted water until just tender. Drain. Combine remaining ingredients in 2-quart bowl. Add carrots; cover. Chill overnight. May be stored for several days. Yield: 8 servings.

Elizabeth Ellmer
Pokono Grange, No. 191
Brookfield Center, Connecticut

COOKED CARROT SALAD

5 c. sliced carrots
½ c. sliced celery
2 c. salad oil
2 c. vinegar
1½ c. sugar
2 tsp. salt

Cook carrots; drain. Set aside. Steam celery; drain. Set aside. Combine remaining ingredients in large jar. Cover; shake well. Combine carrots and celery in salad bowl; cover with dressing. Chill overnight. Serve on lettuce. Yield: 8 servings.

Mrs. Elsie J. Voll
Paradise Valley Grange, No. 389
Bonners Ferry, Idaho

CAULIFLOWER SALAD

1 lb. bacon
1 head cauliflower
1 sm. head lettuce
Onion, chopped (opt.)
¼ c. sugar
¼ c. Parmesan cheese
1 c. salad dressing or mayonnaise

Fry bacon. Drain and crumble. Break head of cauliflower into small flowerets. Arrange in bottom of serving bowl. Break lettuce into bite-sized pieces. Place over cauliflowerets. Add chopped onions. Add bacon. Sprinkle sugar over bacon. Add layer of cheese. Top with salad dressing, spreading to edges to seal. Chill. Toss lightly before serving. Yield: 10 servings.

Reta Mae Tate
Wife of Idaho State Master
Mica Flats Grange, No. 436
Meridian, Idaho

MEXICAN CORN SALAD

3 c. fresh corn, cooked, drained and chilled
½ c. chopped red onion
½ c. sliced green pepper
1 tbsp. chopped parsley
¼ c. sour cream
¼ c. beef broth
2 tbsp. red wine vinegar
½ c. mayonnaise
Salt and pepper to taste
1 tomato, peeled, seeded and diced
4 slices bacon, cooked and crumbled
2 tbsp. chopped green onion

Mix first 4 ingredients in large bowl. Whisk sour cream and broth together in small bowl. Add vinegar and mayonnaise; beat until frothy. Add to vegetable mixture; toss. Season with salt and pepper. Chill. Garnish with tomato, bacon and green onion. Yield: 8 servings.

Mrs. Esther Fry
Mt. Wheeler Grange, No. 696
Arlington, Washington

SCANDINAVIAN CUCUMBERS

½ c. sour cream
1 tbsp. sugar
2 tbsp. snipped parsley
2 tbsp. tarragon vinegar
1 tbsp. finely chopped onion
¼ tsp. dried dillweed
3 sm. cucumbers, sliced

Combine first 6 ingredients. Fold in cucumbers. Cover. Chill for 2 hours.

Cherry Schroeder
Boerne Grange, No. 1545
Boerne, Texas

SEVEN-LAYER SALAD

1 10-oz. package frozen peas
1 head lettuce, shredded
½ c. chopped celery
½ c. chopped green pepper
½ c. chopped onion
1 pt. mayonnaise
2 tbsp. sugar
4 to 6 oz. shredded Cheddar cheese
8 strips bacon, fried and crumbled

Cook peas according to package directions; drain. Fill large salad bowl half full with lettuce. Add celery, green pepper and onion in layers. Add peas. Top with mayonnaise. Sprinkle with sugar. Top with cheese and bacon. Cover with plastic wrap. Chill for 8 hours. Yield: 18 servings.

Mrs. Calvin Kindschuh
South Byron Grange
Brownsville, Wisconsin

TWENTY-FOUR HOUR LAYERED
LETTUCE SALAD

1 head iceberg lettuce
2 green onions, diced
2 stalks celery, thinly sliced
½ c. sliced water chestnuts, drained

1 10-oz. package frozen peas, separated
2 c. mayonnaise
½ tsp. garlic powder
2 tsp. sugar
1 c. Parmesan cheese
2 tbsp. bacon bits

Shred lettuce in large casserole. Layer next 4 ingredients over lettuce. Cover completely with mayonnaise. Sprinkle with remaining ingredients. Refrigerate for 24 hours. Yield: 8-10 servings.

Dorothy Bryant, D.W.A.
Gig Harbor Grange, No. 445
Olalla, Washington

OLD-FASHIONED WILTED LETTUCE

4 strips bacon
¼ c. vinegar
Salt and pepper to taste
Dash of sugar (opt.)
3 qt. leaf lettuce, shredded into 1 in. strips
1 tbsp. chopped green onion

Fry bacon; remove from skillet. Add ¾ cup water, vinegar, sugar, salt and pepper. Bring to a boil. Place lettuce and onion in 3-quart casserole. Pour vinegar mixture over lettuce. Cover for a few minutes. Toss before serving. Yield: 4 servings.

Geneva Atkinson, D.W.A.
Kansas State Grange
St Paul, Kansas

WILTED GREENS WITH FRUIT DRESSING

1 1-lb. 13-oz. can cling peaches, sliced
6 slices bacon
2 tsp. instant dry onion
½ c. vinegar
½ tsp. salt
⅛ tsp. seasoned pepper
1 qt. torn fresh spinach
2 c. torn lettuce

Drain peaches, reserving ½ cup peach syrup. Fry bacon in skillet. Remove bacon. Drain drippings, reserving ¼ cup in skillet. Add peach syrup, onion, vinegar, salt and pepper. Heat through. Add half the peach slices. Heat through; do not boil. Combine remaining ingredients in salad bowl. Add hot dressing; toss. Serve immediately.

Marie Stephens
Roseville Grange, No. 1290
Brookville, Pennsylvania

MOCK CRAB SALAD

2 c. peeled and shredded parsnips
1 c. shredded celery
1 onion, shredded
1 pimento, shredded
8 or 9 ripe or green olives, sliced
½ c. salad dressing

Combine all ingredients; mix well. Chill.

Mrs. Francis Webster
Bell Township Grange, No. 2047
Mahaffey, Pennsylvania

MOLDED CHEF'S SALAD

2 3-oz. packages lemon or lime gelatin
1 tsp. salt
3 tbsp. vinegar
¾ c. diced ham
½ c. cheese strips
⅓ c. chopped onion
¼ c. diced green pepper
¼ c. diced celery
3 tbsp. pimento

Dissolve gelatin and salt in 2 cups boiling water. Add 1 cup cold water and vinegar. Chill until thickened. Fold in remaining ingredients. Pour into mold. Chill 5 hours or until firm. Unmold on lettuce leaves. Garnish with salad dressing and pepper rings. Serve with Ritz crackers.

Clara Blakney
Cimarron Grange
Moscow, Kansas

PEA AND EGG SALAD

1 10-oz. package frozen peas with pearl onions
½ c. chopped celery
3 hard-boiled eggs, chopped
½ c. sliced pimento-stuffed green olives
Mayonnaise

Separate frozen peas in 1½-quart bowl. Add remaining ingredients except mayonnaise; mix well. Stir in mayonnaise just before serving. Yield: 8 servings.

Dorothy Bryant, D.W.A.
Gig Harbor Grange, No. 445
Olalla, Washington

ANNA'S PEA SALAD

1 1-lb. can peas, drained
1 sm. onion, chopped
3 hard-boiled eggs, chopped
½ c. mayonnaise
Dash of salt
½ tsp. prepared mustard

Mix all ingredients. Refrigerate for 1 hour. Place individual servings on a bed of lettuce. Yield: 4-6 servings.

Anna Siemiaczko, C.W.A.
Washington Grange, No. 521
South Charleston, West Virginia

GERMAN POTATO SALAD DELUXE

½ lb. bacon, cut in pieces
½ c. chopped onion
2 tbsp. all-purpose flour
¼ c. sugar
1½ tsp. salt
Dash of pepper
½ c. vinegar
6 c. diced cooked potatoes
3 hard-cooked eggs, sliced (opt.)

Fry bacon until crisp. Drain, reserving ¼ cup drippings. Cook onion in reserved drippings until tender. Blend in flour, sugar, salt and pepper. Add vinegar and 1 cup water. Cook, stirring until thick and bubbly. Add potatoes, bacon and eggs. Heat thoroughly, tossing lightly. Garnish with parsley, pimento and bacon curls. Yield: 5-6 servings.

Esther M. Clay, C.W.A.
Mahoning Co., Smith Grange, No. 1141
Beloit, Ohio

MILDRED'S GERMAN POTATO SALAD

6 med. potatoes
½ c. chopped celery
1 tbsp. chopped onion
Salt and pepper to taste
½ lb. bacon
2 tbsp. flour
⅓ c. vinegar
½ c. sugar

Cook potatoes, until tender-crisp; cool. Slice thin; place in large bowl with celery, onion, salt and pepper. Fry bacon until crisp. Drain all but 2 tablespoons grease from skillet. Crumble bacon; return to skillet. Add flour. Mix thoroughly. Add vinegar, ⅔ cup water and sugar. Stir constantly until mixture begins to boil. Remove from heat; pour over potatoes. Mix gently until potatoes are coated with sauce. Serve at room temperature. Yield: 6 servings.

Mildred W. Eames
Wyoming Co., Perry Grange, No. 1163
Perry, New York

GRANNY'S APPLE-POTATO SALAD

¾ c. mayonnaise
¾ c. sour cream
1 4-oz. package blue cheese, crumbled
1 tsp. salt
½ tsp. dillweed
⅛ tsp. pepper
2 Cape Granny Smith apples, chopped
2 tbsp. lemon juice
6 c. cubed cooked potatoes
3 c. cooked ham, cut in narrow strips

Combine first 6 ingredients in large bowl; mix well. Mix apples with lemon juice. Add to dressing. Add potatoes and ham; mix well. Chill. Yield: 6 servings.

Photograph for this recipe on page 36.

POTATO SALAD WITH BOILED DRESSING

3 pt. cooked chopped potatoes
1 sm. bunch celery, chopped
2 hard-boiled eggs, chopped
Celery seed to taste
Chopped onion (opt.)
2 eggs, well beaten
½ c. vinegar
4 tbsp. sugar
¼ c. butter
1 tsp. cornstarch
Dash of salt
Cream

Combine first 5 ingredients in large bowl. Set aside. Combine remaining ingredients with enough cream to blend well. Bring to a boil; boil, stirring constantly, until thick. Pour dressing over potato mixture; mix well. Garnish with additional hard-boiled egg slices.

Mrs. Evaline Hurley
York Co., Eureka Grange, No. 1915
Carlisle, Pennsylvania

SAUERKRAUT SALAD

1 c. chopped celery
1 green pepper, chopped
1 med. onion, chopped

1 can sauerkraut, drained
1 tsp. celery seed
2 c. sugar
¾ c. vinegar
½ c. salad oil

Mix first 5 ingredients in bowl. Combine remaining ingredients with ½ cup water. Pour over vegetables. Chill overnight. Yield: 8 servings.

Mrs. Hazel Holtz, Pomona
St. Joseph Co., Leonidas Grange, No. 266
Scotts, Michigan

ARIE'S MAYONNAISE

4 eggs, beaten
1 c. sugar
1 tsp. dry mustard
1 tsp. salt
4 tbsp. butter
1 c. milk
1 c. vinegar
1 tbsp. flour

Blend all ingredients in saucepan. Cook over medium heat until thick. Stir often while cooking. Chill.

Arie Nahodil
Washington Grange, No. 521
South Charleston, West Virginia

BACON DRESSING FOR TOSSED SALAD

5 slices bacon
1 tsp. salt
2 to 3 tsp. sugar
2 tbsp. salad oil
2 tbsp. cider vinegar
Pepper to taste (opt.)
Salad greens

Fry bacon until crisp. Remove from skillet. Drain. Pour fat from skillet; let skillet cool. Place next 5 ingredients in skillet. Mix well. Crumble bacon over salad greens; pour dressing over greens. This is a good dressing for head lettuce, radishes, onions, tomatoes and cheese strips.

From a Grange Friend.

GENEVA'S SALAD DRESSING

3⅔ c. sugar
1½ c. catsup
¼ c. vinegar
1 tbsp. salt

1 tbsp. paprika
1 tbsp. garlic salt
¼ c. lemon juice
3 c. Wesson oil
1 tbsp. celery seed
1 tbsp. dry mustard

Boil sugar with 1 quart water to soft-ball stage. Set aside. Combine remaining ingredients in a large bowl. Beat well. Add hot syrup. Beat for 30 minutes until thick.

Geneva R. Byers
Fern Bluff Grange, No. 267
Sultan, Washington

HOMEMADE SALAD DRESSING

2 eggs
1 c. milk
1 tbsp. flour
1 c. sugar
¼ c. vinegar
½ tsp. salt
½ tsp. prepared mustard
1 tsp. mustard seed
1 tsp. celery seed

Beat eggs, milk and flour until thoroughly blended. Add remaining ingredients. Place in saucepan. Cook until thick, stirring frequently. Cool. Use this dressing for macaroni or potato salad.

Mrs. J. Luther Snyder
Valley Grange, No. 1360
Camp Hill, Pennsylvania

RASPBERRY VINEGAR

4 qt. ripe red raspberries
4 c. white or red wine
Vinegar
1½ lb. sugar

Wash 2 quarts of raspberries. Pour the vinegar over raspberries; mash. Place in large container. Cover and let stand for 48 hours at room temperature. Wash remaining 2 quarts raspberries. Place in large bowl. Pour first batch through sieve or cheesecloth. Discard pulp. Let stand 48 hours. Mash all ingredients; strain again. Add sugar to juice. Simmer for 30 minutes. Strain again. Cool. Place in airtight container.

Elizabeth Lowry
Vergennes Grange, No. 406
Vergennes, Vermont

Main Dishes

Hungry families both need and look forward to satisfying and delicious meals. And, because beef, poultry, seafood and pork are tasty and nutritious, they are the most popular main dish foods. That is why smart homemakers everywhere make sure that meat is an essential part of their day-to-day family menus. Those seated around the dinner table appreciate it, too!

Main dish recipes run the gamut from basic pot roast and tender baked poultry to barbecued short ribs and elegant seafood dishes, plus, lamb and veal dishes. So, there is a main dish recipe for every budget, any occasion and all tastes.

Casseroles are favorite main dishes homemakers have come to depend on, and for very good reasons! The homemaker on a budget knows the economy of a casserole—the nutritional value and flavor of a small amount of meat combined with other good foods go a long way in casserole recipes. Busy cooks can count the time they save with meal-in-a-dish cookery. Families love casseroles, too, because the endless flavor combinations are always delicious!

Main dish foods are the basis of good family nutrition, so they should be selected and prepared with care. But, for the same reason, they should always be very tasty. These main dish recipes from Grange will meet the high standards you and your family set for good eating!

BARBECUE BURGERS

1 c. beef gravy
½ c. catsup
¼ c. (firmly packed) brown sugar
1 tbsp. Worcestershire sauce
Dash of red and black pepper
⅛ c. vinegar
2 tsp. barbecue spice
1 tbsp. dried minced onion
2 to 3 lb. cooked roast, thinly sliced

Combine first 8 ingredients with ½ cup water. Simmer for 15 minutes. Add beef; simmer 10 minutes longer. Serve on warm hamburger buns. Yield: 12 servings.

Mrs. Laurie Bedford
Colonel Harper Grange, No. 1508
Jefferson, New York

BEEF STROGANOFF

½ c. diced onion
1 lb. round steak, cubed
2 tbsp. shortening
1 can golden mushroom soup
½ c. sour cream

Brown onion and steak in shortening in electric skillet. Remove from heat. Add soup, sour cream and ⅛ cup water. Blend thoroughly; cover. Simmer for 1 hour or until meat is tender. Serve over cooked noodles. Yield: 4 servings.

Mrs. Ray Wick, C.W.A.
Harlem Springs Grange, No. 2334
Carrollton, Ohio

ORIENTAL STEAK STRIPS

2 lb. round steak, cut 1-inch thick
2 tbsp. fat
⅛ c. soy sauce
2 tsp. sugar
¼ tsp. pepper
1 clove of garlic, minced
3 carrots, cut into thin strips
2 green peppers, cut in 1-in. cubes
8 green onions, cut in 1-in. cubes
½ lb. mushrooms, halved
1 8-oz. can water chestnuts, halved
2 tbsp. cornstarch

Cut steak into ⅛ × 3-inch strips. Brown strips in fat in large skillet. Pour drippings into measuring cup; add enough water to measure 1 cup. Combine dripping mixture with soy sauce, sugar, pepper and garlic; add to steak. Cover tightly. Cook slowly for 45 minutes. Cover. Cook for 15 minutes. Combine cornstarch and ¼ cup water. Pour into skillet. Cook until thickened. Serve with cooked rice. Yield: 6-8 servings.

Mrs. C. Jerome Davis
Ramsey-Spencer Grange
Ramsey, Indiana

GOLDIE'S PASTY

2 c. flour
1 c. chopped suet
½ tsp. salt
1 tsp. baking powder
3 potatoes, peeled and chopped
1 med. onion, chopped
1 or 2 turnips, chopped
2 to 3 lb. flank steak, cubed
Salt and pepper to taste

Combine first 4 ingredients until crumbly. Add 1 cup cold water; mix well. Chill. Roll out on floured board into rectangle. Cut into fourths. Place one-fourth of each of remaining ingredients on each portion of crust. Fold up crust; pinch top together. Place on baking sheet. Bake at 350 degrees until meat and potatoes are tender. Yield: 4 servings.

Goldie A. Feland
Enterprise Grange, No. 25
Arvada, Colorado

BEEF STEW

1½ to 2 lb. beef or lamb, cubed
2 tbsp. fat
Salt and pepper to taste
12 sm. white onions
3 med. carrots, quartered
3 med. potatoes, quartered
1 c. fresh or canned peas
2 tbsp. chopped parsley
1 tbsp. diced green pepper
2 tbsp. flour
1 tsp. Worcestershire sauce

Brown beef cubes in fat on all sides in 3-quart saucepan. Add 3 cups hot water; cover tightly. Simmer for 1 hour and 30 minutes. Season with salt and pepper. Add onions, carrots and potatoes. Cook 30 minutes or until tender. Add peas, parsley and green pepper. Cook 10 minutes. Blend ¼ cup cold water, flour and Worcestershire sauce; pour into stew mixture to thicken. Serve immediately. Extra water can be added if needed. Yield: 6-8 servings.

Mrs. Alice H. Morton
Freeport Grange, No. 2337
Freeport, Ohio

CHUCK WAGON CHILI CASSEROLE

2 slices bacon
¾ lb. beef stew meat, cubed
1 med. onion, chopped
½ tsp. salt
1 8-oz. can tomato sauce
1 sm. can sliced mushrooms, drained
¼ c. coffee
Dash of garlic salt
½ tsp. chili powder
¼ tsp. basil
1 1-lb. can kidney beans

Fry bacon until crisp. Drain, reserving 2 table-spoons drippings. Pour reserved drippings into baking dish; add beef. Bake, covered, at 400 degrees for 20 minutes. Add onion, salt, and ¼ cup water. Bake, covered, at 350 degrees for 1 hour. Add remaining ingredients; mix well. Bake, uncovered, for 1 hour longer. Yield: 4-5 servings.

Mrs. Clyde Wagoner
Chippewa Grange, No. 1592
Beaver Falls, Pennsylvania

MARGARET'S OVEN BEEF STEW

2 tbsp. flour
1 tsp. salt
¼ tsp. pepper
1½ lb. lean cubed stew beef
1 tbsp. butter
1 c. tomato puree
2 tbsp. lemon juice
¼ c. sugar
1 bay leaf
2 whole cloves
4 pearl onions
1 c. green beans
½ c. sliced carrots
¼ c. sliced celery
4 sm. potatoes

Combine flour, salt and pepper. Dredge meat in seasoned flour. Brown beef in butter in large skillet. Place in 3-quart casserole. Add next 5 ingredients and ½ cup hot water; cover. Bake in 300-degree oven for 1 hour. Add remaining ingredients. Bake until tender. Yield: 4 servings.

Mrs. Margaret Shaw
Kennewick Valley Grange, No. 731
Kennewick, Washington

MULLIGAN STEW

1 tbsp. shortening
1 lb. cubed stew beef
1 10½-oz. can tomato soup

3 carrots, sliced
3 potatoes, peeled and quartered
3 onions, halved

Melt shortening in large skillet; add beef. Brown over medium heat. Stir in soup and 1 soup can water. Cover tightly. Simmer 1 hour and 30 minutes or until tender. Add carrots, potatoes and onions; cover. Continue cooking 30 minutes longer. Yield: 4-6 servings.

Naomi Lauchnor
Lehigh Co., Washington Grange, No. 1763
Slotington, Pennsylvania

RUTH'S OVEN STEW

½ c. flour
2 tsp. salt
½ tsp. pepper
2 lb. cubed stew meat
2 tbsp. oil
8 onions, chopped
6 carrots, chopped
6 potatoes, chopped

Combine flour, salt and pepper in plastic bag. Shake meat cubes in flour mixture. Brown in oil in large frypan. Add remaining flour; stir. Add vegetables and 2 cups boiling water. Cover. Bake at 350 degrees for 2 hours and 30 minutes. Yield: 4-6 servings.

Ruth E. Battle
Gifford Grange, No. 1549
Altamont, New York

SENSATIONAL STEW

2 lb. beef stew meat
1 sm. onion, sliced
1 stalk celery, sliced
2 tsp. salt
1 tbsp. sugar
2 tbsp. tapioca
1 6-oz. can V-8 juice
Potatoes, peeled and cubed
Carrots, sliced

Place first 7 ingredients in 1½ to 2-quart casserole. Cover tightly with foil. Bake for 1 hour at 300 degrees. Add potatoes and carrots. Bake 2 hours longer. Stir twice during baking. Yield: 4-6 servings.

Mrs. Emalee Colver
Flora Grange, No. 1762
Capron, Illinois

SPECIAL BEEF CASSEROLE

    1 4-lb. choice rump roast
    Juice of 1 lemon
    1 c. apple juice
    ¼ lb. butter
    1½ lb. mushrooms
    1 qt. sour cream
    3 or 4 garlic cloves, crushed
    1 tsp. paprika
    ½ tsp. marjoram
    1 tsp. freshly ground pepper
    1 c. Sherry
    2 tsp. cornstarch
    Milk or cream

Trim fat from beef. Cut into bite-sized cubes. Place in bowl. Add lemon juice and apple juice. Marinate in refrigerator at least 3 hours. Drain meat, reserving marinade. Melt butter in heavy Dutch oven; add beef. Brown lightly; remove. Saute mushrooms in same Dutch oven. Remove. Place 1 cup reserved marinade, sour cream, garlic, seasonings and Sherry into same Dutch oven. Mix cornstarch with small amount of cold water; add to mixture. Bring to a boil. Place beef and mushrooms in large casserole. Pour gravy mixture over beef. Cover. Bake at 350 degrees for at least 2 hours. Thin gravy with milk if needed. Add more seasoning if desired. Serve with rice. May be prepared the day before and reheated.

Sandy Allen
Potomac Grange, No. 1
Arlington, Virginia

GREEN PEPPER STEAK AND RICE

    1½ lb. sirloin steak, cut in ¼ in. thick strips
    1 tbsp. paprika
    2 cloves of garlic, crushed
    2 tbsp. butter or margarine
    1 c. sliced green onions
    2 green peppers, cut in strips
    2 lg. fresh tomatoes, chopped
    1 c. beef broth
    2 tbsp. cornstarch
    2 tbsp. soy sauce
    3 c. hot cooked rice

Sprinkle steak with paprika. Let stand a few minutes. Cook steak and garlic in butter until browned. Add onions, green peppers, tomatoes and broth; cover. Simmer about 15 minutes. Blend ¼ cup water with cornstarch and soy sauce. Stir into steak. Cook until thickened. Serve over beds of fluffy rice.

Photograph for this recipe on page 46.

CHIPPED BEEF-NOODLE CASSEROLE

¼ lb. chipped beef
¼ c. butter or margarine
½ c. chopped celery
¼ c. chopped green peppers or pimientos (opt.)
¼ c. chopped onions
2 c. dry noodles, slightly packed
1 10-oz. can mushroom soup
Salt and pepper to taste
1 sm. can mushrooms (opt.)

Cut chipped beef into small pieces. Brown in butter in 2-quart saucepan. Add vegetables. Saute until onions are golden. Add remaining ingredients and 2 soup cans water. Stir; cover. Cook over low heat for 20 to 30 minutes. May be placed in casserole. Bake at 350 degrees for 45 minutes or until noodles are done.

Mrs. Elmer W. Franks
Valley College Grange, No. 1892
Wooster, Ohio

BAKED LIVER WITH APPLES

1 lb. beef liver, thinly sliced
2 lg. sour apples, pared and chopped
1 med. onion, chopped
½ tsp. salt
Dash of pepper
6 slices bacon, cut in pieces

Wipe liver with damp cloth. Place in greased casserole. Combine apples, onion, salt and pepper. Cover liver with apple mixture. Top with bacon. Pour ½ cup water over all. Bake, covered, at 350 degrees for 1 hour and 10 minutes. Remove cover. Bake 20 minutes longer. Yield: 6 servings.

From a Grange Friend

FESTIVE BEEF

1 3-lb. chuck roast or brisket
1 bay leaf
1 can beer
⅔ c. catsup
1½ tsp. paprika
½ tsp. celery seed
2 med. onions, chopped or sliced
½ tsp. pepper
¼ tsp. sweet basil (opt.)

Place roast, bay leaf and 1 cup water in large saucepan. Simmer 10 minutes. Remove bay leaf; add remaining ingredients. Simmer on low heat 3 hours or until tender. Remove roast. Simmer until liquid thickens. Pour over meat to serve. Yield: 6 servings.

Elsie Press
Turkey Hill Grange
Belleville, Illinois

BRAISED BEEF RIBS

3 lb. beef ribs
1 tsp. salt
⅛ tsp. pepper
3 tbsp. flour
3 tbsp. Crisco
½ c. carrots, sliced
½ c. onions, sliced
½ c. celery, sliced
1 bay leaf
Flour

Wipe ribs with damp cloth. Sprinkle with salt, pepper and flour. Heat Crisco in skillet; add ribs. Brown slightly. Place ribs in large baking dish. Add remaining ingredients with 2 cups boiling water. Cover tightly. Bake at 325 degrees for 3 hours or until tender. Thicken stock with a small amount of flour mixed with water.

Mrs. Pauline H. Duncan
Old Richmond Grange, No. 675
Pfafftown, North Carolina

CROCK•POT HOME SHORT RIBS

3 or 4 lb. beef short ribs
2 c. catsup
1 c. barbecue sauce
½ c. (firmly packed) brown sugar
8 tbsp. vinegar
4 tbsp. Worcestershire sauce
2 tbsp. dry mustard
2 tbsp. chili powder
½ c. flour

Place ribs in crock•pot. Combine next 7 ingredients. Pour over ribs. Cover. Cook on High for 8 to 10 hours or until meat is tender. Dissolve flour in small amount of water. Stir into sauce. Cook on High for 10 to 15 minutes or until thickened. Serve over wide noodles. Yield: 5-6 servings.

Mrs. Arden Fitch
Olivesburg Grange, No. 2461
Ashland, Ohio

FATHER'S BEEF POT

2 lb. bottom round, cut into 8 pieces
8 lg. onions, chopped
8 carrots, cut into pieces
8 med. potatoes, cut into pieces
2 tbsp. (heaping) flour
2 tbsp. butter
Salt

Brown meat on both sides in hot frypan. Place in roasting pan. Brown onions, carrots and potatoes in skillet. Place on top of meat in roasting pan. Brown flour in frypan; add 3 cups hot water and butter. Cook until thickened. Strain over meat and vegetables. Season with salt to taste. Bake in 350-degree oven for 2 hours or until well done. Yield: 8 servings.

Mrs. Dorathy A. Fox
Hubbardston Grange, No. 126
Gardner, Massachusetts

KANSAS SWISS STEAK

½ c. flour
½ tsp. dry mustard
Seasoned salt and pepper to taste
1 1½ to 2 lb. steak
1 tbsp. brown sugar
1 c. onion, sliced
1 carrot, diced
1½ cans tomatoes
1 tbsp. Worcestershire sauce

Combine first 3 ingredients. Pound into steak. Brown steak in hot fat. Place in shallow covered pan. Add remaining ingredients. Bake in 325-degree oven for 1 hour and 30 minutes. Yield: 6 servings.

Lavonia McIver
Cimarron Grange, No. 1932
Satanta, Kansas

RANCH STEAK

2 lb. top round beef, cut ½ in. thick
¼ c. flour
1 tsp. salt
¼ tsp. pepper
½ c. butter
½ c. catsup
¼ c. lemon juice
½ tsp. Worcestershire sauce
½ clove of garlic, mashed

Cut steak into serving pieces. Combine flour, salt and pepper; pound into both sides of steak. Melt butter in skillet. Brown steaks quickly on both sides. Stir in remaining ingredients; cover. Simmer at least 10 minutes. May be prepared ahead and kept warm, or chill and reheat. Yield: 6 servings.

From a Grange Friend

SAUERBRATEN

3 to 4 lb. bottom round roast
Salt and pepper to taste
1 clove of garlic
1 med. onion, sliced
1 c. vinegar
6 peppercorns
6 cloves
½ lemon, sliced
3 bay leaves
1 onion, chopped
2 tbsp. oil
2 tbsp. tomato sauce
1 carrot, finely grated
Dash of paprika
2 tbsp. sugar
12 gingersnaps
1 c. sour cream

Trim excess fat from roast. Rinse meat. Season with salt and pepper. Cut garlic into several pieces. Cut small slits in meat; insert garlic. Place meat in bowl. Cover with onion slices. Combine next 5 ingredients with 1 quart water in a saucepan. Bring to a boil; pour over meat. Cover lightly. Refrigerate for 24 hours. Saute chopped onion in oil until transparent. Remove meat from marinade. Strain marinade, reserving liquid. Place meat in a Dutch oven. Add sauteed onion, 1 cup marinade liquid and next 4 ingredients. Cover tightly. Bake at 350 degrees for 3 hours and 30 minutes. Crumble gingersnaps; mix well with sour cream. Remove roast from pan. Add sour cream mixture to juices in pan. Blend well until thickened. Thin with marinade liquid if necessary. Serve with sweet and sour red cabbage and potato pancakes. Yield: 4-5 servings.

Diane Schlagel
Homestead Grange, No. 215
Strasburg, Colorado

STEAK AND POTATO CASSEROLE

1½ lb. round steak, cut into serving pieces
¼ c. flour
4 tbsp. vegetable oil
4 to 6 sm. potatoes, peeled
1 sm. onion, chopped
2 tbsp. chopped parsley
½ tsp. salt

⅛ tsp. pepper
2 8-oz. cans tomato sauce

Dredge steak in flour. Brown well on both sides in hot oil. Place meat in casserole. Pour off excess oil. Scrape up browned drippings left in pan; add to meat. Arrange potatoes with meat. Sprinkle onion, parsley, salt and pepper over all. Add tomato sauce; cover. Bake at 350 degrees for 1 hour and 30 minutes. Yield: 4 servings.

Mrs. Charlotte Guodace
Good Will Grange, No. 127
Glastonbury, Connecticut

VEAL STEAK, CORDON BLEU

4 veal cutlets, pounded thin
2 slices cooked ham
2 slices Swiss cheese
Beaten egg
Fine dry bread crumbs
2 to 4 tbsp. margarine
Lemon slices
Parsley

Top 2 veal cutlets with ham and cheese slices, trimming ends, and overlapping if necessary. Dip remaining cutlets in egg. Place firmly on top of each cheese slice. Dip each in egg and then bread crumbs, keeping layers together, coating both sides. Melt margarine in skillet. Add prepared cutlets. Cook over medium heat, turning once about 5 minutes on each side or until golden brown and tender. Garnish with lemon slices and parsley. Yield: 2 servings.

Photograph for this recipe on page 49.

CREAMY CABBAGE ROLLS

1½ lb. veal or beef
3 sprigs fresh dill (opt.)
¾ c. cooked rice
3 tbsp. minced onion
12 lg. cabbage leaves
⅓ c. butter
½ c. sour cream
½ c. milk
Salt and pepper to taste
1 tbsp. catsup

Place veal in large saucepan, add dill and water to cover. Cook until tender. Drain; reserving broth. Cool; grind veal. Add rice and onion to veal. Pour boiling water over cabbage leaves to wilt. Fill each leaf with meat and rice mixture. Fold over; tie securely. Brown cabbage rolls in butter. Place in

lightly greased casserole. Pour reserved broth over all. Cover. Bake in 325-degree oven for 2 hours. Combine remaining ingredients. Heat; use as sauce over cabbage rolls. Yield: 6 servings.

From a Grange Friend

VEAL PARMIGIANO

3 tbsp. butter
½ c. corn flake crumbs
¼ c. Parmesan cheese
Salt and pepper to taste
1 lb. veal cutlets, pounded
1 egg, slightly beaten
1 8-oz. can tomato sauce
½ tsp. oregano
⅛ tsp. sugar
Dash of onion salt
2 thin slices mozzarella cheese

Melt butter in 9 × 13-inch baking dish. Combine next 3 ingredients in small bowl. Dip veal in egg; roll in crumb mixture. Place in baking dish. Bake at 400 degrees for 20 minutes. Turn veal. Bake for 20 minutes longer. Combine sauce, oregano, sugar, and onion salt in saucepan. Bring to a boil. Pour sauce over veal; top with mozzarella cheese. Bake in oven until cheese melts. Yield: 4 servings.

Diana Otte
Papillion Grange, No. 401
Omaha, Nebraska

AMERICAN CHOP SUEY

½ c. uncooked rice
3 med. potatoes, diced
1 med. onion, chopped
1 green pepper, diced (opt.)
1 lb. hamburger
2 c. tomatoes
Salt and pepper to taste

Bring rice to a boil; cook for 10 minutes. Add potatoes. Cook until tender. Saute onions, green pepper and hamburger until brown. Mix all ingredients together well. Season to taste. Pour into well-greased 2½-quart casserole. Bake in 350-degree oven about 1 hour or until brown on top and not juicy. Yield: 5-6 servings.

Mrs. Doris Barnett, C.W.A.
Allegany Pomona Grange, No. 45
Wellsville, New York

BARBECUE SANDWICHES

1 lb. hamburger
1 c. soft bread crumbs
½ c. tomato juice or paste
1 tsp. salt
1 tsp. pepper
1 tbsp. Worcestershire sauce
2 tbsp. sugar
1 tbsp. vinegar
½ c. catsup
Buns

Combine all ingredients except buns and 1 tablespoon water in saucepan; mix well. Simmer slowly until heated. Serve on buns.

Virginia G. Davis
Shavers Creek Grange, No. 353
Petersburg, Pennsylvania

WHOOPIE PIES

1 lb. hamburger
1 tbsp. finely chopped onion
½ c. tomato sauce
½ c. catsup
2 tbsp. Parmesan cheese
¾ tsp. garlic salt
⅛ tsp. oregano
2 tbsp. soft butter
½ tsp. paprika
Rolls
Cheese slices

Brown meat and onion, stirring frequently. Add tomato sauce, catsup, Parmesan cheese, ½ tea

spoon garlic salt and oregano. Cook for 20 minutes. Blend butter, ¼ teaspoon garlic salt and paprika in bowl; mix well. Split rolls. Spread about 1 teaspoon garlic spread on top half of roll. Place meat mixture and 1 slice of cheese on bottom half of roll. Close sandwich. Wrap individually in foil. Bake in 350-degree oven for 15 minutes.

Ellen Foster
Friendship Grange, No. 1018
Uniondale, Pennsylvania

BEEF RING

¾ c. oatmeal
¾ c. milk
1½ lb. hamburger
1½ tsp. salt
7 tbsp. chopped onion or onion powder
½ tsp. pepper
2 tbsp. Worcestershire sauce
3 tbsp. vinegar
3 tbsp. brown sugar
1 c. catsup

Soak oatmeal in milk. Combine hamburger, salt, 1 tablespoon onion, pepper and oatmeal mixture; mix well. Mold into baking dish. Form a ring in center of meat. Bake at 350 degrees for 10 minutes. Combine remaining ingredients, ½ cup water and 6 tablespoons onion; mix well. Pour over meat. Bake at 320 degrees for 1 hour longer, basting often. Yield: 12 servings.

Myrtle Kennard
Lucky Grange, No. 1962
Waverly, Kansas

BROILED BEEF PORKIES

1 lb. ground beef
1 c. crushed corn flakes
1 c. canned tomatoes
1 egg, beaten
1 tsp. salt
⅛ tsp. pepper
1 sm. onion, chopped
8 slices bacon

Combine first 7 ingredients; mix well. Shape into 1-inch thick patties. Wrap bacon slices around each patty; fasten with toothpick. Place patties on broiler rack. Broil 2 to 3 inches from heat for 10 to 12 minutes or until patties are browned. Turn patties over. Broil 8 minutes longer. Yield: 4-6 servings.

Kathryn Kiesecker, Sec.
Anatone Grange, No. 1022
Anatone, Washington

ROLLED BEEF LOAF

2 lb. ground beef
2 eggs, beaten
1 c. powdered milk
1 c. diced onion
1 c. catsup
1 c. oatmeal
Salt and pepper to taste
4 c. fine bread crumbs
¼ c. butter, melted
¼ c. finely chopped celery

Combine first 7 ingredients; mix well. Place on foil. Roll out into thin rectangle. Combine remaining ingredients; season with salt and pepper. Sprinkle over meat. Roll jelly roll fashion, using foil to hold in shape. Place in small roasting pan. Add small amount of water around the foil. Bake, covered, in 350-degree oven for 2 hours or until done. Cool slightly before slicing. Yield: 6-8 servings.

Margaret Francis
Smithfield Grange, No. 1756
Adena, Ohio

SICILIAN MEAT ROLL

2 eggs, beaten
¾ c. soft bread crumbs
½ c. tomato juice
2 tbsp. parsley
½ tsp. oregano
¼ tsp. salt
¼ tsp. pepper
1 sm. clove of garlic, minced
2 lb. ground beef
8 slices precooked ham
6 oz. shredded mozzarella cheese
3 slices mozarella, sliced diagonally

Combine first 8 ingredients; mix well. Add beef; mix well. Shape meat into 10 × 12-inch rectangle on foil. Arrange ham slices on top, leaving small margin around edge. Sprinkle cheese over ham. Roll meat, using foil to lift. Seal edges and ends. Place roll, seam side down, in 9 × 13-inch baking pan. Bake at 350 degrees for 1 hour or until done. Place cheese slices over top of roll; bake for 5 minutes longer. Yield: 8 servings.

Judie L. Roehr
Spurgeon Creek Grange
Olympia, Washington

PINEAPPLE-BEEF BALL BUFFET

1 13½-oz. can pineapple chunks
1 c. rice

1½ tsp. salt
1 1-lb. can stewed tomatoes
½ tsp. dillweed
2 tbsp. chopped parsley
Beef Balls

Drain pineapple, reserving syrup; add enough water to make 1½ cups liquid. Combine pineapple liquid, rice and 1 teaspoon salt in saucepan; bring to a boil. Cover; simmer over very low heat for about 15 minutes or until dry and fluffy. Add pineapple, remaining salt and remaining ingredients. Add Beef Balls; toss to mix well. Place in 2-quart baking dish. Bake in 375-degree oven for 25 minutes or until heated through. Yield: 6 servings.

Beef Balls

1 lb. ground lean beef
1 egg, slightly beaten
1 c. fine soft bread crumbs
1 tbsp. instant minced onion
1¼ tsp. salt
⅛ tsp. pepper
¼ c. milk

Combine all ingredients; shape into 1-inch balls. Brown on all sides in 1 tablespoon fat in skillet.

Photograph for this recipe on page 54.

BURGUNDY MEATBALLS

¾ lb. ground beef
¾ c. sifted bread crumbs
¼ c. minced onion
¾ tsp. cornstarch
Few grains of allspice
1 egg, slightly beaten
¾ c. milk
1 tsp. salt
¼ c. oil
3 tbsp. flour
1 c. Burgundy
2 beef bouillon cubes
⅛ tsp. pepper

Combine first 7 ingredients and ¾ teaspoon salt. Shape into 30 meatballs. Heat oil in skillet. Brown meatballs on all sides, a few at a time. Keep warm. Blend flour with pan drippings. Stir in 2 cups water, ¼ teaspoon salt and remaining ingredients. Cook, stirring constantly, until smooth. Arrange meatballs in sauce; cover. Simmer for 30 minutes. Serve with rice, or noodles. Yield: 6 servings.

Anna I. Marro,
Claremont Grange, No. 9
Claremont, New Jersey

⅓ c. chopped onion
½ tsp. ginger
2 eggs, beaten
1½ tsp. salt
¼ c. milk
1 tbsp. shortening
2 tbsp. cornstarch
½ c. (firmly packed) brown sugar
⅓ c. vinegar
1 tbsp. soy sauce
⅓ c. chopped green pepper
1 can pineapple chunks, drained

Combine first 7 ingredients; mix well. Shape into small balls. Brown in shortening. Combine cornstarch, brown sugar, vinegar and soy sauce in saucepan. Cook until thickened. Add green pepper and pineapple. Pour over meatballs. Serve hot. Yield: 6-8 servings.

Lillian R. Powell, C.W.A.
Golden Harvest Grange
Carmel, Maine

EDUCATED MEATBALLS

1 lb. ground meat
1 egg, beaten
Salt and pepper to taste
1½ tbsp. finely chopped onion
2 tbsp. flour
Oil
1 c. chicken stock or canned chicken soup
4 slices pineapple, cubed
3 green peppers, cut in lg. pieces
3 tbsp. cornstarch
2 tsp. soy sauce
¼ c. vinegar
½ c. sugar

Combine first 4 ingredients. Shape into balls. Roll in flour. Brown lightly in small amount of oil in skillet. Add ⅓ cup chicken stock, 1 tablespoon oil, cubed pineapple and green pepper. Simmer 10 to 15 minutes. Combine cornstarch, soy sauce, vinegar, ¼ cup water, sugar and ⅔ cup chicken stock; mix well. Pour over meatballs. Heat thoroughly. Yield: 6 servings.

Weyona Dodele
Benton Co., Fairmont Grange, No. 252
Albany, Oregon

HAWAIIAN MEATBALLS

1½ lb. ground beef
⅔ c. cracker crumbs

MEATBALL ESPAÑOL

1 lb. lean ground beef
1 c. soft bread crumbs
¼ c. each finely chopped onion and celery
1½ tsp. Worcestershire sauce
1 egg, beaten
1 tbsp. garlic salt
¼ tsp. pepper
1 16-oz. can stewed tomatoes
2½ c. zucchini, thinly sliced
½ tsp. each crushed oregano, basil and sugar
1 tbsp. cornstarch
1 c. beef broth
3 c. hot cooked rice

Combine first 7 ingredients; mix well. Shape into 12 meatballs. Place in greased shallow baking pan. Bake at 375 degrees for 20 minutes. Combine tomatoes and zucchini with remaining seasonings in separate saucepan. Simmer for 5 minutes. Blend cornstarch and broth. Stir into tomato mixture. Pour over meatballs. Bake 10 minutes longer. Serve over fluffy rice. Yield: 6 servings.

Gertrude Hastings
Suffield Grange, No. 27
Suffield, Connecticut

PORCUPINES

2 lb. hamburger
2 eggs, beaten
½ c. uncooked rice
2 potatoes, peeled and grated
½ lg. onion, chopped

Salt and pepper to taste
1 sm. can tomato juice

Combine all ingredients except tomato juice. Shape into balls. Place in casserole. Cover with tomato juice and enough water to cover all. Bake at 350 degrees for 1 hour and 30 minutes. Yield: 6 servings.

Mrs. Emma Wildemuth
Osco Grange, No. 1782
Cambridge, Illinois

BEEF NOODLE–VEGETABLE CASSEROLE

1 lb. ground beef
3 c. noodles
2 tbsp. beef concentrate
6 med. onions, thinly sliced
½ med. red pepper, chopped
½ med. green pepper, chopped
Butter
4 med. carrots, sliced and cooked
1 c. cooked asparagus
4½ oz. can mushrooms
6 oz. grated cheese

Crumble beef; cook until lightly browned. Drain. Combine noodles and beef concentrate in 1 quart water, boil until noodles are tender. Drain. Saute onions and peppers separately in butter. Reserve enough cheese for topping. Alternate layers of beef, noodles, vegetables and cheese in 8 × 14 inch baking pan until all ingredients are used. Top with reserved cheese. Bake at 350 degrees for 1 hour. Best prepared a day ahead and refrigerated. Yield: 10-12 servings.

Florence M. Wells, C.W.A.
Chambers Prairie Grange, No. 191
Turnwater, Washington

BEEF-MUSHROOM CASSEROLE

1½ lb. lean ground beef
1 can cream of chicken soup
1 can cream of mushroom soup
1 c. sour cream
¼ c. chopped pimento
1 4-oz. can sliced mushrooms, drained
¾ tsp. salt
¼ tsp. pepper
3 c. cooked crinkly noodles, drained
Buttered bread crumbs

Brown beef lightly. Add next 7 ingredients; mix well. Stir in noodles. Pour into large casserole. Top with bread crumbs. Bake in 350-degree oven for 30 minutes or until lightly browned. Yield: 8-10 servings.

Mrs. Burdette Goodrich
Georgetown Grange, No. 1540
Erieville, New York

BEST-EVER CASSEROLE

1 lb. ground beef
1 tbsp. shortening
2 med. onions, chopped
1 No. 2½ can tomatoes
½ lb. small noodles, broken
1 green pepper, chopped
4 stalks celery, chopped
1 pkg. frozen mixed vegetables
1 tsp. chili powder
1 tsp. salt
½ tsp. pepper
½ lb. sharp cheese, sliced

Brown ground beef in shortening in large skillet. Add remaining ingredients except cheese. Add ½ cup hot water to cover. Cook for 20 minutes. Layer cheese over mixture. Cook for 5 minutes or longer until cheese melts. Yield: 6-8 servings.

Mrs. Joseph Gannon
Slippery Rock Grange, No. 1441
Slippery Rock, Pennsylvania

CECILIA'S COMPANY CASSEROLE

1 8-oz. package med. noodles
1½ lb. ground round
2 tbsp. butter, melted
1 tsp. salt
Pepper to taste
Minced garlic or garlic salt to taste
1 8-oz. can tomato sauce
1 c. cottage cheese
1 c. sour cream
6 green onions with tops, chopped
¾ c. grated sharp cheese

Cook noodles according to package directions. Drain. Brown meat in butter. Add salt, pepper, garlic and tomato sauce. Simmer for 5 minutes. Combine cottage cheese, sour cream, onions and noodles. Alternate layers of noodles and meat mixture in baking dish until all ingredients are used. Top with grated cheese. Bake at 350 degrees for 45 minutes or until done.

Cecilia Klapstein
Chelon Co., Manson Grange, No. 796
Manson, Washington

CHILI-BURGER SUPPER

1 c. elbow macaroni or spaghetti
1 lb. ground beef
1 can chili-beef soup
1 can tomato soup
3 slices sharp process American cheese

Cook macaroni in boiling salted water until done; drain thoroughly. Brown beef in skillet. Add soups and macaroni. Heat for 5 to 7 minutes or until mixture is bubbly, stirring occasionally. Place cheese slices on top; cover for a few minutes to melt cheese slightly. Yield: 6 servings.

Mrs. Loretta Sechler
Kingwood Grange, No. 1765
Confluence, Pennsylvania

GRANDMA'S CASSEROLE

1 c. chopped onion
1 green pepper, cut in strips (opt.)
2 tbsp. margarine
1½ lb. lean ground chuck
1 tsp. seasoned salt
½ tsp. pepper
1 tbsp. sugar
1 1-lb. 12-oz. can whole tomatoes
1 15-oz. can tomato sauce
1 8-oz. package wide egg noodles, uncooked
1 8-oz. package sliced mozzarella cheese

Saute onion, green pepper and margarine in large skillet for 3 minutes. Add ground chuck. Brown meat; crumble with spoon. Add seasoned salt, pepper and sugar. Stir in tomatoes, tomato sauce and 2 cups water. Bring to a boil. Reduce heat; simmer 15 minutes. Alternate layers of tomato-meat mixture and uncooked noodles until all ingredients are used in a 9 × 13-inch pan. Top with sliced mozzarella cheese. Cover noodles well with sauce. Bake, covered, in preheated 350-degree oven for 45 minutes. Uncover. Bake for about 15 minutes longer. Yield: 8-10 servings.

Mrs. Ruth Baker
Morrow Co., Williamsport Grange, No. 1815
Bellville, Ohio

HAMBURGER-CHEESE BAKE

4 oz. noodles
1 lb. hamburger
¾ tsp. salt
½ tsp. pepper
1 sm. onion, chopped
1 tbsp. green pepper
¼ tsp. garlic salt

1 8-oz. can tomato sauce
½ tsp. oregano
1 3-oz. package cream cheese, softened
¼ c. sour cream
¾ c. cottage cheese

Boil noodles in salted water; drain. Brown next 6 ingredients in skillet. Add tomato sauce and oregano; mix well. Simmer until hot. Mix last 3 ingredients. Pour half the noodles in 8-inch square baking pan. Place cheese mixture on top. Spread remaining noodles over cheese mixture. Place hamburger mixture on top. Bake at 350 degrees for 20 minutes. Yield: 10 servings.

Alice Anderson
Mt. Wheeler Grange
Oso, Washington

WINNING LASAGNA

1 lb. ground beef
¾ c. chopped onion
2 tbsp. salad or olive oil
1 1-lb. can tomatoes
2 6-oz. cans tomato paste
1 tbsp. chopped parsley
1 tsp. sugar
½ to ¾ tsp. garlic powder
½ tsp. pepper
½ tsp. oregano leaves, crushed
8 oz. lasagna noodles
1 lb. ricotta cheese
8 oz. mozzarella cheese, shredded
1 c. grated Parmesan cheese

Saute beef and onion in oil. Drain. Add next 7 ingredients and 2 cups water, chopping tomatoes with spoon. Simmer, uncovered, for 30 minutes, stirring occasionally. Cook lasagna noodles according to package directions. Drain. Spread 1 cup sauce in 9 × 13-inch pan. Alternate layers of noodles, sauce, ricotta, mozzarella and Parmesan cheese, ending with sauce, mozzarella and Parmesan. Bake at 350 degrees for 40 to 50 minutes or until bubbly. Cool 15 minutes before serving. Cut in squares to serve. Yield: 8 servings.

Cheryl Lundgren
Potomac Grange, No. 1
Arlington, Virginia

MICROWAVE MACARONI QUICKIE

½ lb. ground beef
1 c. uncooked elbow macaroni
1 med. onion, chopped
1 8-oz. can tomato sauce
⅛ c. catsup

Pinch of sugar
½ tsp. salt
¼ tsp. pepper
¼ tsp. chili powder

Combine all ingredients with 1½ cups water in 2-quart casserole. Blend well. Microwave, covered tightly for about 15 minutes or until macaroni is tender, stirring occasionally during cooking time. Let stand 4 to 5 minutes to blend flavors. Yield: 4-6 servings.

Barbara Milliron
Blue Ball Grange, No. 1331
Osceola Mills, Pennsylvania

ONE-POT SPAGHETTI SUPPER

1 lb. ground beef
1 med. onion, chopped
1 clove of garlic, minced
1½ tsp. salt
¼ tsp. ground allspice
½ tsp. dry mustard
¼ tsp. pepper
6 oz. uncooked spaghetti, broken into fourths
2½ c. tomato juice
Parmesan cheese

Brown beef with onion and garlic in Dutch oven. Add seasonings. Arrange spaghetti on top. Pour 1 cup water and tomato juice over spaghetti, moistening well; cover. Bring mixture to a boil; reduce heat. Simmer about 15 minutes or until spaghetti is tender, stirring occasionally. Serve with Parmesan cheese. Yield: 4-6 servings.

Photograph for this recipe on page 58.

PAULINE'S SPAGHETTI SAUCE

2 lb. ground beef
1 med. onion, chopped
1 bell pepper, chopped
¼ tsp. garlic powder
1 sm. can tomato paste
1 can tomato sauce
2 cans tomatoes
1 4½-oz. can chopped mushrooms, drained
1 tsp. sugar
½ tsp. oregano
½ tsp. parsley
½ tsp. basil
1 tsp. salt
1 tsp. pepper
1 tbsp. Worcestershire sauce

Brown meat. Add onion, pepper and garlic just before meat is browned. Drain off grease. Set meat aside. Mix remaining ingredients in large saucepan. Add meat mixture. Cook over low heat for 2 to 3 hours. Yield: 8 servings.

Mrs. Pauline E. Wright
Dutch Fork Grange, No. 706
Irmo, South Carolina

QUICK PIZZA

2 c. flour
4 tsp. baking powder
1 tsp. salt
⅓ c. Crisco
1 c. milk
1 sm. onion, chopped
1 lb. ground beef
Salt and pepper to taste
3 c. spaghetti sauce
4 oz. mozzarella cheese, grated

Sift dry ingredients together. Cut in Crisco as for pie crust. Add milk; stir until flour is moist. Spread in well-greased 9 × 13-inch baking pan. Brown onion and ground beef. Add salt and pepper. Spread over crust. Top with spaghetti sauce. Sprinkle grated mozzarella cheese over top. Bake at 375 degrees for 20 minutes. Yield: 4 servings.

Mrs. Calvin Thayer
Center Road Grange, No. 502
Linesville, Pennsylvania

MONTANA SOMBREROS

1 c. chopped onion
⅔ c. chopped celery
⅔ c. chopped green pepper
3 tbsp. fat
2 lb. ground beef
2 to 3 tsp. chili powder
2 tsp. salt
¼ tsp. pepper
½ tsp. thyme
2 6-oz. cans tomato paste
Dash Tabasco sauce
2 tsp. Worcestershire sauce
2 6-oz. packages corn chips
2 c. shredded process American cheese

Saute onion, celery and green pepper in fat in electric skillet. Add remaining ingredients except corn chips and cheese. Add 2 cups water. Simmer for 1 hour, stirring occasionally. Serve meat sauce on corn chips. Top generously with cheese.

Thelma Warfield, Pomona C.W.A.
Walla Walla Co., Pomona Grange, No. 27
Walla Walla, Washington

Cook crumbled beef in butter in large frypan until lightly browned. Add bell pepper and onion. Saute for 3 to 5 minutes or until just tender, stirring often. Combine next 4 ingredients. Drain pineapple, reserving juice. Set pineapple aside. Pour juice into sugar mixture; stir well. Pour sauce into ground beef mixture. Cook, stirring, until thickened. Add pineapple. Heat to serve. Yield: 4 servings.

Meg Wiley
Potomac Grange, No. 1
Arlington, Virginia

BEANS AND BEEF BALLS

1 lb. ground beef
¼ c. dry bread crumbs
2 tbsp. minced onion
1 tsp. salt
Dash of pepper
⅔ c. evaporated milk
5 slices bacon, chopped
1 lg. onion, sliced
½ c. (firmly packed) light brown sugar
¼ c. vinegar
¼ tsp. dry mustard
½ tsp. garlic powder (opt.)
1 15-oz. can kidney beans, drained
1 can lima beans
1 can baked beans

Combine first 6 ingredients in a bowl: mix lightly. Shape into 12 balls. Set aside. Fry bacon until crisp; remove from drippings. Set aside. Brown meatballs slowly on all sides in drippings. Remove meatballs. Add onion to drippings; saute until tender. Drain off drippings. Add next 4 ingredients to onion. Simmer for 5 minutes. Add beans and bacon; cover. Simmer for 20 minutes, stirring occasionally. Place meatballs on top of beans. Simmer for 10 minutes longer. Yield: 6-8 servings.

Mrs. Clyde Diehl
Big Creek Grange, No. 1559
Palmerton, Pennsylvania

SOUTH-OF-THE-BORDER CASSEROLE

1 lb. ground beef
½ c. chopped onion
2 8-oz. cans tomato sauce
1 tbsp. chili powder
1 tsp. salt
12 tortillas, cut in half
8 oz. sharp Cheddar cheese, grated

Brown meat in a frypan. Add onion; cook until tender. Stir in tomato sauce and seasonings. Alternate layers of meat mixture, tortillas and cheese in 1½-quart casserole. Bake at 325 degrees for 20 minutes. Yield: 4-6 servings.

Mrs. Flo Carter
Wife of Texas State Master
Elmendorf, Texas

SWEET AND SOUR BEEF

1 lb. lean ground beef
1 tbsp. butter or margarine, melted
1 sm. seeded red or green bell pepper cut into thin strips
1 med. onion, sliced
⅓ c. (firmly packed) brown sugar
2 tbsp. cornstarch
¼ c. red wine vinegar
3 tbsp. soy sauce
1 1 lb. 4-oz. can pineapple chunks or tidbits

FOUR-BEAN BAKE

1 lb. hamburger or 5 slices bacon, cut-up
1 c. chopped onion
2 15-oz. cans red kidney beans
1 28-oz. can pork and beans
2 cans lima beans
1 can string beans
½ c. (firmly packed) brown sugar or molasses
1 clove of garlic, minced
¼ c. prepared mustard or 1 tbsp. dry mustard
2 tsp. salt

½ tsp. (about) pepper
½ c. catsup or chili sauce
1 to 2 tbsp. vinegar

Brown hamburger and onion in large skillet. Drain kidney beans, reserving liquid. Add kidney beans and remaining ingredients to hamburger; mix well. Pour into 10 × 14-inch baking dish. Add reserved liquid to moisten, if needed. Bake at 300 degrees for 2 to 3 hours or until brown. Yield: 12 servings.

Frances Pierson
Mt. Wheeler Grange, No. 696
Arlington, Washington

BEEF-CARROT CASSEROLE

8 oz. med. noodles
1 lb. ground beef
¼ c. minced onion
1 clove of garlic, minced
1 tbsp. butter or margarine, melted
2 8-oz. cans tomato sauce
1 tsp. salt
¼ tsp. pepper
1 c. cream-style cottage cheese
1 c. sour cream
¼ c. chopped fresh parsley
1 c. sliced cooked carrots
1 c. shredded Cheddar cheese

Prepare noodles according to package directions; drain. Saute beef, onion and garlic in butter until well-browned. Stir in tomato sauce, salt and pepper. Simmer, uncovered, for 5 minutes. Combine cottage cheese, sour cream, parsley and carrots. Add noodles; mix well. Alternate layers of meat mixture and cottage cheese in greased 3-quart casserole, beginning and ending with noodles. Top with Cheddar cheese. Bake in a 350-degree over for 30 minutes or until hot. Yield: 6-8 servings.

Mrs. Helen Molodich
Ekonk Grange, No. 89
Moosup, Connecticut

FAMILY FAVORITE HOT DISH

4 c. sliced potatoes
⅔ c. chopped green pepper
1 c. diced celery
1 c. sliced onion
1 tbsp. salt
⅛ tsp. pepper
1 lb. ground beef
1 can condensed tomato soup

Layer first 6 ingredients in 3-quart casserole. Spread ground beef on top. Combine soup and ½

can water. Pour over all. Bake, covered, at 350 degrees for 1 hour and 30 minutes. Yield: 4-6 servings.

Mary L. Stenberg
Pine Grange, No. 716
Pine River, Montana

HAMBURGER SHEPHERD'S PIE

1 lb. lean ground beef
1 tbsp. shortening
2 tbsp. flour
1 tsp. salt
⅛ tsp. pepper
1 c. beef broth or stock
1 c. thinly sliced celery
1 c. thinly sliced carrots
2 c. fluffly mashed potatoes
1 c. onion rings

Brown beef in shortening. Add flour, salt and pepper. Mix well. Add broth gradually stirring until slightly thickened. Pour into 2-quart casserole. Add carrots and celery; mix well. Top with potatoes and onion rings. Bake at 350 degrees for 45 minutes. Yield: 5-6 servings.

Mildred W. Eames
Perry Grange, No. 1163
Perry, New York

POTATO-TOPPED HAMBURGER CASSEROLE

1 lb. hamburger
1 onion, chopped
4 carrots, peeled and sliced
1 tsp. salt
¼ tsp. pepper
3 tbsp. flour
3 c. mashed potatoes
Butter

Brown hamburger in frypan for 5 minutes; crumble with spoon. Add onion, carrots, salt, pepper and a small amount of hot water. Bring to a boil; cook for 10 minutes. Thicken with flour mixed with a little water. Pour into buttered 2-quart casserole. Cover with potatoes. Dot with butter. Bake at 375 degrees for 30 minutes. Yield: 6-8 servings.

Carrie Sawker C.W.A.
Buxton Grange, No. 95
Gorham, Maine

PEPPY STUFFED PEPPERS

4 med. green peppers
1 lb. ground beef
2 c. cooked rice
¼ c. cooked onion
1½ tsp. salt
⅛ tsp. pepper
2 8-oz. cans tomato sauce

Halve peppers lengthwise. Remove seeds; Wash. Mix next 5 ingredients and ½ cup tomato sauce. Fill pepper halves with mixture. Arrange in 10 × 13-inch baking dish. Pour remaining tomato sauce over peppers; cover tightly. Bake at 350 degrees for 1 hour or until peppers are tender.

Mary Ellen Wiley
Potomac Grange, No. 1
Arlington, Virginia

ZUCCHINI AND GROUND BEEF CASSEROLE

1 lb. ground beef
1 c. chopped celery
2 c. sliced zucchini
Salt and pepper to taste
1 8-oz. can tomatoes
3 tbsp. Worcestershire sauce
1 tsp. sugar
3 tbsp. grated Parmesan cheese

Brown beef and celery in skillet. Drain, reserving drippings; set aside. Saute zucchini in reserved drippings until lightly browned. Alternate layers of beef mixture and zucchini in 1½-quart casserole until all ingredients are used. Sprinkle lightly with salt and pepper. Combine tomatoes, Worcestershire sauce and sugar; mix well. Pour over casserole. Sprinkle with Parmesan cheese. Bake in 350-degree oven for 40 minutes or until bubbly. Yield: 4 servings.

Dollie Belden
Trowbridge Grange, No. 296
Allegan, Michigan

EASY TUESDAY SUPPER

Flour
2 tsp. baking powder
1 tsp. salt
½ c. plus 1 tbsp. shortening
¼ c. (scant) milk
1 egg, beaten
½ to 1 c. leftover chicken, pork, or beef, chopped
1 to 2 c. gravy or broth

1 or 2 potatoes, diced
1 or 2 carrots, sliced
1 stalk celery, sliced
2 onion slices, chopped
½ to 1 c. peas
2 tbsp. cornstarch

Sift together 1 cup flour, baking powder and salt into bowl. Cut in shortening. Add milk to egg; stir into dry mixture. Shape into ball; wrap. Refrigerate. Combine next 7 ingredients together in large saucepan. Cook until vegetables are tender. Season to taste. Combine cornstarch, 1 tablespoon flour and ¼ cup water. Add to hot vegetable mixture. Pat out ⅔ of the dough on floured sheet of waxed paper. Place dough in 9-inch pie pan. Fill with stew, reserving a portion of the gravy for serving. Pat out remaining dough; place on top of stew. Bake in 375-degree oven for 30 minutes or until golden brown.

Mary-Lee Steel
Potomac Grange, No. 1
Washington, D. C.

FRANKS AND CABBAGE CASSEROLE

3 c. shredded cabbage
3 red apples, sliced
4 frankfurters, cut into chunks, or 1 lb. cooked ham, cubed
Butter or margarine
¼ c. (firmly packed) brown sugar
¼ c. vinegar
¾ tsp. salt
2 tbsp. cornstarch
½ c. cracker crumbs

Steam cabbage in small amount of water in covered saucepan until tender-crisp. Drain. Combine cabbage and apples in greased quart casserole. Add frankfurters. Melt 2 tablespoons butter in saucepan. Stir in sugar, vinegar, salt and ¼ cup water. Bring to a boil. Combine cornstarch and ¼ cup water into a paste. Add slowly to hot mixture. Cook, stirring constantly, until thick and clear. Pour sweet-sour sauce over frankfurters. Dot with butter. Sprinkle crumbs on top. Bake, covered, at 350 degrees for 30 minutes. Uncover. Bake 15 minutes longer.

Mrs. Mae Moser
Thurmont Grange, No. 409
Thurmont, Maryland

FRANK AND SAUERKRAUT CASSEROLE

1 sm. onion, chopped
2 tbsp. vegetable oil
1 lb. can sauerkraut, well drained
1 lb. frankfurters, cut into 1-inch pieces

1 peeled apple, sliced
1 c. applesauce
1 8-oz. can tomato sauce

Saute onion in oil until golden. Mix with sauerkraut. Spread half the frankfurters in 1½-quart casserole. Place sauerkraut over frankfurters. Arrange remaining frankfurters over sauerkraut. Top with apple slices. Combine applesauce and tomato sauce; pour over apples. Bake at 350 degrees for 30 minutes. Yield: 4-6 servings.

Ruth E. Sowers
Leonidas Grange, No. 266
Mendon, Michigan

SLICED BAKED HAM

1 tbsp. butter
2 tbsp. brown sugar
½ tsp. dry mustard
1 tbsp. orange juice
1 slice ham, 1⅛ in. thick
1 c. milk

Melt butter in frypan. Add sugar, mustard and orange juice. Blend well. Place ham in mixture; brown lightly on both sides. Pour milk around ham. Bake at 325 degrees for 45 minutes. Remove ham to serving dish. Thicken gravy. Pour over ham. Garnish with pineapple, cranberries or orange sections and parsley. Yield: 4-6 servings.

Edith K. Luce, Home Ec. Chm.
Chelsea Grange, No. 362
Chelsea, Vermont

BROCCOLI AND HAM CASSEROLE

1 10-oz. package frozen broccoli
3½ tbsp. butter or margarine
1½ tbsp. flour
½ tsp. salt
1½ c. milk
2 c. chopped, cooked ham
2 tbsp. chopped green pepper
2 hard-boiled eggs, chopped
¼ c. grated cheese
1 tsp. chopped onion
4 tsp. lemon juice
½ c. bread crumbs

Cook broccoli according to package directions. Drain; chop into 1½ inch pieces. Melt 1½ tablespoons butter in a saucepan. Add flour and salt; cook 1 minute. Add milk. Cook, stirring constantly, until thickened. Place broccoli in 1½ quart buttered casserole. Combine next 6 ingredients. Cover broccoli with ham mixture. Pour white sauce over

all. Combine 2 tablespoons melted butter with bread crumbs. Sprinkle over top. Bake at 350 degrees for 20 minutes or until hot and bubbly. Green beans or asparagus may be substituted for broccoli. Yield: 10 servings.

Iva Guiter
Leonidas Grange, No. 266
Scotts, Michigan

DEEP DISH HAM PIE

¼ c. butter
¼ c. flour
½ tsp. salt
1 tsp. dry mustard
½ tsp. pepper
1 tsp. minced onion
2 c. milk
2½ c. diced cooked ham
2 hard-boiled eggs, chopped
1 8½-oz. can peas, drained
1 recipe biscuit dough or pastry

Melt butter; blend in flour, salt and mustard. Add pepper, onion and milk. Cook over medium heat, stirring constantly, until thick. Add ham, eggs and peas. Pour into 1½-quart casserole. Roll out dough; cover casserole. Fold edges under. Prick dough with fork to allow steam to escape. Bake at 450 degrees for 20 minutes or until top is browned.

Nora Wilson
Clearwater Grange, No. 299
Kooskia, Idaho

HAM BALLS

1 lb. smoked ham, ground
1½ lb. fresh pork, ground
2 c. dried bread crumbs
1 c. milk
1 tsp. salt
2 eggs, beaten
½ c. vinegar
1½ tsp. dry mustard
1 c. (firmly packed) brown sugar

Combine first 6 ingredients; mix well. Form into balls. Place in baking dish. Combine remaining ingredients with ½ cup water. Pour over ham balls. Bake at 350 degrees for 1 hour and 30 minutes. Balls may be shaped the day before and refrigerated. Yield: 30 balls.

Mrs. Marjorie Radford
Burns Grange, No. 1839
Kewanee, Illinois

ETHEL'S HAM LOAF

1½ lb. lean smoked ham, ground
¾ lb. lean fresh pork, ground
1½ tsp. Worcestershire sauce
1½ c. soft bread crumbs
1 egg, beaten
½ tbsp. horseradish (opt.)
⅛ tsp. pepper
Flour

Combine all ingredients except flour; mix thoroughly. Shape into loaf. Sprinkle with flour. Place in roaster. Bake in 350-degree oven for 1 hour.

Mrs. Ethel Petars
Half Moon Grange, No. 290
Port Matilda, Pennsylvania

TREVA'S HAM LOAF

1½ lb. ground ham
¾ lb. ground pork
1 c. bread crumbs
1 c. milk
2 eggs, beaten
1 c. (firmly packed) brown sugar
½ c. vinegar
1 tsp. mustard

Combine first 5 ingredients; mix well. Place in 9x13-inch baking pan; shape into loaf. Combine remaining ingredients with ½ cup water. Blend well. Baste loaf with sauce. Bake in 300-degree oven for 2 hours and 30 minutes. Yield: 8 servings.

Treva Leese
York Co., Gideon Grange, No. 2010
Hanover, Pennsylvania

STUFFED SHOULDER OF LAMB

1 3 to 4-lb. lamb shoulder, boned
Salt and pepper to taste
1 recipe bread stuffing
Flour

Wipe shoulder; sprinkle inside with salt and pepper. Place bread stuffing inside. Fasten edges securely with skewers. Sprinkle outside with salt and pepper; dredge lightly with flour. Place on rack, fat side up, in roasting pan. Bake in 325-degree oven for 2 hours and 30 minutes or to 182 degrees on meat thermometer. Make gravy with pan drippings, if desired. Yield: 6 servings.

From a Grange Friend

LAMB CHOPS WITH MUSHROOMS

½ lb. large mushrooms
1 egg, slightly beaten
Fine cracker crumbs
Butter
6 lamb chops
Toast slices, buttered

Cut mushrooms in half lengthwise. Dip each half in egg. Roll in crumbs. Fry slowly in 3 tablespoons butter in heavy skillet for 10 minutes or until golden brown. Stir frequently. Remove; keep warm. Saute chops slowly in pan drippings for 12 to 18 minutes. Serve chops on toast; cover with mushrooms. Garnish with parsley. Yield: 6 servings.

From a Grange Friend

FRENCH CANADIAN TOURTIERE

2 lb. ground pork
2 med. onions, chopped
3 med. potatoes, chopped
1½ tsp. cinnamon
½ tsp. allspice
Salt and pepper to taste
½ tsp. cloves
1 tsp. sugar
Pastry for 2-crust pie
1 egg, beaten
Milk

Brown pork. Add vegetables and 3 cups water. Cook 1 hour. Add spices and seasonings; mix well. Cool. Roll out crust. Place in pie plate. Add filling and top-crust. Brush top crust with mixture of egg and milk. Bake at 375 degrees for 1 hour or until brown. Yield: 6-8 servings.

Lillian F. Brown
Hudson Grange, No. 11
Hudson, New Hampshire

TOUCHIE PIE

2 lb. lean ground pork
1 lb. ground beef
1 lg onion, ground
1 tsp. salt
¼ tsp. pepper
½ tsp. cinnamon
½ tsp. sage
3 potatoes, cooked and mashed
Pastry for 2-crust pie

Simmer meat in 2 cups water for 45 minutes. Add onion and seasonings. Simmer 15 minutes longer. Mix in mashed potatoes; cool. Line pie pan with pastry. Add filling. Top with second crust. Slash top for steam vents. Bake at 400 degrees for 30 minutes or until brown. Serve hot or cold. This makes enough filling for 2 pies. It freezes well.

Mrs. Skip Rossman
Roxy Ann Grange, No. 792
Medford, Oregon

FRENCH-FRIED LIVER

1 lb. pork or beef liver
½ c. flour
½ c. cornmeal
1 egg, beaten
Salt and pepper to taste

Cut liver in thin strips. Combine flour and cornmeal. Dip liver in egg; roll in flour mixture until well-coated. Heat enough bacon grease to measure 1 inch deep, in fry-pan. Add liver. Fry until golden brown. Drain on absorbent paper. Season with salt and pepper. Serve with spicy tomato sauce, if desired. Yield: 4 servings.

Mrs. William Corey
Harbor Springs Grange, No. 730
Harbor Springs, Michigan

LOUISIANA YAM AND PORK SURPRISE

4 pork chops, 1-in. thick
½ tsp. salt
¼ tsp. pepper
3 tbsp. salad oil
2 16-oz. cans Louisiana yams, undrained
1 8¼-oz. can sliced pineapple, undrained
⅛ tsp. each ground cinnamon, ground nutmeg and ground allspice
½ tsp. basil leaves, crushed
1 8½-oz. can water chestnuts, drained and sliced

Sprinkle chops with salt and pepper. Brown chops in hot oil in large heavy skillet; remove. Drain fat from skillet. Drain syrup from yams and pineapple into skillet. Cut pineapple slices in half. Set yams and pineapple slices aside. Stir spices into syrup in skillet; add chops. Cover. Simmer chops for 45 minutes, basting occasionally. Add yams, pineapple slices and water chestnuts. Simmer, covered, 15 minutes longer, basting occasionally. Transfer to serving dish. Yield: 4 servings.

Photograph for this recipe on page 63.

CRANBERRY PORK CHOPS

6 pork chops
½ tsp. salt
4 c. ground cranberries
¾ c. honey
½ tsp. cloves

Brown chops quickly on both sides in hot frypan. Sprinkle with salt. Place 3 chops in greased baking dish. Combine cranberries, honey and cloves. Spread half of mixture over chops. Arrange remaining 3 chops on top. Cover with remaining cranberry mixture. Cover. Bake in 350-degree oven for 1 hour.

From a Grange Friend

PORK CHOPS AND DRESSING

4 pork chops
3 c. toasted bread cubes
2 tbsp. chopped onion
¼ c. melted butter or margarine
¼ tsp. poultry seasoning
1 can cream of chicken soup

Brown pork chops. Place in baking dish. Combine next 4 ingredients with ¼ cup water. Top pork chops with bread mixture. Dilute soup with ⅛ cup water. Pour over dressing. Bake at 350 degrees for 1 hour. Boned chicken or turkey may be substituted for pork chops. Yield: 4 servings.

Mrs. Robert White, Sr.
Painter Creek Grange, No. 1923
Mt. Victory, Ohio

PORK CHOPS AND ZUCCHINI PARMESAN

3 tbsp. flour
4½ tbsp. Parmesan cheese
1½ tsp. salt
½ tsp. dillweed
¼ tsp. pepper
4 or 6 lean pork chops
2 med. onions, sliced
3 or 4 sm. zucchini, sliced
½ tsp. paprika

Combine flour, 1½ tablespoons cheese, salt, dillweed and pepper. Dredge chops with seasoned flour, reserving leftover flour. Brown chops in oil in large skillet on all sides. Spread onions over chops. Add ⅓ cup water. Simmer, covered, for 15 minutes. Add zucchini. Combine leftover flour with 3 tablespoons Parmesan cheese and paprika. Sprinkle over zucchini. Simmer, covered, 25 minutes longer. Transfer to serving dish. Garnish with tomatoes and parsley. Yield: 4-6 servings.

Mrs. Lenore Brake
Capital Grange, No. 540
Bellaire, Michigan

SMOTHERED PORK CHOPS

6 pork chops, center cut
Salt and pepper to taste
1 can mushroom soup
½ tsp. thyme
1 tsp. parsley flakes
½ c. sour cream
1 3½-oz. can French-fried onions

Brown chops; arrange in baking pan. Season with salt and pepper. Combine soup, ½ can of water, and thyme. Heat. Add parsley, sour cream and half the onions. Pour over chops; cover. Bake at 350 degrees for about 1 hour. Remove cover. Add remaining onions. Bake 5 minutes longer. Yield: 6 servings.

Mrs. Margaret Warner
Wife of Master of Connecticut State Grange
Hamden Grange, No. 99, Hamden, Connecticut

PORK SAUSAGE CASSEROLE

1 lb. pork sausage links
1 can tomato soup
1 sm. onion, chopped
1 c. flour
1 egg, beaten
1 tsp. baking powder
½ c. milk

Fry sausages; drain. Place sausage in a casserole. Add soup and onion. Combine remaining ingredients; mix well. Pour over sausage mixture. Bake in 375-degree oven for 20 to 30 minutes.

Mrs. Eli Therriault
Leon Grange
Charlo, Montana

SAUSAGE BEAN POT

1 lb. pork sausage
1 16-oz. can kidney beans
1 16-oz. can white beans
1 16-oz. can diced carrots, drained
1 16-oz. can stewed tomatoes
1 clove of garlic, minced
1 tbsp. parsley flakes
4 slices crisp bacon, crumbled

Brown sausage in Dutch oven over medium heat, stirring until brown. Pour off drippings. Add remaining ingredients except bacon. Cook for 15 minutes. Add bacon. Yield: 6-8 servings.

Catherine L. Marolf
Beaver Falls Grange, No. 554
Castorland, New York

SAUSAGE CHILI

2 lb. lean sausage
4 onions, chopped
1 ½ c. tomato puree
1 lb. 14-oz. can red kidney beans
1 12-oz. can tomato paste
2 tbsp. chili powder
3 tsp. salt
¼ c. sugar
2 tbsp. chili powder

Crumble sausage in skillet. Cook until lightly browned. Cook onions in ½ cup water until tender. Dillute tomato puree with 2 cups water; add to onions. Combine all ingredients in a large saucepan. Add 1 cup water. Bring to a boil. Let cool. Refrigerate overnight to allow flavors to blend. Reheat to serve. May be frozen.

Mrs. Eugene Young, C.W.A.
Athens Co., York Grange, No. 2436
Nelsonville, Ohio

ZUCCHINI CASSEROLE WITH SAUSAGE

1 lb. sweet Italian sausage
4 c. sliced zucchini
2 c. spaghetti sauce

¼ to ½ lb. extra sharp Cheddar cheese, diced
¼ c. seasoned bread crumbs
¼ c. grated Italian cheese

Remove casing from sausage. Form into small balls. Fry until lightly browned. Drain on paper towel. Simmer zucchini in small amount of salted water in saucepan until just tender. Drain. Combine sausage, zucchini, spaghetti sauce and Cheddar cheese. Pour into 2-quart casserole. Sprinkle crumbs over top. Add Italian cheese. Bake in 350-degree oven for 30 minutes.

Mary Stimson
Spencer Grange, No. 1110
Spencer, New York

BARBECUED SPARERIBS

Salt
Pepper
3 lb. spareribs
¾ c. sliced onion
1 clove of garlic, minced
1 tsp. dry mustard
1 c. catsup or chili sauce
2 tbsp. vinegar
2 tbsp. brown sugar
2 tbsp. lemon juice
2 tbsp. Worcestershire sauce
1 c. chopped celery

Salt and pepper ribs. Place in 9x13-inch baking pan. Brown in 350-degree oven. Drain fat, reserving 2 tablespoons. Place reserved fat in saucepan. Saute onion and garlic in fat until browned. Add remaining ingredients with 1 cup water, 1 teaspoon salt and ⅛ teaspoon pepper. Simmer for 20 minutes, stirring occasionally. Pour over ribs. Bake in 350-degree oven for 1 hour to 1 hour and 30 minutes. Baste occasionally. Yield: 6-8 servings.

Mrs. Clovis St. Jean
Stevenson Grange, No. 121
Stevenson, Washington

SAUERKRAUT AND SPARERIBS WITH POTATO DUMPLINGS

1 qt. sauerkraut
3½ to 4 lb. country-style spareribs
¼ tsp. pepper
⅛ tsp. garlic powder (opt.)
2 tbsp. sugar
¼ tsp. caraway seed (opt.)
2 c. mashed potatoes
⅔ c. flour
½ tsp. salt
1 tsp. baking powder

1 egg
3 to 4 tbsp. milk

Place half the sauerkraut in Dutch oven. Arrange ribs over sauerkraut. Sprinkle with pepper and garlic powder. Cover with remaining sauerkraut. Sprinkle with sugar and caraway seed. Pour 1½ cups water carefully over all. Cover. Bring to a boil. Reduce heat. Simmer slowly for 2 hours and 30 minutes. Combine remaining ingredients; mix well for dumplings. Drop dumpling mixture by teaspoons on cooked kraut and ribs. Cover. Cook over medium heat for 15 to 20 minutes longer.

Mrs. Mary Gluck, C.W.A.
Fairview Grange, No. 2177
Elkhart, Indiana

BARBECUE SAUCE FOR SPARERIBS

2⅓ c. tomato juice
2 tbsp. brown sugar
2 tsp. salt
1 tsp. dry mustard
3 tbsp. vinegar
1 tbsp. Worcestershire sauce

Combine all ingredients in a saucepan. Simmer for 15 minutes.

Mrs. Mark W. Deerwester
Hancock Co., Shawtown Grange, No. 2404
McComb, Ohio

CHICKEN CROQUETTES WITH CRANBERRY SAUCE

3 c. cooked chicken
½ sm. onion
1 sm. rib celery
2 c. cooked rice
2 tsp. salt
½ tsp. pepper
1 tbsp. lemon juice
3 eggs
1 c. fine dry bread or cracker crumbs
Hot whole cranberry sauce

Grind chicken, onion and celery. Add rice, seasonings, lemon juice and 2 eggs; mix well. Chill. Shape into 12 croquettes. Beat remaining egg with 2 tablespoons water. Dip croquettes into egg mixture. Roll in crumbs. Fry in deep fat 5 to 7 minutes. Serve croquettes topped with hot cranberry sauce.

Photograph for this recipe on page 65.

CHICKEN BREAST ROLLS

2 chicken breasts, split and boned
⅔ c. butter
4 slices ham
4 slices Swiss cheese
1 tsp. each basil and oregano
½ tsp. garlic salt
¼ tsp. salt
Flour
1 egg, beaten
½ c. fine dry bread crumbs

Pound chicken breasts in waxed paper until thin. Divide butter into 4 portions. Place 1 slice each of ham and cheese on each chicken breast. Sprinkle with basil, oregano, garlic salt and salt. Insert 1 portion of butter on top of cheese. Roll up; fasten with toothpick. Roll in flour; dip in egg. Roll in bread crumbs. Place in 9-inch square pan. Bake in preheated 350-degree oven for 50 minutes or until brown, basting once. Yield: 4 servings.

A. Maude Harlow
Fidelity Grange
South Hampton, New Hampshire

CHICKEN BREASTS SUPREME

4 chicken breasts, split and boned
¼ c. flour
1¼ tsp. salt
½ tsp. paprika
¼ c. butter or margarine
2 tsp. cornstarch
1½ c. evaporated milk or light cream
¼ c. Sherry

½ tsp. grated lemon peel
1 tbsp. lemon juice
¾ c. grated Cheddar cheese

Remove skin from chicken. Combine next 3 ingredients in bag. Shake a few pieces of chicken at a time in bag to coat. Melt butter in skillet; add chicken. Cook 15 minutes or until brown on both sides. Add ¼ cup water; cover. Simmer 30 minutes. Remove chicken, reserving drippings. Place in 9x12-inch casserole. Combine cornstarch with ¼ cup milk; blend until smooth. Add mixture to pan drippings. Add remaining milk, Sherry, lemon peel and lemon juice. Cook 3 minutes or until thick. Pour over chicken; cover. Bake in 350-degree oven for 35 minutes or until fork-tender. Sprinkle cheese on chicken. Return to oven for 2 minutes longer or until cheese is melted. Yield: 4 servings.

May V. Wiles
Jeremiah Smith Grange
Durham, New Hampshire

CHICKEN ENCHILADAS WITH SOUR CREAM

1 lb. chicken breasts
1 sprig parsley
1 sm. carrot, chopped
Salt
1 clove of garlic, chopped
4 tbsp. olive oil
1½ c. canned green chili peppers
5 ripe peeled tomatoes, chopped
2 med. onions, chopped
Pinch of oregano
½ lb. grated Cheddar cheese
1 pt. sour cream
12 tortillas

Place chicken breasts, parsley and carrot in a saucepan. Salt slightly; cover with water. Bring to a boil; cook until tender, about 45 minutes. Remove chicken; cool. Remove skin and bones; shred chicken into a bowl. Saute garlic in olive oil; add chili peppers, tomatoes, onions, oregano and a pinch of salt. Cover with water; cook over low heat until thick. Add cheese and sour cream to chicken; mix thoroughly. Saute tortillas, one at a time, for a few seconds or until soft. Dip tortillas into chili sauce. Fill with chicken mixture; roll up. Place in flat casserole. Cover with remaining chili sauce. Bake at 350 degrees for 10 to 15 minutes or until thoroughly heated. Serve with shredded lettuce, green salad or guacamole.

Rosemary Worthy
Boerne Grange, No. 1545
Boerne, Texas

CHICKEN WITH TAJ MAHAL BARBECUE SAUCE

2 c. orange juice
½ c. (firmly packed) brown sugar
½ c. sugar
½ tsp. ginger
1 tsp. curry powder
2 tbsp. Sherry
8 whole chicken breasts

Combine first 6 ingredients in large saucepan. Bring to a boil. Add chicken. Simmer 10 minutes per side. Remove to large baking dish. Bake in 350-degree oven for 1 hour, basting occasionally with remaining sauce. Yield: 8 servings.

From a Grange Friend

MY MOTHER'S CHICKEN PIE

4 lb. cut-up chicken
2 stalks celery, cut in pieces
1 onion, diced
1 clove of garlic (opt.)
2 tsp. salt
Flour
3 tsp. baking powder
¼ c. shortening
¾ c. milk

Combine first 4 ingredients and 1 teaspoon salt in large saucepan. Cover with water. Cook until chicken falls from bones. Remove chicken from stock; cut into bite-sized pieces. Arrange evenly in 9x13 inch baking dish. Combine ¼ cup flour and ½ cup water. Add to stock; stir until thick. Pour gravy over chicken. Bake in 400-degree oven until bubbly. Sift 2 cups flour with baking powder and 1 teaspoon salt into large bowl. Cut in shortening. Stir in milk to form soft dough. Knead lightly. Roll out dough to ½ inch thick. Cut biscuits with 2-inch cutter. Place over chicken. Bake at 400 degrees for 10 minutes or until well browned. Reduce temperature to 350 degrees. Bake for 10 to 15 minutes longer. Yield: 12-16 servings.

Mrs. Loana S. Shibles
St. Alabans Grange, No. 114
Newport, Maine

ROSEMARY CHICKEN

¼ c. flour
1 tsp. salt
3 lg. chicken breasts, cut in halves
¼ c. Mazola oil or butter
2 tsp. crushed rosemary
½ c. chopped green onions

4 oz. sliced mushrooms
1 7-oz. bottle of lemon-lime beverage
1 c. sour cream
½ c. cream Sherry
1 tsp. Accent

Combine flour and salt. Coat chicken with flour-salt mixture. Heat Mazola oil in large skillet. Add chicken, skin side down. Brown evenly. Sprinkle rosemary, onion and mushrooms over chicken. Pour beverage into skillet; cover. Cook over low heat for 45 minutes or until tender. Remove chicken to 9x15-inch serving platter. Add sour cream, Sherry, and Accent to sauce, stirring constantly. DO NOT BOIL. Spoon over chicken.

Mary Fairbanks
Lompoc Grange, No. 646
Lompoc, California

BARBECUED CHICKEN

½ c. vinegar
½ c. molasses
¼ c. prepared mustard
2 tbsp. Worcestershire sauce
1 c. catsup
Salt
1 chicken, cut up
Flour

Combine first 5 ingredients; set aside. Salt chicken; roll in flour. Brown lightly in fat in skillet. Remove from skillet; pour off fat. Return chicken to skillet. Pour sauce over chicken; mix well. Cover, simmer slowly for 1 hour.

Mrs. Ruby Stoops
Highland Grange, No. 1771
Norwich, Ohio

BUTTERMILK-FRIED CHICKEN

½ c. flour
½ tsp. curry powder
½ tsp. salt
½ tsp. paprika
⅛ tsp. pepper
1 3-lb. fryer, cut up
⅔ c. buttermilk

Combine first 5 ingredients. Dip chicken pieces in buttermilk. Coat in flour mixture. Brown slowly in frypan in ¼-inch hot shortening. Place on broiler pan. Bake at 350 degrees for 40 to 50 minutes.

Mrs. Rosella Smith
Steuben Co., Big Creek Grange, No. 324
Hornell, New York

COUNTRY-STYLE CHICKEN POTPIE

1 chicken, cut up
1 stalk celery, chopped
1 tsp. chopped onion
Salt
⅓ c. flour
Pepper to taste
2 potatoes, sliced
½ c. cooked peas
½ c. cooked sliced carrots

Cook first 3 ingredients with 1 teaspoon salt in water to cover until tender. Remove chicken. Add enough water to broth to measure 2 cups. Combine flour and ½ cup water; add to broth. Cook stirring, until thick. Add salt and pepper to taste. Remove bones from chicken. Place potatoes, peas, carrots and chicken in casserole. Pour broth mixture over.

Biscuit Topping

2½ c. flour
2 tsp. baking powder
½ tsp. salt
⅓ c. shortening or butter
Milk

Combine first 4 ingredients. Add enough milk to make soft dough. Place on top of casserole. Bake in 375-degree oven for 35 minutes.

Mrs. Alice Menear
Bell Township Grange, No. 2047
Mahaffey, Pennsylvania

ELIZABETH'S CHICKEN PAPRIKA

1 lg. onion, chopped
¼ c. shortening
2½ to 3 lb. chicken, cut into pieces
2 tsp. paprika
1½ tsp. salt
Pepper to taste
2 bouillon cubes
2 tbsp. flour
1 c. sour cream
Dumplings

Saute onions in shortening in Dutch oven. Remove onion. Add chicken; brown. Add paprika, salt, pepper, bouillon cubes, onion and 2 cups water. Cook until chicken is tender. Remove chicken to serving dish. Mix flour with small amount of water until smooth; add to sour cream. Mix well. Add to chicken stock. Pour over chicken. Serve with Dumplings. Yield: 4-6 servings.

Dumplings

2 c. flour
2 eggs
½ tsp. salt

Combine all ingredients with enough water to make a stiff batter. Bring 2 quarts salted water to a boil. Drop batter by spoonsfuls into water. Remove with slotted spoon as they rise to the top.

Elizabeth Ames
Pleasant Valley Grange
Bath, New York

LOW-CAL CHICKEN

1½ c. skim milk
1 tsp. paprika
¼ tsp. pepper
1 tsp. salt
1 3-lb. fryer, cut up

Combine first 4 ingredients in 9x13-inch pan; add chicken. Bake at 375 degrees for 1 hour and 15 minutes, turning twice. Yield: 4 servings.

Joan L. Mohler
Stark Co., Marlboro Grange, No. 1401
Hartville, Ohio

MATTIE TAVERN'S OVEN-FRIED CHICKEN

1 fryer
Butter, melted
Red wine
Salt and Pepper to taste

Split chicken into 4 parts. Place, skin side down, in flat baking pan. Baste twice with butter and wine. Add salt and pepper. Place in 350-degree oven for 45 minutes or until brown. Turn chicken. Bake until browned. Yield: 4 servings.

Marie Olsen
Santa Ynez Valley Grange, No. 644
Solvang, California

VIENNESE CHICKEN

1 onion, minced
2 tbsp. butter
1 roasting chicken, cut up
1 green pepper, chopped
2 carrots, chopped
6 mushrooms, chopped
1 fresh tomato, chopped or ¼ c. canned tomato
Salt and pepper to taste
1 tbsp. flour
½ c. sour cream

Saute onion in butter in large saucepan until tender. Add chicken. Cook until chicken is evenly brown. Add next 5 ingredients. Simmer for 1 hour or until tender. Combine flour and sour cream. Pour into chicken mixture. Cook 3 minutes stirring constantly.

Mrs. Ned Rieth
Ramsey-Spencer Grange
Ramsey, Indiana

CHICKEN ROYALE

3 c. chopped cooked chicken
2 c. soft bread crumbs
1½ c. cooked rice
2 eggs, beaten
1 c. chicken broth or bouillon
1 c. milk
¼ c. chopped pimento
½ tsp. salt
½ tsp. paprika
¼ tsp. pepper
Cream of Mushroom Sauce

Combine first 10 ingredients in large bowl. Turn into 1½-quart buttered loaf dish. Place in pan of hot water. Bake in preheated 350-degree oven for 1 hour. Let stand for 10 minutes; invert onto serving platter. Serve with Cream of Mushroom Sauce.

Cream of Mushroom Sauce

1 chicken bouillon cube
½ c. milk
1 can cream of mushroom soup
½ c. sour cream
2 tbsp. chopped parsley

Dissolve bouillon cube in milk in saucepan over low heat. Stir in soup and sour cream. Heat to serving temperature; do not boil. Add parsley; mix well.

Photograph for this recipe on page 71

SCALLOPED CHICKEN AND STUFFING

2 c. cooked diced chicken
1 can cream of mushroom soup
1 tsp. sage or rosemary
½ tsp. celery salt or seed
3 c. toasted bread cubes
¼ c. butter or margarine
¼ c. dry bread crumbs
⅓ c. chopped onion
1 tbsp. grated Parmesan cheese

Combine chicken, soup and 4 tablespoons water. Add sage and celery salt to toasted bread cubes. Melt butter in small skillet. Add 1 tablespoon melted butter to dry bread crumbs; reserve. Add onion to remaining butter in skillet. Saute until tender. Add to bread cube mixture; mix well. Place half the chicken mixture in ungreased 1-quart casserole. Place stuffing over chicken; top stuffing with remaining chicken mixture. Combine buttered bread crumbs with cheese; sprinkle over top of casserole. Bake in 350-degree oven for 30 minutes.

Florence Waters
Elmore Co., Pamona Grange, No. 10
Mountain Home, Idaho

CHICKEN TAMALE PIE

3 med. onions, chopped
½ c. oil
1 lg. can whole tomatoes, chopped
1 lg. can white hominy, ground
1 tbsp. salt
3 eggs, beaten
3 c. chicken broth
1½ c. yellow cornmeal
1 cooked chicken, cubed
3 tbsp. chili powder
1 can pitted black olives

Saute onions in oil. Add next 5 ingredients. Heat well. Add cornmeal. Add remaining ingredients. Place in 9 × 13-inch greased casserole. Bake at 400 degrees for 30 minutes. Can be made ahead or may be frozen. Yield: 15 servings.

Sandy Powell, C.W.A.
McFarland Grange
McFarland, California

CHICKEN SPAGHETTI

1 chicken
1 pkg. spaghetti
1 green pepper, chopped
1 bunch celery, chopped
1 onion, chopped
Garlic and pepper to taste
Butter
1 lb. Velveeta, cubed
1 can mushrooms
1 can mushroom soup
1 can tomatoes
½ can Ro-Tel

Boil chicken until tender. Remove skin and bones; chop chicken. Boil spaghetti in broth; drain. Saute next 4 ingredients in small amount of butter until tender. Combine vegetables, spaghetti and cheese in large saucepan. Add mushrooms, soup, tomatoes, Ro-Tel and chicken. Cook until cheese is melted.

Mrs. Gilbert Downey
Boerne Grange, No. 1545
Boerne, Texas

SCALLOPED CHICKEN

1 2½ to 3-lb. chicken
2½ tsp. salt
6 c. stale bread cubes
⅛ c. butter, melted
¼ c. minced onions
½ tsp. poultry seasoning
⅛ tsp. pepper
4 tbsp. flour
4 tbsp. fat

Place chicken in 2½ cups water with 2 teaspoons salt in large saucepan. Cook until chicken falls from bones. Reserve broth; cube chicken. Combine next 5 ingredients and ½ teaspoon salt; mix well. Place chicken in 9 × 13-inch baking dish; top with dressing mixture. Combine flour and fat in saucepan. Stir in 2 cups reserved broth. Heat until thick, stirring constantly. Pour over dressing. Bake in 375-degree oven until brown. Yield: 6-8 servings.

Mrs. Alfred Crowell, C.W.A.
Livingston Co., Pomona Grange
Nunda, New York

CHICKEN WITH RICE

1 3 to 4-lb. chicken
3 c. celery, sliced
½ c. chopped onion
¼ green pepper, diced
¼ red pepper, diced
¼ sm. box parsley
2 cans mushroom soup
1 c. salad dressing
1 14-oz. box rice, cooked and drained
1½ c. bread crumbs
½ c. margarine, melted

Cook chicken until meat falls from bones; chop. Return chicken to broth. Cook celery, onion, and peppers together in small amount of water until tender. Combine vegetables and liquid with chicken and broth. Add parsley, mushroom soup, salad dressing and rice; mix well. Place in casserole. Combine crumbs and margarine. Pour over top. Bake at 350 degrees for 1 hour or longer. Yield: 6-8 servings.

Mary Harris
White Pigeon Grange, No. 1345
White Pigeon, Michigan

CHICKEN-BROCCOLI CASSEROLE

2 10-oz. packages broccoli
2 cans cream of chicken soup
1 c. mayonnaise
1 tsp. lemon juice
⅛ tsp. curry powder
2 lb. cooked chicken, diced
¾ c. grated cheese
¾ c. bread crumbs

Cook broccoli according to package directions. Combine next 4 ingredients. Alternate layers of broccoli, chicken soup mixture and cheese in 9 × 13-inch pan. Top with bread crumbs. Bake at 350 degrees for 1 hour. Yield: 6-8 servings.

Elizabeth Bauknecht
Studley Grange, No. 1174
Midland, Michigan

BINGO NOODLES

1 egg
3 egg yolks
Salt
2 c. (about) flour
1 chicken
2 carrots, diced
2 stalks celery, diced

Combine first 2 ingredients with 1 teaspoon salt and ¼ cup water; beat well. Add enough flour for stiff dough. Divide dough into 2 parts. Roll out very thin. Cut dough into strips. Let dry. Bring 3 quarts water and 1 tablespoon salt to a boil. Drop noodles in slowly keeping water boiling. Cook until tender. Drain; wash noodles in cold water. Drain well. Place remaining ingredients in large saucepan with 1 tablespoon salt and water to cover. Boil until chicken falls off bone. Remove carrots and celery. Remove chicken. Bone and dice. Return chicken to broth. Add noodles. Bring broth to a boil. Boil for 6 minutes. Yield: 8 servings.

Ella E. Wise
New England Grange, No. 1785
Durand, Illinois

HARVEST DINNER

1 10-lb. turkey
Salt and pepper to taste
¼ c. butter or margarine
6 to 8 med. Louisiana yams
1 16-oz. jar spiced crab apples
2 tbsp. cornstarch
½ c. Rhine wine
1 6-oz. can unsweetened pineapple juice
½ c. dark corn syrup
1½ tsp. lemon juice

Sprinkle inside of turkey with salt and pepper. Place on rack in shallow roasting pan. Melt butter in saucepan; brush turkey with part of the butter. Bake at 325 degrees for 2 hours. Cook yams in boiling salted water until almost done; drain. Peel and cut in half. Drain crab apples, reserving syrup. Blend cornstarch and wine; stir into remaining butter. Add reserved crab apple syrup, pineapple juice, corn syrup, lemon juice and ¼ teaspoon salt. Cook, stirring constantly, until sauce boils for 30 seconds. Drain fat from roasting pan. Arrange yams around turkey; brush both with sauce. Bake for 30 minutes longer or until meat thermometer registers 185 degrees, brushing once with sauce. Heat crab apples in remaining sauce. Arrange turkey, yams and crab apples on platter. Serve with hot sauce.

Photograph for this recipe on page 73.

RABBIT BARBECUE

1 frying rabbit
1 c. catsup
½ c. sugar
½ c. vinegar

Boil rabbit until tender. Debone; cut meat into bite-sized pieces. Place in casserole. Combine catsup, sugar and vinegar; mix with rabbit. Sprinkle 2 tablespoons water over top. Bake at 350 degrees

for 30 minutes. Serve on buns. Recipe good with wild or tame rabbit. Old rabbit is best.

Mrs. Margaret Lockcuff
Pine Run Grange, No. 250
Linden, Pennsylvania

HALIBUT-LOBSTER CASSEROLE

Butter
3 tbsp. flour
2 c. milk
1 c. cream
5 tbsp. chopped onion
1 tbsp. chopped green pepper
3 c. cooked rice
2 c. boiled flaked halibut
1 c. lobster
1 can pimentos, sliced
2 tbsp. Sherry
¼ c. shredded cheese
Bread or cracker crumbs

Melt ¼ cup butter; blend in flour. Add milk and cream. Cook, stirring constantly, until thickened. Saute onion and green pepper in small amount of butter. Add to cream sauce. Mix next 6 ingredients; stir into sauce. Place in buttered baking dish. Cover with crumbs. Bake in 350-degree oven for 30 minutes. Yield: 8-10 servings.

Mrs. Hilda Tucker
Henry Wilson Grange, No. 205
New Durham, New Hamsphire

FISH IN BATTER

½ c. flour
½ c. cornmeal
1 egg
1 tsp. salt
Beer
Fish

Combine first 4 ingredients in bowl. Add enough beer to make pancake type batter. Dip fish into batter. Coat well. Fry in French fryer or in 1-inch melted shortening in skillet.

Martha Long
Paulding Grange, No. 332
Paulding, Ohio

FISH SHORTCAKE

2 to 3 tbsp. chopped onion
4 tbsp. fat
4 tbsp. flour
2 c. milk
⅓ c. grated cheese
1½ c. flaked cooked fish
Salt and pepper to taste

Saute onion in fat in skillet until tender. Blend in flour. Add milk gradually, stirring constantly. Cook until sauce is thickened. Add cheese, fish and seasonings. Heat mixture through, stirring occasionally. Serve over biscuits or corn bread.

Marylee Smith
Norton Grange, No. 2566
Norton, Ohio

MOCK LOBSTER

1 tbsp. pickling spice
1 bay leaf
¼ c. vinegar
1 to 1½ lb. haddock fillets
Butter
Paprika

Combine pickling spice, bay leaf and vinegar with 3 quarts water in large saucepan. Bring to a boil. Place fillets in seasoned water. Boil for 3 to 5 minutes or until fish turns white. Remove fillets from water; place in 9 × 13-inch pan. Dot with butter; sprinkle generously with paprika. Broil for 5 to 10 minutes until butter melts. Serve hot.

June D. Lull
Westbrook Grange, No. 123
Westbrook, Connecticut

BAKED SALMON LOAF

1 lg. can salmon, boned and flaked
2 c. bread crumbs
1 to 1½ c. milk
½ tsp. dry mustard
½ tsp. salt
Dash of pepper
2 eggs, separated

Combine first 6 ingredients with beaten egg yolks. Beat egg whites until stiff. Fold into salmon mixture. Shape into loaf in baking dish. Bake at 350 degrees for 30 minutes. Any cooked vegetables may be added to mixture before baking. Serve with tomato sauce or tomato soup poured over loaf.

Mrs. S. Isobel Oesterling, C.W.A.
Newport Co., Pomona Grange, No. 4
Middletown, Rhode Island

BETTE'S SALMON LOAF

2 eggs, beaten
¼ c. milk
1 can salmon, shredded
½ tsp. salt
¼ tsp. pepper
1 tbsp. minced parsley
2 c. corn flakes

Combine eggs and milk. Mix salmon with remaining ingredients; add to egg mixture. Press into greased loaf pan. Bake in 350-degree oven for 45 minutes. Serve with tomato sauce.

Bette Davis
Campville Grange, No. 1492
Endicott, New York

SUPER SALMON LOAF

1 can cream of celery soup
⅓ c. mayonnaise
1 egg, beaten
½ c. chopped onion
¼ c. chopped green pepper
1 tsp. lemon juice
1 16-oz. can salmon, drained
1 c. cracker crumbs

Combine all ingredients; mix well. Place in greased loaf pan. Bake at 350 degrees for 40 minutes.

Mrs. Milton E. Retz
Wife of the Master
Prairie Center Grange, No. 2179
Ryan, Iowa

POTLUCK CASSEROLE

1 can cream of mushroom soup
1 7-oz. can chunk tuna
1 No. 303 can peas, drained
2½ c. cooked macaroni
Grated cheese

Mix soup, tuna and peas in saucepan. Heat until mixture bubbles. Place macaroni in buttered casserole; add tuna mixture. Sprinkle with cheese, if desired. Bake in 350-degree oven for 25 to 30 minutes.

Mrs. Florienze Williams
Sacramento Grange, No. 12
Sacramento, California

TUNA AND NOODLE CASSEROLE

1 8-oz. package noodles
1 No. 2 can condensed celery or cream of mushroom soup
1 c. milk
1 tbsp. butter
1 7-oz. can tuna, flaked
1 tsp. salt
1 c. crushed corn flakes or cracker crumbs

Cook noodles in boiling salted water for 20 minutes. Drain. Combine soup and milk; add to noodles. Add remaining ingredients in order listed. Place in large baking dish. Bake in preheated 400-degree oven for 30 to 40 minutes.

Darlene G. Phillips
Buffalo Grange, No. 1523
Washington, Pennsylvania

CLAM-CHEESE CASSEROLE

¼ c. butter or margarine
⅛ c. flour
2 c. milk
1 c. grated sharp Cheddar cheese
2 c. chopped clams
2 c. cooked spinach or 2 c. zucchini
½ c. buttered bread crumbs

Melt butter in skillet; blend in flour. Add milk. Cook until thickened, stirring frequently. Add cheese and clams. Place spinach in buttered 8-inch casserole dish. Pour clam mixture over spinach. Top with bread crumbs. Bake in 350-degree oven for 30 minutes or until bubbly. Yield: 4 servings.

Mrs. Helen D. Pearl
Little River Grange, No. 36
Hampton, Connecticut

FRIED CLAMS

1 egg, separated
½ c. milk
¼ tsp. salt
1 tbsp. butter, melted
½ c. sifted all-purpose flour
1 pt. shucked clams, drained

Beat egg white until stiff. Combine milk, salt, butter and egg yolk; beat together well. Add sifted flour; stir. Fold in egg white. Dip each clam into batter. Fry in deep fat at 375 degrees until golden brown. Drain before serving. Yield: 4 servings.

Beatrice Dow, C.W.A.
Albion Grange, No. 181
Albion, Maine

BAKED AVOCADO AND CRAB CASSEROLE

1½ c. flaked crab meat
¾ tsp. Worcestershire sauce
2 tbsp. minced green pepper
¼ c. finely diced celery
¾ tsp. salt
½ c. chili sauce
3 avocados
Buttered crumbs or corn flakes

Combine first 6 ingredients. Cut avocados in half lengthwise; remove seed. Fill center with crab mixture. Top with crumbs. Bake at 400 degrees for 15 minutes or until browned. Serve immediately.

Mrs. Mary Maskew
Leon Valley Grange, No. 1581
San Antonio, Texas

LOBSTER SCALLOP

1½ c. lobster meat, cut up
1 c. soft bread crumbs
1 c. half and half
1 egg, well beaten
2 tbsp. margarine
1 tbsp. lemon juice
Onion juice to taste
½ tsp. prepared mustard
Buttered crumbs

Combine first 7 ingredients; mix well. Place in greased baking dish. Top with buttered crumbs. Bake in 350-degree oven for 30 minutes.

D. Brackett
Sabbathday Lake Grange, No. 365
Poland Spring, Maine

SCALLOPED OYSTERS

1 qt. oysters
Saltine crackers, crushed
Butter
Salt and pepper to taste
1 egg
½ c. milk

Drain oysters, reserving liquor. Alternate layers of cracker crumbs and oysters in buttered casserole dotting each layer with butter, salt and pepper until all ingredients are used. Beat egg with milk and reserved oyster liquor. Pour over casserole. Bake at 350 degrees for 30 minutes.

From a Grange Friend

GRANDMOTHER'S SCALLOPED OYSTERS

2 pt. select large oysters, cleaned
4 tbsp. butter
2 c. finely crushed cracker crumbs
Salt and pepper to taste
2 to 3 c. milk or half and half

Drain oysters, reserving liquor. Grease bottom and sides of deep casserole generously with butter. Sprinkle thin layer of crumbs over bottom of casserole. Place layer of oysters over crumbs. Sprinkle lightly with salt and pepper; dot with butter. Cover with layer of crumbs. Repeat layers until casserole is filled to within ¾ inch of top. Dot with butter. Combine reserved oyster liquor with half the milk. Pour over casserole. Add enough milk to come to top of dish. Let stand for 20 minutes. Bake in 350-degree oven about 1 hour.

Mrs. Franklin F. Karn
Cuba Grange, No. 799
Belfast, New York

CREAMED SCALLOPS AND MUSHROOMS

1 c. sliced fresh mushrooms
1 lb. scallops, rinsed and drained
4 tbsp. butter or margarine
4 tbsp. flour
1½ c. light cream
2 tbsp. minced parsley
½ tsp. salt
¼ tsp. pepper
½ c. grated cheese
Paprika

Simmer mushrooms for 5 minutes in ½ cup water. Arrange scallops in greased casserole. Melt butter in saucepan. Add flour, stirring constantly. Add cream gradually, stirring until thick and smooth. Add mushrooms and liquid; mix well. Add parsley, salt and pepper. Pour gently over scallops. Sprinkle with cheese and paprika. Bake in 350-degree oven for 25 to 30 minutes or until cheese is bubbly.

Mrs. Evelyn R. Nelson
Blue Mountain Grange, No. 263
Ryegate, Vermont

SEAFOOD CASSEROLE SUPREME

2 tbsp. butter
2 tbsp. flour
1 c. milk or light cream
½ tsp. salt
⅛ tsp. pepper
¼ c. dry Sherry
½ lb. scallops, cooked
½ lb. lobster meat, cooked
½ lb. crab meat, cooked
½ lb. shrimp, peeled and cooked
Buttered crumbs

Melt butter; stir in flour. Stir in milk gradually until mixture boils and thickens. Cook 3 minutes longer, stirring occasionally. Add seasonings and Sherry. Pour sauce into buttered casserole; add seafood. Cover with buttered crumbs. Bake at 350 degrees for 30 to 40 minutes or until crumbs are browned. Sauteed mushrooms may be added.

From a Grange Friend

SHRIMP CREOLE

1 onion, peeled and sliced
1 green pepper, diced
½ c. sliced celery
½ bay leaf
2 tbsp. butter
1 tbsp. flour
3 c. chopped canned tomatoes
1 tsp. salt
½ tsp. sugar
⅛ tsp. cayenne pepper
1½ lb. cooked shrimp
3 c. cooked rice

Saute first 4 ingredients in butter for 8 minutes. Add flour; stir. Mix smoothly for 2 or 3 minutes. Add tomatoes, salt, sugar and cayenne pepper. Simmer for 15 minutes. Add shrimp. Simmer until shrimp is heated. Serve over rice.

Sandy Adams
Potomac Grange, No. 1
Arlington, Virginia

Vegetables
and Side Dishes

What better way is there to add a sparkle to mealtime than with the sumptuous flavor of garden-fresh vegetables? They add color, plus a wealth of vitamins and minerals to the table, and adapt deliciously to the addition of herbs, spices, and other seasonings. Then, for added mealtime interest, there is a great variety of family-favorite side dishes featuring pasta, cereals, potatoes and fruits.

Vegetable cookery to please family tastes is really no mystery—in fact, it's easy! First of all, for maximum flavor and nutrition, vegetables need only to be cooked until they are tender-crisp. Mushy, overcooked vegetables are tasteless and totally unappetizing. Secondly, vegetable cookery is perfectly suited to imaginative trial and error. If your family doesn't like a particular vegetable one way, prepare it another way—baked instead of stewed, with a cheese sauce rather than with herbs and butter. Chances are, they'll love it!

Side dishes add still another dimension of flavor and nutrition to family meals. Ranging from steaming dishes of macaroni and cheese or a hearty baked potato to a complementary serving of spiced, baked fruit or even a savory pudding, side dishes belong at every dinner table.

Colorful, zesty, nutritious, budget-pleasing—all these words describe what these vegetable and side dish recipes can bring to your family menu plan—all from Grange cooks!

SWEET-SOUR ASPARAGUS

½ c. sugar
¼ c. wine vinegar
3 whole cloves
1 cinnamon stick
½ tsp. celery seed
½ tsp. salt
1 15-oz. can asparagus spears, drained

Combine first 6 ingredients with ¼ cup water in saucepan. Bring to boiling point; stir until sugar dissolves. Pour mixture over asparagus; cool. Cover. Refrigerate for 6 to 24 hours. Garnish with mashed hard-boiled egg before serving. Yield: 4-6 servings.

Mrs. Elsie M. Luther
Boerne Grange, No. 1545
Boerne, Texas

GREEN BEANS AND GERMAN CABBAGE

3 slices bacon, cut into 1-in. pieces
½ c. vinegar
⅛ c. sugar
3 tbsp. chopped onion
3 c. shredded cabbage
¾ tsp. salt
¼ tsp. pepper
1 1-lb. can green beans, drained

Cook bacon in skillet until crisp. Remove bacon; drain on absorbent paper. Add next 6 ingredients to remaining fat in skillet. Cover; simmer for 5 minutes. Stir in beans; cook for 5 minutes. Spoon into serving dish. Top with bacon. Yield: 4-6 servings.

Verl Woods
Richwall Grange, No. 671
Monmouth, Oregon

MAINE BAKED BEANS

2 lb. dried beans
1 med. onion, peeled and quartered
½ lb. salt pork
½ c. molasses
2 tsp. dry mustard
¼ tsp. red pepper
1½ tbsp. salt

Soak beans in cold water overnight. Parboil beans until skins crack; drain. Place onion in large saucepan. Add beans. Cut ½-inch deep slashes through pork rind. Place on top of beans. Combine remaining ingredients with 1 pint boiling water. Pour over beans. Add more boiling water if neces-sary. Bake at 300 degrees for 8 hours. Yield: 12 servings.

Halice Bemis
Minerva Grange, No. 383
Levant, Maine

NEW YORK BAKED BEANS

2 lb. dried white beans
2 c. maple syrup
½ c. sugar
2 tbsp. salt
½ to 1 lb. salt pork, sliced

Soak beans overnight in water to cover. Drain. Place in large saucepan. Cover with cold water. Cook until tender, adding more water if needed. Drain; return to saucepan. Add syrup, sugar, salt and enough water to cover. Bring to boiling point. Pour into 9 × 10-inch baking dish. Cover with salt pork. Bake at 350 degrees for 2 or 3 hours or until browned. Yield: 15-20 servings.

Mrs. Lawrence Wagstaff, Sr. C.W.A.
Winthrop Grange, No. 538
Winthrop, New York

HOLLANDAISE SAUCE

3 egg yolks
2 to 3 tbsp. lemon juice
¼ tsp. salt
½ cup soft margarine

Blend together egg yolks, lemon juice and salt in small saucepan. Add margarine; stir constantly over very low heat until margarine melts and sauce thickens. Serve hot or at room temperature. Any leftover sauce can be stored in the refrigerator. Stir in small amount of hot water to serve. Yield: Approximately ¾ cup sauce.

Fluffy Hollandaise: Just before serving, beat 2 egg whites until soft peaks form, or ½ cup heavy cream, whipped, into the Hollandaise Sauce. Yield: Approximately 1½ cups sauce.

Maltaise Sauce: Reduce lemon juice to 1 table-spoon. Add 1 teaspoon grated orange rind and 3 or 4 tablespoons orange juice. Yield: Approximately 1 cup sauce.

Béarnaise Sauce: Boil ¼ cup wine vinegar with 1 teaspoon finely minced onion, ½ teaspoon leaf tarragon, and ⅛ teaspoon each salt and black pepper, until reduced to 2 tablespoons. Substitute for lemon juice in Hollandaise Sauce. Yield: Approximately ⅔ cup sauce.

Photograph for this recipe on page 80.

PRUSSIAN CABBAGE PIE

1 onion, chopped
1 med. cabbage, shredded
3 tbsp. margarine, melted
2 3-oz. packages cream cheese, softened
1 can mushrooms
1 sm. can evaporated milk
Marjoram, tarragon, sweet basil, salt and pepper
  to taste
4 hard-boiled eggs
1 recipe 2-crust pie pastry

Fry onion and cabbage in skillet with margarine until limp. Add cream cheese; mix well. Turn off heat. Add mushrooms, milk, spices and eggs; mix well. Place in pie shell; cover with second crust. Make small slits in top crust with knife. Bake at 400 degrees for 15 minutes. Reduce heat to 350 degrees; bake for 25 minutes or until browned. Yield: 6 servings.

Patsy Bianchi
Cedar Creek Grange, No. 586
Blythewood, South Carolina

SKILLET CABBAGE

4 c. shredded cabbage
1 green pepper, shredded
2 c. diced celery
2 lg. onions, sliced
2 tomatoes, chopped
¼ c. bacon drippings

2 tsp. sugar
Salt and pepper to taste

Combine all ingredients in large skillet. Cover. Bring to boiling point. Reduce temperature to medium. Cook for 5 minutes. Yield: 8 servings.

Leta Adair
Col. Harper Grange
Bloomville, New York

CAMP MEAL-IN-ONE

1 peeled potato per person
1 lg. zucchini, peeled
2 or 3 ribs celery
2 lg. onions
2 sweet peppers
Salt and pepper to taste

Cube vegetables. Combine; mix well. Place 1 cup full on a square of foil for each person served. Season with salt and pepper or seasoning salt to taste. A tablespoon of diced bacon or sliced hot dogs or a hamburger patty may be added on top of vegetables in each foil square. Tightly seal each package. Roast on grill or in pan in oven for 30 minutes or until done.

Mabel C. Peter
Avis Grange, No. 1959
Lock Haven, Pennsylvania

CARROT CASSEROLE

4 c. sliced carrots
¼ c. chopped celery
½ stick margarine or butter
½ c. minced onion
¼ c. flour
2 c. milk
¼ tsp. dry mustard
1 tsp. salt
⅛ tsp. pepper
1½-inch block Velveeta cheese

Place carrots and celery in saucepan with water to cover. Bring to boiling point. Reduce heat. Simmer until tender. Drain. Place in casserole. Place margarine in saucepan over low heat until melted. Add onion. Blend in flour. Add remaining ingredients. Cook, stirring constantly, until thickened and bubbly. Pour over carrots. Bake at 350 degrees for 45 minutes. Yield: 6-8 servings.

Arlene Pharis, C.W.A.
Tamarack Grange, No. 1388
Renovo, Pennsylvania

SWEET AND SOUR CARROTS

3 bunches carrots
1 med. green pepper, sliced
1 lg. onion, sliced
1 10½-oz. tomato soup
1 c. sugar
½ c. vinegar
½ c. salad oil
1 tsp. dry mustard
1 tsp. Worcestershire sauce
Salt and pepper to taste

Peel carrots; cook in salted water until tender. Slice. Combine with green pepper and onion. Combine remaining ingredients in small saucepan. Simmer about 10 minutes. Pour over vegetables. Refrigerate overnight. Serve hot or cold. Keeps well in refrigerator.

Opal Robinson
Guernsey Co., Birds Run Grange, No. 366
Newcomerstown, Ohio

CAULIFLOWER CASSEROLE

1 tsp. sesame seed
1 med. head cauliflower
Salt and pepper to taste
½ c. sour cream
½ c. sharp Cheddar cheese, shredded

Place sesame seed in shallow pan. Toast at 350 degrees for 10 minutes. Cook cauliflower in water until tender; drain. Place half the cauliflower in 1-quart casserole; season with salt and pepper. Spread with half the sour cream and half the cheese. Layer remaining ingredients. Top with sesame seeds. Bake at 350 degrees for 10 to 12 minutes.

Mrs. James Waring
Hilltop Grange, No. 225
Ree Heights, South Dakota

BAKED CORN

1 c. (scant) sugar
2 tbsp. flour
Salt to taste
Milk
2 eggs, beaten
1 pt. corn
2 tbsp. butter, melted

Combine sugar, flour and salt. Add enough milk to beaten eggs to measure 1 cup. Combine all ingredients; mix well. Pour into 2-quart casserole. Bake at 350 degrees for 45 minutes.

Mrs. Helen Wertman
Delaware Grange, No. 1895
Watsontown, Pennsylvania

CORN FRITTERS

8 ears of corn
2 eggs, separated
3 tbsp. flour
3 tbsp. sugar
1 tsp. salt
½ tsp. baking pwder
1 tbsp. melted butter
4 tbsp. milk

Remove corn from cob. Beat egg yolks. Add corn and next 6 ingredients, thinning with more milk, if needed. Beat egg whites until stiff. Fold into batter. Drop by spoonfuls into hot oil. Fry until brown. Yield: 8 servings.

Mrs. Howard Braucher
Fleetwood Grange, No. 1839
Leesport, Pennsylvania

CORN PUDDING

3 eggs, beaten
2 c. corn
2 tbsp. melted butter
½ tsp. salt
2 c. milk
2 tbsp. sugar

Combine all ingredients. Pour into buttered 2-quart baking dish. Place dish in pan of hot water. Bake in 350-degree oven about 40 minutes or until mixture is firmly set. Yield: 6 servings.

Mrs. Elwyn Wrisley
Fossett Grange, No. 1567
Gillett, Pennsylvania

PATTY'S CORN PUDDING

1 tbsp. flour
⅓ c. sugar
1 tsp. salt
4 eggs, well beaten
1 can evaporated milk
2 c. drained corn
¼ c. melted butter
Nutmeg to taste

Combine flour, sugar and salt. Add eggs and milk. Combine first mixture with corn and butter. Pour into buttered baking dish. Sprinkle with nutmeg. Place in pan of water. Bake at 350 degrees for 1 hour or until firm in center.

Patty Myers
Thurmont Grange, No. 409
Thurmont, Maryland

SCALLOPED CORN

1 No. 3 can cream-style corn
¼ c. diced onion
½ c. cracker crumbs
½ c. milk
Butter
Salt and pepper to taste

Pour corn into 1-quart casserole. Add onion, cracker crumbs and milk. Dot with butter, pushing down into corn mixture. Sprinkle with salt and pepper. Bake in preheated 350-degree oven for 30 minutes. Yield: 4 servings.

Patty Gaulropp
Galt Grange, No. 1853
Rock Falls, Illinois

EGGPLANT PARMESAN

1 lg. eggplant, peeled
Salt
3 eggs
Bread crumbs or wheat germ
Mozzarella cheese, sliced
1 sm. can mushrooms, drained
¼ c. chopped onion
1 sm. can tomato paste
1 tsp. oregano
½ tsp. basil
1 tsp. parsley
Parmesan cheese, grated

Cut eggplant into ½-inch slices. Salt each slice. Let stand for 1 hour. Rinse eggplant; pat dry. Dip each slice in 1 beaten egg, then bread crumbs. Fry in oil until golden brown. Layer with mozzarella cheese in 10-inch casserole. Beat 2 eggs; pour over eggplant. Brown mushrooms and onion in small amount of oil. Add tomato paste and 1½ tomato paste cans water. Add oregano, basil, parsley and 1 teaspoon salt. Cool slightly. Pour over eggplant. Sprinkle with Parmesan cheese. Bake at 325 degrees for 30 minutes or until bubbly. Yield: 4-6 servings.

Mary E. Rehm
Wayne Co., Smithville Grange
Smithville, Ohio

SCALLOPED EGGPLANT

1 med. eggplant
4 tbsp. shortening
2 tbsp. green pepper, chopped
2 tbsp. onion, chopped
2 c. canned tomatoes
1 tsp. salt

1 tsp. pepper
¾ c. bread cubes

Pare eggplant; cut into small pieces. Melt 2 tablespoons shortening in skillet; add green pepper and onion. Cook until tender. Add tomatoes, salt, pepper and eggplant. Simmer for 10 minutes. Pour into greased baking dish. Melt remaining shortening; mix with bread cubes. Spread over top of eggplant mixture. Bake at 350 degrees for 20 minutes or until eggplant is tender and bread cubes are brown. Yield: 4 servings.

Mrs. J. W. Larkin
Blue Mound Grange, No. 2230
Walker, Missouri

MELINDA'S JUBILADE

2 sm. onions, chopped
1 carrot, sliced
2 stalks celery, chopped
Sprig of parsley, minced
4 cloves of garlic, minced
¼ c. oil
2 10-oz. cans tomatoes
1 6-oz. can tomato paste
1 tbsp. sugar
Salt to taste
6 to 12 eggs

Saute vegetables in oil in large skillet until tender. Add tomatoes and paste. Simmer 1 hour. Add 1 tablespoon sugar and salt to taste. Break eggs, 2 to 3 at a time, into same skillet. Poach in sauce. Simmer 30 minutes. Serve on hard bread. Other vegetables can be added, if desired.

Melinda Lampariello
Petries Corners Grange, No. 561
Lowville, New York

BAKED ONION SLICES

6 lg. onions, peeled
Butter
Brown sugar
Dash of salt
Dash of pepper

Slice onions into ½-inch slices. Place in shallow pan. Place ½ teaspoon butter, ½ teaspoon brown sugar and a dash of salt and pepper on each onion slice. Bake, uncovered, in 350-degree oven for 1 hour or until tender. Yield: 4 servings.

Beatrice Dow, C.W.A.
Albion Grange, No. 181
Albion, Maine

CREAMED ONIONS

1 c. white table wine
Salt
2 lb. small white onions, peeled
¼ c. butter or margarine
¼ c. flour
1 c. cream
2 tbsp. minced parsley
Pepper to taste
2 tsp. grated Parmesan cheese

Place 2 cups water, wine and ½ teaspoon salt in saucepan. Bring to boiling point. Add onions; cook, uncovered, for 20 minutes. Drain, reserving liquid. Melt butter; stir in flour. Add cream and 1 cup reserved liquid. Cook, stirring constantly, until mixture is thickened and smooth. Add parsley, salt to taste, pepper and onions. Turn into greased casserole. Sprinkle Parmesan cheese over top. Bake at 375 degrees for 20 to 25 minutes. Yield: 5-6 servings.

Mrs. Gertrude Hyde
Williamstown Grange, No. 366
Williamstown, Massachusetts

CRISP ONION RINGS

1 c. flour
1½ tsp. baking powder
½ tsp. salt
1 egg, beaten
½ tsp. lemon juice
1 tbsp. melted shortening
Onions, peeled and sliced

Combine first 6 ingredients with ¾ cup water. Blend. Dip onions into batter. Drop into fat heated to 375 degrees. Fry 2 minutes or until light brown on each side. Drain on paper towels. Drain on paper towels. Keep warm in 325-degree oven. Yield: 4 servings.

Vickie Powell
Huntington Grange, No. 731
Bidwell, Ohio

DILLED ONION RINGS

1 lg. sweet onion
⅓ c. sugar
2 tsp. salt
½ tsp. dried dillweed
½ c. white vinegar

Cut onion into thin slices; separate into rings. Combine remaining ingredients in saucepan with ¼

cup water. Bring to a boil. Pour over onion rings; cool. Chill for at least 5 hours.

Ethel Gruner
Lower Naches Grange
Yakima, Washington

SCALLOPED OYSTER PLANT

2 c. pared cooked oyster plant, sliced
1 c. finely-crushed cracker crumbs
¼ tsp. salt
¼ tsp. pepper
¼ c. melted butter
Milk or cream

Dip oyster plant slices into bowl of salted water or juice of ½ lemon to prevent discoloration. Drain. Place in saucepan with small amount of water. Cook 10 minutes or until just tender. Drain. Mix cracker crumbs with salt, pepper and butter. Layer oyster plant and crumbs in greased 1½-quart casserole ending with crumbs. Fill just to top of layers with milk. Bake in 425-degree oven for 20 minutes or until brown and bubbly. Yield: 4 servings.

Mrs. Lorena D. Stigers
Potomac Grange, No. 1
Falls Church, Virginia

CROWD-PLEASIN' POTATOES

8 med. potatoes
1 bay leaf
Butter
1 can cream of mushroom soup
1 c. sour cream
½ tsp. salt
¼ tsp. pepper
1 can mushrooms
5 green onions, chopped with tops
2 c. grated Cheddar or Monterey Jack cheese
1 can Ortega chilies

Place potatoes and bay leaf in saucepan with water to cover. Boil until just tender. Drain. Peel; slice into ½-inch slices. Combine ¼ cup butter, soup, sour cream, salt and pepper in large bowl. Saute mushrooms and onions in butter in skillet. Add to soup mixture. Add potatoes and 1 cup cheese. Place half the mixture in buttered casserole. Add chilies. Add soup mixture. Top with remaining cheese. Bake at 350 degrees for 30 minutes. Yield: 4-6 servings.

Ann Larson
Riverdale Grange, No. 624
Laton, California

GERMAN POTATO PANCAKES

3 eggs, separated
1 tsp. salt
1 tbsp. sugar
3 c. milk
2½ c. sifted flour
1 tbsp. shortening, melted
3 c. grated potatoes
Finely chopped onion, (opt.)

Beat egg yolks in bowl. Add salt, sugar and milk. Add flour and shortening gradually, beating well. Stir in potatoes. Beat egg whites in small bowl until stiff. Fold egg whites into first mixture. Cook on greased, hot griddle. Onion may be placed on top of batter on griddle. Serve hot with meat. Yield: 24 pancakes.

From a Grange Friend

GOLDEN POTATO SQUARES

5 lb. potatoes, peeled
⅔ c. melted butter
1 c. chopped onion
1 13-oz. can evaporated milk
4 eggs, beaten
2½ tsp. salt
¼ tsp. pepper
2¼ c. shredded Cheddar cheese

Place potatoes in cold water. Melt butter in skillet. Saute onion until tender. Add milk. Bring to a boil; remove from heat. Combine eggs, salt and pepper in large bowl. Beat until frothy. Shred potatoes, using medium blade. Place immediately into egg mixture to prevent discoloration. Turn to coat well. Add milk mixture and 1½ cup cheese. Turn into greased 9 × 13-inch baking dish. Bake in preheated 350-degree oven for 1 hour. Top with ¾ cup cheese. Bake 30 minutes longer. Cut into squares to serve. Freezes well. Yield: 12-15 servings.

Mrs. Albert Christiansen
Fairfield Grange, No. 679
Delavan, Wisconsin

PIROGHY

1 c. flour
1 egg
¼ tsp. salt
2 c. mashed potatoes
1 med. onion, diced
1 egg, beaten
Salt and pepper to taste

Mix first 3 ingredients with enough cold water to make medium soft dough. Knead until dough is easily handled. Roll into thin rectangle on lightly floured board. Cut into squares. Combine remaining ingredients for filling. Place 1 teaspoon filling on each square of dough. Fold in half to make triangles. Moisten edges with water; pinch well to seal. Prepare all piroghy; set aside to dry slightly. Drop in boiling, salted water a few at a time. Piroghy will rise to top. Cook 5 minutes longer. Drain. Serve with butter. Piroghy may also be deep-fried until golden brown. Yield: 4 servings.

Jean A. Grata
Banner Grange, No. 1115
Ebensburg, Pennsylvania

POTATO CASSEROLE

2 c. cottage cheese
1 c. sour cream
1 tsp. salt
⅓ c. diced onion
Garlic (opt.)
5 c. cooked diced potatoes
½ c. grated cheese

Combine first 5 ingredients in bowl. Mix with potatoes. Add part of grated cheese. Place in greased casserole. Sprinkle remaining cheese on top. Bake at 350 degrees for 40 minutes. May be reheated in oven or double boiler. Yield: 8-12 servings.

Esther Hoag, C.W.A.
Hamburg Grange, No. 1293
Eden, New York

REFRIGERATOR MASHED POTATOES

5 lb. potatoes (9 large), peeled and sliced
2 3-oz. packages cream cheese, softened
1 c. sour cream
2 tsp. onion salt
1 tsp. salt
¼ tsp. pepper
2 tbsp. butter or margarine

Cook potatoes in boiling, lightly salted water. Drain. Mash; Add remaining ingredients. Beat until light and fluffy. Cool. Cover; place in refrigerator. May be used any time within 2 weeks. Place in buttered casserole. Dot with butter. Bake at 350 degrees about 30 minutes. Yield: 12 servings.

Mrs. Ralph Roush
Jerusalem Grange, No. 2089
West Union, Ohio

SCALLOPED MAINE POTATOES

1 can Cheddar cheese soup
1 c. milk
Salt and pepper to taste
4 c. sliced potatoes
4 beef hot dogs, sliced
1 sm. onion, chopped
Butter or margarine
Dash of paprika

Combine soup, milk, salt and pepper in bowl. Place potatoes, hot dogs, onion and soup mixture in alternate layers in buttered casserole. Dot with 1 tablespoon of butter. Sprinkle with paprika. Cover. Bake at 350 degrees for 1 hour or until potatoes and onion are tender. Uncover last 10 minutes of baking time.

Althea Stevens
Forest Grange, No. 125
Lee, Maine

ANNA'S SCALLOPED POTATOES

1 can Cheddar cheese soup
½ c. milk
Dash of pepper
4 c. thinly-sliced potatoes
1 sm. onion, thinly sliced
Butter
Paprika

Blend soup, milk and pepper in bowl. Arrange alternate layers of potatoes, onion and sauce in buttered 1½-quart casserole. Dot with 1 tablespoon butter. Sprinkle with paprika. Cover. Bake at 375 degrees for 1 hour. Uncover; bake 15 minutes longer.

Anna Siemiaczko, C.W.A.
Washington Grange, No. 521
South Charleston, West Virginia

JOAN'S ACORN SQUASH CASSEROLE

½ stick margarine
2 c. acorn or butternut squash
1 c. sugar
½ c. flour
2 eggs, beaten
Pinch of salt and soda
1 c. milk
1 tsp. vanilla extract
Cinnamon

Melt margarine in 8×8-inch baking dish. Parboil squash in small amount of water. Scoop pulp out. Place in bowl. Add remaining ingredients except cinnamon. Mix well. Pour into baking dish. Sprinkle

with cinnamon. Bake at 450 degrees 25 to 30 minutes. Yield: 6 servings.

Joan O'Day
Reliance Grange, No. 58
Seaford, Delaware

FRIED SUMMER SQUASH

1 med. summer squash, thinly sliced
1 or 2 eggs, well beaten
Flour or cracker crumbs
Oil for deep-frying
Salt to taste

Dip squash in egg, then in flour to coat. Fry in hot deep fat for 8 to 10 minutes, turning once to brown both sides. Drain on paper towel. Season with salt. This can take the place of meat in summer.

Jeannette Lewis, D.W.A.
Ohio State Grange,
Lebanon, Ohio

MARJORIE'S SUMMER SQUASH

2 small crookneck squash, sliced
1 onion, sliced
1 16-oz. can tomatoes
American cheese, grated
Salt and pepper to taste

Layer squash, onion, tomatoes with juice in greased 1½ quart casserole. Top each layer with cheese. Season with salt and pepper. Bake, covered, in 325-degree oven for 1 hour and 30 minutes. Remove lid. Bake additional 30 minutes or until lightly browned. Yield: 4 servings.

Marjorie A. Pittaway
Friendship Grange, No. 1018
Herrick Center, Pennsylvania

MRS. MURPHY'S COLASHE

2 tbsp. butter
1 med. onion, chopped
1 green pepper, sliced
3 med. zucchini, sliced
1 lg. tomato, diced
1 can whole kernel corn or fresh corn
Salt and pepper to taste

Melt butter in skillet. Saute onion and green pepper. Add zucchini and ⅓ cup water. Simmer for 5 minutes. Add tomato, corn, salt and pepper. Simmer 5 minutes longer or until vegetables are tender. Freezes well. Yield: 8 servings.

Marie Olsen
Santa Ynez Valley Grange, No. 644
Solvang, California

SQUASH AND VEGETABLE SAUTE

3 tbsp. butter or margarine
3 c. sliced yellow squash or zucchini
3 c. shredded cabbage
¾ c. chopped green pepper
1½ tsp. salt
⅛ tsp. pepper
¼ tsp. dried oregano
¼ tsp. dried thyme
1 tbsp. vinegar

Melt butter in large skillet. Add squash and cabbage; cover. Cook over medium heat for 5 minutes. Remove cover; add green pepper. Cook over low heat 10 minutes or until squash is tender, turning occasionally with spatula. Stir in seasonings, herbs and vinegar. Yield: 6 servings.

Ethel Smith
Spencer Grange, No. 1110
Lockwood, New York

SUMMER SQUASH MELANGE

1 tsp. butter
1 sm. zucchini, thinly sliced
2 summer crookneck squash, thinly sliced
1 patty pan squash, thinly sliced
1 tbsp. semi-hot red pepper, finely chopped
1 sm. onion
1 tsp. salt

Melt butter in skillet over medium heat. Add vegetables and salt. Cover. Cook 1 minute or until steam begins to form. Remove cover. Continue cooking, stirring occasionally, until just tender. Moisture should be absorbed. Yield: 4-6 servings.

Mrs. George Huston
Sandusky Co., Townsend Grange
Clyde, Ohio

KATHLEEN'S ZUCCHINI CASSEROLE

4 c. sliced zucchini
2 eggs, beaten well
1 c. mayonnaise
1 onion, chopped
¼ c. chopped green pepper
1 c. grated Parmesan cheese
Salt and pepper to taste
1 tbsp. butter or margarine
2 tbsp. buttered bread crumbs

Cook zucchini in 2 cups boiling water until just tender. Drain. Combine next 6 ingredients in large bowl. Add zucchini. Pour into greased 1½-quart baking dish. Dot with butter. Sprinkle with bread crumbs. Bake at 350 degrees for 30 minutes. Yield: 4-6 servings.

Kathleen White
Blue Mountain Grange
Ryegate, Vermont

SWEET POTATO SOUFFLE

3 c. cooked mashed sweet potatoes
½ c. milk
2 eggs, well beaten
1 c. sugar
1 tsp. vanilla extract
Margarine
1 c. (firmly packed) brown sugar
½ c. flour
1 c. chopped nuts

Combine first 5 ingredients with ⅓ stick margarine. Place in greased casserole. Combine brown sugar, flour, nuts and ½ stick margarine. Sprinkle over potato mixture. Bake at 350 degrees for 30 minutes. Yield: 6-8 servings.

Catherine Murphy
Woodpecker Community Grange No. 942
Petersburg, Virginia

TOMATO TOAST

2 tomatoes
1 sm. onion
1 oz. ham
1 oz. butter
2 eggs, beaten
Salt and pepper to taste
6 slices toast, buttered

Chop tomatoes; mince onion and ham. Cook with butter in saucepan for 10 minutes. Remove from heat; add beaten eggs, salt and pepper. Heat; stir until set. Serve on buttered toast.

Mrs. Dorothy Pray
Gilman Grange, No. 1
Exeter, New Hampshire

FINNISH TURNIP

1 lg. cooked turnip, mashed
2 eggs, beaten
2 tbsp. butter
⅛ c. (firmly packed) brown sugar
1 tsp. salt
1 c. corn flakes
1 c. cream or condensed milk

Combine all ingredients. Mix thoroughly with electric mixer. Pour into casserole. Bake at 350 degrees for 45 minutes. Yield: 6-7 servings.

Mrs. Karl S. Woerner
Schenevus Valley Grange, No. 1201
Westford, New York

VEGETABLE SOUFFLE

3 tbsp. butter
⅓ c. flour
⅓ c. cream or milk
⅔ c. vegetable stock
Chopped spinach or chopped broccoli, cooked and drained
3 eggs, separated
Salt and pepper to taste

Melt butter in skillet over low heat. Blend in flour. Add cream and stock, stirring slowly, until sauce reaches boiling point. Add spinach. Beat egg yolks; add to sauce. Cook for 1 minute, stirring constantly. Season with salt and pepper. Cool slightly. Beat egg whites until stiff peak form. Fold lightly into spinach mixture. Pour into greased 7-inch casserole. Bake at 350 degrees about 40 minutes. Serve immediately. Yield: 4 servings.

Jennifer R. Nelson
Blue Mountain Grange, No. 263
Ryegate, Vermont

BAKED PINEAPPLE

3 eggs, beaten
½ c. sugar
2 tbsp. flour
1 No. 2 can crushed pineapple
1 stick margarine or butter, melted
4-5 slices bread, crusts removed

Combine eggs, sugar, flour and pineapple with juice. Mix well. Spread in casserole. Cover with buttered bread cubes. Do not mix. Bake at 350 degrees until lightly browned and bubbling. Yield: 12 servings.

Mrs. Ruth Skinner
Asbury Grange, No. 563
New Bethlehem, Pennsylvania

CHEESE RAREBIT FONDUE

8 slices bread, buttered
1 lb. cheese, grated
7 or 8 eggs
½ c. milk

2 tsp. brown sugar
½ tsp. salt
¼ tsp. pepper
¾ tsp. seasoned salt
1 tsp. Worcestershire sauce

Cut 6 slices bread into cubes. Cut 2 slices into triangles. Place half the cubes in buttered 2-quart casserole. Layer half the cheese over bread cubes. Repeat bread and cheese layers. Arrange triangles of bread around the edge. Place remaining ingredients in blender container. Blend thoroughly on high speed. Pour over bread and cheese in casserole. Cover. Refrigerate until ready to bake. Bake, uncovered, in 325-degree oven for 1 hour and 15 minutes or until puffy and golden. Best if made with homemade bread.

Mrs. Janet T. Stoddard, C.W.A.
Morris Grange, No. 119
Lakeside, Connecticut

MOCK CHEESE SOUFFLE

6 slices bread, buttered
½ lb. sharp cheese, shredded
½ tsp. salt
¼ tsp. pepper
¼ tsp. mustard (opt.)
3 eggs
3 c. milk

Cut bread into cubes; place in buttered casserole. Add cheese, salt, pepper and mustard. Beat eggs and milk together. Pour over bread-cheese mixture. Refrigerate 3 hours. Bake, uncovered, at 375 degrees for 1 hour. Serve with crisp bacon and onion rings.

Lydia E. McClure
Presumpscot Grange, No. 15
South Portland, Maine

QUICHE

½ lb. sausage, ham, or bacon
½ c. chopped onion
1½ c. shredded sharp Cheddar cheese
2 tbsp. flour
1 10-inch unbaked pie shell
2 eggs, beaten
⅔ c. milk
2 tsp. parsley flakes (opt.)

Cook sausage. Drain. Combine with onion, cheese, and flour. Spread in pie shell. Add milk and parsley to eggs. Pour over meat mixture. Bake at 375 degrees for 35 to 40 minutes. Yield: 6-8 servings.

Mrs. Ella S. Murray
Stevenson Grange, No. 121
Stevenson, Washington

Combine 1 cup flour and ½ teaspoon salt in a bowl. Cut in margarine until mixture resembles coarse meal. Add 2 tablespoons cold water; mix thoroughly. Form into a smooth ball. Cover; refrigerate 15 minutes. Roll out on a lightly floured board. Transfer to a 9-inch pie plate; shape edge. Set aside. Combine Swiss cheese, onion, peanuts and 1 tablespoon flour in a bowl. Toss gently to mix. Sprinkle evenly into pie shell. Combine eggs, cream, ¼ teaspoon salt and dry mustard in a bowl. Beat until smooth. Pour evenly over cheese mixture. Bake at 425 degrees for 15 minutes. Reduce heat to 300 degrees. Bake for 30 minutes longer or until a knife inserted 1-inch from edge comes out clean. Yield: 8 servings.

Photograph for this recipe on page 88.

DRESSING FOR TURKEY

2 loaves bread, cubed
2 c. mashed potatoes
3 tsp. crushed sage leaves
Salt and pepper to taste
Onion, (opt.)
Celery, (opt.)
Eggs, (opt.)
Melted butter, (opt.)
Giblets, (opt.)

Combine first 4 ingredients; mix well. Add onion, celery, eggs, butter and giblets. Add water or turkey broth to make dressing consistency desired. Stuff turkey cavities. Place extra dressing around turkey in roaster. Roast according to turkey directions. Enough for 13-pound turkey. Yield: 15 servings.

Mrs. Lucille Pierson, C.W.A.
St. Joseph Co., Leonidas Grange, No. 266
Vicksburg, Michigan

PEANUT QUICHE

Flour
¾ tsp. salt
½ c. margarine, softened
1½ c. shredded Swiss cheese
⅓ c. minced onion
¼ c. chopped peanuts
3 eggs
1 c. light cream
¼ tsp. dry mustard

PENNSYLVANIA DUTCH STUFFING

2 lb. potatoes, peeled and quartered
2 c. milk
1 tsp. salt
¼ tsp. pepper
2 eggs, beaten
¼ c. minced parsley
1 1-lb. loaf bread, cubed
2 lg. onions, chopped
2 stalks celery, chopped
1 stick margarine, melted

Cook potatoes in saucepan until tender in water to cover. Drain. Add milk, salt and pepper. Mash. Add eggs and fresh parsley. Place bread in bowl. Saute onion and celery in margarine in skillet. Pour over bread cubes. Mix well. Combine all ingredients with potatoes. Place in 2 quart baking dish. Dot with butter. Bake at 350 degrees for 30 minutes. This may be used to stuff turkey or roasting chicken. Yield: 8 servings.

Mrs. Stanley L. G. Oswald
Trexlestown Grange, No. 1755
Allentown, Pennsylvania

GRITS AND CHEESE CASSEROLE

1 c. quick grits
1 tbsp. salt
2 c. milk
Butter or margarine
2 eggs, well beaten
1 roll nippy sharp cheese, thinly sliced
1 roll garlic cheese, thinly sliced
Corn flake crumbs

Combine grits, 2½ cups water, salt and milk in a saucepan. Cook over low heat until thick, stirring occasionally. Stir small amount of hot mixture into eggs. Add remaining eggs, 1 stick butter and cheeses. Stir until cheese is melted and all ingredients are blended smoothly. Pour into 10 × 13-inch greased baking dish. Cover with corn flake crumbs. Dot with butter. Bake at 350 degrees until set.

Cora Belle Dennis
Wharton Grange, No. 2034
Gibbon Glade, Pennsylvania

EGG-CHEESE CASSEROLE

1 1-lb. can peas
Milk
¼ c. butter
⅛ c. flour
¼ tsp. salt
½ tsp. dry mustard
1½ c. grated American cheese
5 c. bread crumbs
6 eggs, well beaten

Drain peas, reserving liquid. Add enough milk to pea liquid to measure 2 cups. Melt butter in large saucepan. Blend in flour, seasonings and liquid. Cook until thick, stirring constantly. Add cheese and peas. Stir until cheese melts. Arrange layer of crumbs in 8 × 10-inch baking dish. Spoon cheese sauce over crumbs. Pour on eggs, carefully. Repeat crumb and cheese layers. Bake at 350 degrees for 40 minutes. Yield: 8 servings.

Mrs. Leo Peterson
Weissert Grange, No. 419
Berwyn, Nebraska

HUEVOS RANCHEROS SAUCE

3 lg. onions, diced
1 med. can tomatoes
1 or 2 med. jalapeno peppers, chopped
Salt and pepper to taste
Grated Parmesan cheese (opt.)

Saute onions in 2 tablespoons bacon fat. Add tomatoes and peppers. Add salt and pepper. Simmer until thick. Cheese may be added. Serve over scrambled or fried eggs. Yield: 6 servings.

Marie Olsen
Santa Ynez Valley Grange, No. 644
Solvang, California

MITZI'S EGG DISH

8 slices of bread, crusts removed
⅔ lb. Velveeta cheese, diced

4 c. milk
8 eggs, slightly beaten
1 tsp. salt
¼ tsp. pepper
¼ tsp. dry mustard
6 to 8 slices of bacon, chopped

Cut bread into cubes. Place in 8 × 8-inch greased baking dish. Top with cheese. Combine remaining ingredients, except bacon in bowl. Pour over cheese and bread. Chill overnight. Place bacon on top of casserole. Bake at 350 degrees for 30 minutes. Yield: 6-8 servings.

Mitzi Furst
Hopewell Grange, No. 1747
Washington, Illinois

GERMAN NOODLES

1 c. of flour
2 eggs, beaten
2 tbsp. oil
Meat broth

Combine all ingredients in bowl. Form into 2 balls. Roll thin. Let dry a short time. Cut in narrow strips. Cook 10 to 15 minutes in broth. These noodles can be frozen when completely dried. Yield: 1½ pints.

Mrs. Ruth F. Williams
Eagle Grange, No. 2726
Findlay, Ohio

LASAGNA ROLL

6 lasagna noodles
1 c. cream-style cottage cheese
1 8-oz. package cream cheese, softened
1 garlic clove, minced
½ tsp. salt
⅛ tsp. pepper
2 tbsp. Parmesan cheese
1 8-oz. can tomato sauce
1 8-oz. can tomatoes
1 tsp. dried oregano, crushed

Cook noodles according to package directions. Overlap noodles across width of 6 × 10-inch baking dish. Combine next 5 ingredients and 1 tablespoon of Parmesan cheese. Beat until well-blended. Spread over noodles. Fold ends of noodles over top. Turn over; place seam side down. Combine tomato sauce, tomatoes, and oregano in saucepan; heat until bubbly. Pour over noodles. Sprinkle remaining cheese over top. Bake in a 350-degree oven for 35 to 40 minutes. Yield: 4-6 servings.

Nancy N. Perkins
Blue Mountain Grange, No. 263
Wells River, Vermont

MACARONI AND CHEESE

2 tsp. salt
½ lb. elbow macaroni
½ lb. Velveeta cheese, diced
¼ c. Parmesan cheese
4 tbsp. (heaping) mayonnaise

Add salt to 4 quarts of boiling water. Add macaroni. Cook until tender; drain. Stir cheeses into hot macaroni until melted. Add mayonnaise. Mix well. Leftover cooked chicken or tuna may be added.

Mrs. Edward Knicely
New Concord Grange, No. 2416
Norwich, Ohio

SPAGHETTI SAUCE

1 onion, chopped
1 clove of garlic, crushed
Olive oil
1 lg. can tomatoes
1 lg. can tomato puree
1 lg. can tomato paste
1 tsp. oregano
½ tsp. chopped parsley
Salt and pepper to taste
Tomato juice (opt.)

Place onions and garlic in Dutch oven. Saute in small amount of olive oil until transparent. Add remaining ingredients except tomato juice. Simmer, covered, for several hours. Thin sauce with tomato juice if necessary. Yield: 16 servings.

Jean Albert, C.W.A.
Amity Grange, No. 1540
Washington, Pennsylvania

FRIED RICE WITH BACON AND MUSHROOMS

½ c. chopped green onions and tops
1 c. diced celery
1 c. sliced mushrooms
3 c. barely cooked rice
2 tbsp. soy sauce
1 egg, slightly beaten
½ lb. crisp bacon, crumbled

Heat 3 tablespoons bacon drippings in 10-inch skillet. Add onions and celery. Cook until tender. Add mushrooms, rice and soy sauce. Cook 10 minutes on low heat, stirring occasionally. Stir in beaten egg; cook only until egg is set. Add bacon; mix well.

Margaret C. Fish
Chatham Grange, No. 2487
Lodi, Ohio

HOPPING JOHN

2 c. dried cowpeas or black-eyed peas
¼ lb. salt pork, diced
2 c. cooked rice
¼ tsp. salt
Dash of pepper
2 tbsp. butter

Soak peas overnight in large pan. Simmer with salt pork 2 hours or until peas are tender. There should be only a small quantity of liquid left. Add remaining ingredients: cover. Simmer 15 minutes. Yield: 8-10 servings.

Margaret Shaw
Kennewick Valley Grange, No. 731
Kennewick, Washington

RICE PILAF

4 tbsp. butter
1 c. egg noodles
2 c. rice
Salt to taste
4 c. chicken broth

Melt butter in skillet. Break noodles into small pieces. Saute noodles in butter until golden brown. Rinse rice with hot water. Bring broth to boiling point. Add noodles, rice and salt. Cook until liquid is absorbed. Place in baking dish. Bake in 275-degree oven until rice is well done. Yield: 6 servings.

Elizabeth Mellian
North Andover Grange, No. 128
Andover, Massachusetts

SPANISH RICE

1 lb. ground beef
1 med. onion, chopped
1 sm. sweet green pepper, chopped
1 12-oz. can tomato paste
1 tbsp. salt
2 c. rice, cooked and salted

Brown ground beef in frypan. Remove beef from pan, reserving drippings. Saute onion and green pepper in drippings. Dilute tomato paste with 2 cups water; add salt. Mix rice, meat, onion, pepper and tomato mixture together. Pour in 3-quart baking dish. Bake at 350 degrees for 45 minutes. Yield: 10 servings.

Mrs. Norman F. Sprague, D.W.A.
New York State Grange
Falconer, New York

Breads

For an age-old way to take the routine away from your family's meals, serve homemade breads! Baking all your own breads "from scratch" is not only a very rewarding task, but also a lot of fun. Home bread baking is also an excellent family project, and a very inexpensive and personal way to create grifts for birthdays and other special occasions.

Bread making has been one of the most important household duties since the beginning of recorded history. Even early in this century one of the most disheartening kitchen failures was when the bread failed to rise or bake properly. Then, in the decades after World War II, it became more common—even a status symbol—to serve "store-bought" bread to family and guests.

Today, however, that is changing as the art of bread making is once again gaining importance in the American kitchen. People realize that homemade bread is tastier and more nutritious than commercially prepared breads. And, in your own home bakery, you can easily surpass the variety offered in the stores. Believe it or not, it's easy to make feathery-light biscuits, mouth-watering sweet breads and doughnuts, as well as a variety of loaves, dinner rolls and muffins. Think of the money you can save!

For many cooks, there is another reason to bake your own bread that is just as important as nutrition, taste and variety—it's the marvelous aroma that fills the house as bread bakes in the oven. Grange cooks recommend you try baking many of the breads that follow—they'll make a believer out of you!

DEAR FRIENDS:

If you've never smelled homemade bread being baked or fresh from the oven, you've missed one of life's treats.

As a child I remember mother getting the yeast crock in which the starter was mixed, setting it on top of the warming closet for the night and the next morning carefully filling a quart jar for the next baking. (In case the starter "died" a neighbor was always glad to share from hers.)

Into the bread pan (a large aluminum dish pan) went the flour and a nest was made in the center and the remaining starter added. Then came the mixing with both hands until the flour was used up. Turning the dough onto a floured board she kneaded for at least 10 minutes.

One of the secrets of good bread making is learning to get the feel of the dough. This comes with practice.

Back into the big pan the dough went to rise until it formed a dome. Then it was punched down, and left to rise again after which it was time to divide into loaves. After rising in the loaf pans it was into the oven for about an hour. Mother would remove a loaf from its pan, tap it on the bottom then touch it to the end of her nose. If it didn't feel warm to the touch, it was baked.

Mrs. Dorothy Scott
Unionville Grange, No. 1971
Mechanicsburg, Pennsylvania

COFFEE CAN BREAD

4 c. flour
1 pkg. dry yeast
½ c milk
⅓ c. butter or margarine
¼ c. sugar
1 tsp. salt
2 eggs, beaten
Raisins or nuts (opt.)

Mix 2 cups flour with yeast. Combine ½ cup water and next 4 ingredients in saucepan. Stir over low heat until butter melts. Cool for 5 minutes. Add yeast and flour mixture. Add remaining flour, eggs and raisins. Knead dough until smooth and elastic. Divide dough into 2 parts. Place in 2 greased coffee cans. Cover with lids. Let rise to top of can. Remove lids. Bake at 375 degrees for about 35 minutes or until top sounds hollow when tapped. Yield: 2 loaves.

Dorothy Sainio
Evening Star Grange, No. 183
Washington, Maine

DILLY BREAD

1 c. cottage cheese, drained
2 tbsp. sugar
1 tbsp. chopped onion
1 tbsp. margarine
2 tsp. dillseed
¼ tsp. soda
1 egg
Salt
1 pkg. yeast
2½ c. flour
Melted butter

Combine first 7 ingredients with 1 teaspoon salt in large bowl. Dissolve yeast in ¼ cup warm water. Add to first mixture. Mix well. Add flour; mix well. Cover. Let rise 50 to 60 minutes or until doubled in bulk. Stir. Place in 2-quart greased casserole. Let rise 30 to 40 minutes. Bake at 350 degrees for 40 to 50 minutes or until golden brown. Brush with butter and salt.

Mrs. Marion Schilliger
Delaware Co., Ashley Grange
Ashley, Ohio

DOROTHY'S FRENCH BREAD

2 tbsp. sugar
Salt
1 pkg. yeast
2 tbsp. oil
7 or 8 c. flour
2 tsp. cornstarch
Sesame seed

Place 2½ cups warm water, sugar, 1 tablespoon salt and yeast in large bowl; let stand for 5 minutes. Add oil and flour; mix well. Let rise until doubled in bulk. Punch down; divide into 2 parts. Let stand 5 minutes. Shape into 2 oblong loaves on cookie sheet; let rise until doubled in bulk. Cook cornstarch, ¼ cup water and salt until thick. Spread paste over loves with pastry brush. Sprinkle with sesame seed. Cut gashes in tops of loaves. Bake in 450-degree oven for 15 minutes. Reduce temperature to 275 degrees. Bake for 30 minutes longer. Yield: 10 servings.

Mrs. Dorothy M. Waters
Hurricane Creek Grange, No. 608
Joseph, Oregon

BRAIDED FRENCH BREAD

5½ to 6 c. all-purpose flour
2 tsp. salt
1 tbsp. sugar
2 pkg. dry yeast
3 tbsp. shortening
1 egg, beaten
Sesame seed

Combine 3 cups flour, salt, sugar and yeast in mixer bowl. Stir at low speed to blend. Add shortening, and 2 cups very warm water. Blend at low speed. Mix at high speed for 3 minutes, scraping bowl occasionally with rubber spatula. Add 2½ to 3 cups flour. Mix by hand enough to make a stiff dough. Turn onto lightly floured surface. Knead for 5 to 7 minutes or until smooth and elastic; add flour to keep from sticking to surface. Shape into a ball. Place in lightly greased bowl. Turn, greasing all surfaces. Cover with cloth. Let rise in warm place for 1 hour or until doubled in bulk. Punch down. Turn dough out of bowl; cut into 2 equal parts. Cut each part into 3 equal pieces. Roll each piece into a rope about 12 inches long. Braid ropes together loosely. Seal ends by pinching together gently. Place on greased baking sheet. Cover with towel. Let rise until doubled in bulk. Brush top gently with egg. Sprinkle with sesame seed. Bake in preheated 375-degree oven for 30 to 35 minutes or until loaves are golden brown. Remove from baking sheet. Cool on racks. Yield: 2 loaves.

Mrs. Vera S. Young
Goodwill Grange, No. 959
Troutdale, Virginia

GRANOLA BEER BREAD

2 pkg. yeast
1½ c. warm beer
½ c. (firmly packed) brown sugar
1½ tsp. salt
2 eggs, beaten
¼ c. melted butter
4 c. flour
¾ c. wheat germ
1 c. granola
3 tbsp. caraway seed

Dissolve yeast in beer. Add next 4 ingredients and 2 cups flour; beat until smooth. Stir in wheat germ, granola and caraway seed. Add remaining flour to make a soft dough. Turn out on lightly floured board. Knead for about 5 minutes until smooth and elastic. Place in a greased bowl, turning to grease surface. Cover; let rise in warm place for about 1 hour and 30 minutes or until doubled in bulk.

Punch down; divide in half. Shape into loaves. Place in 2 greased loaf pans. Let rise about 45 minutes or until doubled in bulk. Bake at 325 degrees for 50 minutes or until brown. Brush with additional melted butter. Yield: 2 loaves.

Eleanor Trefry
Delrio Grange, No. 828
Mansfield, Washington

HEALTH BREAD

1 env. dry yeast
2¼ c. buttermilk
1 tsp. salt
1¼ c. rye flour
1¼ c. whole wheat flour
Wheat germ
2 c. all-purpose flour

Dissolve yeast in ¼ cup warm water in mixing bowl. Add next 4 ingredients and ¼ cup wheat germ. Stir with wooden spoon until well blended. Add all-purpose flour gradually, beating until smooth. Turn onto floured board. Knead until smooth and elastic. Cover. Let rest 30 minutes. Divide into 2 round 6-inch loaves. Brush with water. Press dough in wheat germ. Place on greased baking sheet. Let rise 1 hour or until doubled in bulk. Cut a crisscross pattern on top with sharp knife. Bake in preheated 400 degree oven for 30 minutes or until brown. Cool on rack.

Mrs. Thomas Brian, Wife of Master
Fairview Grange, No. 817
Osceola, Pennsylvania

HONEY-GRAHAM BREAD

4¾ c. all-purpose flour
2½ c. graham flour
1 tbsp. salt
2 pkg. dry yeast
2 c. milk
⅓ c. honey
½ c. margarine

Combine all-purpose and graham flours; mix well. Blend thoroughly 2½ cups flour mixture, salt and undissolved yeast in a large mixer bowl. Combine milk, ½ cup water, honey and margarine in saucepan. Heat over low heat until warm. Margarine need not melt. Add gradually to dry ingredients; beat 2 minutes at medium speed of electric mixer. Add 1 cup flour mixture, or enough to make a thick batter. Beat at high speed for 2 minutes, scraping bowl occasionally. Stir in additional flour to make a soft dough. Turn dough onto lightly floured board; knead 8 to 10 minutes or until smooth and elastic. Cover with towel; let rest 20 minutes. Divide in half. Shape each piece into loaf; place into 2 greased 5 × 9-inch loaf pans. Cover; let rise in warm place, free from draft for 1 hour or until doubled in bulk. Bake in 350-degree oven for 45 minutes, or until brown. Remove from pans; cool on wire racks.

Mrs. Ted Christensen
Raymond Grange, No. 391
Raymond, Nebraska

LAZY MAN'S BREAD

1½ c. milk
2 pkg. dry yeast
1 tsp. salt
6 tbsp. sugar
¼ lb. margarine or butter, melted
4 eggs
8 c. all-purpose flour

Mix 1½ cups water and milk in saucepan. Heat to lukewarm. Place in large bowl. Add yeast, stir to mix. Add next 3 ingredients. Beat 3 eggs. Add to mixture; mix well. Add flour. Mix well with wooden spoon or with hands until dough is moist and sticky. Cover with damp cloth. Let rise in warm place for 1 hour or until doubled in bulk. Punch down. Divide into 2 parts. Place into 2 greased loaf pans. Brush tops with beaten egg. Bake at 400 degrees for 1 hour. Cool. Let stand for 24 hours for easier cutting. Freezes well.

Mrs. Marjorie G. Conklin
Evening Star Grange, No. 183
Washington, Maine

OATMEAL BREAD

1 c. oatmeal
½ c. molasses
2 tsp. salt
1 tbsp. butter
1 pkg. dry yeast
5 c. flour

Add 2 cups boiling water to oatmeal. Let stand for 2 hours. Add next 3 ingredients. Dissolve yeast in ½ cup lukewarm water. Stir into mixture. Add flour; beat well. Let rise until doubled in bulk. Beat again. Place in 2 greased loaf pans. Let rise until doubled in bulk. Bake at 375 degrees for 40 to 60 minutes.

Lucy Streeter
Good Will Grange, No. 127
Glastonbury, Connecticut

PILGRIMS' BREAD

½ c. yellow cornmeal
⅓ c. (firmly packed) brown sugar
1 tbsp. salt
¼ c. cooking oil
2 pkg. dry yeast
¾ c. whole wheat flour
½ c. rye flour
4¼ to 4½ c. unbleached flour

Combine first 3 ingredients. Stir gradually into 2 cups boiling water. Add oil; mix well. Cool to lukewarm. Soften yeast in ½ cup warm water. Stir into cornmeal mixture. Add whole wheat and rye flours; mix well. Stir in enough unbleached flour to make a moderately stiff dough. Turn out onto a lightly floured surface. Knead for 6 to 8 minutes or until smooth and elastic. Shape into ball. Place in lightly greased bowl, turning once to grease surface. Cover. Let rise in warm place for 50 to 60 minutes or until doubled in bulk. Punch dough down. Turn out onto lightly floured surface; divide in half. Cover. Let stand 10 minutes. Shape dough into 2 loaves. Place in 2 greased 5 × 9-inch loaf pans. Cover. Let rise in warm place for 30 minutes or until doubled in bulk. Bake at 375 degrees for about 45 minutes or until done. Remove from pans. Cool on wire racks. Yield: 2 loaves.

Donna Jeffers
Hopewell Grange, No. 1747
Washington, Illinois

RICH EGG BREAD

2 pkg. dry yeast
1½ c. lukewarm milk
¼ c. sugar
1 tbsp. salt
3 eggs, beaten
¼ c. butter or margarine, softened
7½ cups (about) flour

Dissolve yeast in ½ cup warm water. Add next 5 ingredients and 4 cups flour. Beat until smooth. Mix in enough of remaining flour to make dough easy to handle. Turn dough onto lightly floured board. Knead for about 5 minutes or until smooth and elastic. Place in greased bowl; turn once. Cover. Let rise in warm place for 1 hour and 30 minutes to 2 hours or until doubled in bulk. Punch down. Divide in half. Roll each half into 9 × 18-inch rectangle. Roll up, beginning at short side. Press each end to seal. Fold ends under; place seam side down in greased 5 × 9-inch loaf pan. Cover. Let rise about 1 hour or until doubled in bulk. Bake in 425-degree oven for about 30 minutes.

Bertha Marrow
North Adrian Grange, No. 721
Tipton, Michigan

OLD-FASHIONED ANADAMA BREAD

> ½ c. old-fashioned or quick oats
> 3 tbsp. corn oil
> ¼ c. molasses
> 2 tsp. salt
> 1 pkg. dry yeast
> 1 egg, beaten
> 2¾ c. sifted flour
> Melted margarine or butter

Mix ¾ cup boiling water, oats, corn oil, molasses and salt in large mixing bowl. Cool to lukewarm. Dissolve yeast in ¼ cup warm water. Add yeast, egg and half the flour to oats mixture. Beat for 2 minutes with electric mixer at medium speed or 300 vigorous strokes with spoon, scraping side and bottom of bowl frequently. Stir in remaining flour. Mix with spoon until thoroughly blended. Spoon into 2 greased 1-pound coffee cans or greased loaf pan. Smooth top with floured hand. Let rise in warm place for about 1 hour or until dough is ¾ inch from top of coffee cans or to top of loaf pan. May place pans on rack over bowl of hot water; cover with towel to rise if kitchen is cool. Sprinkle top of bread with additional salt. Bake in preheated 375-degree oven for 40 minutes for loaves in coffee cans or 50 to 55 minutes for loaf in loaf pan or until bread sounds hollow when tapped. Remove from pans immediately. Place, free from draft, on cooling rack or across edges of baking pans. Brush tops of bread with margarine. Cool before slicing.

Photograph for this recipe on page 96.

CARAWAY RYE BREAD

> 2 pkg. dry yeast
> 1 tbsp. salt
> ¼ c. dark molasses
> 2 tbsp. butter or margerine
> 3 c. rye flour
> Caraway Seed
> 3 c. flour
> Cornmeal

Dissolve yeast in 2 cups warm water. Add next 4 ingredients with 1 or 2 tablespoons caraway seed. Beat until smooth. Add remaining flour; knead until smooth. Place in lightly greased bowl. Cover. Let rise in warm place for 1 hour or until doubled in bulk. Grease cookie sheet. Sprinkle with cornmeal or caraway seed. Punch down dough. Divide in half. Make into 2 balls. Place on cookie sheet. Cover with towel. Let rise in warm place for 1 hour or until doubled in bulk. Bake at 375 degrees for 40 to 50 minutes or until sounds hollow when tapped.

Jean Dake
Ashland Co., Ruggle Grange, No. 2119
Nova, Ohio

DILL-WHEAT GERM BREAD

2 pkg. yeast
⅓ c. sugar
1 tsp. salt
2 tsp. dillseed
2 tbsp. onion flakes
5½ to 6½ c. all-purpose flour
1½ c. warm milk
3 eggs
½ c. butter, melted and cooled
1⅓ c. wheat germ

Combine first 5 ingredients and 3 cups flour in large bowl. Stir milk and ½ cup warm water into flour mixture. Add 2 eggs and 1 egg yolk; stir. Add butter. Stir in wheat germ and enough additional flour to make soft dough. Knead on floured board for 10 minutes or until smooth and elastic. Place in greased bowl; turn to grease top. Let rise until doubled in bulk. Punch down. Divide into 2 parts. Cut in half. Twist 2 pieces together. Place in 4×8½-inch greased pan. Repeat with remaining dough. Let rise until doubled in bulk. Brush top with beaten egg white. Bake at about 325 degrees for 35 to 40 minutes. Freezes well.

Julia H. Sanger
Orwell Grange, No. 1562
Orwell, Ohio

JANE'S WHOLE WHEAT BREAD

1 pkg. dry yeast
½ c. (firmly packed) brown sugar
3 tsp. salt
¼ c. shortening
3 c. whole wheat flour
5 c. white flour

Soften yeast in ¼ cup warm water. Combine 2½ cups hot water, sugar, salt and shortening. Cool to lukewarm. Stir in whole wheat flour and 1 cup white flour; beat well. Stir in yeast. Add enough remaining flour to make a soft dough. Turn onto lightly floured surface. Knead for 10 to 12 minutes or until smooth and satiny. Shape into ball. Place in

lightly floured bowl; cover. Let rise about 1 hour and 30 minutes or until doubled in bulk. Punch down. Cut in 2 portions. Shape each into a smooth ball; cover. Let stand 10 minutes. Shape into 2 loaves. Place in greased 4×8-inch baking pans. Let rise about 1 hour and 15 minutes or until doubled in bulk. Bake at 375 degrees about 45 minutes. Cover with foil last 20 minutes, if necessary.

Mrs. Jane Treichler
Wife of Berks County Pomona Grange Master
Kutytown, Pennsylvania

HONEY-WHOLE WHEAT BREAD

2 pkg. dry yeast
4 tbsp. honey or brown sugar
5 c. stirred whole wheat flour
2 c. milk
2 tsp. salt
¼ c. oil
Egg white

Combine yeast, ¾ cup warm water and 2 tablespoons honey. Let stand until foamy. Combine 1 cup flour and milk in saucepan. Cook until thick and smooth, stirring constantly. Add salt, oil, 2 tablespoons honey and 1 cup flour; mix well. Cool to warm. Add yeast mixture and about 3 cups flour; mix well. Cover. Let rise for about 1 hour or until doubled in bulk. Turn onto floured board. Knead until smooth and elastic. Cover. Let rise for 15 minutes. Shape into 2 loaves; fold edges to make a tight loaf. Place into 2 greased glass loaf pans. Press down to fit corners. Cover. Let rise until doubled in bulk. Brush lightly with egg white. Bake at 400 degrees for 45 to 50 minutes. Remove from pans. Cool on rack. Yield: 2 loaves.

Mrs. Nelson Pierce
Aldonquin Grange, No. 1570
Bainbridge, New York

PIZZA DOUGH

1 ¼-oz. package yeast
2 tbsp. mayonnaise
½ tsp. salt
⅛ tsp. sugar
3½ c. flour

Dissolve yeast in 1 cup warm water in medium bowl. Stir in mayonnaise. Add remaining ingredients; mix well. Knead for several minutes. Let rise for at least 10 minutes. Divide into 2 parts; spread out on oiled pizza pans. Add sauce and toppings. Bake as desired. Yield: 2 pizza crusts.

Patricia Fitch
Oliveburg Grange, No. 2641
Ashland, Ohio

KASE KEGLA (Cottage Cheese Puffs)

1 c. large-curd cottage cheese
1 tbsp. butter
½ tsp. salt
1 egg
Flour

Rinse cottage cheese in boiling water. Drain until dry. Mix cottage cheese with butter, salt and egg; blend well. Add enough flour to make stiff dough. Roll out very thin. Cut into triangles. Let set to dry for several minutes. Fry in hot deep fat until lightly brown. Drain on absorbent paper. Sprinkle with cinnamon and sugar. Dough will puff if dry enough and rolled thin enough. Serve warm. This is a family recipe from France.

Florence Keil
Hopewell Grange, No. 1747
Washington, Illinois

CLOUD BISCUITS

2 c. flour
1 tbsp. sugar
4 tsp. baking powder
½ tsp. salt
½ c. shortening
1 egg, beaten
⅔ c. milk

Sift dry ingredients together. Cut in shortening until mixture resembles coarse crumbs. Add egg and milk. Knead. Roll until ¾-inch thick; cut with biscuit cutter. Place on ungreased baking sheet. Bake in 450-degree oven for 10 to 14 minutes. Yield: 2 dozen.

Margarette Thomas
Brown Co., Pleasant Grange, No. 2077
Georgetown, Ohio

BISCUIT SUPREME

2 c. flour
½ tsp. cream of tartar
½ tsp. salt
4 tsp. baking powder
½ c. shortening
⅔ c. milk

Sift dry ingredients together. Add shortening; cut into coarse crumbs. Add milk. Bake at 425 degrees for 10 to 12 minutes. Mix well. Yield: 10 servings.

Mrs. Carolee J. Kissel
Union Grange, No. 1648
Shelby, Ohio

RANCH-STYLE BISCUITS

1½ sticks butter
2 c. flour
1 tbsp. baking powder
¾ tsp. salt
1¼ c. buttermilk

Place ½ stick butter in 9 × 13-inch baking pan. Place in 450-degree oven to melt. Sift dry ingredients together. Cut in 1 stick butter until mixture resembles coarse meal. Stir in buttermilk to make a soft dough. Turn onto lightly floured board. Pat into 9 × 12-inch rectangle. Cut into six 3 × 6-inch biscuits. Remove 1 tablespoon butter from baking pan; set aside. Place biscuits in baking pan. Drizzle with reserved butter. Bake in 450-degree oven for 20 minutes. Yield: 6 servings.

From a Grange Friend

SOURDOUGH BISCUITS

1 tbsp. dry yeast
⅓ c. sugar
½ tsp. salt
1 c. Sourdough Starter
5 c. flour
Butter or margarine, melted

Dissolve yeast in 2 cups lukewarm water in glass or plastic bowl. Add sugar, salt, Sourdough Starter and flour. Cover; let rise until doubled in bulk. Roll out dough to ¾-inch thickness. Cut with biscuit cutter. Dip both sides in butter. Place on well-greased baking pan. Let rise 15 minutes. Bake at 425 degrees for 20 minutes. Yield: 10-12 servings.

Sourdough Starter

1 tbsp. dry yeast
¼ c. sugar
4 c. flour

Combine all ingredients with 4 cups lukewarm water in glass bowl. Do not use metal bowl. Mix well. Cover with cloth. Let stand for 4 days, stirring daily. Add 1 cup water and 1 cup flour to Starter after a portion has been used. Cover; let stand at room temperature. Stir daily to keep Starter active.

Shirley Engler
La Plata Pomona Grange, No. 10
Ignacio, California

JOY'S CORN BREAD

1 c. sifted flour
1 c. cornmeal

¾ tsp. salt
½ c. sugar
4 tsp. baking powder
1 c. plus 2 tbsp. milk
1 egg, slightly beaten
4 tbsp. oil

Sift dry ingredients together in bowl. Add remaining ingredients; beat for 2 minutes. Pour into a well-greased 9 × 13-inch pan. Bake in 425-degree oven for 25 minutes. Yield: 6-8 servings.

Joy Beatie, D.W.A.
California State Grange
Anderson, California

ESTHER'S CORN MUFFINS

⅓ c. shortening, melted
⅓ c. sugar
1 egg, beaten
1¼ c. milk
1 c. flour
4 tsp. baking powder
½ tsp. salt
2 c. cornmeal

Combine shortening with ⅓ cup sugar. Add remaining ingredients in order given. Mix well. Pour into greased muffin tins. Sprinkle tops with small amount of sugar. Bake at 450 degrees for 10 minutes.

Esther Johnson
Neighborhood Grange, No. 891
Valleyford, Washington

CORNMEAL BUNS

2 c. milk
1 c. cornmeal
½ c. sugar
½ c. shortening
2 tsp. salt
1 pkg. yeast
2 eggs, beaten
Flour

Heat milk; stir in cornmeal. Cook to a mush, not too thick. Cool to lukewarm. Add sugar, shortening and salt. Dissolve yeast in 1 cup warm water; add to mush mixture. Add eggs to mixture. Stir in enough flour to thicken to consistency of light bread dough. Turn onto floured board. Knead until it springs back. Let rise in a greased bowl until doubled in bulk. Roll out as biscuit dough; cut with biscuit cutter. Let rise until doubled its bulk. Bake at 350 degrees for about 20 minutes.

Pauline H. Atkins
Harrisonville Grange, No. 1734
Rutland, Ohio

CRACKLING BREAD

2 c. yellow cornmeal
½ tsp. soda
¼ tsp. salt
1 c. buttermilk
1 c. cracklings, diced

Sift dry ingredients together. Add buttermilk; stir in cracklings. Place in greased 9 × 12-inch baking pan. Bake at 450 degrees for 30 minutes. This recipe was used by my Great, Great Grandmother back in 1863 during Civil War days.

Gladys Richards
Steele Community Grange, No. 841
Springdale, Arkansas

SOUTHERN SPOON BREAD

1 c. yellow cornmeal
1½ tsp. baking powder
½ tsp. salt
2 eggs, beaten
2 tbsp. melted butter
2¼ c. milk

Mix cornmeal, baking powder and salt together. Pour eggs and butter into greased 1-quart casserole. Bring milk to boiling point, stirring to avoid scorching. Sprinkle in dry ingredients; stirring vigorously with wooden spoon. Cook, stirring constantly, for 2 or 3 minutes, or until thickens. Add slowly to eggs. Bake at 425 degrees for 45 minutes. Serve from casserole with spoon. Top each serving with butter. Yield: 6 servings.

Mrs. Vera S. Young
Goodwill Grange, No. 959
Troutdale, Virginia

CURRIED CORNMEAL MUFFINS

¼ c. chopped green onion
3 tbsp. vegetable oil
1¼ c. cornmeal
¾ c. sifted all-purpose flour
¾ tsp. salt
1 tbsp. baking powder
2 tbsp. sugar
1 tbsp. curry powder
1 egg
1 c. milk

Preheat oven to 425 degrees. Cook onion in oil until tender; set aside. Sift cornmeal, flour, salt, baking powder, sugar and curry powder together into bowl. Add egg, milk and onion; stir until just combined. Fill greased medium-sized muffin cups ⅔ full. Bake for 15 to 18 minutes. Serve hot.

Photograph for this recipe on page 100.

Heat 2 cups water. Add shortening, sugar and salt. Cool to lukewarm. Dissolve yeast in 1 cup lukewarm water. Mix a small amount of flour with first mixture. Add yeast and eggs; beat well. Add enough flour to make stiff dough. Knead well; cover dough. Let rise in warm place until doubled in bulk. Form dough into balls. Place in 2 greased 9 × 12-inch pans, 20 to each pan. Let rise about 45 minutes or until doubled in bulk. Bake at 375 degrees until brown. May mix and refrigerate overnight. Form rolls and bake next day. Yield: 40 servings.

Charlotte Mock
Spring Valley Grange, No. 814
Schellsburg, Pennsylvania

DELICIOUS HOT ROLLS

2 c. milk
⅔ c. yellow cornmeal
1 stick margarine
½ c. sugar
1½ tsp. salt
2 pkg. yeast
3 eggs, beaten
Flour

Combine milk, cornmeal and margarine in saucepan. Cook, stirring continuously, until thick. Remove from heat; add sugar and salt. Cool until lukewarm. Dissolve yeast in ½ cup warm water. Add eggs and yeast mixture. Add enough flour to make stiff dough. Knead well. Let rise in warm place until doubled in bulk. Punch down; shape into rolls. Place on greased baking pan. Let rise until doubled in bulk. Bake at 375 degrees until brown. Yield: 12 servings.

Mrs. Clyde Akins
Blue Mound Grange, No. 2230
Nevada, Missouri

ANNA'S OVERNIGHT BUNS

Sugar
2 pkg. dry yeast
1 c. oil
3 tsp. salt
15 c. flour

Mix 2 tablespoons sugar with ½ cup warm water. Add yeast. Let mixture stand for 10 minutes. Mix with 1½ cups sugar, 4 cups lukewarm water, oil, salt and flour. Let rise 3 hours. Punch down. Let rise 1 hour and 30 minutes. Form buns; place on baking pans. Let stand overnight. Bake at 350 degrees for 20 minutes. Yield: 5 dozen rolls.

Mrs. Anna Gould
Bell Township, No. 2047
Mahaffey, Pennsylvania

BUTTERMILK BUNS

4¼ c. all-purpose flour
¼ c. sugar
1¼ tsp. salt
2 tsp. baking powder
½ c. butter
2 pkg. dry yeast
1¼ c. buttermilk

Combine flour, sugar, salt and baking powder in large bowl. Cut in butter until mixture looks like cornmeal. Dissolve yeast in ¾ cup warm water. Make a "well" in center; pour in buttermilk and yeast mixture. Stir; knead to blend. Add more flour, if necessary. Knead until dough is smooth and satiny. Cover; let rise in warm place until doubled in bulk. Punch down; divide into 24 equal pieces. Shape each piece into smooth ball. Place about 3 inches apart on lightly greased baking sheet. Cover; let rise until doubled in bulk. Bake at 350 degrees for 15 to 20 minutes. May use for 2 loaves of bread.

Alice L. Pearson
Dalbo Grange, No. 670
Ogilvie, Minnesota

CHARLOTTE'S ROLLS

½ c. Crisco
¼ c. sugar
2 tbsp. salt
3 pkg. dry yeast
9 c. flour
2 eggs

DINNER ROLLS

1 pkg. yeast
1 c. milk
6 tbsp. sugar
2 tsp. salt
Margarine
5 c. flour
1 egg, slightly beaten

Dissolve yeast in 1 cup warm water. Heat milk; add sugar, salt, ¼ cup margarine and 2 cups flour. Mix well. Add yeast mixture and egg. Add 3 cups flour, mixing to make soft dough. Let rise in warm place until doubled in bulk. Divide dough into 3 pieces. Place 1 piece on floured board. Roll into 15-inch circle. Spread with melted margarine. Cut into 16 pie-shaped pieces. Roll up, beginning at wide end. Place on greased baking pan, point side down. Let rise until doubled in bulk. Bake at 375 degrees for 10 minutes or until brown. Repeat process with remaining dough. Yield: 35 servings.

Mrs. Robert Jellison, C.W.A.
Union Grange, No. 2516
Van Wert, Ohio

RICH DINNER ROLLS

1 c. milk
¼ c. sugar
1 tsp. salt
¼ c. margarine
2 pkg. yeast
2 eggs, beaten
5¼ c. unsifted flour
Butter

Scald milk. Stir in sugar, salt and margarine. Cool to lukewarm. Place ½ cup warm water in large warm bowl. Sprinkle in yeast; stir until dissolved. Add milk mixture, eggs and 2 cups flour. Beat until smooth. Stir in enough remaining flour to make soft dough. Turn onto lightly floured board. Knead 8 to 10 minutes or until smooth and elastic. Place in greased bowl, turning to grease top. Cover; let rise in warm place until doubled in bulk. Punch down. Shape into small balls. Place on greased pans. Cover; let rise in warm place until doubled in bulk. Bake in 375-degree oven about 15 minutes. Brush top with butter. Yield: 30 servings.

Mrs. Jane McVay
Knox Co., Morgan Grange
Mt. Vernon, Ohio

LIGHT DINNER ROLLS

2 pkg. dry yeast
½ c. sugar
1 tbsp. salt
2 tbsp. cooking oil
2 eggs
4 c. flour
Butter

Add yeast to ½ cup warm water to soften. Combine sugar, salt, oil and 2 cups hot water in large bowl. Stir until dissolved. Beat eggs until light. Add to sugar mixture. Add yeast mixture. Beat in flour with electric mixer until of consistency to handle. Place on floured surface; knead until dough is smooth and elastic. Place in greased bowl. Let rise 3 hours or until doubled in bulk. Shape into 24 dinner rolls. Place on greased baking pan. Let rise 2 hours and 30 minutes or until doubled in bulk. Bake at 350 degrees for 30 minutes. Remove from oven. Butter tops of rolls. Yield: 12-24 rolls.

Irene F. Hastings
Willard Grange, No. 2106
Willard, Ohio

PARKER HOUSE ROLLS

2 tbsp. shortening
1 tsp. salt
¼ c. sugar
1 pkg. yeast
3½ c. sifted flour
1 egg, well beaten
Melted butter

Add shortening, salt, sugar and yeast to 1½ cup lukewarm water. Stir until shortening is melted. Stir in sifted flour; mix well. Cover. Let rise in a warm place, free from drafts until doubled in bulk. Add egg; mix well. Knead lightly. Let rise until doubled in bulk. Roll out ½-inch thick on well-floured board. Cut with 2-inch biscuit cutter. Crease in center with dull knife; brush with melted butter. Fold over, pinching dough at sides to make a pocketbook. Place on baking sheet; brush tops with melted butter. Let rise until doubled in bulk. Bake in 400-degree oven about 20 minutes. Yield: 24 rolls.

Mrs. Kenneth Palmer
Adirondack Grange, No. 1019
St. Regis Falls, New York

QUICK LIGHT ROLLS

2 pkg. yeast
2 c. buttermilk, lukewarm
¼ tsp. baking powder
¼ tsp. soda
1 egg, beaten
3 tbsp. lard or shortening
2 tsp. sugar
1 tsp. salt
Flour

Dissolve yeast in buttermilk. Add remaining ingredients. Work in enough flour to form stiff dough. Place on floured surface. Knead until dough is smooth. Roll out on floured surface; cut with biscuit cutter. Place in two 9×13-inch baking pans. Let rise until doubled in bulk. Bake at 375 degrees for 25 to 30 minutes. This makes delicious cinnamon rolls and hamburger buns.

Millie E. Patterson
Crystal Grange, No. 1126
Poulsbo, Washington

REFRIGERATOR ROLL DOUGH

½ c. sugar
1 tbsp. salt
3 tbsp. shortening
2 pkg. dry yeast
1 egg, beaten
6 c. sifted flour

Combine sugar, salt, shortening and 1¾ cups hot water; cool to lukewarm. Dissolve yeast in ¼ cup lukewarm water. Combine both mixtures. Add egg and 3 cups flour. Beat until smooth. Add about 3 cups flour. Mix; knead thoroughly. Place dough in greased bowl; brush top with soft shortening. Cover tightly with aluminum foil. Store in refrigerator until doubled in bulk. Punch down. Cut off dough as needed. Roll to ½-inch thickness; cut with round cutter. Spread with butter. Crease through center with dull knife; fold over. Place on greased cookie sheets. Let rise 2 hours. Bake in 400-degree oven for 12 to 15 minutes. Yield: 25 servings.

Janice Edwards
Licking Co., Bennington Grange, No. 977
Johnstown, Ohio

BUTTERMILK WHEAT ROLLS

1 pkg. yeast
2 c. buttermilk
¼ c. sugar
1 tsp. salt
¼ c. melted shortening
½ tsp. soda
2½ c. whole wheat flour
2 c. white flour
Melted butter

Soften yeast in ¼ cup lukewarm water. Scald buttermilk. Add sugar, salt, shortening and soda. Cool to lukewarm. Add to yeast mixture; stir. Add flour; mix well. Knead. Shape into rolls. Place in greased pan; brush with melted butter. Cover; let rise until doubled in bulk. Bake at 425 degrees for 20 minutes. Yield: 3 dozen rolls.

Mrs. Howard Miller
Hall of Fame Grange
Bonner Springs, Kansas

HONEY WHEAT BUNS

2 pkg. dry yeast
2 c. scalded milk
¼ c. safflower or vegetable oil or shortening
1 tbsp. salt
⅔ c. honey
4½ c. whole wheat flour
6 c. unbleached flour
1 egg, beaten

Soften yeast in ½ cup warm water. Combine milk, 1½ cups hot water, oil, salt and honey. Stir until salt and honey dissolve. Cool to lukewarm. Add 2 cups whole wheat flour and 2 cups unbleached flour. Beat until smooth. Beat in yeast mixture and egg. Stir in 2½ cups whole wheat flour and enough remaining unbleached flour to make a soft dough. Knead until smooth and elastic. Place in greased bowl. Let rise hour and 30 minutes or until doubled in bulk. Form into 48 buns. Let rise until doubled in bulk. Bake in 350-degree oven for 25 to 30 minutes.

Mrs. George R. McConnell
Montour Grange, No. 2005
Clinton, Pennsylvania

WHOLE WHEAT ROLLS

¾ c. milk
Sugar
3 tsp. salt
Butter
⅓ c. molasses
1 tbsp. yeast
4 c. whole wheat flour
4 c. (unsifted) white flour

Scald milk; stir in ⅓ cup sugar, salt, ⅓ cup butter and molasses. Cool to lukewarm. Place 1½ cups warm water in bowl. Add yeast with a small amount of sugar. Stir until dissolved. Add to lukewarm milk mixture. Mix in 2 cups whole wheat flour and 2 cups white flour. Beat until smooth. Add enough remaining flour to make a soft dough. Knead 8 to 10 minutes or until smooth and elastic. Place in greased bowl, turning to grease top. Cover; let rise in warm place free from draft, until doubled in bulk. Punch down; let rest 10 to 15 minutes. Shape into desired rolls. Place in 2 greased 9-inch pans or 2 muffin pans. Brush lightly with butter. Let rise in warm place until doubled in bulk. Bake at 425 degrees for 15 to 18 minutes. Yield: 24 servings.

Mrs. Francis E. Thomas
Kent Co. Delaware Bethesda Grange, No. 64
Marydel, Maryland

WHOLE WHEAT SANDWICH BUNS

½ c. sugar
½ c. nonfat dry milk
1 tbsp. salt
¾ c. cooking oil
4½ to 5 c. sifted all-purpose flour
2 pkg. dry yeast
3 eggs
3½ c. stirred whole wheat flour
Whole milk

Combine 2 cups water, sugar, dry milk, salt and oil in saucepan. Heat to lukewarm. Stir 4 cups all-purpose flour and yeast in bowl. Add warm liquid and eggs. Beat with electric mixer at low speed for 30 seconds, scraping sides and bottom of bowl constantly. Beat at high speed for 3 minutes, scraping bowl occasionally. Stir in whole wheat flour by hand. Add enough remaining all-purpose flour to make a soft dough. Knead on floured surface about 5 minutes or until smooth and elastic. Place in greased bowl, turning to grease top. Cover; let rise one hour and 30 minutes or until doubled in bulk. Punch dough down; divide into 3 parts. Cover; let rest for 5 minutes. Divide each third into 8 portions. Shape into balls; place on greased baking sheet. Press down with palm of hand to make 3½-inch rounds. Cover. Let rise 35 to 45 minutes or until doubled in bulk. Brush with milk. Bake at 375 degrees about 12 minutes or until golden brown. Yield: 24 buns.

Corliss M. Larson
Wolf River Community Grange
Weyauwega, Wisconsin

WATER BAGELS

4 to 5 c. unsifted flour
3 tbsp. sugar
1 tbsp. salt
1 pkg. dry yeast
1 egg white, beaten

Mix 1½ cups flour, sugar, salt and undissolved yeast in large bowl thoroughly. Add 1½ cups hot water gradually to dry ingredients. Beat for 2 minutes at medium speed of electric mixer, scraping bowl occasionally. Add ½ cup flour, or enough flour to make a thick batter. Beat at high speed 2 minutes, scraping bowl occasionally. Stir in enough additional flour to make soft dough. Turn onto lightly floured board. Knead until smooth and elastic, about 8 to 10 minutes. Place in ungreased bowl. Cover; let rise in warm place, free from draft, for 20 minutes. Dough will not be doubled in bulk. Punch dough down. Turn onto lightly floured board. Roll dough into 12 × 10-inch rectangle. Cut dough into twelve 1-inch strips. Pinch ends of strips together to form circles. Place on ungreased baking sheets. Cover; let rise in warm place, free from draft, for 20 minutes. Dough will not be doubled in bulk. Fill a large shallow pan with water to 1¾-inch depth. Bring to a boil. Lower heat; add few bagels at a time. Simmer for 7 minutes. Remove from water. Place on towel to cool. Cool 5 minutes. Place on ungreased baking sheets. Bake in 375-degree oven for 10 minutes. Remove from oven. Combine beaten egg white and 1 tablespoon cold water. Brush on each bagel. Return to oven; bake about 20 minutes longer, or until done. Remove from baking sheets. Cool on wire racks.

Photograph for this recipe on page 106.

ALMOND COFFEE CAKE

½ c. butter or margarine
1¼ c. sugar
2 eggs, well beaten
2 c. flour, sifted
1 tsp. baking powder
1 tsp. soda
Pinch of salt
1 c. sour cream
1½ tsp. vanilla extract
½ c. chopped walnuts
½ tsp. almond extract

Cream butter. Add 1 cup sugar; beat until fluffy. Add eggs. Sift dry ingredients together. Add to egg mixture alternately with sour cream. Blend thoroughly; add 1 teaspoon vanilla. Combine walnuts, almond extract, ½ teaspoon vanilla and ¼ cup sugar. Pour half the batter into a well-greased and floured 10-inch tube pan. Sprinkle all but 1 heaping tablespoon of walnut mixture on batter. Add remaining batter. Top with reserved walnut mixture. Bake in 350-degree oven for 45 minutes. Cool for 15 minutes before removing from pan.

Angela Maxham
Farmington Grange, No. 12
Farmington, Maine

ANNA'S COFFEE CAKE

¼ lb. butter, softened
1¼ c. sugar
2 eggs, beaten
2 c. sifted flour
1 tsp. each soda and baking powder
1 c. sour cream
½ c. milk
1 tsp. vanilla extract
½ tsp. cinnamon
¾ c. chopped nuts

Cream butter with 1 cup sugar; beat until fluffy. Add eggs, one at a time, beating well after each addition. Sift flour, soda and baking powder together; add to creamed mixture alternately with sour cream and milk. Add vanilla; mix well. Combine cinnamon, nuts and ¼ cup sugar. Pour half the batter into greased and floured tube pan. Sprinkle half the nut mixture over batter. Repeat layers. Bake at 350 degrees for 55 minutes.

Anna Peterka
Friendship Grange, No. 1018
Forest City, Pennsylvania

CARDAMOM BRAID

2 pkg. yeast
2 c. milk
Sugar
1½ tsp. salt
1 tsp. crushed cardamom seed
Butter
2 eggs, beaten
9 c. flour
2 tbsp. hot coffee

Dissolve yeast in ½ cup warm water. Scald milk. Stir in 1¼ cups sugar, salt, cardamom and ½ cup soft butter. Cool. Add yeast mixture, eggs and half the flour. Beat. Stir in enough flour for soft dough. Knead on floured board 10 minutes or until smooth and elastic. Place in greased bowl. Cover; let rise until doubled in bulk. Punch down. Let rest 10 minutes. Divide into thirds. Divide each third into 3 equal pieces. Shape each into 14-inch rope. Place 3 ropes side by side. Pinch together at one end. Braid loosely. Pinch ends to seal. Place in greased loaf pan. Repeat with remaining dough. Combine 2 tablespoons melted butter and hot coffee. Spoon over loaves. Sprinkle with 3 tablespoons sugar.

Cover. Let rise until doubled in bulk. Bake at 350 degrees for 35 to 40 minutes.

Elsie Mathews, Master
Chiawana Grange, No. 1141
Pasco, Washington

COFFEE KRINGLE

¼ c. milk, scalded
2 c. flour
Sugar
½ tsp. salt
¼ c. butter
2 pkg. yeast
1 egg, beaten
1½ c. chopped stewed prunes
3 tbsp. lemon juice
½ tsp. grated lemon peel

Cool milk to lukewarm. Combine flour, ¼ cup sugar and salt. Cut in butter with pastry cutter. Dissolve yeast in ½ cup warm water in large bowl. Stir in milk, egg and flour mixture; mix well. Place in a greased bowl, turning to grease top. Cover; let rise in warm place 40 minutes or until doubled in bulk. Combine prunes, 3 tablespoons sugar, lemon juice and lemon peel. Set aside. Punch dough down; turn out on well floured board. Divide in half. Roll each half to a 2 × 16-inch rectangle. Place in a greased 10 × 15-inch pan. Spread with prune mixture. Cover with second half. Seal edges. Cover. Let rise in warm place 30 minutes or until doubled in bulk. Bake at 350 degrees for 20 minutes. Turn out of pan at once. Ice with confectioners' sugar frosting when cool, if desired.

Mrs. Marcella Burris
Bryant Grange, No. 791
Stanwood, Washington

CRANBERRY COFFEE CAKE

1 stick margarine, softened
1 c. sugar
2 eggs
2 c. flour
1 tsp. each baking powder and soda
½ tsp. salt
1 c. sour cream
1½ tsp. almond flavoring
1 7-oz. can whole cranberry sauce
½ c. chopped nuts
¾ c. confectioners' sugar

Cream margarine and sugar together. Add eggs one at a time beating well after each addition. Sift dry ingredients together; add to creamed mixture alternately with sour cream. Add 1 teaspoon almond flavoring. Grease and flour 8-inch tube pan. Put layer of batter in bottom of pan. Add half the cranberry sauce, evenly distributed. Repeat layers. Sprinkle with nuts. Bake at 350 degrees for 55 minutes. Mix confectioners' sugar with 2 tablespoons warm water and ½ teaspoon almond flavoring. Spread over top of warm cake.

Gertrude Hastings
Suffield Grange, No. 27
Suffield, Connecticut

FRENCH COFFEE CAKE

2 c. flour
1 tsp. baking powder
½ tsp. salt
1 stick butter or margarine, softened
1½ c. sugar
2 eggs
1 tsp. soda
1 c. sour cream
1 tsp. vanilla extract
½ c. chopped nuts
½ tsp. cinnamon

Sift flour, baking powder and salt together. Cream butter with 1 cup sugar. Add eggs, one at a time, beating well after each addition. Add soda to sour cream; mix. Add flour to creamed mixture alternately with sour cream. Add vanilla. Combine nuts, cinnamon and ½ cup sugar. Pour half the batter into greased and floured 9-inch springform pan. Sprinkle with half the nut mixture. Repeat layers. Bake at 350 degrees for 40 to 45 minutes.

Gladys G. Howe
Otsego Co., Red Creek Valley Grange, No. 1583
Cooperstown, New York

QUICK COFFEE CAKE

2 c. flour, sifted
2 tsp. baking powder
¾ tsp. salt
½ c. sugar
6 tbsp. shortening
1 egg, well beaten
½ c. milk
Preserves

Sift together all dry ingredients. Cut in shortening. Combine egg and milk; add to flour mixture. Stir until well blended. Pour into greased 9-inch round pan. Bake at 350 degrees for 25 minutes. Top with preserves; bake 5 minutes longer. Serve with whipped cream, if desired. Given to me by my grandmother.

Mrs. Jim Reimann, C.W.A.
St. Clair Co., Pomona Grange
Lebanon, Illinois

SOUR CREAM COFFEE CAKE

1 c. butter, softened
Sugar
2 eggs
1 tsp. vanilla extract
1 c. sour cream
2 c. all-purpose flour
1 tsp. each salt and baking powder
½ tsp. soda
½ c. finely chopped nuts (opt.)
½ tsp. cinnamon
Confectioner's sugar

Cream butter and 1½ cups sugar until fluffy. Add eggs one at a time, beating well after each addition. Add vanilla and sour cream. Sift dry ingredients together; add to creamed mixture. Combine nuts, cinnamon and 2 tablespoons sugar. Spread half of batter in 9 or 10-inch tube pan. Sprinkle with half the nut mixture. Repeat layers. Bake at 350 degrees for 45 minutes. Cool 10 minutes. Invert on wire rack. Cool. Sprinkle with confectioners' sugar.

Georgia M. Taylor
Potomac Grange, No. 1
Arlington, Virginia

APPLE DOUGHNUTS

2 c. thick unsweetened applesauce
½ c. undiluted frozen orange juice
2 eggs, beaten
1 tsp. lemon extract
1½ c. sugar
1 c. powdered milk
5 c. sifted flour
½ tsp. nutmeg
2 tsp. soda
1 tsp. salt
1 tsp. baking powder
Oil for frying

Combine applesauce, orange juice, eggs and lemon extract. Sift together dry ingredients; combine with applesauce mixture. Mix well. Roll ½-inch thick on floured board. Cut as desired. Fry at 360 degrees in deep oil 1 minute on each side or until brown. Drain. Glaze or frost as desired. Store in stone crock in cool dry place. Will keep for several days. A doughnut gun may also be used for this recipe.

Adelaide J. Mathison
Stemjt Hill Grange, No. 1095
Wenatchee, Washington

DOUGHNUTS

6 c. flour
1½ tsp. soda

4 tsp. baking powder
1 tsp. nutmeg
3 eggs, beaten
1 c. sugar
1 c. margarine
3 c. warm mashed potatoes
1 c. buttermilk
Lard for frying

Sift dry ingredients together. Combine eggs, sugar, margarine and potatoes; mix well. Add buttermilk. Add dry ingredients all at once; stir until flour is moistened but not smooth. Roll out; cut half the dough at a time. Fry in lard heated to 375 degrees. Yield: 5 dozen.

Helen Miles
Moosilauka Grange, No. 214
North Haverhill, New Hampshire

COUNTRY-RAISED DOUGHNUTS

1 tbsp. yeast
1 tbsp. sugar
¾ c. sugar
1 tsp. salt
¼ c. butter
1 c. scalded milk
4½ to 5 c. flour
2 eggs, beaten
1 tbsp. flavoring, vanilla, orange, or spice
Oil for frying
2 c. confectioners' sugar

Dissolve yeast and sugar in ¼ cup warm water. Combine sugar, salt, and butter in large mixer bowl. Stir in milk until sugar dissolves. Cool to lukewarm. Stir in about 2 cups flour; beat until smooth. Stir in yeast, eggs and flavoring. Stir in enough additional flour to make a soft dough. Knead for 5 to 9 minutes or until smooth and satiny. Shape into ball in bowl. Grease lightly; cover. Let rise in warm place for 1 hour and 30 minutes or until doubled in bulk. Punch down. Turn dough onto lightly floured pastry board. Roll ½ inch thick. Cut with floured doughnut cutter. Place dougnuts on lightly floured board. Let rise in warm place until doubled in bulk. Heat cooking oil ½ to 2-inches deep in saucepan. Fry doughnuts for 45 seconds on each side. Drain on paper towels. Combine confectioners' sugar and 4 tablespoons cold water; mix well. Dip hot doughnuts into mixture. Place on rack to drip. Cool.

Margaret S. Robinson
Kent Co., Bethesda Grange, No. 64
Marydel, Maryland

BUTTERMILK DOUGHNUTS

2 eggs, beaten
1¼ c. sugar
Cooking oil
2 c. sifted all-purpose flour
1 tbsp. baking powder
½ tsp. salt
½ tsp. nutmeg
1½ tsp. soda
½ c. milk
¾ c. buttermilk
1 c. confectioners' sugar

Combine eggs, sugar and 2 tablespoons oil. Mix next 5 ingredients together. Combine 2 mixtures in mixer bowl. Add milk and buttermilk; mix thoroughly with electric mixer. Preheat Doughnut Machine for 10 minutes. Add batter. Add ½ teaspoon oil to each circular cavity at top of unit within first 2 minutes of baking time. Bake for 5 minutes or until oil no longer bubbles for crispier doughnut. Add ½ cup boiling water gradually to confectioners' sugar; mix well. Dip warm doughnuts into warm glaze. Yield: 20 servings.

Mrs. Jean Bagnich
Hope Grange, No. 898
Waymart, Pennsylvania

GRANDMOTHER TOWNSENDS' DOUGHNUTS

1 egg
1 c. sugar
½ tsp. soda
1½ c. buttermilk
1 tbsp. (heaping) lard or melted shortening
Pinch of salt
3 c. flour
Oil for frying

Beat egg and sugar. Mix soda in ½ cup buttermilk; add to egg and sugar mixture. Combine remaining ingredients, adding flour last. Roll out; cut into rounds. Fry in hot oil. Turn to brown.

Janet Whetstone
Papillion Grange, No. 401
Omaha, Nebraska

KIGLEYS

6 c. flour
¾ c. sugar
2 tsp. salt
2 eggs, sightly beaten
2 pkg. yeast
1 c. lukewarm milk
Shortening, softened
Oil for frying
Confectioners' sugar

Mix flour, sugar and salt in large bowl. Make a well in center. Add eggs. Dissolve yeast in ½ cup warm water. Add ½ cup shortening and yeast mixture, stirring after each addition. Mix with some of the flour. Add milk; mix well. Knead with hands, adding more flour, if needed. Spread enough shortening over dough to coat surface. Cover dough with cloth. Let rise in warm place to doubled in size. Punch down. Let stand 30 minutes longer. Place some dough on floured board; roll out to ⅛ inch thickness. Cut in desired shapes. Let rest for 10 to 15 minutes. Fry in 375 degree deep fat, turning to brown on both sides. Remove from fat. Drain on absorbent paper. Shake several at a time in bag of confectioner's sugar. May also use a mixture of sugar and cinnamon or icing.

Eunice Wilson
Central Square, Subordinate Grange, No. 583
West Monroe, New York

RAISED DOUGHNUTS

¾ c. scalded milk
⅓ c. sugar
1 tsp. salt
¼ c. shortening
1 pkg. yeast
4¼ c. all-purpose flour
1 tsp. nutmeg
2 eggs, beaten
Oil for frying

Combine first 4 ingredients. Cool to lukewarm. Dissolve yeast in ¼ cup warm water. Add to milk mixture. Pour into large bowl. Add 2 cups flour and nutmeg. Beat well; stir in eggs. Add remaining flour; stir. Turn out on floured board. Knead. Place in greased bowl; let rise for 1 hour and 30 minutes. Do not punch down. Place on floured board; roll ⅛ inch thick. Place doughnut cutter in flour; cut out doughnuts. Place trimmings back in bowl. Let rise until doubled in bulk. Roll. Cut. Let doughnuts rise uncovered for 30 to 40 minutes to form crust. Fry in oil at 375 degrees for 3 to 5 minutes. Yield: 2 dozen.

Mrs. Ronald R. Dillie
Buffalo Grange, No. 1523
Washington, Pennsylvania

1 tbsp. lemon juice
Evaporated milk
Oil for frying
3 c. confectioners' sugar
1 tsp. grated orange rind
2 tbsp. orange juice

Beat eggs, sugar and butter in large bowl of electric mixer. Beat in pumpkin. Sift together flour, baking powder, soda, salt, cinnamon and nutmeg. Add lemon juice to evaporated milk. Add dry ingredients to egg-sugar mixture alternately with 1 cup evaporated milk, beginning and ending with dry ingredients. Blend well after each addition. Cover; chill 2 hours. Turn dough out on well floured pastry board or cloth. Knead 5 or 6 times. Roll dough to ¼ inch thickness. Cut with floured doughnut cutter. Fry in deep 375-degree oil until golden, about 3 to 4 minutes, turning once. Drain on absorbent paper. Beat together until smooth confectioners' sugar, grated orange rind, orange juice and 1 tablespoon evaporated milk. Frost doughnuts while warm. Yield: 2 dozen.

Photograph for this recipe on page 110.

SWEET MILK DOUGHNUTS

1 c. sugar
2 eggs, beaten
½ tsp. salt
¼ tsp. nutmeg
4 tbsp. melted shortening
3 tsp. triple acting baking powder
1 c. milk
Flour
Oil for frying

Combine first 7 ingredients with enough flour to make a stiff dough. Roll out on floured board to ⅛-inch thickness. Cut with doughnut cutter. Fry in 380-degree oil. Brown both sides. Yield: 30 large doughnuts.

Mrs. Rose Cleason
Bennington Grange, No. 497
Bennington, Vermont

FROSTED PUMPKIN DOUGHNUTS

2 eggs
1 c. sugar
2 tbsp. butter, softened
1 c. canned pumpkin
4 c. sifted all-purpose flour
2 tsp. baking powder
1 tsp. soda
½ tsp. salt
½ tsp. cinnamon
½ tsp. nutmeg

LOTTIE'S BANANA BREAD

½ c. butter
1 c. sugar
2 eggs, beaten
3 lg. bananas, mashed
¼ tsp. salt
1 tsp. baking powder
½ c. chopped nuts
2 c. flour

Cream butter and sugar. Add eggs, bananas and salt; mix well. Fold in baking powder and nuts. Beat in flour. Pour into greased loaf pan. Bake at 350 degrees for 45 minutes or until done.

Lottie V. Owen
South Bay Grange
Olympia, Washington

APPLE-BANANA NUT BREAD

⅔ c. sugar
⅛ c. soft shortening
2 eggs, beaten
3 tbsp. sour milk or buttermilk
½ c. mashed banana
½ c. grated unpeeled apple or applesauce
2 c. flour
1 tsp. baking powder
½ tsp. soda
½ tsp. salt
½ c. chopped nuts

Cream sugar and shortening. Add eggs; mix well. Add milk, banana and apple. Sift dry ingredients. Add to banana mixture; mix well. Stir in nuts. Pour into well-greased 5 × 9-inch loaf pan. Let stand 20 minutes before baking. Bake at 350 degrees for 50 to 60 minutes.

Marge Bush
Oakfield Grange
Bosom, New York

BANANA-DATE BREAD

½ c. shortening
1 c. sugar
2 eggs, well-beaten
2 c. sifted flour
1 tsp. soda
3 med. bananas, mashed
¼ c. chopped nuts
¼ c. dates

Combine all ingredients; mix well. Pour into greased 6 × 9-inch loaf pan. Bake at 350 degrees for 45 minutes. Yield: 15 servings.

Mrs. Mary Welton
Slippery Rock Grange, No. 1444
Slippery Rock, Pennsylvania

ALICE'S BANANA BREAD

5 lg. bananas
4 eggs, well-beaten
1 c. shortening
2 c. sugar
4 c. sifted flour
2 tsp. soda
1 tsp. salt
1 c. walnuts

Beat bananas until liquid. Add eggs; set aside. Cream shortening and sugar until fluffy. Add banana mixture; blend well. Add flour, soda and salt; stir until smooth. Fold in walnuts. Pour into 3 well-greased 5 × 9-inch loaf pans. Bake at 350 degrees for 45 to 50 minutes.

Alice Anderson
Mt. Wheeler Grange
Oso, Washington

APPLESAUCE BROWN BREAD

2 c. unsweetened applesauce
⅔ c. molasses
1 c. flour
1½ tsp. soda
½ tsp. salt

1 c. cornmeal
1 c. oatmeal
⅔ c. raisins

Combine applesauce and molasses; mix well. Sift flour, soda and salt. Add to applesauce mixture. Stir in cornmeal and oats; mix well. Add raisins, stirring quickly. Pour into 2 greased 1-quart coffee cans. Cover cans with foil. Place in water bath. Steam in oven at 350 degrees for 2 hours.

Annie W. Thompson
Wilmot Grange, No. 309
Wilmot Flat, New Hamsphire

BESSIE'S BROWN BREAD

2 c. graham flour
2 c. white flour
½ tsp. salt
2 tsp. soda
½ c. sugar
⅓ c. dark molasses
1½ c. sour milk or buttermilk
½ c. walnuts (opt.)
1 c. seeded muscat raisins

Combine dry ingredients in bowl. Stir to mix. Add remaining ingredients all at once. Mix well with a spoon until smooth. Pour into greased 5 × 9-inch loaf pan. Let stand for 30 minutes at room temperature. Bake at 375 degrees for 45 minutes or until loaf tests done. Four cups stone-ground whole wheat flour may be substituted for 2 cups white flour.

Bessie Storms
Plummer Grange, No. 273
Plummer, Idaho

BAKED BOSTON BROWN BREAD

1½ c. flour
2½ tsp. soda
1½ tsp. salt
¼ c. sugar
2 c. whole wheat flour
⅓ c. shortening
2 c. sour milk or buttermilk
1 egg, beaten
¾ c. molasses
1 c. raisins (opt.)

Sift first 4 ingredients. Add whole wheat flour; mix well. Cut in shortening. Add remaining ingredients; mix until flour is moist. Pour into 2 greased 3½ × 7½-inch loaf pans. Bake in 325-degree oven for about 45 minutes.

Barbara H. Young
Mount Hope Grange, No. 77
Landaff, New Hampshire

DOROTHY'S BROWN BREAD

1½ c. flour
2 tsp. soda
1½ tsp. salt
1 c. wheat germ
1 c. graham cracker crumbs
2 eggs, beaten
⅓ c. vegetable oil
1 c. light molasses
2 c. buttermilk

Combine all ingredients; mix well. Pour into 2 greased 1-pound coffee cans. Bake at 350 degrees for 50 to 55 minutes. Cool in cans for 10 minutes.

Dorothy Shores
Benton Grange, No. 358
Augusta, Maine

EASY BROWN BREAD

1½ c. raisins
2 tbsp. shortening
1 c. sugar
2 eggs, beaten
2 tsp. soda
2¾ c. flour
1 tsp. salt
1 tsp. vanilla extract
1 c. nuts

Bring raisins and 1½ cups water to boil. Add shortening. Cool. Add remaining ingredients; mix well. Fill 4 greased No. 303 cans ½ full. Bake at 350 degrees for 1 hour. Cool. Wrap in foil. Freeze.

Mrs. Mabel Barry, C.W.A.
Carlton Grange, No. 264
Hastings, Michigan

MILDRED'S BROWN BREAD

1 c. cornmeal
2 c. rye or graham flour
1 c. sour milk or buttermilk
½ c. sugar
½ c. molasses
1 tsp. soda
Dash of salt
1 c. raisins

Combine first 7 ingredients. Soak raisins in 1 cup hot water. Drain, reserving liquid. Add enough water to reserved liquid to measure 1 cup. Pour into a saucepan. Bring to a boil. Add raisins to dry ingredients. Stir well to coat each with flour. Add the boiling water from raisins to dry ingredients. Pour immediately into 2 greased 1-pound coffee cans. Cover with foil. Steam for 3 hours in boiling water. Yield: 6-8 servings.

Mrs. Mildred Ward
Cavendish Grange, No. 275
Cavendish, Vermont

STEAMED BROWN BREAD

1 c. cornmeal
1 c. oatmeal
1 c. flour
1 c. buttermilk
1 c. molasses
1 tsp. salt
1 tsp. soda

Combine first 7 ingredients; mix well. Add 1 cup boiling water; stir. Pour immediately into 2 well-greased 1 pound coffee cans. Cover with foil. Place in kettle of boiling water. Steam at least 3 hours. Slice hot using twine. Yield: 6-8 servings.

Emma Jordan, C.W.A.
Old Town Grange, No. 522
Old Town, Maine

CARROT-APPLE BREAD

1½ c. shredded apples
½ c. shredded carrots
¼ c. butter or margarine
2 eggs, beaten
1 tsp. lemon peel
1¾ c. flour
⅔ c. sugar
1 tsp. baking powder
1 tsp. soda
½ tsp. salt
½ c. chopped nuts or ¼ c. nuts and ¼ c. raisins

Combine first 5 ingredients; mix well. Mix dry ingredients together; add to first mixture. Beat for 3 minutes. Stir in nuts. Pour into greased 5 × 9-inch loaf pan. Bake in preheated 350-degree oven for 50 to 60 minutes or until loaf tests done.

Mrs. Mamie Bosic
Linganore Grange, No. 410
New Windsor, Maryland

DATE AND NUT BREAD

1 c. chopped dates
2 tbsp. butter, softened
1¾ c. sugar
1 egg, beaten
1 c. chopped English walnuts

3¾ c. flour
2 tsp. soda
1 tsp. vanilla extract

Pour 1½ cups boiling water over dates; cool. Cream butter and sugar. Add egg, walnuts and date mixture; mix thoroughly. Stir in flour, soda and vanilla. Pour into 2 greased and floured loaf pans. Bake at 350 degrees for 1 hour.

Mrs. Emil Peters
Half Moon Grange, No. 290
Port Matilda, Pennsylvania

DATE NUT BREAD

¾ c. chopped nuts
1 c. chopped dates
1½ tsp. soda
½ tsp. salt
¼ c. margarine
2 eggs, sightly beaten
½ tsp. vanilla extract
1 c. sugar
1½ c. sifted flour

Combine first 4 ingredients in mixer bowl. Add margarine and ¾ cup boiling water. Let stand 15 minutes. Stir to blend. Combine eggs and vanilla. Add sugar and flour; mix well. Add to date mixture; mix lighty. Pour into greased loaf pan. Bake at 350 degrees for 1 hour or until loaf tests done.

Amelia Schwaegel
Enterprise Grange
O'Fallon, Illinois

GREEN TOMATO MINCEMEAT BREAD

½ c. shortening
¾ c. sugar
1 egg, beaten
2 c. flour
1 tsp. soda
½ tsp. salt
1 tsp. baking powder
1 c. green tomato mincemeat

Cream shortening and sugar. Add egg; mix well. Sift dry ingredients together. Add half the dry ingredients to creamed mixture; mix well. Add mincemeat; mix well. Add remaining dry ingredients; mix well without beating. Pour into greased 5 × 9-inch loaf pan. Bake in preheated 375-degree oven for 45 to 55 minutes. Yield: 12 servings.

Mrs. Verlie Vaughan
Poultney Valley Grange, No. 533
Poultney, Vermont

NUT BREAD

Milk
1 egg
1 c. sugar
4 c. flour
4 tsp. baking powder
1 c. chopped nuts
Salt to taste

Add enough milk to beaten egg to measure 1 cup. Pour into bowl. Add 1 cup milk. Add remaining ingredients; mix well. Pour into greased 5 × 9-inch loaf pan. Let stand for 1 hour. Bake at 350 degrees for 1 hour.

Marjorie C. Pendleton
Quonochontaug Grange, No. 48
Bradford, Rhode Island

PERSIMMON BREAD

1 c. sugar
¾ c. margarine, softened
2 eggs, beaten
2 c. flour
1 tsp. soda
1 c. persimmon pulp
½ c. chopped pecans

Cream sugar and margarine until light and fluffly. Add eggs; mix well. Mix flour and soda. Add to creamed mixture. Add persimmon pulp and pecans; mix well. Pour into 4 × 8-inch greased loaf pan. Bake at 325 degrees for 1 hour. Good served with cream cheese. Yield: 12-15 servings.

From a Grange Friend

PINEAPPLE-NUT BREAD

2 c. sifted all-purpose flour
½ c. sugar
1 tsp. baking powder
½ tsp. salt
1 c. raisins
½ c. coarsely chopped walnut
1 egg, beaten
1 tsp. vanilla extract
2 tbsp. melted shortening
1 tsp. soda
1 c. crushed pineapple, undrained

Sift first 4 ingredients into mixing bowl. Add raisins and walnuts. Combine egg, vanilla and shortening. Add to mixture. Dissolve soda in pineapple. Add to mixture; stir until blended. Pour into greased 4 × 8-inch loaf pan. Bake at 350 degrees about 1 hour or until loaf tests done.

Annabelle Loomis
Sunnyridge Grange, No. 898
Toledo, Oregon

ORANGE-DATE BREAD

2 tbsp. butter, softened
1 c. sugar
1 egg, beaten
1 c. finely chopped dates
½ c. orange juice
1 tsp. soda
2 c. flour
1 tsp. salt
1 tsp. baking powder
½ c. broken nuts
Grated rind of 1 orange

Cream butter and sugar. Add egg; beat well. Mix dates, orange juice, soda and ½ cup hot water in bowl. Cool. Add to creamed mixture. Sift together flour, salt and baking powder. Add to creamed mixture. Stir in nuts and orange rind. Pour into greased 5 × 9-inch loaf pan. Bake at 350 degrees for 60 minutes.

Eileen Wurster
Hopewell Grange, No. 1747
Washington, Illinois

PRUNE-NUT BREAD

2 c. chopped prunes
1½ c. sugar
1 tsp. salt
2 eggs
5 c. flour
2 tsp. soda
2 tsp. baking powder
1½ tsp. vanilla extract
1 c. chopped nuts
3 tbsp. butter, melted

Soak prunes in 3 cups boiling water for 10 minutes. Combine remaining ingredients in bowl. Add prune mixture; mix well. Pour into greased 5 × 9-inch loaf pan. Let rise 10 minutes. Bake at 350 degrees for 1 hour.

Rosemond Jones
Spencer Grange, No. 1110
Spencer, New York

PUMPKIN BREAD

3½ c. flour
2 tsp. soda
1½ tsp. salt
1 tsp. cinnamon
1 tsp. nutmeg
3 c. sugar
1 c. cooking oil
4 eggs, beaten
2 c. canned pumpkin

Mix all dry ingredients in mixer bowl; add remaining ingredients and ⅔ cup water. Mix until smooth.

Pour into 2 greased and floured loaf pans. Bake at 350 degrees for 1 hour.

Eunice Trible
Papillion Grange, No. 401
Papillion, Nebraska

STRAWBERRY-NUT LOAF

1 c. butter, softened
1½ c. sugar
1 tsp. vanilla extract
1¼ tsp. lemon extract
4 eggs, beaten
3 c. sifted flour
1 tsp. salt
¾ tsp. cream of tartar
⅛ tsp. soda
1 c. strawberry jam
½ c. sour cream
½ c. chopped walnuts

Cream first 4 ingredients. Add eggs; beat well. Sift dry ingredients. Combine jam and sour cream. Add jam mixture and flour alternately to creamed mixture. Add walnuts. Pour into 2 greased loaf pans. Bake at 350 degrees for 50 minutes. Cool 10 minutes.

Mrs. Marvyn Harris
Hebron Grange, No. 845
Cottage Grove, Oregon

ESTHER'S ZUCCHINI BREAD

1½ c. flour
2 tsp. baking powder
½ tsp. salt
½ tsp. soda
½ tsp. cinnamon
1 c. grated zucchini
2 eggs, beaten
1 c. sugar
½ c. cooking oil
1 tsp. vanilla extract
½ c. nuts or raisins

Combine all ingredients; mix well. Pour into greased loaf pan. Bake in a 375-degree oven for 60 to 65 minutes.

Mrs. Esther Shaw
Pleasant Grange, No. 2077
Georgetown, Ohio

FAYE'S ZUCCHINI BREAD

3 eggs, beaten
1 c. oil

2 c. sugar
2 c. peeled grated zucchini
2 tsp. cinnamon
½ tsp. baking powder
1 tsp. soda
2 tsp. vanilla extract
1 c. chopped nuts, (opt.)
1 c. raisins or dates, chopped
3 c. flour
1 tsp. salt

Combine ingredients in order listed; mix well. Pour into 2 greased loaf pans. Bake at 350 degrees for 1 hour.

Faye Cousino
Pittsford Grange, No. 133
Pittsford, Michigan

GAIL'S ZUCCHINI BREAD

1 c. oil
2 c. sugar
3 eggs, beaten
2 c. grated unpeeled zucchini
½ tsp. salt
3½ c. flour
2 tsp. soda
½ tsp. nutmeg
⅛ tsp. cinnamon
½ tsp. vanilla extract
2 c. seedless raisins
1 c. chopped walnuts

Combine oil and sugar in bowl. Add eggs and zucchini; mix well. Add remaining ingredients; mix well. Pour into 2 greased and floured loaf pans. Bake at 350 degrees for 1 hour and 15 minutes.

Gail Older
Ballston Grange
Ballston Spa, New York

THREE-IN-ONE CEREAL BREAD

1 tsp. soda
1 c. buttermilk
1 c. flour
1 c. oatmeal
1 c. All-Bran
1 c. sugar
1 egg, beaten

Dissolve soda in ½ cup buttermilk. Combine all ingredients; mix. Pour into a greased loaf pan. Let stand for at least 20 minutes. Bake in 350-degree oven for 1 hour.

Marion Judd, Master
Lake Harbor Grange, No. 1185
Muskegon, Michigan

BUTTERSCOTCH ROLLS

2 c. flour
4 tsp. baking powder
1 tsp. salt
4 tbsp. shortening
⅔ c. milk
¼ c. walnuts
½ tsp. cinnamon
Brown sugar
Melted butter

Combine first 5 ingredients. Roll out to ½-inch thickness. Combine walnuts, cinnamon, ⅔ cup firmly packed brown sugar and 1 tablespoon butter. Spread over dough. Roll up jelly roll fashion. Cut into 1 inch pieces. Combine ¼ cup firmly packed brown sugar and 1 tablespoon butter in baking pan. Place rolls close together in pan, cut side down. Bake at 400 degrees or 25 to 30 minutes.

Veronica B. Schuster
Litchfield Grange, No. 107
Litchfield, Connecticut

BUTTER RINGS

¼ c. milk
Sugar
1 pkg. yeast
3 egg yolks, beaten
1 c. evaporated milk
3 c. flour
1 tsp. salt
Butter
1 c. coconut
1 c. chopped nuts or slivered almonds
1 c. confectioners' sugar
¼ tsp. vanilla extract
1 tbsp. cream

Scald ¼ cup milk and 2 teaspoons sugar. Cool to lukewarm. Add yeast, egg yolks and canned milk. Set aside. Sift flour, 2 tablespoons sugar and salt. Mix ½ cup butter into flour mixture with pastry blender. Add liquid ingredients; beat until smooth. Place in greased bowl; cover. Refrigerate several hours or overnight. Knead lightly; divide into 12 equal portions. Shape each into long rope; form in spiral on 2 greased cookie sheets. Mix ½ cup melted butter with coconut and nuts. Sprinkle over rolls. Let rolls rise 1 hour and 30 minutes or until doubled in bulk. Bake at 350 degrees for 15 to 20 minutes. Combine confectioners' sugar, vanilla and cream. Mix well. Drizzle over hot rolls. Yield: 12 rolls.

Mrs. Barry Watson
Delrio Grange, No. 828
Mansfield, Washington

BUTTER BRIGHT PASTRIES

2 pkg. dry yeast
⅓ c. sugar
⅛ tsp. salt
1 c. cold milk
4 to 4½ c. sifted flour
2 eggs
Butter
1 c. confectioners' sugar
2 tbsp. evaporated milk
½ tsp. vanilla extract

Dissolve yeast in ¼ cup warm water. Combine yeast mixture, sugar, salt and milk. Beat in 2 cups flour. Add eggs, beating well. Stir in enough flour to make a soft dough. Cover; refrigerate 15 minutes. Roll dough on lightly floured surface into 15 × 18-inch rectangle. Cut ⅓ cup butter into small pieces. Dot surface with butter, leaving 1 inch around edge. Fold into thirds making 3 layers. Rotate a quarter turn. Fold into thirds again making 9 layers. Wrap in floured aluminum foil. Chill 15 minutes. Repeat procedure twice more, from "roll dough" using remaining butter. Chill 15 minutes longer. Divide dough into fourths. Roll and cut into desired shapes. Let rise until doubled in bulk. Bake at 400 degrees for 8 minutes or until golden brown. Combine confectioners' sugar, 2 tablespoons butter, evaporated milk and vanilla. Blend well. Glaze pastries.

Betty Master
Scrubgrass Grange, No 1705
Harrisville, Pennsylvania

C.D.Q. SWEET DOUGH

2 pkg. dry yeast
1¼ c. buttermilk, lukewarm
2 eggs, beaten
½ c. softened butter or margarine
½ c. sugar
2 tsp. baking powder
2 tsp. salt
5½ c. flour

Dissolve yeast in ½ cup warm water in mixer bowl. Add remaining ingredients with 2½ cups flour. Mix for 30 seconds on low speed, scraping sides and bottom of bowl. Beat 2 minutes on medium speed. Stir in remaining flour. Dough should remain soft and slightly sticky. Knead 5 minutes on lightly floured board. Shape as desired. Place on baking pans. Let rise in 100-degree oven for 1 hour or until doubled in bulk. Remove rolls from oven. Increase oven temperature to 375 degrees. Return rolls to oven. Bake about 20 minutes. Dough may be made into loaves. Bake loaves for 45 minutes.

Emma Martin
Neighborhood Grange, No. 891
Mica, Washington

DORIS' CINNAMON ROLLS

1 pkg. yeast
1 c. milk, scalded
2 tbsp. sugar
2 tbsp. shortening
1 tsp. salt
3½ c. flour
1 egg, beaten
Butter, melted
¾ c. (firmly packed) brown sugar
1 tsp. cinnamon
1 tbsp. light corn syrup

Soften yeast in ¼ cup warm water. Combine milk, sugar, shortening and salt. Cook to lukewarm. Add 1 cup flour; beat well. Beat in yeast and egg. Add remaining flour; beat well. Cover. Let rise in warm place for about 1 hour or until doubled in bulk. Roll dough on lightly floured surface into a 12 × 18-inch rectangle. Brush with ¼ cup butter. Combine ¼ cup brown sugar and cinnamon; sprinkle on top of dough. Roll lengthwise; cut in 1 inch slices. Combine ½ cup brown sugar, ¼ cup butter and corn syrup in 12 × 18-inch baking dish. Heat slowly; stirring often. Place rolls, cut side down, over mixture. Cover. Let rise until doubled in bulk. Bake at 375 degrees for 20 minutes. Cool 2 or 3 minutes. Invert pan on rack. Yield: 24 rolls.

Doris Bruns
Rupert Grange, No. 114
Rupert, Idaho

ESTHER'S CINNAMON ROLLS

1½ pkg. yeast
Sugar
4½ c. flour
1 c. milk, scalded
1½ tsp. salt
Margarine or butter
2 eggs, beaten
⅓ c. mashed potatoes
1½ c. confectioners' sugar
2 tsp. cornstarch
½ c. (firmly packed) brown sugar
2 tsp. cinnamon
1 tsp. vanilla extract

Dissolve yeast in large bowl in ½ cup warm water. Let stand 5 minutes. Add 2 teaspoons sugar and ½ cup flour; beat well. Let stand ½ hour. Combine milk, salt, ⅓ cup sugar and ⅓ cup margarine. Cool. Add eggs and mashed potatoes; beat well. Pour into yeast mixture. Add remaining flour, 1 cup at a time. Mix well; let stand 10 minutes. Mix again. Place tight lid on bowl. Chill at least 10 hours. Combine ½ cup confectioners' sugar, 2 tablespoons sugar, cornstarch, brown sugar and cinnamon. Place dough onto a floured board; knead. Cut dough in half. Roll each half to 9 × 15-inches; butter. Sprinkle with cinnamon mixture. Roll up from long side. Cut into 1-inch slices. Place on oiled cookie sheet, cut side up, 1-inch apart. Let rise 1 hour in a warm place until light. Bake in a 350-degree oven for 15 to 20 minutes. Combine 2 tablespoons hot water, 1 tablespoon margarine, vanilla and 1 cup confectioners' sugar. Spread 1 teaspoon of mixture over each hot roll. Yield: 30 rolls.

Esther Chatham
Fairplain Osage Co. Grange, No. 1719
Burlingame, Kansas

EASY NUT ROLLS

2 pkg. yeast
Sugar
4½ c. flour
Butter
2 eggs, separated
1 tsp. salt
1 lb. ground nuts
½ c. milk, heated
1 tsp. lemon juice

Dissolve yeast in 1 cup lukewarm water and 4 tablespoons sugar. Combine flour and ⅛ cup butter as for pie crust. Mix well; add egg yolks, salt and yeast mixture. Mix. Knead until dough is smooth. Divide into 4 pieces. Roll out as thin as possible. Combine nuts, ½ cup sugar, milk, lemon juice and 1 tablespoon butter. Mix well. Spread dough with filling. Place on greased 12 × 18-inch pan; brush with egg whites. Let rise in warm place about 1 hour or until doubled in bulk. Bake at 350 degrees for 30 to 45 minutes.

Mrs. Julius Toth
Carlisle Grange, No. 1503
Elyria, Ohio

HOT CROSS BUNS

2 pkg. dry yeast
⅓ c. milk, heated
⅓ c. sugar
¾ tsp. salt
½ c. Wesson oil
3½ c. flour
1 tsp. cinnamon
3 eggs
¾ c. raisins or currants
1½ c. confectioners' sugar

Soften yeast in ⅓ cup warm water. Place milk in large bowl. Add sugar, salt and oil. Cool to lukewarm. Add 1 cup flour and cinnamon. Beat by hand. Add unbeaten eggs. Beat by hand until smooth. Stir in yeast and raisins. Add enough of remaining flour for a soft dough. Let rise until doubled in bulk. Turn dough out on floured surface; knead lightly. Roll to ½-inch thickness. Cut in rounds with biscuit cutter; place in greased shallow pans. Snip top of each bun with scissors to form a cross. Let rise until almost double. Bake at 375 degrees for 15 to 20 minutes or until lightly browned. Turn out on rack; cool. Combine confectioners' sugar with enough warm water to make glaze. Drizzle glaze on buns in cross shape.

Mrs. Marion T. Jones
Daniel Webster Grange, No. 100
Contoocook, New Hampshire

GLAZED ORANGE ROLLS

3¼ to 3½ c. all-purpose flour
1 pkg. yeast
1 c. milk
1 c. sugar
Butter, softened
½ tsp. salt
3 eggs, beaten
1½ tsp. shredded orange rind
1½ c. sifted confectioners' sugar
2 to 3 tbsp. orange juice

Combine 2 cups flour and yeast in large mixer bowl. Heat milk; combine with ½ cup sugar, 3 tablespoons butter and salt in saucepan until warm and butter melts. Add to dry mixture; add eggs. Beat with mixer on low speed for 30 seconds, scraping bowl. Beat 3 minutes at high speed. Stir in enough remaining flour to make a moderately soft dough. Knead on floured surface for 3 to 5 minutes or until smooth. Place in greased bowl; turn once. Cover. Let rise 1 hour to 1 hour and 30 minutes or until doubled in bulk. Punch down; divide in half. Cover; let rise 10 minutes. Roll each half into an 8 × 12-inch rectangle. Combine 6 tablespoons butter, ½ cup sugar and orange rind. Spread over dough. Roll up, starting with long side. Seal seams. Slice each into 12 rolls. Place, cut side down, in greased 2½-inch muffin pans. Cover; let rise 1 hour and 30 minutes or until doubled in bulk. Bake at 375 degrees for 15 to 20 minutes. Remove from pan immediately. Combine confectioners' sugar and orange juice. Drizzle over warm rolls.

Sarah Jeffers, 1979 National Princess
Hopewell Grange, No. 1747
Washington, Illinois

ORANGE ROLLS

1 env. dry yeast
Sugar
Salt
2 eggs, beaten
1 c. sour cream
Butter, melted
3½ c. flour
2 tbsp. grated orange rind
2 tbsp. orange juice concentrate

Dissolve yeast in large mixer bowl in ¼ cup warm water. Beat in ¼ cup sugar, small amount of salt, eggs, ½ cup sour cream and 6 tablespoons melted butter. Add 2 cups flour. Beat until smooth. Knead in remaining flour. Let rise until doubled in bulk. Knead; divide in half. Roll each half into a rectangle. Combine 2 tablespoons butter, ¾ cup sugar and orange rind. Spread ½ mixture onto each rectangle. Roll each rectangle jelly roll fashion; cut each roll into 12 slices. Place in buttered 9 × 13-inch pans. Cover. Let rise until doubled in bulk. Bake at 350 degrees for 20 minutes. Combine ¾ cups sugar, ½ cup sour cream, orange juice and ¼ cup butter in saucepan. Bring to a boil. Boil for 3 minutes, stirring constantly. Pour warm sauce over hot rolls. Yield: 24 rolls.

Mabel Kegel
Narcisse Grange, No. 301
Colville, Washington

SWEET ROLL YEAST DOUGH

2 c. milk, scalded
1 pkg. yeast
¼ c. sugar
2 eggs, beaten
3 tsp. salt
6 c. flour
¼ c. butter, melted

Cool milk to lukewarm. Add yeast; stir well. Add sugar, eggs, salt and 3 cups flour. Beat well. Add melted butter. Beat thoroughly. Add remaining flour or enough to make a soft dough. Place on floured board; knead into smooth dough. Place in greased bowl. Cover; let rise until doubled in bulk. Knead down; let rise 45 minutes. Shape as desired. Place on oiled pans; let rise until light. Bake in preheated 400-degree oven for 12 to 20 minutes. Yield: 18 servings.

Helen M. Hall
Springfield Grange, No. 114
Springfield, Vermont

SNAILS

1½ c. milk, heated
Butter, melted
½ c. mashed potatoes
⅔ c. sugar
Salt
1 pkg. yeast
2 eggs, beaten
7 to 8 c. flour
2 c. confectioners' sugar
½ tsp. vanilla extract

Combine milk, ½ cup butter, potatoes, sugar and 2 teaspoons salt in large mixer bowl. Let stand until lukewarm. Soften yeast in ½ cup warm water. Add to potato mixture. Add eggs. Add 1½ cups flour; mix well. Add remaining flour. Knead until smooth on lightly floured board. Place in greased mixer bowl, turning once to grease surface. Cover. Let rise until doubled in bulk. Turn onto lightly floured board. Roll out ¼-inch thick. Spread with melted butter; cut in ¾ × 12-inch strips. Twist each strip in circle to form the snail. Place on greased cookie sheet. Let rise until doubled in bulk. Bake at 350 degrees for 15 to 20 minutes. Combine confectioners' sugar, 3 tablespoons boiling water, 2 tablespoons melted butter, pinch of salt and vanilla; beat well. Spread on warm snails. Yield: 18 rolls.

Eileen Walker, C.W.A.
Whitman Co. Pomona, Winona Grange, No. 1038
Endicott, Washington

SWEET CLOVERLEAF ROLLS

2 c. milk
2 tsp. salt
8 tbsp. sugar
6 tbsp. shortening or lard
2 pkg. dry yeast
6 c. flour

Bring milk to boiling point. Add salt, sugar and shortening; mix well. Cool. Add yeast to ½ cup warm water; stir until dissolved. Add to milk mixture. Add flour gradually; mix well. Let rise in warm draft-free place until doubled in bulk. Knead dough on well floured surface until smooth and elastic. Let rise again until doubled in bulk. Grease muffin pans. Shape dough into 1-inch balls. Place 3 balls in each muffin cup; let rise until doubled in bulk. Bake in preheated 375-degree oven for 12 to 15 minutes. May brush tops of warm rolls with melted butter. Pan rolls, crescents or pinwheels may be made with this recipe. Yield: 30-36 rolls.

Mrs. Mabel Rohrer
Washington Co., Waterford Grange, No. 231
Waterford, Ohio

MARY'S SWEET ROLLS

3 c. milk
⅔ c. oil
1½ c. sugar
5 or 6 eggs
2 pkg. yeast
8 to 10 c. flour
1½ tsp. salt

Heat milk, oil and sugar in large saucepan. Add eggs, yeast and 2 cups flour; mix well; Let stand 10 to 15 minutes at room temperature. Add salt and remaining flour. Turn onto floured board. Knead until smooth and elastic. Place in large bowl; cover. Let rise in warm place until doubled in bulk. Place on floured board; knead well. Form into rolls. Place on greased baking pan. Let rise until doubled in bulk. Bake at 350 degrees for 20 minutes. Yield: 4 to 6 dozen.

Mary E. Doane
Tioga Co., Stony Fork Grange, No. 1033
Wellsboro, Pennsylvania

APPLE MUFFINS

⅓ c. shortening
2 c. flour
4 tsp. baking powder
¾ tsp. salt
¾ tsp. cinnamon
¼ tsp. nutmeg
6 tbsp. sugar
¾ c. chopped apples
1 egg
1 c. milk

Combine shortening and dry ingredients; mix well. Add apples. Beat egg and milk together. Add to first mixture, beating to blend. Fill greased muffin tins ⅔ full. Sprinkle tops with mixture of sugar and cinnamon. Bake at 350 degrees for 20 minutes.

Mrs. Dale M. Burns
Half Moon Grange, No. 290
Port Matilda, Pennsylvania

BLUEBERRY-SUGAR MUFFINS

1 c. sugar
½ tsp. salt
½ c. shortening
3 eggs, beaten
2 c. flour
2 tsp. baking powder
1 c. milk
¾ c. fresh blueberries, rinsed and drained

Work sugar and salt into shortening in large bowl with wooden spoon until well blended. Stir in eggs. Sift flour and baking powder together; add to mixture. Add milk gradually; beat mixture until dough is smooth and satiny. Fold in blueberries carefully. Pour batter into well-greased muffin tins. Bake in preheated 400-degree oven until toothpick comes out dry, about 15 to 20 minutes.

Photograph for this recipe on page 120.

GRANDMA'S BLUEBERRY MUFFINS

1 egg
½ c. milk
¼ c. vegetable oil
1½ c. flour
½ c. sugar
2 tsp. baking powder
½ tsp. salt
1 c. fresh blueberries

Beat egg in large bowl; stir in milk and oil. Sift flour, sugar, baking powder and salt into egg mixture. Stir just enough to moisten dry ingredients. Batter should be lumpy. Fold blueberries into batter. Fill greased 12-cup muffin pan ⅔ full. Bake in preheated 400-degree oven for 20 to 25 minutes or until golden brown. Remove from pan immediately and serve warm with butter. May substitute ¾ cup frozen blueberries, thawed and drained, for fresh blueberries.

Kara Arnold
Westminster Grange
Westminster, Colorado

EMILY'S BRAN MUFFINS

6 c. Bran Buds
3 c. sugar
1 c. oil
4 eggs
1 qt. buttermilk
5 c. flour
5 tsp. soda
1 tsp. salt

Combine 2 cups boiling water with 2 cups Bran Buds. Cool. Combine sugar, oil and eggs in mixer bowl; blend. Add Bran Buds mixture. Add buttermilk; mix well. Stir flour, soda and salt together. Add to first mixture. Blend in 4 cups Bran Buds. Fill greased muffin tins ¾ full. Bake at 400 degrees for 20 minutes. May be refrigerated in covered container for 1 month or more. Bake as needed.

Emily K. Hayes
Wolcott Grange, No. 348
Wolcott, New York

MAKE-AHEAD BRAN MUFFINS

2 c. All-Bran
5 c. sifted flour
5 tsp. soda
1 tsp. salt (opt.)
2 c. sugar
1 c. shortening
1 qt. buttermilk
4 eggs, well beaten
4 c. Bran Buds
1 lb. white raisins (opt.)

Pour 2 cups boiling water over All-Bran; cool. Sift together flour, soda, and salt. Cream sugar and shortening in large mixer bowl until light. Blend in buttermilk, eggs, raisins, Bran Buds and soaked All-Bran. Add dry ingredients. Fill greased muffin tins ⅔ full. Bake at 350 degrees about 20 minutes. Batter may be stored in refrigerator 6 weeks. Yield: 60 muffins.

Frances E. White, C.W.A.
Bellbrook Grange, No. 2702
Bellbrook, Ohio

MARVIS'S MUFFIN MIX

4 lg. shredded wheat biscuits
¾ c. shortening
1 c. margarine
3 c. sugar
4 eggs, beaten

5 c. flour
5 tsp. soda
1 tsp. salt
1 qt. buttermilk
4 c. All-Bran
½ c. raisins or nuts

Combine 2 cups boiling water with shredded wheat. Let stand to cool. Cream shortening, margarine and sugar in large bowl. Add eggs; beat well. Combine flour, soda and salt. Combine all mixtures and remaining ingredients. Stir just enough to blend. Fill greased muffin tins ⅔ full. Bake at 400 degrees for 20 minutes. May be stored in refrigerator for 6 weeks. Bake as needed.

Mrs. Wilma Purdy
Oklahoma State Master's Wife
Bethel Grange, No. 129
Tonkawa, Oklahoma

REFRIGERATOR TWO-BRAN MUFFINS

1 c. 100% bran cereal
1¼ c. sugar
½ c. salad oil
2 eggs, beaten
2½ c. all-purpose flour
2½ tsp. soda
½ tsp. salt
2 c. buttermilk or 2 c. yogurt
2 c. All-Bran
1 c. golden raisins or dates
1 c. chopped nuts

Pour 1 cup boiling water over 100% bran cereal; let stand. Mix sugar with salad oil. Add eggs; beat well. Sift flour with soda and salt; add to creamed mixture alternately with buttermilk. Add All-Bran, 100% bran mixture, raisins and nuts. Spoon into well-greased muffin tins or into paper bake cups set in muffin tins. Bake at 350 degrees about 30 minutes, or until muffins test done. Batter may be refrigerated in a covered plastic container for 3 weeks. Do not stir batter again. Yield: 3-4 dozen.

Viola Anderson
Mt. Wheeler Grange, No. 696
Oso, Washington

REFRIGERATOR DATE MUFFINS

5 tsp. soda
1 c. shortening
2 c. sugar
4 eggs, beaten
6 c. flour
1 tsp. salt
4 c. All-Bran

2 c. 40% bran flakes
2 c. chopped dates or raisins
1 qt. buttermilk

Add soda to 2 cups boiling water. Cool. Cream shortening and sugar. Add remaining ingredients, including cooled soda mixture. Do not over blend. Spoon into greased muffin tins. Bake at 375 degrees for 20 minutes. Batter may be refrigerated in covered dish for about 6 weeks. Bake as needed. Yield: 8 dozen.

Mrs. Clinton Dougherty
Filer Grange, No. 215
Filer, Idaho

REFRIGERATOR MUFFINS

4 c. All-Bran
2 c. 100% bran cereal
1 c. raisins or chopped dates (opt.)
1 c. shortening
2 c. sugar
4 eggs, beaten well
1 qt. buttermilk
5 c. flour
5 tsp. soda
1 tsp. salt

Mix first 2 ingredients with 2 cups boiling water. Add raisins. Cream shortening and sugar together in large mixer bowl. Add eggs; mix well. Add buttermilk. Sift dry ingredients together. Blend into creamed mixture. Fill greased muffin tins ½ full. Bake at 375 degrees for 20 to 25 minutes. Batter may be refrigerated in airtight container for 4 weeks.

Gay Smith
Enterprise Grange, No. 784
Fruitland, Washington

PINEAPPLE BRAN MUFFINS

2 eggs, beaten
Sugar
¾ c. buttermilk
1½ c. All-Bran
¾ c. crushed pineapple, lightly drained
1 c. sifted flour
½ tsp. soda
3 tsp. baking powder
½ tsp. salt
¼ c. melted shortening, cooled

Combine eggs, ¼ cup sugar, buttermilk, All-Bran and pineapple. Let stand for 5 minutes. Sift flour with soda, baking powder and salt. Add dry ingredients to bran mixture stirring only until flour

is moistened, adding shortening as you stir. Fill greased muffin pans ⅔ full. Sprinkle with sugar. Bake at 400 degrees for about 25 minutes. Let stand 5 minutes before removing from pans. Yield: 12 large muffins.

Blanche Rice, Chaplain
Hamburg Grange, No. 1293
Hamburg, New York

PINEAPPLE MUFFINS

½ c. whole wheat flour
½ c. soy flour
2 c. unbleached flour
3¼ tsp. baking powder
¾ c. Grape Nuts
½ tsp. salt
⅔ c. sugar
1 can crushed pineapple, drained
1 egg, beaten
3 tbsp. shortening

Combine all dry ingredients in large bowl. Drain pineapple; reserve juice. Add enough water to juice to measure ¾ cup. Combine egg, shortening and liquid; mix well. Add to dry ingredients; stirring only enough to blend. Fold in pineapple. Fill buttered muffin cups ⅔ full. Bake at 425 degrees for 20 minutes until muffins test done. Yield: 8-12 muffins.

Ruth M. Shallies
Green Mountain Grange, No. 347
Woodstock, Vermont

LAPLANDS MUFFINS

2 egg yolks
⅔ c. all-purpose flour
⅔ c. milk
1 tbsp. sugar
1 tbsp. butter, melted
¼ tsp. salt
2 egg whites, stiffly beaten

Beat egg yolks 4 to 5 minutes or until thick and lemon-colored. Blend in flour, milk, sugar, butter and salt. Beat 2 to 3 minutes. Fold in egg whites gently. Fill well-greased 2-inch muffin pans ⅔ full. Bake at 375 degrees for 30 to 35 minutes. Serve with butter and jam. Yield: 10 muffins.

Patty Gaulropp
Galt Grange
Rock Falls, Illinois

1 c. buttermilk
1½ c. diced rhubarb
½ c. chopped walnuts
2½ c. flour
1 tsp. soda
1 tsp. baking powder
½ tsp. salt
1 tbsp. butter, melted
⅓ c. sugar
1 tsp. cinnamon

Combine first 5 ingredients in mixer bowl; beat well. Stir in rhubarb and walnuts. Combine flour, soda, baking powder, and salt in separate bowl. Stir into rhubarb mixture just enough to blend. Fill 20 greased medium-sized muffin cups ⅔ full. Combine butter with sugar and cinnamon. Sprinkle over muffins. Press lightly into batter. Bake in 400-degree oven for 20 to 25 minutes or until muffins test done. Yield: 20 muffins.

Mrs. Mildred Williams, D.W.A.
Mondovi Grange, No. 822
Reardan, Washington

SPICY-NUT COFFEE CAKE MUFFINS

Flour
½ c. sugar
2 tsp. baking powder
½ tsp. salt
¼ c. shortening
1 egg, beaten
½ c. milk
½ c. (firmly packed) brown sugar
½ c. chopped walnuts or pecans
2 tsp. cinnamon
2 tbsp. melted butter

Sift 1½ cups flour, sugar, baking powder and salt. Cut shortening into dry mixture until resembles coarse crumbs. Blend egg and milk; add to flour mixture. Stir just until dry ingredients are moistened. Combine brown sugar, walnuts, 2 tablespoons flour, cinnamon and butter; mix well. Alternate layers of batter and spicy nuts in greased muffin pans, ending with batter. Fill ⅔ full. Bake at 375 degrees for 20 minutes. Yield: 12 muffins.

Judy McLure
Blue Mountain Grange, No. 263
Wells River, Vermont

RHUBARB MUFFINS

1¼ c. (firmly packed) brown sugar
½ c. salad oil
1 egg
2 tsp. vanilla extract

BLENDER POPOVERS

3 eggs
1 c. flour
1 c. milk
2 tsp. butter
Dash of salt

Place all ingredients, except Crisco, in blender container. Process for 13 seconds. Stop blender; scrape down sides and bottom. Process for 13 seconds longer. Pour into well-greased muffin pans. Bake at 400 degrees for about 30 minutes. Yield: 12 popovers.

Judy McLure
Blue Mountain Grange, No. 263
Wells River, Vermont

RICE DOLLAR PANCAKES

1 c. sifted flour
1 tsp. baking powder
½ tsp. soda
¼ tsp. salt
1 tsp. sugar
2 eggs, separated
1 c. buttermilk
3 tbsp. melted butter, margarine or oil
½ c. cooked rice

Sift together dry ingredients. Beat egg yolks until light. Add milk and butter; mix well. Stir in dry ingredients; beat only until smooth. Add rice. Beat egg whites until stiff but not dry. Fold into rice mixture. Bake on a hot griddle, using about 1 tablespoon butter for each cake. Yield: 3 dozen.

Photograph for this recipe on page 122.

EARLY BREAKFAST PANCAKES

1½ c. flour
1 egg
¼ c. sugar
¼ tsp. salt
1 tbsp. Mazola oil or shortening
1½ tsp. baking powder
Milk

Combine all ingredients, adding enough milk to make a medium batter. Cook as for pancakes in hot skillet. Serve with butter, syrup, jelly or honey. Yield: 6-8 pancakes.

Mildred Limprecht
La Plata Co., Animas Valley Grange, No. 194
Durango, Colorado

MIRACLE PANCAKES

1 stick butter
½ c. milk
½ c. flour
3 eggs, beaten

Melt butter in 9 × 13-inch pan. Combine remaining ingredients; mix well. Pour over melted butter. Bake in preheated 400-degree oven for 25 minutes. Do not open oven door. Cut into squares. Serve with syrup. Yield: 3-4 servings.

Dorothy Svinth
Gig Harbor Grange, No. 445
Gig Harbor, Washington

OLD-FASHIONED BUCKWHEAT CAKES

1 pkg. dry yeast
2 tsp. salt
1 c. buttermilk
1 c. flour
2 c. buckwheat flour
½ tsp. soda

Dissolve yeast in 1 cup warm water. Add salt, buttermilk and 2 cups water. Stir in flours; beat well. Let rise overnight at room temperature. Dissolve soda in ½ cup water; add to batter. Pour spoonfuls of batter on hot griddle. Turn when bubbles appear; brown on second side. Reserve 1 cup of batter to use as starter. Store in refrigerator

for up to 1 month. Use starter in place of yeast and 1 cup warm water. Yield: 4 servings.

Mrs. Opal S. Wetzel
Marion Center Grange, No. 1910
Indiana, Pennsylvania

PANCAKES

1½ c. sifted flour
½ tsp. soda
½ tsp. salt
1 tsp. sugar
1 egg, slightly beaten
3 tbsp. cooking oil
1½ c. sour milk

Combine all ingredients; mix until smooth. Cook on hot griddle or iron skillet. Yield: 6 servings.

Maxine B. Nichols
Stevenson Grange, No. 121
Stevenson, Washington

FRIED CAKES

1 c. hot mashed potatoes
2 tbsp. shortening
1 c. sugar
2 eggs or 4 egg yolks
1 c. milk
4 c. flour
1 tsp. each nutmeg and vanilla extract
4 tsp. baking powder
1 tsp. salt

Cream first 3 ingredients; let stand until cool. Add remaining ingredients; mix well. Fry by spoonfuls in hot deep fat. Yield: 20 servings.

Joanne Shea
Sherrill Grange, No. 1567
Munnsville, New York

DELUXE WAFFLES

2 c. sifted flour
3 tsp. baking powder
½ tsp. salt
1 c. milk
3 eggs, separated
6 tbsp. melted shortening

Sift dry ingredients. Combine beaten egg yolks, milk and shortening. Mix only until blended. Beat egg whites until stiff. Fold in first mixture. Bake in preheated waffle iron until steam ceases to escape from sides of iron. Yield: 4 waffles.

Patsey M. Mathes
Poe Valley Grange, No. 710
Klamath Falls, Oregon

Desserts

A good American meal is just not complete without dessert! Family members love something sweet, even at the end of a filling meal, because it is just too good to pass by. But, cooks love preparing desserts, too, because it's a culinary art that puts all of their creative cooking talents to work, and always with delicious results!

Preparing desserts, especially when it's cookies, cakes, candies and homemade ice cream, becomes extra rewarding when the whole family joins in the process. And, creating desserts "from scratch" is always worth any added work because the results are absolutely fresh, and therefore, far tastier. For added convenience, prepare double recipes of cookies and cookie dough, cakes, candy, and pie crusts, and freeze for future use.

These happy endings to mealtime never have to fall short of the nutrition standards you set for your family's menus, either. Choose dessert recipes that feature eggs, milk, nuts, fresh fruit, gelatin or cheese, and the desserts you serve will be as wholesome as they are delicious. For this same reason, don't neglect serving desserts because they are "too fattening" or "just empty calories." Desserts can be a vital part of a balanced meal plan, and an easy way to please finicky eaters.

For Grange members, a good meal is not over until dessert has been served. And, as the following recipe repertoire proves, homemade dessert should be served often!

ALMOND ROCHA

1 lb. sugar
1 lb. butter
1 lb. unblanched whole almonds
1 12-oz. package semisweet chocolate chips,
   melted
1 c. ground walnuts

Place sugar and butter in heavy skillet over medium heat. Stir constantly until melted. Add almonds. Continue cooking until creamy, stirring constantly. Pour onto buttered cookie sheet. Cover mixture with ½ of the chocolate chips and ½ of the walnuts. Cool. Turn over. Spread on remaining chocolate chips and walnuts. Cool. Break into pieces.

Faye Clarke
Quartz Hill, California

APPLE CANDY

2 tbsp. unflavored gelatin
1¼ c. canned applesauce
1½ c. sugar
2 tsp. vanilla extract
1 c. nuts
Confectioners' sugar

Soak gelatin in ½ cup applesauce. Blend well. Place ¾ cup applesauce in heavy saucepan; add sugar. Bring to a boil, stirring constantly. Add softened gelatin mixture. Boil hard for 15 minutes. Remove from heat. Add vanilla and nuts. Pour into buttered 8-inch square pan. Chill overnight. Cut in squares. Roll in confectioners' sugar. Variations: Use lemon, coconut or pineapple flavoring.

Anita Graves, C.W.A.
Crystal Grange, No. 1126
Bremerton, Washington

CANDY APPLES

2 c. sugar
⅔ c. light corn syrup
2 tsp. red food coloring
1 tsp. oil of cinnamon
12 med. apples
Sticks

Combine first 3 ingredients in saucepan. Cook to 300 degrees on candy thermometer or to hard-crack stage. Add cinnamon just before this stage is reached. Place apples on wooden sticks. Dip into

syrup. Place on greased waxed paper. Cool until coating is firm. Wrap in waxed paper.

Mrs. Joetta R. Carles
Hancock Co., Eagle Grange
Findlay, Ohio

APRICOT CANDY

½ c. canned apricots, pureed
½ c. applesauce
1½ c. sugar
2 tbsp. unflavored gelatin
1 c. nuts
2 tsp. vanilla extract
Confectioners' sugar

Combine apricots, applesauce and sugar in heavy saucepan. Boil, stirring constantly, for 15 minutes. Add gelatin. Cook for 15 minutes longer. Remove from heat. Add nuts and vanilla. Pour into buttered 8-inch square pan. Chill overnight. Cut into squares. Roll in confectioners' sugar.

Dorothy Bryant, D.W.A.
Gig Harbor Grange, No. 445
Olalla, Washington

BASIC MOLDED CANDY

2 1-lb. boxes confectioners' sugar
1 8-oz. package cream cheese, softened
½ tsp. peppermint oil
Coloring (opt.)
Superfine sugar

Combine sugar and cream cheese. Add peppermint oil and food coloring. Knead by hand until smooth. Dip candy mold into sugar. Dip a small amount of candy into sugar. Press into candy mold. Let dry for 1 day.

Susan Straw
Blue Ball Grange, No. 1331
West Decatur, Pennsylvania

BOLOGNA CANDY

3 c. sugar
1 c. milk
1 lb. dates
1 lb. English walnuts
1 lb. Brazil nuts

Combine milk and sugar in saucepan. Bring to a boil. Add dates. Cook to soft-ball stage. Remove from heat. Beat well. Cool slightly. Roll candy in

long strip of damp cloth. Fasten securely. Hang up
to dry. Slice as needed.

Mrs. Ervin Ebner
Lightstreet Grange, No. 31
Bloomsburg, Pennsylvania

PLAIN CARAMELS

1 c. sugar
1 c. corn syrup
1 c. half and half
¼ c. butter

Combine all ingredients. Cook to 240-degrees on
candy thermometer, stirring frequently. Stir constantly when caramelizing begins. Turn into buttered 8-inch square pan. Chill. Remove from pan;
cut into pieces. Wrap each piece in waxed paper.
Yield: 40 caramels.

Mrs. Kenneth E. Wilkin
Newark Grange, No. 1004
Heath, Ohio

COCONUT CANDY BALLS

2 sticks margarine, melted
1 can condensed milk
3 c. coconut
2 lb. confectioners' sugar
1 12-oz. package chocolate chips
1 2-inch sq. paraffin

Combine first 5 ingredients in order given. Shape
into balls. Place on cookie sheet; let harden. Chill.
Melt chocolate chips and paraffin in double boiler.
Dip balls into chocolate mixture. Cool.

Verna Bicheler
Glen Grange, No. 658
Fultonville, New York

ENERGY CANDY

¼ c. molasses
¼ c. honey
⅓ c. peanut butter
1 c. dry powdered milk
½ c. raisins
½ c. sunflower seed

Combine all ingredients in bowl. Mix well. Place in
loaf pan. Chill. Slice to serve.

Hazel M. Duncan
Lewis Co., Adna Grange, No. 417
Chehalis, Washington

CHOCOLATE FUDGE

2 c. sugar
2 sq. baking chocolate
1 tbsp. light corn syrup
⅔ c. milk
Dash of salt
1 tbsp. butter
1 tsp. vanilla extract

Combine first 5 ingredients in saucepan. Boil to
soft-ball stage. Remove from heat. Add butter and
vanilla; mix well. Beat until thick and dull-looking.
Pour onto buttered platter. Yield: 1 pound.

Peggy Beezer, Pomona
Blue Ball Grange, No. 1331
Philipsburg, Pennsylvania

CREAM CHEESE FUDGE

2 3-oz. packages cream cheese, softened
2 tbsp. cream or milk
4 c. confectioners' sugar
4 oz. unsweetened chocolate, melted
1 tsp. vanilla extract
1½ c. walnuts, chopped
1 tsp. rum
Dash of salt

Beat cream cheese and cream until smooth. Beat in
sugar gradually. Blend chocolate into cream cheese
mixture thoroughly. Stir in vanilla, walnuts, rum
and salt. Press into lightly greased 8 x 8-inch pan.
Let set 15 minutes. Cut into pieces. Store in
airtight container. Keeps well in refrigerator.

Karen Gorby
Encinitas Grange, No. 634
Encinitas, California

MEXICAN FUDGE

3 c. sugar
½ c. milk
Grated rind of 2 oranges
½ c. butter
1 c. nuts

Caramelize 1 cup sugar. Add milk, remaining sugar
and orange rind. Cook to 236 degrees on candy
thermometer. Add butter. Cool until lukewarm.
Beat until creamy. Add nuts. Turn into a buttered
pan. Cool. Cut into squares.

Ruth Whitehill Freeman
Prosperity Grange, No. 1985
Clarion County, Pennsylvania

PEANUT BUTTER FUDGE

4 c. sugar
2 tbsp. light corn syrup
1 c. evaporated milk
1 tsp. vinegar
2 tbsp. cocoa
1 pt. marshmallow cream
1 pt. peanut butter

Combine first 5 ingredients in saucepan. Bring to a rolling boil. Boil for 3 minutes. Remove from heat; add marshmallow cream and peanut butter; mix well. Pour into greased pan; cool.

Evelyn Barnes
Friendship Grange, No. 1018
Herrick Center, Pennsylvania

SKILLET PEANUT BUTTER FUDGE

2 c. sugar
3 tbsp. margarine
1 c. evaporated milk
1 c. miniature marshmallows
1 12-oz. jar chunk-style or regular peanut
   butter
1 tsp. vanilla extract

Combine sugar, margarine and evaporated milk in electric skillet. Set temperature control at 280 degrees. Bring mixture to a boil. Boil for 5 minutes, stirring constantly. Turn off heat. Add remaining ingredients. Stir until marshmallows and peanut butter are blended. Pour into buttered 8-inch square pan. Cool. Cut into squares. Yield: 2 pounds.

Barbara Fry, C.W.A.
Rocksprings Grange
Pomeroy, Ohio

GLASS CANDY

2 c. sugar
½ c. light corn syrup
2 to 3 drops of food coloring
1 tsp. flavoring

Combine sugar, syrup and ½ cup hot water in saucepan. Boil, without stirring, until 300 degrees on candy thermometer or hard-crack stage. Add food coloring and flavoring. Pour into greased 7 x 11-inch dish. Break or crack into pieces. If sticky loosen candy from dish in warm water.

Mrs. Lucille Pierson, C.W.A.
St. Joseph Co., Leonidas Grange, No. 266
Vicksburg, Michigan

SUGAR AND SPICE NUTS

1 egg white
3 c. nuts
1½ c. sugar
1 tsp. cinnamon
¼ tsp. nutmeg
½ tsp. salt
¼ tsp. cloves

Whip egg white lightly with fork. Blend in nuts. Combine remaining ingredients. Add to nuts; mix well. Place on cookie sheet. Bake at 300 degrees for 30 minutes, stirring twice. Place on waxed paper. Separate into clusters. Dry for 2 hours.

Irene Mason
Blue Ball Grange, No. 1331
West Decatur, Pennsylvania

PEANUT BRITTLE

1 tbsp. butter
1 c. chopped salted peanuts
1½ c. sugar

Melt butter in small sauce pan. Add peanuts; keep warm. Caramelize sugar in heavy frypan. Stir sugar with slotted spoon until golden. Remove from heat. Stir in peanuts. Pour into lightly buttered aluminum cake pan. Cool. Break into small pieces. Yield: 25-30 pieces.

Mrs. Charles C. Smith
Metichewan Grange, No. 190
New Milford, Conn.

PEANUT PRALINES

1 1-lb. box light brown sugar
1 6¾-oz. can peanuts
Margarine
½ teaspoon vanilla exract

Combine brown sugar and ¼ cup water in large saucepan. Cook, stirring, over medium heat until mixture begins to simmer. Add peanuts and 2 tablespoons margarine. Bring to a boil, stirring constantly. Remove from heat; let stand 5 minutes. Stir vanilla into candy mixture. Drop from tablespoon onto lightly-greased baking sheets. Set aside to harden. Yield: 24 candies.

Photograph for this recipe on page 129.

NUT CLUSTERS

1 12-oz. package chocolate chips
1 can condensed milk
2 c. chopped nuts

Melt chocolate chips in saucepan. Add to milk in mixing bowl. Beat until thick. Add nuts. Drop by spoonfuls onto waxed paper. Cool until set.

> Harriet Fenn
> Moosilauke Grange, No. 214
> Pike, New Hampshire

PEANUT TAFFY

1 c. sugar
1 tbsp. cornstarch
¼ tsp. salt
⅜ c. light corn syrup
Margarine
½ c. finely chopped peanuts
¼ tsp. vanilla extract

Combine sugar, cornstarch and salt in saucepan. Add corn syrup, ½ cup water and 1 tablespoon margarine. Heat, stirring constantly, until sugar and margarine are melted. Heat over medium heat, without stirring, until mixture reaches 256 degrees. Remove from heat; stir in peanuts and vanilla. Pour onto plate coated with margarine. Cool until mixture can be handled. Pull taffy with well greased hands until light tan in color and quite firm. Stretch into roll about 1 inch in diamter; cut off 1-inch pieces using kitchen shears. Wrap each piece of taffy in waxed paper or clear plastic wrap; twist ends tightly to seal. Yield: 50 pieces

Photograph for this recipe on page 129.

PEANUT BRITTLE

3 c. sugar
1 c. light corn syrup
3 c. salted peanuts
2 tsp. soda

Combine sugar, corn syrup and ½ cup water in heavy saucepan. Cook over medium heat, stirring constantly, until sugar dissolves and mixture comes to a boil. Continue cooking without stirring, until temperature reaches 280-degrees on candy thermometer. Stir in peanuts gradually; continue to boil mixture. Cook, stirring often, until temperature reaches 300 degress on candy thermometer. Remove from heat; add soda. Stir in gently but quickly. Pour at once onto 2 large greased cookie

sheets without spreading. Cool; break into pieces. Yield: 2½ pounds candy.

> Dorothy Cousino
> Pittsford Grange, No. 133
> Pittsford, Michigan

CARAMEL CORN

2 c. (firmly packed) brown sugar
3 tbsp. butter or margarine
¼ tsp. salt
¼ tsp. soda
4 qt. popped popcorn

Combine brown sugar, ½ cup water, butter and salt in saucepan. Cook to firm-ball stage. Add soda; stir until mixture foams up. Add popcorn; stir until well coated. Spread on floured baking sheets. Let harden. Yield: 6 servings.

> Helen Ott
> Meridian Grange, No. 265
> Kent, Washington

TAFFY PULL

3 c. sugar
½ c. vinegar
2 tsp. butter
1 tsp. vanilla extract
½ tsp. soda

Combine first 3 ingredients in saucepan with ½ cup water. Boil to hard-crack stage. Add vanilla and soda. Pour into shallow dishes. Cool. Fold in edges. Start pulling. Pull until white.

> Mrs. Charles Moseley
> Ledge Grange
> Thompson, Ohio

TEXAS MILLIONAIRES

1 c. sugar
1 c. (firmly packed) brown sugar
2 sticks margarine
1 c. dark syrup
2 c. evaporated milk
1 tbsp. vanilla extract
1 lb. pecans
3 lg. chocolate bars
½ stick paraffin

Combine sugars, margarine, syrup and 1 cup milk in saucepan. Bring to a boil, stirring constantly. Add remaining milk gradually, stirring slowly. Cook to soft-ball stage. Remove from heat. Add vanilla and pecans. Beat hard. Pour into buttered 9 x 12-inch pan. Chill overnight. Cut into squares. Combine chocolate bars and paraffin in double boiler. Dip squares into chocolate mixture. Place on waxed paper to dry. Yield: 30 squares.

Velma Hockett
Cimarron Grange, No. 1932
Ulysses, Kansas

WALNUT-DATE ROLL

3 c. sugar
½ c. canned milk
2 tbsp. white corn syrup
1 lb. seeded dates, diced
Juice of 1 lemon
1½ c. chopped walnuts
1 tsp. vanilla extract

Combine sugar, milk and syrup in saucepan. Stir until sugar is dissolved. Place over low heat. Add dates. Cook until soft-ball stage is reached, stirring constantly. Add lemon juice, walnuts and vanilla. Beat until stiff. Place on damp cloth. Form into rolls. Chill for 24 hours; slice. Yield: 20 servings.

Mae L. Britton
Hayfork Valley Grange, No. 710
Hayfork, California

WEDDING MINTS

1 3-oz. package cream cheese, softened
2 c. confectioners' sugar
1 tsp. peppermint flavoring
2 drops of food coloring

Combine first 3 ingredients. Add coloring. Blend evenly. Roll into small balls. Press down with fork or into powdered mold. Wait several seconds; turn onto waxed paper or foil. Let set overnight. Store in airtight container.

Mrs. Thelma Hartsel
Ashland Co., Ruggles Grange
Greenwich, Ohio

STRAWBERRY CONFECTIONS

Chocolate Strawberries

1 6-oz. package semisweet chocolate pieces
2 c. strawberries, washed and drained

Place chocolate in top of double boiler; heat over hot water until melted. Remove from heat. Dip strawberries in chocolate to coat, holding by stem ends. Set on waxed paper; let stand at room temperature until chocolate is set.

Snowcap Strawberries

1 egg white
¾ c. sugar
1½ tsp. light corn syrup
¼ tsp. salt
¼ tsp. vanilla extract
4 c. fresh strawberries, washed and drained

Combine egg white, sugar, ¼ cup water, syrup and salt in top of double boiler. Blend with electric mixer. Place over rapidly boiling water; beat at high speed until mixture forms peaks when beater is raised. Remove from heat; add vanilla. Beat until thick and of spreading consistency. Remove from heat. Dip strawberries into vanilla mixture to coat, holding by stem end. Set on waxed paper; let stand at room temperature until coating is set.

Photograph for this recipe on page 132.

ANGEL CHEESECAKE

1 c. graham cracker crumbs
Sugar
2 tbsp. melted butter
2 8-oz. packages cream cheese, softened
1 tbsp. lemon juice
1 tsp. vanilla extract
¼ tsp. salt
5 eggs, separated
2 c. sour cream
Pie filling

Mix crumbs, 2 tablespoons sugar and butter. Press onto bottom of 9-inch ungreased springform pan. Beat cream cheese until smooth. Add ½ cup sugar, lemon juice, vanilla and salt. Blend in beaten egg yolks; add sour cream. Beat egg whites until soft peaks form. Add ½ cup sugar gradually. Beat until stiff peaks form. Fold whites into cheese mixture. Pour gently into prepared springform pan. Bake in 325-degree oven for 1 hour and 15 minutes or until set. Cool 10 minutes; run spatula around edge to loosen. Cool completely. Remove sides of pan. Top with favorite pie filling. Yield: 12-16 servings.

Mrs. Myrna List, C.W.A.
Genesee Co. Pomona Grange, No. 10
Bergen, New York

1 c. finely chopped pecans
3 eggs, separated
2 env. unflavored gelatin
¾ c. sugar
2 tsp. vanilla extract
2 8-oz. pkg. cream cheese, softened

Combine chocolate and ¼ cup milk in saucepan. Heat slowly until chocolate melts. Reserve ⅓ cup chocolate mixture. Add remaining chocolate to butter, coconut and pecans; mix well. Press mixture into bottom of 9 x 13-inch pan. Combine remaining milk and egg yolks; beat well. Add gelatin and ½ cup sugar. Pour mixture in saucepan. Stir over low heat 5 minutes or until gelatin dissolves. Add vanila. Beat cream cheese in large bowl until smooth. Add gelatin mixture. Beat well. Chill, stirring occasionally, until mixture mounds when dropped from spoon. Beat egg whites until soft peaks form. Add ¼ cup sugar gradually; beat until stiff. Fold into cheese mixture. Divide cheese mixture in half. Mix reserved chocolate into one half. Pour other cheese mixture into prepared pan. Marble chocolate cheese mixture through pan mixture. Yield: 15 servings.

Joan Conard
Capital Grange, No. 18
Dover, Delaware

ADALINE'S CHEESECAKE

20 to 22 graham crackers, crushed fine
Sugar
¾ stick margarine, melted
3 8-oz. packages cream cheese, softened
4 eggs
1 tsp. vanilla extract
Dash of salt
1 can crushed pineapple
1 tbsp. cornstarch

Mix crumbs and 2 tablespoons sugar. Add butter; mix well. Press onto bottom and sides of 9-inch pie pan. Blend cream cheese until smooth. Add eggs to cheese one at a time, beating well after each addition. Add 1 cup sugar, vanilla and salt; beat well. Pour into crust. Bake at 350 degrees for 35 minutes. Turn oven off; open door. Allow to stand in oven for 25 minutes. Remove cake; cool. Combine 1 cup sugar and remaining ingredients in saucepan. Cook until thick. Cool. Pour over cake.

Adaline Howell
Shavers Creek Grange, No. 353
Petersburg, Pennsylvania

ELVA'S GERMAN CHOCOLATE CHEESECAKE

1 4-oz. bar German's sweet chocolate
2 c. milk
¼ c. butter, melted
1 c. flaked coconut

LEMON REFRIGERATOR CHEESECAKE

1⅛ c. sugar
2 env. unflavored gelatin
¼ tsp. salt
2 eggs, separated
1 6-oz. can evaporated milk
1 tsp. grated lemon peel
12 oz. cream cheese
2 tbsp. lemon juice
1½ tsp. vanilla extract
1 c. whipping cream
1½ c. finely crushed corn flakes
½ tsp. cinnamon
¼ tsp. nutmeg
⅓ c. butter or margarine, melted

Combine ¾ cup sugar, gelatin, salt, egg yolks and milk in double boiler. Stir constantly until gelatin dissolves and mixture thickens slightly. Remove from heat. Add lemon peel, cream cheese, lemon juice and vanilla. Chill, stirring occasionally, until mixture is partially set. Beat egg whites until soft peaks form. Add ¼ cup sugar gradually, beating until stiff. Fold into gelatin mixture. Whip cream; fold into gelatin mixture. Combine remaining ingredients with ⅓ cup sugar. Reserve ½ of the mixture. Press remaining on bottom of 8-inch square pan. Chill. Pour filling over crust. Top with reserved crumb mixture.

Alice Sprague
Aroostook Union Grange, No. 143
Presque Isle, Maine

BLITZ TORTE

4 egg whites
2 c. plus 2 tbsp. sugar
½ c. soft butter
1¾ c. sifted cake flour
2¼ tsp. baking powder
¾ tsp. salt
⅔ c. minus 1 tbsp. milk
1 tsp. vanilla extract
2 eggs
¼ c. slivered almonds
1 to 2 cans pineapple filling
Whipped cream

Beat egg whites until foamy. Add 1 cup sugar gradually. Beat until stiff. Set meringue aside. Cream butter lightly. Sift in remaining sugar, flour, baking powder and salt. Add milk and vanilla. Mix until flour is dampened. Beat for 2 minutes on low speed of electric mixer. Add eggs; beat 1 minute longer. Pour into two 9-inch layer pans lined with greased waxed paper. Spread meringue on batter; sprinkle with almonds. Bake in preheated 350-degree oven for 35 minutes. Cool 5 minutes. Cut around edge with sharp knife. Turn out on rack; remove waxed paper. Turn meringue side up immediately. Cool. Spread pineapple filling between layers. Spread whipped cream on sides and top.

Vivian F. LeBeau
Little Compton Grange, No. 32
Little Compton, Rhode Island

ORANGE AND CRANBERRY TORTE

2¼ c. sifted flour
2 c. sugar
¼ tsp. salt
1 tsp. soda
1 tsp. baking powder
1 c. chopped walnuts
1 c. diced dates
1 c. fresh chopped cranberries
Grated rind of 2 oranges
2 eggs, beaten
1 c. buttermilk
¾ c. salad oil
1 c. orange juice

Sift flour, 1 cup sugar, salt, soda and baking powder together into large bowl. Stir in walnuts, dates, cranberries and orange rind. Combine eggs, buttermilk and salad oil. Add to flour-fruit mixture; stir until blended. Pour into well-greased 10-inch tube pan. Bake at 350 degrees for 1 hour. Let stand in pan until lukewarm. Remove to rack placed over wide dish. Combine orange juice with 1 cup sugar; pour over cake. Repeat using drippings several times. Set in deep dish; let stand. Wrap in heavy foil. Chill for 24 hours. Serve with whipped cream. Can be kept in refrigerator for 2 weeks or longer.

Minnie M. Benson, C.W.A.
Mt. Pleasant Grange, No. 73
Washougal, Washington

PINEAPPLE TORTE

½ c. butter
¾ c. confectioners' sugar
4 eggs, separated
1 c. flour
1 tsp. baking powder
3 tbsp. milk
2 tsp. vanilla extract
1 c. sugar
1½ c. nuts
1 can crushed pineapple, drained
1 c. cream, whipped

Combine butter, confectioners' sugar and egg yolks. Add flour, baking powder, milk and 1 teaspoon vanilla. Pour into two 8 x 8-inch cake pans. Beat egg whites until soft peaks form. Add sugar gradually. Beat until stiff peaks form. Fold in 1 cup nuts. Pour mixture evenly into cake pans. Bake at 325 degrees for 1 hour. Cool. Combine pineapple, whipped cream, 1 teaspoon vanilla and ½ cup nuts; mix well. Place filling between cooled cake layers. May be served with whipped cream topping.

Rosemond Jones
Spencer Grange, No. 1110
Spencer, New York

BANANA SPLIT CAKE

2 c. graham cracker crumbs
Margarine or butter, softened
2 c. confectioners' sugar
2 egg whites
4 bananas, sliced
1 lg. can crushed pineapple, drained
1 lg. carton Cool Whip
1 c. chopped pecans

Combine cracker crumbs with 6 tablespoons margarine. Press into 9 x 13-inch pan. Combine sugar, egg whites and 1 stick margarine; beat 10 minutes. Pour over cracker crumbs. Top with remaining ingredients, layered in order given. Chill for 2 to 3 hours. Cut into squares. Serve with chocolate syrup, if desired. Yield: 10-12 servings.

Mrs. Charles Parnacott
Crystal Springs Grange, No. 2676
Navarre, Ohio

CHAMPAGNE-WALNUT SQUARES

1 3-oz. package cherry flavored gelatin
1 c. vanilla wafer crumbs
½ c. finely chopped walnuts
⅓ c. melted butter, divided
2 env. unflavored gelatin
¼ c. sugar
1 6-oz. can frozen limeade concentrate
1 c. Champagne or ginger ale
1 c. whipping cream
½ c. halved seedless green grapes
½ c. chopped toasted walnuts

Prepare cherry flavored gelatin, using only 1½ cups water. Chill in 8-inch square pan until firm. Cut about ⅔ of the firm gelatin into ½-inch cubes. Cut remaining gelatin into fancy shapes to decorate top of finished dessert. Combine wafer crumbs, walnuts and melted butter; reserve 2 tablespoons. Press remaining onto bottom of greased 9-inch square pan. Add unflavored gelatin and sugar to ½ cup cold water in saucepan, stir over low heat until dissolved. Stir in frozen limeade and Champagne. Chill until thick but not firm. Whip cream stiff; with same beaters whip limeade mixture. Gently fold whipped cream, grapes, toasted walnuts and diced cherry flavored gelatin into limeade mixture. Pour over crumb crust. Decorate with cherry flavored gelatin cut-outs. Chill until firm. Sprinkle reserved crumb mixture around edges.

Photograph for this recipe on page 134.

ORANGE FLUFF

2 pkg. Knox gelatin
2 c. sugar

2 c. orange juice
Few drops of orange food coloring
1 lg. carton Cool Whip
½ of 10-in. angel food cake, torn into sm. pieces

Soften gelatin in ½ cup cold water for 5 minutes. Add ½ cup boiling water. Stir in sugar, orange juice and food coloring. Cool until syrupy. Fold in Cool Whip. Arrange cake in 10 x 13-inch pan. Pour gelatin mixture over cake. Chill for 4 hours. Keeps well for several days. Yield: 15 servings.

Bertha Holaday
Southside Grange, No. 99
Kuna, Idaho

PEACHES AND CREAM DESSERT

1½ c. vanilla wafer crumbs
¼ c. butter or margarine, melted
½ lb. marshmallows
2 tbsp. orange juice
2 tbsp. lemon juice
2 c. chopped fresh peaches
1 c. whipping cream, whipped

Mix crumbs with butter; reserve ½ cup. Pat remainder into 9-inch round cake pan. Heat marshmallows and juices over low heat until marshmallows are almost melted. Chill marshmallow mixture until partially thickened. Fold in peaches and whipped cream. Pour over crust. Sprinkle with reserved crumbs. Chill. Yield: 8 servings.

Lois M. Mecklenburg
Lincoln Co., Bluestem Grange, No. 776
Davenport, Washington

STRAWBERRY FLUFF

10-oz. package frozen strawberries or 1 pt. fresh
  strawberries
1 env. unflavored gelatin
¼ c. sugar

Puree strawberries in blender. Soften gelatin in ¾ cup cold water. Beat gently, stirring with rubber spatula, until dissolved. Add gelatin to strawberry puree in blender container. Add sugar. Blend until frothy. Pour into wine glasses or dessert cups. Chill to set. Yield: 6 servings.

Mrs. Bess M. Jones
Portland Grange
Ionia, Michigan

RASPBERRY DELIGHT

1⅔ c. graham cracker crumbs
¼ c. chopped nuts
¼ c. melted butter
50 lg. marshmallows
1 c. milk
1 c. whipping cream, whipped
2 10-oz. packages frozen or fresh raspberries
½ c. sugar
2 tsp. lemon juice
1 tbsp. cornstarch

Combine crumbs, nuts and butter. Pat into 8 x 10-inch pan. Place marshmallows and milk in double boiler over hot water. Stir until melted. Cool. Fold whipped cream into marshmallows. Pour over crust. Cook raspberries, sugar, lemon juice and cornstarch with ¼ cup water until clear. Cool. Pour over marshmallow mixture. Best if made the night before.

Mary Ruth Mills
Snoqualmie Valley Grange, No. 283
Fall City, Washington

LEMON BUTTER

6 eggs, beaten
Juice of 3 lemons, strained
2 c. sugar
2 tbsp. butter

Combine all ingredients in double boiler. Cook, stirring occasionally, until thick.

Dorothy E. Dempsey, C.W.A.
Harmony Grange, No. 12
Newark, Delaware

HOT FUDGE SAUCE

3 sq. unsweetened chocolate
5 tbsp. butter
3 c. confectioners' sugar
1 c. evaporated milk
1 tsp. vanilla extract

Melt chocolate and butter in saucepan over low heat. Stir in sugar alternately with milk, stirring constantly. Bring to a slow boil, stirring constantly. Cook until sauce thickens. Remove from heat; stir in vanilla. Cool. Store in glass jars. Keeps in refrigerator for weeks. Reheat over very low heat. Yield: 2 cups.

Mrs. Judy T. Massabny
Potomac Grange, No. 1
Arlington, Virginia

PEANUT BUTTER-CARAMEL SUNDAE SAUCE

½ c. (firmly packed) brown sugar
⅔ c. light Karo syrup
3 tbsp. butter
½ c. canned milk
2 tbsp. peanut butter

Combine first 3 ingredients in saucepan. Bring to a boil. Cook 5 minutes, stirring frequently. Add milk. Bring to a boil. Remove from heat. Add peanut butter; beat until smooth. Yield: 2 cups.

Irene Mackrell
Slippery Rock Grange
Slippery Rock, Pennsylvania

SPANISH CAKE SAUCE

2 tbsp. flour
1 c. sugar
½ tsp. nutmeg
1 tbsp. butter
2 tbsp. vinegar
1 tsp. vanilla extract

Mix first 5 ingredients with 1 cup boiling water. Boil over low heat, stirring occasionally until thick. Remove from heat; add vanilla. Spoon hot or cold over yellow or white cake slices. This is a very old recipe which has been used in my husband's family for over 70 years.

Mrs. Mendal Jordan, C.W.A.
Meigs Co., Pomona Grange, No. 46
Albany, Ohio

ELLEN'S APPLE CRISP

6 or 8 apples, sliced
¾ c. sugar
½ c. cake flour
1 tsp. cinnamon
6 tbsp. butter

Place apples in baking dish. Pour ⅓ cup water over apples. Blend remaining ingredients with butter until crumbly. Sprinkle over apples. Bake at 375 degrees for 30 minutes.

Ellen Foster
Friendship Grange, No. 1018
Uniondale, Pennsylvania

NELLIE'S BROWN BETTY

3 c. peeled chopped apples
2 c. bread crumbs
2 tbsp. butter
½ tsp. cinnamon
½ c. (firmly packed) brown sugar

Place layer of chopped apples in buttered 8 x 10-inch baking dish. Sprinkle with layer of bread crumbs. Dot with butter. Sprinkle with cinnamon and brown sugar. Repeat layers until all ingredients are used. Pour ¼ cup water over top. Bake in 350-degree oven for 30 minutes or until apples are tender. Serve with cream or hard-sauce, if desired. Yield: 6 servings.

Nellie E. Trotter
Princeton Grange, No. 426
Potlatch, Idaho

DANISH PASTRY

1 c. milk
1¼ oz. package yeast
Sugar
3½ c. flour
1½ tsp. salt
¾ c. shortening
3 eggs, slightly beaten
Melted butter
Chopped nuts

Scald milk; cool to lukewarm. Add yeast and 3 tablespoons sugar. Let stand 15 minutes. Combine flour and salt, cut in shortening. Add milk mixture and eggs, folding into flour mixture. Chill overnight. Roll ¼-inch thick. Spread with butter. Cut in triangles. Roll up. Let rise until very light. Bake on cookie sheet in 400 degree oven 12 to 15 minutes. Frost with sugar and chopped nuts. Yield: 24 pastries.

Thelma Hughes, C.W.A.
Johnson Co., Pomona Grange, No. 20
Clarksville, Arkansas

APPLE BROWN BETTY

Stale bread crumbs
Butter
6 or 7 tart apples, pared and sliced
½ c. molasses
2 tbsp. brown sugar

Sprinkle layer of bread crumbs in baking dish. Dot with butter; add a layer of apples. Repeat layers until all ingredients are used, ending with crumbs.

Add ½ cup water to molasses; stir in brown sugar. Pour sugar mixture over crumbs. Dot with butter. Bake in 350-degree oven for 1 hour. Serve hot with whipped cream or hard sauce.

From a Grange Friend

OLD-FASHIONED APPLE CRUNCH

8 tart apples, peeled and sliced
1 c. (firmly packed) brown sugar
1 tsp. cinnamon
1 c. flour
1 c. sugar
1 tsp. baking powder
½ tsp. salt
1 egg
½ c. butter, melted

Place apples in square cake pan. Mix brown sugar and cinnamon. Sprinkle half of mixture over apples. Mix together flour, sugar, baking powder, salt and egg. Sprinkle over apples. Top with remaining brown sugar mixture. Pour butter over brown sugar. Bake at 350 degrees for 30 minutes or until apples are tender.

Mrs. Hubert Birkenholz
Sugar Grove Grange, No. 2044
Newton, Iowa

SWEDISH PANCAKE MOUND

1½ c. flour
Sugar
½ tsp. salt
3 eggs, well beaten
1½ c. milk
4 tbsp. butter or margarine, melted
2 c. chunky applesauce
1 c. heavy cream

Sift together flour, ¼ cup sugar and salt in mixer bowl. Combine eggs, milk and butter; add gradually to dry ingredients. Beat until batter is smooth. Heat 8-inch frypan. Brush generously with oil. Pour in 3 tablespoons batter. Tilt pan quickly to spread the batter evenly and thinly over bottom of pan. Brown lightly on one side. Turn carefully with spatula. Brown lightly; remove. Cool pancakes completely. Spread each pancake with applesauce. Stack pancakes like a many-layered cake. Beat cream with 2 tablespoons sugar until stiff and shiny. Cover pancake mound with whipped cream. Chill. Cut in pie-shaped wedges to serve. Yield: 6 servings.

From a Grange Friend

APPLE-DANISH PASTRY SQUARES

2¾ c. sifted flour
1 tsp. salt
½ c. plus 2 tbsp. shortening
Milk
1 egg, separated
1 c. crushed corn flakes
8 c. sliced, peeled apples
⅔ c. sugar
½ tsp. cinnamon
1 c. sifted confectioners' sugar
½ tsp. vanilla extract

Sift together flour and salt. Cut in shortening until crumbly. Add enough milk to beaten egg yolk to make ⅔ cup. Add to flour mixture; mix to blend. Divide dough into 2 parts. Roll half the dough to fit a 10½ x 15½-inch jelly roll pan. Sprinkle bottom crust with corn flakes. Combine apples, sugar and cinnamon, stirring gently. Spread apple mixture over corn flakes. Roll out other half of dough; place over apple mixture. Pinch edges together to seal. Beat egg white stiff; brush over top crust. Bake in 400-degree oven for 50 to 60 minutes or until golden. Cool slightly. Mix confectioners' sugar, vanilla and 1 to 2 tablespoons water. Frost while crust is warm. May be served warm or cold. Yield: 16 servings.

Mrs. Mae Moser
Thurmont Grange, No. 409
Thurmont, Maryland

GERMAN APPLE TORTE

¼ c. shortening
2 c. sugar
1 tsp. salt
2 tsp. vanilla extract
2 eggs
2 c. flour
2 tsp. soda
1 tsp. cinnamon
4 c. finely chopped unpeeled apples
1 c. chopped nuts

Cream shortening, sugar, salt and vanilla. Add eggs; beat well. Sift together dry ingredients; add to creamed mixture. Fold in apples and nuts. Place in greased 9 x 13-inch pan. Bake at 350 degress for 35 minutes. Serve with whipped cream, if desired. May be frozen. Yield: 12 servings.

Mrs. LeRoy Rahn
Rock Creek Grange, No. 1908
Polo, Illinois

SPICED BANANA CHIPS

1 green banana
Paprika
Ground cuminseed or mango powder

Cut banana, on the bias, into 24 to 26 very thin slices or chips. Fry in deep 365-degree oil for about 1½ minutes, or until golden brown and crisp. Drain on paper towels. Dust lightly with paprika and ground cuminseed while still warm. Mango powder can be purchased at an Indian or Far Eastern food specialty shop.

From a Grange Friend

BLUEBERRY BATTER CAKE

2 c. blueberries
Juice from ½ lemon
1¼ c. sugar
3 tbsp. shortening
1 c. flour
1 tsp. baking powder
½ tsp. salt
½ c. milk
1 tbsp. cornstarch

Place blueberries in well greased 8 x 8-inch baking pan. Sprinkle with lemon juice. Cream ¾ cup sugar and shortening. Sift flour, baking powder and ¼ teaspoon salt together; add to creamed mixture alternately with milk. Spread evenly over berries. Combine ½ cup sugar, cornstarch and ¼ teaspoon salt. Sprinkle over batter. Pour 1 cup boiling water over cake. Bake in 375-degree oven for 45 to 50 minutes. Serve warm. Yield: 8 servings.

Mary Ann Gilligan
Weston Grange, No. 555
Weston, Vermont

BOOZY FRUIT STARTER

Mixed mandarin oranges, pineapple chunks,
sliced peaches and maraschino cherries
6 c. sugar

Combine fruits to measure 1½ cups fruit in 1-quart jar. Add 1½ cups sugar; mix well. Cover with lid tilted slightly to allow air in jar to cause fermentation. Let stand for 10 days, stirring daily. Add 1½ cups each kind of remaining fruit, one fruit at a time, at 2-week intervals. Add 1½ cups sugar at the same time. Transfer to apothecary jar when mixture increases. Do not close tightly; allow air to escape. This is a delicious dessert topping.

Lola Chandler
Nezperce Grange, No. 295
Nezperce, Idaho

CHERRY CAKE

1 egg, beaten
1 c. sugar
2 tbsp. melted butter
Pinch of salt
2 c. flour
2 tsp. baking powder
¾ to 1 c. milk
1 tsp. vanilla extract
Cherries

Cream egg and sugar together. Add melted butter; beat. Sift together dry ingredients; add to creamed mixture alternately with milk. Add vanilla; mix well. Cover bottom of 7 x 11-inch pan with cherries. Top with batter. Bake at 350 degrees for 20 to 30 minutes. Serve with cream, if desired. This recipe may be doubled and cooked in 9 x 13-inch pan. May substitute other berries for cherries. I have had this recipe for 49 years.

Helen A. Myers, C.W.A.
Thurmont Grange, No. 409
Thurmont, Maryland

CHERRY DUMPLINGS

1½ c. real sour cherries, pitted
½ c. cherry juice
¼ c. butter
¾ c. sugar
Salt
1 c. sifted flour
1½ tsp. baking powder
½ tsp. vanilla extract
½ c. milk

Combine cherries, juice, 1½ cups boiling water, 2 tablespoons butter, ½ cup sugar and a dash of salt in heavy saucepan or electric skillet. Simmer 5 minutes. Combine remaining ingredients with a dash of salt. Drop by spoonfuls into hot cherry sauce. Cover. Steam for 20 minutes. Serve warm. Yield: 6 servings.

Mrs. John W. Scott
Unionville Grange, No. 1971
Michanicsburg, Pennsylvania

CHERRY PUDDING

2 c. sugar
Pinch of salt
2 c. flour
2 tsp. baking powder
¼ c. shortening
1 c. milk

1½ c. canned cherries, drained
2 tbsp. butter

Combine 1 cup sugar, salt, flour and baking powder. Cut in shortening. Add milk; mix well. Place in baking pan. Combine remaining ingredients with 1 cup boiling water. Pour over batter. Bake at 350 degrees for 45 minutes. Serve with cream, if desired. This recipe is 50 years old.

Mona L. Ayers
Huntingdon Co., Shavers Creek Grange, No. 353
Petersburg, Pennsylvania

FRESH FRUIT COBBLER

3 c. chopped fruit
Sugar
Flour
½ tsp. cinnamon (opt.)
2 tbsp. butter
1½ tsp. baking powder
½ tsp. salt
⅓ c. shortening
3 tbsp. milk
1 egg, beaten

Arrange fruit in 9 x 9-inch baking pan. Mix ⅔ cup sugar, 2 tablespoons flour and cinnamon; sprinkle over fruit. Dot with butter. Sift together 1 cup flour, 2 tablespoons sugar, baking powder and salt. Add shortening, milk and egg. Stir with fork until well blended. Drop from heaping teaspoons over top of fruit. Bake at 350 degrees for 25 to 30 minutes. Do not use cinnamon with any fruit except peaches and apples. Serve with whipped cream or milk, if desired.

Mrs. Clyde Stubbs,
Franklin Grange, No. 1858
Coshocton, Ohio

CLARA'S QUICK COBBLER

¼ lb. butter or margarine
1 c. milk
1 c. flour
1 c. sugar
2 tsp. baking powder
1 lg. can fruit

Melt butter in 9-inch skillet. Mix next 4 ingredients; pour over butter. Top batter with fruit. Do not stir. Bake at 350 degrees for 40 minutes. Yield: 12 or more servings.

Mrs. Clara Black
Kingsriner Grange, No. 562
Loton, California

FRUIT COBBLER

1 stick butter or margarine, melted
1 c. sugar
¾ c. milk
¾ c. self-rising flour
2 c. fruit

Melt butter in 2-quart baking dish. Mix next 3 ingredients together. Pour over butter. Do not stir. Top with fruit, evenly distributed. Do not stir. Bake at 350 degrees for 1 hour.

Mrs. Maurice Baker
Leonidas Grange, No. 266
Fulton, Michigan

GRANOLA AND STRAWBERRIES

1 c. uncooked old-fashioned oats
1 c. wheat germ
½ c. graham cracker crumbs
½ c. flaked coconut
½ c. slivered blanched almonds
1 to 2 tbsp. light brown sugar
1 tsp. vanilla extract
Milk
3 pt. California strawberries

Combine oats, wheat germ, cracker crumbs, coconut, almonds, brown sugar and vanilla in shallow baking pan; mix well. Bake in 275-degree oven for 1 hour, stirring occasionally. Cool. Store granola in tightly covered container in refrigerator. Combine ½ cup granola, ½ cup milk and about ¾ cup whole strawberries for each serving. Recipe may be doubled, if desired.

Photograph for this recipe on page 140.

BAKED PINEAPPLE DESSERT

5 slices stale bread, cubed
1 lg. can crushed pineapple, drained
1 c. sugar
3 eggs, well beaten
½ c. milk
2 tbsp. margarine, melted
¼ tsp. salt

Combine all ingredients in large mixer bowl in order given. Mix well. Pour into a greased 2-quart casserole. Bake in a preheated 350-degree oven for 45 minutes. Yield: 6-8 servings.

Mrs. Edythe J. Harding
Forest Grange, No. 853
Tionesta, Pennsylvania

PINEAPPLE CASSEROLE

¾ c. sugar
2 eggs
¼ c. butter
¼ c. milk,
1 15½-oz. can crushed pineapple

Combine all ingredients; mix lightly. Pour into 7-inch casserole. Bake at 350 degrees for 1 hour. Yield: 5-6 servings.

Nathalie B. Nuite, Lecturer
South Sangerville Grange, No. 335
Dexter, Maine

RHUBARB COBBLER

4 c. rhubarb, cut into ½-in. pieces
Sugar
Butter or margarine
1 c. flour
1 tsp. baking powder
½ tsp. salt
⅛ tsp. nutmeg
1 egg, beaten
¼ c. milk

Place rhubarb in 9 x 13-inch baking pan. Add 1¾ cups sugar; dot with butter. Pour ½ cup water over all. Sift dry ingredients with 1 tablespoon sugar. Cut in ¼ pound butter until fine crumbs form. Combine egg and milk; add to dry ingredients. Stir only until flour is moistened. Spread over rhubarb. Bake at 350 degrees for 40 to 45 minutes. Yield: 10 servings.

Rosanna Lookabaugh
Ashtabula Co., Saybrook Grange, No. 1739
Ashtabula, Ohio

RHUBARB DREAM DESSERT

1¼ cup flour
½ c. margarine or butter, softened
⅓ c. confectioners' sugar
2 c. finely chopped rhubarb
2 eggs, well beaten
1½ c. sugar
¾ tsp. salt
½ tsp. vanilla extract

Blend 1 cup flour with margarine and confectioners sugar. Press into 9 x 9-inch baking pan. Bake at 350 degrees for 15 minutes. Spread rhubarb over hot crust. Combine remaining ingredients with ¼ cup flour. Pour evenly over rhubarb. Bake at 350 degrees for 35 minutes or until lightly browned.

Serve warm with ice cream, if desired. Keep well in refrigerator. Yield: 16 servings.

Mrs. William Stock
Mariposa Grange, No. 2167
Laurel, Iowa

RHUBARB CRUNCH

1¼ c. flour
½ c. butter, softened
5 tbsp. confectioners' sugar
2 eggs, well beaten
1½ c. sugar
¾ tsp. baking powder
Dash of salt
2 c. chopped rhubarb

Mix 1 cup flour with butter and confectioners' sugar. Press into 8 x 8-inch baking pan. Bake at 350 degrees for 15 minutes. Combine remaining ingredients with ¼ cup flour; blend well. Pour over crust. Bake at 350 degrees for 35 minutes. Yield: 9 servings.

Verl E. Woods
Polk Co., Pomona Grange, No. 3
Monmouth, Oregon

RHUBARB FLOAT

¼ c. butter, softened
Sugar
1 egg, beaten
1 c. flour
1 tsp. baking powder
¼ tsp. salt
¼ c. milk
3 c. diced rhubarb, fresh or frozen
½ tsp. nutmeg

Cream butter; add ½ cup sugar. Stir in egg. Sift together flour, baking powder and salt; add to creamed mixture alternately with milk. Place in greased 8 x 8-inch cake pan. Combine rhubarb with ½ to ¾ cup sugar, nutmeg and ½ cup boiling water. Pour over batter. Bake at 375 degrees for 45 to 55 minutes. Yield: 9 servings.

Mrs. David Goodlaxson
Rising Sun Grange, No. 718
Waupun, Wisconsin

RHUBARB TORTE

3 c. flour
2 tsp. baking powder
6 tbsp. shortening

2 eggs, slightly beaten
4 tbsp. milk
4 c. diced rhubarb
2 sm. packages strawberry Jell-O
2 c. sugar
½ c. butter, softened

Combine 2 cups flour and baking powder. Cut in shortening. Add eggs and milk; mix well. Pat into 9 x 13-inch baking pan. Spread rhubarb over crust. Sprinkle with dry Jell-O. Combine sugar, butter and 1 cup flour. Sprinkle over Jell-O. Bake at 350 degrees for 40 minutes. Yield: 12 servings.

Mrs. Wyn Davis
Amberg Granite Grange, No. 729
Amberg, Wisconsin

STRAWBERRY SHORTCAKE

2 eggs, well beaten
1 c. sugar
1 c. flour
1 tsp. baking powder
1 tsp. vanilla extract
½ tsp. salt
Strawberries
Cream

Combine eggs and sugar; beat well. Add flour and baking powder; beat. Add vanilla and salt. Add ½ cup boiling water; mix well. Batter will be thin. Pour into well-greased 9-inch square pan. Bake at 325 degrees until it leaves side of pan and springs back when tests done. Cool. Cut into squares. Cover with strawberries; top with cream. Yield: 6-9 servings.

Mrs. Charles R. Redman
Licking Co., Madison Grange
Newark, Ohio

APRICOT SHERBET

1 qt. apricots, sieved
Juice of 3 oranges
Juice of 3 lemons
1 lg. can evaporated milk
3 c. sugar
Milk

Combine first 4 ingredients. Add sugar. Mix well. Pour into 1-gallon ice cream freezer container. Fill to top with milk. Stir. Freeze according to manufacturer's directions. Yield: 16 servings.

Grace Edna Willett
Cimarron Grange, No. 1932
Satanta, Kansas

OLD-FASHIONED LEMON SHERBET

Juice of 4 oranges
Juice of 3 lemons
3½ c. sugar
Orange and lemon rind to taste
3 c. cream
1 qt. milk
3 egg whites, beaten stiff

Combine juices, sugar and rind. Boil for 5 minutes. Remove rind. Cool. Add remaining ingredients. Mix well. Freeze in ice cream freezer. Yield: 1 gallon.

Bertha C. Smith, C.W.A.
Clifton Springs Grange, No. 1042
Clifton Springs, New York

ALICE'S ICE CREAM

½ gal. milk
6 eggs, beaten
½ tsp. salt
3 c. sugar
1 pt. cream
1 tbsp. vanilla extract

Combine milk, eggs, salt and sugar in saucepan. Heat to scalding. Add cream and vanilla. Place in ice cream freezer container. Follow freezer manufacturer's directions.

Alice McTyer
Cimarron Grange, No. 1932
Satanta, Kansas

CHOCOLATE ICE CREAM

4 c. milk
4 c. whipping cream
2 c. sugar
1 tbsp. vanilla extract
Dash of salt
1 can Hershey's chocolate syrup

Combine all ingredients. Mix well. Pour into 1 gallon ice cream freezer container. Follow freezer manufacturer's directions.

Shirley Zimmerman
Glade Valley Grange
Walkersville, Maryland

FROZEN CHOCOLATE DESSERT

1 c. butter, softened
2 c. sifted confectioners' sugar
3 sq. unsweetened chocolate, melted

5 egg yolks
½ tsp. peppermint flavoring
2 tsp. vanilla extract
1 c. cream, whipped
1 c. chopped walnuts
½ c. vanilla wafer crumbs

Cream butter and sugar together until fluffy. Add chocolate; continue beating. Add egg yolks and flavorings. Fold in whipped cream and walnuts. Sprinkle crumbs in 18 cupcake liners. Spoon in chocolate mixture. Freeze overnight. Keeps well in freezer. Yield: 18 servings.

Mary Blum
Morton Grange, No. 1066
Morton, Washington

FROZEN LEMON PIE

5 egg whites
2 tbsp. sugar
½ c. lemon juice
1 can sweetened condensed milk
1 baked pie shell

Beat egg whites. Add sugar gradually. Beat until stiff. Combine lemon juice and milk; fold into egg whites. Pour into pie shell. Freeze for 12 hours. Serve frozen.

Mrs. Emil Peters
Half Moon Grange, No. 290
Port Matilda, Pennsylvania

STRAWBERRY FROZEN DESSERT

1 egg white
½ c. sugar
1 10-oz. package frozen strawberries, thawed
1 tbsp. lemon juice
1 tsp. vanilla extract
1 c. whipping cream, whipped

Beat egg white; add sugar gradually beating until stiff. Add next 3 ingredients. Beat for 20 minutes at high speed. Fold in whipped cream. Freeze for 24 hours. Yield 12-15 servings.

Joan L. Mohler
Stark Co., Marlboro Grange, No. 1401
Hartville, Ohio

FLOATING ISLAND WITH FRUIT

Milk
2 eggs, separated
Pinch of salt

¾ c. sugar
1 tbsp. cornstarch
½ tsp. vanilla extract
Sliced fruit

Scald 2 cups milk in a double boiler. Beat egg yolks with salt and ¼ c. sugar in a small bowl. Add slowly to hot milk, stirring constantly. Blend cornstarch with a small amount of cold milk; add slowly to custard. Continue cooking, stirring constantly, until custard thickens and coats spoon. Remove from heat. Add vanilla. Beat egg whites until frothy; add 4 tablespoons sugar gradually, beating until stiff peaks form. Place custard in shallow, serving dish. Spoon meringue slowly into custard, 1 spoonful at a time. Serve very cold over sliced fruit. Yield: 6 servings.

Gertrude G. Platt
Pokono Grange, No. 191
Brookfield Center, Connecticut

APPLE PUDDING

¼ c. butter
1 c. sugar
1 egg, beaten
2 c. finely chopped peeled apples
1 c. flour
1 tsp. soda
1 tsp. cinnamon
¼ tsp. nutmeg
¼ tsp. cloves

Cream butter and sugar until fluffy. Add egg and apples. Sift dry ingredients together. Add to apple mixture; mix well. Spread into greased 8-inch square baking pan. Bake at 350 degrees for 40 minutes. Cool. Serve with milk or whipped cream, if desired.

Iva H. Cameron
Stevenson Grange, No. 121
Stevenson, Washington

APRICOT-RICE PUDDING

1½ c. cooked rice
½ c. shredded coconut
1½ c. apricot nectar
⅔ c. sugar
½ tsp. salt
3 eggs, separated
1 tsp. grated lemon peel
1 tsp. vanilla extract
¼ tsp. almond extract
½ c. apricot preserves

Combine rice and coconut. Place in 10 x 6 x 2-inch baking dish. Heat apricot nectar, ½ cup water, ⅓ cup sugar and salt to boiling point. Combine egg yolks, lemon peel and flavoring; beat slightly. Stir in hot apricot nectar mixture gradually. Pour over rice and coconut. Place in pan of hot water. Bake at 350 degrees for 45 minutes or until set. Cool slightly. Spread top with apricot preserves. Beat egg whites with remaining sugar gradually until stiff but not dry to form meringue. Spread meringue over pudding. Bake 15 minutes longer or until lightly browned. Cut into squares. Serve warm or cold. Yield: 8 servings.

Photograph for this recipe on page 146.

DOUBLE BOILER BREAD PUDDING

1 c. (firmly packed) light brown sugar
3 eggs, slightly beaten
2 c. milk
1 tsp. vanilla extract
½ tsp. salt
4 slices bread
Raisins (opt.)
Nutmeg to taste

Place brown sugar in top of double boiler. Combine eggs, milk, vanilla and salt. Pour over brown sugar. Place whole slices of bread, one at a time, into milk mixture. Add raisins. Sprinkle with nutmeg. Cook over boiling water for 1 hour or until custard is set. Remove from heat. Turn out into serving dish. Brown sugar makes a sauce for pudding. Serve warm or cold. Yield: 4-6 servings.

Marian N. Plumb
Litchfield Grange, No. 107
Litchfield, Connecticut

ORANGE-BREAD PUDDING

2 c. bread cubes
2 eggs, beaten
½ c. sugar
1⅓ c. milk
¼ tsp. salt
1 c. orange juice
1 tsp. grated orange rind

Place bread cubes in buttered 5 x 9-inch baking dish. Combine next 4 ingredients. Stir in orange juice and rind. Pour over bread. Bake in 350 degree oven 45 minutes or until set. One half cup raisins may be added. Yield: 6-8 servings.

Gertie Hess
Douglas Co., Evergreen Grange, No. 460
Roseburg, Oregon

CHOCOLATE PUDDING

6 c. milk
1 c. sugar
1 c. flour
2 tbsp. (heaping) cocoa
1 tsp. salt
1 tsp. vanilla extract

Heat 5 cups milk in a double boiler. Combine next 4 ingredients in a bowl. Blend in 1 cup cold milk; mix well. Pour slowly into hot milk. Cook, stirring constantly, until thick. Remove from heat. Add vanilla. Cool. Eggs may be added for extra richness. Yield: 6-8 servings.

Wanneta P. Wilson, C.W.A.
Wolf Creek Grange, No. 596
North Powder, Oregon

DATE PUDDING

1 tsp. soda
1 c. chopped dates
2 tbsp. butter
1 c. sugar
1 egg, beaten
1¾ c. flour
1 tsp. baking powder
1 tsp. vanilla extract
½ c. chopped nuts (opt.)
¼ tsp. salt

Combine first 3 ingredients with 1 cup boiling water. Cool. Add remaining ingredients; mix well. Place in greased pan. Steam for 1 hour. Cool. Serve with whipped cream.

Mrs. Elrena Eddy, C.W.A.
Champion Grange, No. 18
Jefferson County, New York

ESTERBROOK PUDDING

Milk
¼ c. sugar
½ c. flour
3 tbsp. butter
4 eggs, separated
2 c. confectioners' sugar
1 tsp. vanilla extract

Bring 2 cups milk to a boil. Mix sugar and flour with a small amount of cold milk. Stir sugar mixture slowly into boiling milk. Cook, stirring constantly, over low heat until thickened. Beat egg yolks. Stir into milk mixture. Beat egg whites until stiff. Fold into custard. Pour into shallow 2-quart baking dish.

Set dish in pan of water. Bake in 400-degree oven until pudding rises in the middle and browns. Combine remaining ingredients with a small amount of boiling water to make a hard sauce. Serve with sauce. This pudding is like a souffle. It may fall but the flavor remains delicious. Yield: 4 servings.

Mrs. Charlotte Leeman
Woolwich Grange, No. 68
Woolwich, Maine

DATE AND NUT PUDDING

1 c. chopped dates
8 tbsp. butter
1 c. (firmly packed) brown sugar
½ c. nuts
1 tsp. soda
1½ c. flour

Pour 1 cup hot water over dates and butter. Cool. Add remaining ingredients; mix well. Pour into greased 7 x 11-inch cake pan. Bake at 325 degrees for 1 hour.

Dorothy O. Reichart
Gideon Grange, No. 2010
Hanover, Pennsylvania

GRAHAM PUDDING

1 c. milk
1 c. molasses
1½ c. graham or whole wheat flour
2 tsp. soda
½ c. white flour
1 tsp. salt
½ tsp. cinnamon
½ tsp. cloves
Raisins (opt.)
½ c. butter
1 c. confectioners' sugar
2 eggs, beaten
Vanilla or lemon extract

Combine all ingredients; mix well. Steam in greased 4 quart pan for 2 hours. Cream butter and sugar. Add eggs; beat until fluffy. Add vanilla. Chill. Serve pudding with fluffy sauce. Yield: 6 servings.

Anna W. Fenton
Middletown Springs Grange, No. 476
Middletown Springs, Vermont

IRIS' RAISIN PUDDING

1 c. flour
1 c. sugar
2 tsp. baking powder
1 c. raisins
½ c. milk
1 c. (firmly packed) brown sugar
1 tsp. vanilla extract
1 tbsp. butter

Sift first 3 ingredients together. Add raisins and milk; mix well. Place in greased 8 x 10-inch baking pan. Combine remaining ingredients with 2 cups boiling water. Stir to dissolve sugar. Pour over raisin mixture. Bake at 350 degrees for 45 minutes. Yield: 8 servings.

Iris Brollier
Cimarron Grange, No. 1932, Grant Co.
Ulysses, Kansas

DOLLY'S RAISIN PUDDING

2 c. (firmly packed) brown sugar
2 tbsp. butter
⅛ tsp. salt
1 c. milk
1 tbsp. cinnamon
2 c. flour
1 tbsp. baking powder
1 c. raisins

Combine 1 cup brown sugar and 1 tablespoon butter with 4 cups hot water in 9 x 13-inch baking pan. Keep warm while mixing batter. Combine next 5 ingredients with remaining butter and sugar. Mix; do not beat. Add raisins; mix thoroughly. Spoon batter evenly over hot water mixture. Swirl with spatula. Bake in 350-degree oven for 30 minutes or until browned. Invert on serving dish. Yield: 12 servings.

Dolly Yeckley
Blair Co., Pomona Grange
Duncansville, Pennsylvania

GRANDMOTHER'S RICE PUDDING

2 c. cooked rice
¾ c. sugar
1 14½-oz. can evaporated milk
2 c. whole milk
½ c. golden raisins
1 tsp. vanilla extract
Nutmeg

Combine first 6 ingredients in a large bowl; mix well. Place in lightly greased 2-quart casserole.

Sprinkle with nutmeg. Bake in preheated 350-degree oven for 1 hour or until lightly browned. This recipe is almost 200 years old and is a favorite of all generations. Yield: 10-12 servings.

Mrs. Edythe J. Harding
Forest Grange, No. 853
Tionesta, Pennsylvania

RASPBERRY HEAVENLY RICE PUDDING

½ tsp. salt
1 tbsp. butter
1 c. rice
1 c. evaporated milk
2 tbsp. lemon juice
1 c. confectioners' sugar
1 pt. fresh raspberries

Combine 2 cups water, salt, butter and rice in a saucepan. Cover tightly. Bring to a boil; reduce heat. Cook, covered, stirring occasionally, for 15 to 20 minutes or until liquid is absorbed. Refrigerate for 1 hour. Chill evaporated milk in refrigerator tray until soft ice crystals form around edges. Transfer to chilled mixer bowl. Whip with chilled beaters until stiff, about 1 minute. Add lemon juice. Whip for 2 minutes longer. Fold whipped milk, confectioners' sugar and raspberries into rice mixture. Chill in serving dish. Yield: 6-8 servings.

Mrs. Barbara Bean
Moss Glen Grange, No. 554
Rochester, Vermont

BARBARA'S STEAMED PUDDING

1 c. molasses
1 egg, beaten
1 tsp. ginger
1 tsp. soda
Flour
½ c. sugar
2 tbsp. butter
Vinegar (opt.)

Combine first 4 ingredients with 1½ cups flour; mix well. Place in greased pan. Steam 2 hours and 30 minutes to 3 hours. Combine remaining ingredients with 2 tablespoons flour and 2 cups boiling water in a saucepan. Cook over low heat, stirring constantly, until thickened.

Barbara Chapman
Petines Corner Grange, No. 561
Lawville, New York

FAVORITE HOLIDAY PUDDING

2 eggs, beaten
2 c. (firmly packed) brown sugar
1 c. seeded raisins
1 c. dark or golden raisins
1 tsp. grated lemon peel
2 c. sifted flour
1 tsp. salt
2 tsp. soda
2 tsp. cinnamon
1 tsp. nutmeg
1 tsp. cloves
2 c. grated apple
2 c. grated potato
2 c. grated carrot
¼ c. melted butter

Mix eggs, brown sugar, raisins and lemon peel in a large bowl. Sift flour with salt, soda and spices. Stir into egg mixture. Add remaining ingredients, mixing well. Turn into well-buttered 2½-quart mold; cover tightly. Place mold on rack in deep kettle. Add enough boiling water to come half way up side of mold; cover kettle. Simmer for 3 hours and 30 minutes to 4 hours. Replenish boiling water as needed. Serve hot with hard sauce. Freezes well. Yield: 12-16 servings.

Helen Shore
Black Diamond Grange, No. 1128
Port Angeles, Washington

HEALTH PUDDING AND TASTY SAUCE

1 c. (firmly packed) brown sugar
¼ c. shortening
1 c. oatmeal, wheaties or other cereal
2 c. milk
1 c. whole wheat flour
1 c. white flour
2 tsp. (scant) soda
Salt to taste
1 tsp. allspice
½ tsp. nutmeg
½ tsp. cinnamon
1 c. chopped raisins
1 c. chopped nuts (opt.)
½ tsp. vanilla extract
½ tsp. lemon extract
Tasty Sauce

Cream brown sugar and shortening in a large mixing bowl. Add cereal and milk; mix well. Beat in next 9 ingredients. Beat thoroughly. Add remaining ingredients; mix well. Place in two 1-pound coffee cans. Steam for 2 hours. Serve with whipped cream, cream cheese, fruit or Tasty Sauce. Yield: 10 servings.

Tasty Sauce

1 c. (firmly packed) brown sugar
½ tsp. nutmeg
2 tbsp. flour
½ tsp. vanilla extract
½ tsp. lemon extract

Combine sugar and nutmeg into a saucepan. Add flour to 3 cups water. Blend well. Add to sugar mixture. Boil for 5 minutes, stirring constantly. Remove from heat. Add remaining ingredients. Mix well. Cool.

Mary Richmond
Kahlotus Grange, No. 939
Pasco, Washington

STEAMED CHRISTMAS PUDDING AND HARD SAUCE

2 c. loosely-packed freshly ground suet
1 c. sugar
½ c. molasses
5 eggs, beaten
3½ c. flour
1 tsp. each: salt, cloves, cinnamon, nutmeg and allspice
3 tsp. baking powder
½ tsp. soda
1 c. milk
1 lb. pitted dates
2 c. golden raisins
1 lb. candied fruit mixture
1 lb. currants
1 lb. seeded muscat raisins
1 c. coarsely chopped nuts
Hard Sauce

Combine first 4 ingredients in large bowl; mix well. Sift 2½ cups flour with remaining dry ingredients. Add milk and flour mixture to egg mixture; mix well. Combine fruits and nuts with 1 cup flour. Combine all ingredients. Mix thoroughly. Pour into two 3-pound coffee cans. Steam for 3 hours and 30 minutes to 4 hours. Serve warm with Hard Sauce. Will freeze.

Hard Sauce

½ c. butter, softened
1 c. confectioners' sugar
½ tsp. vanilla extract or rum flavoring
Nutmeg

Beat butter in small mixer bowl at high speed until very creamy. Beat in sugar gradually. Stir in vanilla. Place in serving bowl. Sprinkle with nutmeg. Chill 1 hour.

Bessie Storms
Plummer Grange, No. 273
Plummer, Idaho

BROWNIE PUDDING CAKE

1 c. flour
2 tsp. baking powder
¾ c. sugar
½ tsp. salt
Cocoa
½ c. milk
1 tsp. vanilla extract
2 tbsp. oil
¾ c. chopped nuts
¾ c. (firmly packed) brown sugar

Sift first 4 ingredients with 2 tablespoons cocoa into 2-quart bowl. Stir in milk, vanilla and oil. Add nuts; mix well. Combine brown sugar and ¼ cup cocoa in small bowl. Spoon over pudding mixture. Pour 1¾ cups hot water over all. Bake at 350 degrees for 40 to 45 minutes. Serve with whipped cream. Yield: 6 servings.

Mrs. Norman Sprague, D.W.A.
New York State Grange
Ross Grange No. 305
Falconer, New York

CHOCOLATE PUDDING CAKE

1 c. flour
6 tbsp. cocoa
1 tsp. baking powder
½ tsp. salt
2 tbsp. melted margarine
1 c. sugar
1 tsp. vanilla extract
½ c. milk
½ c. chopped walnuts

Sift flour, 3 tablespoons cocoa, baking powder and ¼ teaspoon salt together. Combine margarine, ½ cup sugar and vanilla. Add alternately with ½ cup milk to flour mixture. Add walnuts. Mix remaining sugar, cocoa and salt with 1⅜ cup boiling water. Turn sugar mixture into 8-inch square baking pan. Drop batter by spoonfuls into sugar mixture. Bake in 350-degree oven for 40 to 45 minutes.

Marion W. Kuhn
Greenfield Hill Grange, No. 133
Fairfield, Connecticut

CINNAMON PUDDING CAKE

1¾ c. (firmly packed) brown sugar
4 tbsp. butter
1 c. sugar
2 c. sifted flour
2 tsp. baking powder
½ tsp. salt
2½ tsp. cinnamon
1 c. milk
½ c. chopped nuts

Combine brown sugar, 2 tablespoons butter and 1½ cups water in a saucepan. Bring to a boil. Cool. Cream 2 tablespoons butter with sugar in a bowl. Sift dry ingredients together; add to creamed mixture alternately with milk, beginning and ending with dry ingredients. Blend well after each addition. Spread in greased 9-inch square pan. Pour brown sugar mixture over batter. Sprinkle with nuts. Bake at 350 degrees for 35 to 40 minutes. Serve warm with whipped cream. Yield: 8-10 servings.

Loretta Marteney
Carroll Co., Petersburg Grange, No. 1819
Carrollton, Ohio

HOT FUDGE PUDDING CAKE

1 c. flour
2 tsp. baking powder
¼ tsp. salt
¾ c. sugar
Cocoa
½ c. milk
2 tbsp. shortening, melted
1 c. chopped nuts
1 c. (firmly packed) brown sugar

Sift first 4 ingredients with 2 tablespoons cocoa into a bowl. Stir in milk and shortening. Blend in nuts. Spread in 9-inch square pan. Combine brown sugar and ¼ cup cocoa. Sprinkle over mixture in pan. Pour 1¾ cups hot water over entire batter. Bake at 350 degrees for 45 minutes. Cake mixture rises to top during baking; chocolate sauce settles to bottom. Invert squares of pudding onto dessert plates. Dip sauce from pan over each. Serve warm with whipped cream or vanilla ice cream.

Mrs. Virginia Shaw
Indian River Grange, No. 19
Antwerp, New York

VIOLA'S PUDDING

3 tbsp. butter
½ c. sugar
1 c. flour
1 tsp. baking powder
1 tsp. soda
¼ tsp. nutmeg
Pinch of salt
½ c. milk
1 tsp. vanilla extract
½ c. raisins
1 c. (firmly packed) brown sugar

Cream 1 tablespoon butter and sugar. Sift dry ingredients together. Add to creamed mixture alternately with milk. Stir in vanilla and raisins. Pour into well-greased deep casserole. Combine brown sugar, 2 tablespoons butter and 2 cups boiling water. Bring to a boil. Pour over mixture. Bake at 325 degrees for 25 minutes. Yield: 6-8 servings.

Mrs. Viola Anderson
Mt. Wheeler Grange, No. 696
Oso, Washington

DANISH APPLE BARS

2½ c. all-purpose flour
1 tsp. salt
1 c. vegetable shortening
1 egg, separated
Milk
1 c. corn flake crumbs
4 c. sliced apples
⅓ c. sugar
½ tsp. cinnamon
1 c. confectioners' sugar
½ tsp. vanilla extract

Sift together flour and salt. Cut in shortening. Combine egg yolk and enough milk to measure ⅔ cup. Add to flour mixture; blend well. Divide dough in half. Place one half in 10 x 15 inch jelly roll pan. Press upon sides of pan. Sprinkle with corn flake crumbs. Combine apples, sugar and cinnamon. Spread over cornflakes. Roll out remaining pastry to fit over top of apple mixture. Beat egg white until stiff packs form. Spread over pastry. Bake at 375 degrees for 35 to 40 min. Combine confectioners' sugar, 1 tablespoon hot water and vanilla. Drizzle over top while still warm. Cut into bars. Yield: 36 servings.

Mrs. Hal Sundberg
Mt. Wheeler, Grange, No. 696
Arlington, Washington

BROWN ICEBOX COOKIES

1 c. butter or margarine
2 c. (firmly packed) brown sugar
3 eggs, well beaten
1 tsp. vanilla extract
4½ c. flour, sifted
1 tsp. cinnamon
1 tsp soda
1 tsp. cream of tartar
½ tsp. salt
1 c. chopped nuts

Cream butter and brown sugar until smooth. Add eggs and vanilla. Sift dry ingredients together. Add to butter and egg mixture gradually. Add nuts. Shape into 2-inch rolls. Wrap in waxed paper. Refrigerate for 24 hours. Slice dough into ¼-inch thick cookies. Place on greased cookie sheet. Bake at 350 degrees until browned.

Harriet Guthrie, Wife of Master of Colorado State Grange
Mountain View Grange, No. 411
Calhan, Colorado

APPLE BARS

2 c. flour
1 tsp. baking powder
½ tsp. salt
1 tsp. cinnamon
1¾ c. sugar
3 eggs
1 c. cooking oil
1 tsp. vanilla extract
2 c. thinly sliced apples
1 c. chopped nuts (opt.)

Sift dry ingredients together. Beat sugar and eggs. Add to dry ingredients; mix well. Add oil and vanilla. Fold in apples and nuts. Place in greased 9 x 13-inch pan. Bake at 350 degrees for 40 minutes. Place pan on rack to cool; cut in squares. May be frozen.

Delores C. Moore
Holden Grange, No. 544
East Holden, Maine

APPLE BAR COOKIES

½ c. margarine, melted
1 c. sugar
1 c. flour
1 egg
½ tsp. baking powder
¼ tsp. salt
2 lg. apples, peeled and chopped
½ c. raisins
¼ c. nuts

Combine first 7 ingredients, mix well. Stir in raisins and nuts. Pour into greased 8-inch square pan. Bake in preheated 350-degree oven for 35 to 40 minutes. Yield: 16 squares.

Mrs. Mamie Bosic
Linganore Grange, No. 410
New Windsor, Maryland

APPLE-RAISIN COOKIES

1 c. golden raisins
1 c. thick applesauce
1 c. (firmly packed) light brown sugar
½ c. butter, softened
1 egg
2 c. unbleached flour
½ tsp. salt
1 tsp. soda
1 c. chopped pecans

Mix raisins and applesauce; let stand for 30 minutes. Combine next 3 ingredients; beat until fluffy. Stir in applesauce and raisins. Sift dry ingredients together; add to applesauce mixture. Stir in pecans. Drop from teaspoon about 2 inches apart on greased cookie sheet. Bake at 350 degrees for 12 to 15 minutes.

Pearl Rader
Mariposa Grange, No. 2167
Newton, Iowa

DOROTHY'S BANANA COOKIES

1 c. (firmly packed) brown sugar
¾ c. shortening
1 egg
1 c. mashed bananas
1½ c. flour
½ tsp. each soda and salt
¼ tsp. nutmeg
¾ tsp. cinnamon
1¾ c. oatmeal
½ c. chopped nuts

Combine brown sugar, shortening, egg and bananas; mix well. Add dry ingredients and nuts; mix well. Drop from teaspoon onto greased cookie sheet. Bake at 350 degrees for 8 to 10 minutes. Yield: 3 dozen.

Dorothy Clapper
Norton Grange, No. 2566
Norton, Ohio

JOAN'S BANANA COOKIES

1½ c. sugar
1½ c. whole bran
½ tsp. cinnamon
¼ c. butter, softened
½ c. shortening
2 eggs
1½ tsp. vanilla extract
1 c. mashed bananas
2½ c. flour

½ tsp. salt
3 tsp. baking powder

Place ½ cup sugar, bran and cinnamon on sheet of waxed paper. Roll until fine to use as coating mixture. Combine 1 cup sugar, butter, shortening, eggs and vanilla in a mixing bowl. Beat with rotary or electric beater until smooth. Add bananas and sifted dry ingredients all at once. Stir to make a soft dough. Drop dough from teaspoon onto coating mixture. Shape with fingers into balls. Roll in mixture to coat well. Place on greased baking sheet about 2½ inches apart. Bake at 400 degrees 10 minutes or until cookie tests done. Yield: 4 dozen.

Joan L. Mohlu
Stark Co., Marlboro Grange, No. 1401
Hartville, Ohio

BANANA-SPICE COOKIES

½ c. shortening
1 c. (firmly packed) brown sugar
2 eggs
1 c. mashed bananas
2 c. sifted flour
2 tsp. baking powder
½ tsp. each soda, salt, cloves and cinnamon
½ c. chopped nuts

Combine shortening, brown sugar, and eggs; mix well. Stir in bananas. Sift dry ingredients; stir into banana mixture. Blend in nuts. Chill about 1 hour. Drop from tablespoon 2 inches apart on lightly greased baking sheet. Bake at 375 degrees for 8 to 10 minutes. May be frosted with thin yellow tinted confectioners' sugar icing. Yield: 2½ dozen.

Mary Beth Bowen, Sec.
Vermont State Grange
Moss Glen Grange, No. 554, Granville, Vermont

BUTTERSCOTCH BROWNIES

1 c. shortening
1 c. (firmly packed) brown sugar
2 eggs
¾ c. flour
¾ tsp. baking powder
½ tsp. salt
1 tsp. vanilla extract
½ c. chopped nuts

Melt shortening in 2-quart saucepan over low heat; remove from heat. Add brown sugar; mix well with spoon. Add eggs, one at a time, stirring well after each addition. Mix dry ingredients, blend with first mixture. Add vanilla; mix well. Stir in nuts. Pour into 8-inch square pan. Bake in 350-degree oven for 25 to 30 minutes. Yield: 16 brownies.

Debbie Wade
Hopewell Grange, No. 1747
Washington, Illinois

CHERYL'S BROWNIES

4 sq. unsweetened chocolate
⅔ c. shortening
2 c. sugar
4 eggs, beaten
1¼ c. flour
1 tsp. salt
1 tsp. baking powder
1 c. nuts (opt.)

Melt chocolate and shortening in top part of double boiler over about 1-inch boiling water; stir occasionally. Remove from heat. Beat in sugar and eggs with egg beater. Sift flour, salt and baking powder; add to chocolate mixture. Stir in nuts. Spread in greased 9½ × 13-inch baking pan. Bake at 350 degrees for 30 minutes.

Cheryl L. Myers
Thurmont Grange, No. 409
Thurmont, Maryland

ETHEL'S CHOCOLATE BROWNIES

3 c. sugar
¼ c. cocoa
1¼ c. melted butter
4 eggs, beaten
2 tsp. vanilla extract
1½ c. sifted flour
Salt
½ c. chopped English walnuts or coconut
⅓ c. milk
1 sq. chocolate

Mix 2 cups sugar and cocoa together. Stir in 1 cup butter. Add eggs and vanilla. Beat well. Sift flour and 1 teaspoon salt together; stir into cocoa mixture. Fold in walnuts. Pour into greased 10 × 15-inch jelly roll pan. Bake in 375-degree oven for 25 minutes. Cool. Combine 1 cup sugar, milk, dash of salt, chocolate and ¼ cup butter in saucepan. Bring to a boil; boil for 1 minute, stirring constantly. Cool in pan of ice water about 5

minutes. Beat until of spreading consistency. Frost brownies.

Mrs. Ethel Peters
Half Moon Grange, No. 290
Port Matilda, Pennsylvania

CHOCOLATE-NUT BROWNIES

4 oz. chocolate
¾ cup margarine
4 eggs
2 c. sugar
¼ tsp. salt
1 tsp. vanilla extract
1 c. sifted all-purpose flour
1 c. broken nuts
Confectioner's sugar

Melt chocolate over hot water. Add margarine; cool. Beat eggs until light. Add sugar, salt and vanilla; beat well. Stir in chocolate mixture and flour; beat until smooth. Add nuts. Bake in 325-degree oven for about 20 minutes. Cool; cut in rectangles. Roll in confectioners' sugar. Yield: 12 servings.

Wanetta Radekin
Laurel Grange
Albany, Ohio

CHOCOLATE-TOPPED BROWNIES

¾ c. butter or shortening
2 c. sugar
4 eggs
1 can chocolate syrup
¼ tsp. salt
½ c. chopped nuts
½ tsp. baking powder
1¼ c. flour
1½ tsp. vanilla extract
¼ c. milk
½ c. chocolate chips

Cream ½ cup butter and 1 cup sugar. Add eggs one at a time, beating well after each addition. Blend in chocolate syrup. Add salt, nuts, baking powder, flour and 1 teaspoon vanilla; mix well. Pour into greased and floured 9 × 13-inch pan. Bake at 350 degrees for 35 to 40 minutes. Combine 1 cup sugar, milk and ¼ cup butter in saucepan. Bring to a boil; boil for 1 or 2 minutes. Remove from heat; add chocolate chips and ½ teaspoon vanilla. Beat until blended. Frost brownies. Yield: 24 pieces.

Nina M. Nystrom, C.W.A.
King Co., North Side Grange, No. 727
Seattle, Washington

ELMA BELLE'S BROWNIES

1½ c. margarine
4 eggs
2 c. sugar
1½ c. flour
Cocoa
1 tsp. salt
1½ c. nuts (opt.)
2 tsp. vanilla extract
1 c. miniature marshmallows
¼ c. cream
¾ lb. confectioners' sugar

Cream 1 cup margarine, eggs and sugar. Add flour, ⅓ cup cocoa, ½ teaspoon salt, nuts and 1 teaspoon vanilla. Mix well. Place in greased 9 × 13-inch pan. Bake at 350 degrees until tests done. Top with miniature marshmallows. Return to oven until marshmallows begin to brown. Cool. Combine ½ cup margarine, cream, confectioners' sugar, 1 tsp. vanilla, ¼ cup cocoa and ½ teaspoon salt. Mix until of spreading consistency. Spread over brownies.

Elma Belle Rufence
Warren Co., Mason Grange, No. 1680
Mason, Ohio

LILLIAN'S BROWNIES

¾ c. flour
½ tsp. baking powder
¼ tsp. salt
2 eggs
1 c. sugar
½ c. butter or shortening
2 sq. unsweetened chocolate
¾ c. chopped nuts
1 tsp. vanilla extract

Sift flour, baking powder and salt. Beat eggs until light and fluffy. Add sugar; beat well. Melt butter and chocolate together in top of double boiler over hot water. Add to egg mixture; mix thoroughly. Add flour mixture, nuts and vanilla; beat only enough to blend well. Spread in greased 8-inch square pan. Bake at 350 degrees for 20 to 25 minutes. Do not overbake! Yield: 16-20 servings.

Mrs. Lillian Merrill, C.W.A.
Bethlehem Grange, No. 121
Litchfield, Connecticut

MARSHMALLOW BROWNIES

¼ c. butter or margarine
Chocolate chips
¾ c. flour

⅓ c. (firmly packed) brown sugar
1 tsp. baking powder
¼ tsp. salt
½ tsp. vanilla extract
1 egg, beaten
1 c. miniature marshmallows

Melt butter and ½ cup chocolate chips in heavy saucepan over medium heat, stirring constantly. Remove from heat; cool to lukewarm. Add next 6 ingredients to chocolate mixture in saucepan; mix well. Fold in marshmallows and 1 cup chocolate chips into first mixture until just combined. Spread in greased 9-inch square pan. Bake in 350-degree oven for 20 to 25 minutes. Do not overbake. Center will not be firm but becomes firm when cool. Cool before cutting. Yield: 12 to 18 bars.

Louise M. Hanna
Jefferson Grange, No. 197
Augusta, Maine

MARSHMALLOW-BROWNIE DELIGHT

Butter
2 c. sugar
1 tsp. vanilla extract
2 eggs, well beaten
½ c. cocoa
2 c. flour
1 tsp. baking powder
1 c. chopped walnuts
Marshmallows
½ c. (firmly packed) brown sugar
2 sq. unsweetened chocolate
1½ c. confectioners' sugar
Milk
¼ c. chopped nuts

Cream 1 cup butter and sugar. Add vanilla and eggs. Add cocoa, flour and baking powder. Beat until smooth. Add walnuts. Place in greased 10 × 15-inch baking pan. Bake at 375 degrees for 25 minutes or until tests done. Place enough marshmallows on top to cover. Return to oven for 3 minutes. Mash marshmallows down with a fork until top is covered. Combine brown sugar, chocolate and ¼ cup water. Boil for 3 minutes. Add 3 tablespoons butter; cool. Add confectioners' sugar; beat. Thin with milk until the right consistency for spreading. Spread over marshmallow topping. Sprinkle with nuts.

Mary Harris
White Pigeon Grange
White Pigeon, Michigan

EASY BUTTER COOKIES

Sugar
2 sticks margarine, softened
2 egg yolks
Pinch of salt
1½ tsp. soda
1½ tsp. lemon extract
2½ c. flour

Cream 1 cup sugar and margarine. Add remaining ingredients; mix well. Form into balls the size of walnuts. Dip top side in additional sugar. Press flat with fork. Bake at 350 degrees for 8 to 10 minutes.

Mrs. Kenneth E. Wilkin
Newark Grange, No. 1004
Heath, Ohio

CHEESECAKE DREAMS

⅓ c. (firmly packed) light brown sugar
1 c. all-purpose flour
½ c. chopped walnuts
⅓ c. butter or margarine, melted
1 8 oz. package cream cheese, softened
¼ c. sugar
1 egg
2 tbsp. milk
1 tbsp. lemon juice
1 tsp. vanilla extract

Combine brown sugar, flour and walnuts in small bowl; mix well. Stir in butter. Reserve ⅓ cup crumbs. Pat remaining crumbs gently into greased 8-inch square baking pan. Bake in preheated 350-degree oven for 12 to 15 minutes. Beat cream cheese and sugar in small bowl with electric mixer at medium speed until smooth. Beat in remaining ingredients. Pour over baked crust; sprinkle with reserved crumbs. Bake 25 minutes longer or until set. Cool on wire rack. Cut into 2-inch squares; cut each square diagonally in half. Yield: 32 cookies.

Mrs. Linda M. Bell,
Claibourne Grange, No. 2679
Richwood, Ohio

ROCKY ROAD DROPS

½ c. butter
⅔ c. (firmly packed) brown sugar
1 tsp. vanilla extract
1 egg, slightly beaten
½ c. semisweet chocolate morsels, melted
½ c. chopped walnuts
1½ c. sifted all-purpose flour
½ tsp. soda
¾ tsp. salt
1 tsp. instant coffee powder

⅓ c. milk
12 to 14 marshmallows
36 to 40 walnut halves
Chocolate Frosting

Cream butter, brown sugar and vanilla until light and fluffy. Beat in egg. Add chocolate and walnuts, mixing well. Resift flour with soda, salt and coffee powder. Add to creamed mixture along with milk; stir until well blended. Drop from rounded teaspoons onto greased cookie sheets. Bake at 350 degrees for 10 minutes until cookies test done. Be careful not to overbake so cookies will be moist. Cut marshmallows into thirds, crosswise. Top hot cookies with marshmallow slice; return to oven 1 minute to set marshmallows. Remove cookies to wire racks. Top each marshmallow with walnut half, pressing down lightly. Cool. Place racks over waxed paper. Spoon warm Chocolate Frosting carefully over top of each cookie. Let stand until set.

Chocolate Frosting

¼ c. butter or margarine
⅓ c. milk or light cream
½ c. semisweet chocolate morsels
¼ tsp. salt
1 tsp. vanilla extract
2½ c. sifted confectioners' sugar

Combine butter, milk, chocolate and salt in double boiler. Place over hot water; stir occasionally until melted and smooth. Add vanilla. Beat in confectioners' sugar until smooth. Spoon warm frosting over baked cookies.

Photograph for this recipe on page 154.

CHOCOLATE CHIP COOKIES

1 c. sugar
1 c. (firmly packed) brown sugar
1 c. shortening or margarine
2 eggs
4½ c. flour
1 tsp. baking powder
1 tsp. soda
1 c. sour milk
1 tsp. vanilla extract
1 tsp. salt
1 lg. package chocolate chips

Cream first 4 ingredients together. Add next 6 ingredients. Add chocolate chips to mixture. Stir. Drop by spoonfuls onto cookie sheet. Bake at 375 degrees for 12 minutes. One cup coconut may be added for variation.

Beverly Durko
Friendship Grange, No. 1018
Uniondale, Pennsylvania

CONGO SQUARES

2¾ c. sifted flour
2½ tsp. baking powder
½ tsp. salt
⅔ c. shortening
2¼ c. (firmly packed) light brown sugar
3 eggs
1 c. broken nuts
1 pkg. chocolate chips

Sift flour, baking powder and salt. Melt shortening; add sugar. Cool slightly. Add eggs one at a time, beating well after each addition. Add dry ingredients, nuts and chocolate chips. Bake at 350 degrees for 25 to 30 minutes. Cut when almost cool. Yield: 48 squares.

Orpha Inman,
Holden Grange, No. 544
East Holden, Maine

FORGOTTEN COOKIES

2 egg whites
¾ c. sugar
6 oz. package chocolate chips
¼ tsp. mint flavoring
½ tsp. vanilla extract

Whip egg whites until soft peaks form; add sugar gradually. Beat until stiff. Fold in chips and flavorings. Drop from teaspoon onto foil-covered cookie sheet. Place in preheated 375-degree oven. Shut door of oven. Turn oven off at once. Let stand in oven 6 hours or overnight.

Emily Jacobsen
Fruitland Grange, No. 16
Marydel, Delaware

FUDGE-NUT BARS

Butter or margarine, softened
2 c. (firmly packed) brown sugar
2 eggs
4 tsp. vanilla extract
2½ c. sifted flour
1 tsp. soda
1½ tsp. salt
3 c. quick cooking oats
1 12-oz. package semisweet chocolate chips
1 c. sweetened condensed milk
1 c. chopped walnuts

Cream together 1 cup butter and brown sugar in mixer bowl until light and fluffy. Beat in eggs and 2 teaspoons vanilla. Sift together flour, soda and 1 teaspoon salt. Add flour mixture and oats to creamed mixture; mix well. Combine chocolate chips, condensed milk, 2 tablespoons butter and ½ teaspoon salt in top of double boiler. Place over hot water; stir until melted. Remove from heat. Add walnuts and 2 teaspoons vanilla. Spread ⅔ of the batter in greased 10½×15½-inch jelly roll pan. Cover with chocolate mixture. Swirl remaining batter over filling. Bake in 350-degree oven for 25 minutes or until done. Cool in pan on rack. Cut into 1×2-inch bars. Yield: 72 bars.

Andrea J. Myers
Thurmont Grange, No. 409
Thurmont, Maryland

JUMBLES

2 c. sugar
½ c. lard
2 eggs
½ c. sour milk
1 tsp. baking soda
2 c. flour
1 tsp. baking powder
2 sq. unsweetened chocolate, melted

Cream sugar and lard. Add eggs one at a time, beating well after each addition. Combine sour milk and soda. Combine flour and baking powder. Add to creamed mixture alternately with milk mixture. Add chocolate; beat well. Add 1 cup boiling water; stir in carefully. Batter will be thin. Pour into greased 9×13-inch baking pan. Bake at 350 degrees for 25 to 30 minutes.

Florence Keil,
Hopewell Grange, No. 1747
Washington, Illinois

MARY ELLEN'S CHOCOLATE COOKIES

2 sq. chocolate
¼ c. butter or margarine
1 c. sugar
2 eggs
1 c. flour
1 tsp. baking powder
¼ tsp. salt
Confectioners' sugar

Melt chocolate and butter in saucepan. Cool. Add sugar and eggs; beat well. Sift next 3 ingredients; add to egg mixture. Chill for 2 to 3 hours. Roll dough into 1-inch balls. Roll in confectioners' sugar. Place on greased cookie sheet. Bake at 350 degrees for 8 minutes. Yield: 24 cookies.

Evelyn F. Vadney, C.W.A.
Oak Hill Grange, No. 32
Francestown, New Hampshire

CHOCOLATE CRINKLES

½ c. vegetable oil
4 sq. unsweetened chocolate, melted
2 c. sugar
4 eggs
2 tsp. vanilla extract
2 c. sifted flour
2 tsp. baking powder
½ tsp. salt
1 c. crushed nuts
1 c. confectioners' sugar

Combine oil, chocolate, and sugar. Add eggs one at a time, beating well after each addition. Add vanilla. Stir flour, baking powder and salt into oil mixture. Add nuts. Chill for several hours or overnight. Roll dough into balls by teaspoonfuls. Roll in confectioners' sugar. Place 2 inches apart on greased baking sheet. Bake at 350 degrees for 10 to 12 minutes. Do not overbake. Yield: 6 or 7 dozen cookies.

Mrs. Catherine S. Pulling, Master
Skaneateles Grange, No. 458
Skaneateles, New York

CHOCOLATE JUMBLES

1 c. shortening
1 c. sugar
2 egg yolks
1 c. molasses
4½ c. flour
2 tsp. soda
1 tsp. salt
1 tsp. cinnamon
3 sq. chocolate
⅔ c. cold coffee

Cream shortening and sugar; add egg yolks and molasses. Combine next 4 ingredients in bowl. Melt chocolate; cool slightly. Combine mixture together alternately with the coffee. Let stand overnight. Roll out on floured board. Cut into desired shapes. Place on cookie sheet. Bake at 375 degrees for 10 to 12 minutes. Cover with white frosting. Yield: 3 dozen.

Mrs. Agnes Williams
Norwich Township Grange, No. 1581
Norwich, New York

SEAFOAM SQUARES

¾ c. shortening
½ c. sugar
Brown sugar
3 eggs, separated
2 c. flour
¼ tsp. soda
1 tsp. baking powder
¼ tsp. salt
1 tsp. vanilla extract
1 sm. package chocolate chips

Cream together shortening, sugar and ½ cup firmly packed brown sugar. Add beaten egg yolks and 1 tablespoon water. Mix next 4 ingredients together; add to creamed mixture. Add vanilla. Press evenly into 9 × 13-inch baking pan. Sprinkle with chocolate chips; press into dough. Beat egg whites until stiff peaks form. Add ⅓ cup firmly packed brown sugar gradually. Beat until stiff. Spread over chocolate chips. Bake at 350 degrees for 25 minutes. Cool. Cut into squares. Yield: 20 squares.

Helen Verge
Fidelity Grange, No. 300
Amesbury, Massachusetts

CRISSCROSS COOKIES

1¾ c. sugar
1 c. shortening
2 eggs
3 tbsp. sweet or sour cream
1 tsp. vanilla extract
½ tsp. lemon extract
3 c. sifted all-purpose flour
½ tsp. soda
Salt
1½ c. chopped dates
½ c. chopped walnuts
1 tbsp. light corn syrup
1 tsp. vinegar

Add 1½ cups sugar to shortening gradually; cream until fluffy. Beat in eggs, one at a time, beating well after each addition. Add cream and flavorings. Sift flour with soda and ½ teaspoon salt; stir into mixture. Chill thoroughly. Place on sugared board; roll ¼ of the dough to ⅛-inch thickness. Cut two each ½-inch circles, hearts, diamonds, etc. Place 1 inch apart on ungreased cookie sheet. Combine ¼ cup sugar, dash of salt with remaining ingredients in saucepan. Cook for 2 or 3 minutes, stirring constantly. Remove from heat. Cool. Spread cooled date filling onto each cookie, leaving ¼-inch margin. Cut narrow strips from rolled-out dough. Crisscross strips over filling, lightly press ends to cookie edges, trimming if necessary. Bake at 375 degrees for 10 to 12 minutes or until lightly browned. Yield: 4-5 dozen cookies.

Photograph for this recipe on page 158.

COCONUT CHEWS

½ c. (firmly packed) light brown sugar
½ c. margarine, softened
Flour
2 eggs, well beaten
½ c. (firmly packed) dark brown sugar
½ c. light corn syrup
1 tsp. vanilla extract
1 tsp. baking powder
½ tsp. salt
1 c. shredded coconut
⅛ to ¼ c. English walnut halves

Blend first 2 ingredients; add 1 cup flour. Pat mixture in ungreased 9-inch square pan. Bake at 350 degrees for 10 minutes. Cool 5 minutes. Combine 2 tablespoons flour with remaining ingredients; blend well. Pour over first layer. Bake 25 to 35 minutes longer or until golden brown. Cool. Cut into squares. Yield: 2 dozen cookies.

Mrs. Marjorie Radford,
Burns Grange, No. 1839
Kewanee, Illinois

CORNUCOPIAS

3 eggs, beaten
1 c. sugar
1 c. flour
1 tsp. baking powder
Whipped cream
Strawberries

Combine first 4 ingredients with 2 tablespoons cold water. Drop from tablespoon onto cookie sheet, allowing room for spreading. Bake at 350 degrees until slightly brown. Remove from oven. Lap the edges together while hot to form a cornucopia. Hold in shape for a few seconds. Cool. Fill with whipped cream and strawberries. Yield: 12 cookies.

Mrs. John E. Patch
Saxtons River Grange, No. 298
Saxtons River, Vermont

ROMANCE COOKIES

Flour
1 tbsp. sugar
Butter, softened
1½ tsp. vanilla extract
2 eggs, beaten
1 c. (firmly packed) brown sugar
1 tsp. baking powder
½ c. sliced maraschino cherries
1 c. coconut
1 c. nuts, finely chopped

1 c. confectioners' sugar
1 tbsp. milk
½ tsp. almond extract

Blend 1 cup flour, sugar and ½ cup butter. Press into 8 × 10-inch baking pan. Bake at 325 degrees for 20 minutes or until lightly brown. Cool. Combine 2 tablespoons flour and 1 teaspoon vanilla with next 6 ingredients. Pour over crust. Bake in 325-degree oven for 20 minutes. Cool. Combine remaining ingredients with 3 tablespoons butter, ½ teaspoon vanilla and 1 tablespoon boiling water, mix well. Ice cookies. Cut into desired shapes.

Frances Pierson,
Mt. Wheeler Grange, No. 696
Arlington, Washington

DESSERT BARS

1 c. butter
1 c. sugar
1 c. (firmly packed) brown sugar
3 eggs
1 c. pecans, chopped
1 tsp. vanilla extract
1 c. flour
Confectioners' sugar

Cream butter and sugars. Add eggs, one at a time, beating well after each addition. Add pecans and vanilla. Add flour; mix well. Spread in 9 × 13-inch pan. Bake at 325 degrees for 35 to 40 minutes. Cut into bars while warm; roll in confectioners' sugar.

Enez Birkett
South Prairie Grange, No. 2077
West Liberty, Iowa

FIESTA FRUIT BARS

½ c. margarine
⅔ c. sugar
⅛ c. molasses
1 tsp. lemon extract
1 egg, beaten
2 tbsp. orange juice
½ tbsp. grated orange rind
1¾ c. flour
¼ tsp. soda
½ tsp. salt
1 tsp. baking powder
1 tsp. nutmeg
½ c. raisins
½ c. chopped nuts
½ c. chopped dates
⅔ c. candied fruit

Cream margarine; add sugar. Beat until light and fluffy. Stir in molasses and lemon extract. Add egg; mix well. Add orange juice and rind. Add dry ingredients; mix well. Fold in raisins, nuts and fruit. Spread in 12 × 15-inch baking pan. Bake in 350-degree oven for 15 to 20 minutes. Ice with lemon frosting or sprinkle with confectioners' sugar while still warm, if desired.

Ona Dresser
Calidonia Grange, No. 9
East Hardwick, Vermont

FRUIT BARS

Sugar
2 eggs
1 1-lb. can fruit cocktail, undrained
2¼ c. flour
1½ tsp. soda
½ tsp. salt
Vanilla extract
1⅛ c. flaked coconut
½ c. chopped walnuts
½ c. butter
¼ c. evaporated milk

Combine 1⅛ cups sugar, eggs, fruit cocktail, flour, soda, salt and ½ teaspoon vanilla in mixer bowl. Blend at slow speed; increase to medium speed for several minutes. Pour into greased and floured jelly roll pan. Sprinkle with coconut and walnuts. Bake in preheated 350 degree oven for 30-35 minutes. Combine ¾ cup sugar, butter, milk, and ½ teaspoon vanilla. Boil 2 minutes, stirring constantly. Beat with a spoon until slightly thickened. Drizzle over warm bars. Cool. Cut into bars. Yield: 56 bars.

Tammy Williams
Mondovi Grange, No. 822
Reardan, Washington

FRUIT COCKTAIL COOKIES

¾ c. butter
1½ c. (firmly packed) brown sugar
1 tsp. vanilla extract
2 tsp. almond extract
1 egg
1 No. 303 can fruit cocktail, drained
3 c. all-purpose flour
½ tsp. salt
1 tsp. (heaping) soda

Cream butter with sugar and flavorings. Beat in egg. Add fruit cocktail. Combine remaining ingredients; stir into creamed mixture. Drop from teaspoon 2-inches apart on greased baking sheet. Bake in preheated 350-degree oven for 10 to 12 minutes or until brown. Crushed pineapple may be substituted for fruit cocktail. Yield: 6 dozen cookies.

Mrs. June Meyers,
Unity Grange
Pemberton, Ohio

FROSTED COFFEE BARS

¼ c. shortening
1 c. (firmly packed) brown sugar
1 egg
1½ c. flour
½ tsp. baking powder
½ tsp. soda
½ tsp. cinnamon
½ c. hot coffee
½ c. raisins
¼ c. nuts (opt.)
1 recipe confectioners' sugar frosting

Cream shortening and brown sugar. Add egg. Sift dry ingredients together. Add to creamed mixture alternately with coffee. Add raisins and nuts. Pour into 10½ × 15⅛-inch pan. Bake at 350 degrees for 15 to 20 minutes. Ice with confectioners' sugar frosting. Cut into squares.

Mrs. Melvin Zipse
Ogle Co., Blackhawk Grange, No. 1822
Leaf River, Illinois

EVELYN'S GINGERSNAPS

Sugar
1½ c. shortening
2 eggs, beaten
4 c. flour
2 tsp. soda
2 tsp. cinnamon
2 tsp. cloves
2 tsp. ginger
½ c. molasses

Cream 2 cups sugar and shortening together. Add eggs. Sift dry ingredients together; add to creamed mixture alternately with molasses. Roll into balls. Dip in additional sugar. Place on cookie sheet about 2-inches apart. Bake at 375 degrees for 15 to 18 minutes.

Evelyn Barnes
Friendship Grange, No. 1018
Herrick Center, Pennsylvania

MY GINGERBREAD MEN COOKIES

1 c. sorghum or molasses
1 c. shortening
1 c. sugar
1 egg
1 tsp. vanilla extract
2 tsp. soda
6 c. flour
½ tsp. cloves
1 tsp. salt
2 tsp. cinnamon
1 tsp. ginger

Simmer sorghum and shortening for 15 minutes. Cream sugar, egg and vanilla together. Dissolve soda in ½ cup hot water; add to sugar mixture. Sift remaining ingredients together. Add sorghum mixture to sugar mixture. Stir in flour mixture until well-blended. Roll thin; cut with gingerbread man cookie cutter or cutters of your choice. Place on greased cookie sheet. Bake at 375 degrees for 10 minutes. Remove immediately. Cool. Frost if desired. Yield: 5 dozen.

Mrs. Janet Price, C.W.A.
Carroll Co. Perry Township Grange, No. 1945
North Canton, Ohio

GERMAN GINGERSNAP COOKIES

¾ c. shortening
1 c. (firmly packed) brown sugar
¼ c. molasses
1 egg
2¼ c. sifted flour
2 tsp. soda
½ tsp. salt
1 tsp. ginger
1 tsp. cinnamon
½ tsp. cloves
Sugar

Cream together first 4 ingredients until fluffy. Blend together dry ingredients; stir into molasses mixture. Form into small balls; roll in granulated sugar. Place 2-inches apart on greased cookie sheet. Bake at 375 degrees for about 10 minutes. Cool slightly; remove from pan. Yield: 5 dozen cookies.

Mrs. Louise U. Summers
New Market Grange, No. 362
Ijamsville, Maryland
Patty Wedding
Levicks Mill Grange, No. 2239
Jacksonville, Missouri

GINGER CREAMS

¼ c. shortening
1¼ c. sugar
1 lg. egg
½ c. molasses
2 c. flour
½ tsp. soda
1 tsp. ginger
½ tsp. saffron
¼ tsp. each nutmeg, cloves and cinnamon

Cream shortening and ½ cup sugar. Add egg, molasses and ½ cup warm water. Add next 5 ingredients; mix well. Chill dough. Drop by spoonfuls onto greased cookie sheets. Bake in 400-degree oven for 7 to 8 minutes. Combine ¾ cup sugar with vanilla and cream. Spread on cookies. Yield: 4 dozen.

Mabel E. Alley, C.W.A.
Meenahga Grange, No. 555
Waldoboro, Maine

GRAHAM CRACKER BARS

⅔ c. evaporated milk
1 c. sugar
1 tbsp. flour
½ c. butter
1 egg, beaten
Graham crackers
1 c. chopped walnuts
1 c. flaked coconut
1 c. graham cracker crumbs
2 tsp. vanilla extract
1 recipe butter frosting

Mix first 5 ingredients in saucepan. Bring to a boil over medium heat, stirring constantly. Remove from heat. Arrange graham crackers in bottom of 7 × 11-inch baking pan. Add remaining ingredients to cooked mixture. Spoon over crackers in pan. Top with graham cracker squares. Press slightly into filling. Frost with butter frosting. Chill. Cut into bars.

Darlene Morton, C.W.A.
Lamont Grange, No. 889
Lamont, Washington

HAWAIIAN DROP COOKIES

2 c. all-purpose flour, sifted
2 tsp. baking powder
½ tsp. salt
⅔ c. shortening

1¼ c. sugar
½ tsp. vanilla extract
½ tsp. almond extract
1 egg
¾ c. crushed pineapple, drained
½ c. shredded coconut, finely chopped

Sift first 3 ingredients together. Cream shortening and sugar. Add extracts; mix thoroughly. Beat in egg until mixture is fluffy. Blend in pineapple and dry ingredients. Drop from teaspoon 3-inches apart on ungreased cookie sheet. Sprinkle with coconut. Bake at 325 degrees about 20 minutes or until lightly browned. Store cookies for 24 hours. Yield: 4½ dozen.

Lila R. Erickson
Rickreall Grange, No. 671
Independence, Oregon

HONEY COOKIES

1 pt. honey
1 pt. light corn syrup
⅓ c. sugar
Flour
1 tbsp. soda
Juice of 1 lemon
1 c. (firmly packed) brown sugar
1 c. candied fruit, finely cut
1 c. nuts, finely chopped
1 tbsp. cinnamon
3 eggs
Grated rind of 1 lemon

Mix first 3 ingredients with 3 cups flour. Dissolve soda in lemon juice. Add next 6 ingredients with 1 cup flour; mix well. Add honey mixture; blend well. Chill overnight. Roll out; cut with cookie cutters. Place on cookie sheets. Bake at 375 degrees until light brown. Cool. Frost, if desired.

Mrs. Edna Bidlack, Sec.
Union Grange, No. 2516
Van Wert, Ohio

SUGAR WAFERS

½ c. sugar
½ c. shortening
1 egg, well beaten
¾ c. flour
½ tsp. salt
½ tsp. flavoring
English walnuts or pecans

Blend sugar and shortening thoroughly. Add egg. Sift flour with salt; add to creamed mixture. Beat

Desserts / 163

vigorously. Add flavoring. Form into small balls. Place on cookie sheet. Place whole walnut in center of each cookie. Bake in 400-degree oven for 10 to 15 minutes or until edges brown. Yield: 40 small wafers.

Mrs. Donald Peck
Litchfield Grange, No. 107
Litchfield, Connecticut

S.C. LEMON BARS

2¼ c. all-purpose flour
Confectioners' sugar
2 sticks margarine, softened
4 eggs, beaten
2 c. sugar
⅓ c. lemon juice

Mix 2 cups flour and ½ cup confectioners' sugar. Cut in margarine until crumbly. Press into well-greased 9 x 13-inch baking pan. Bake in 350-degree oven for 15 minutes. Combine eggs, sugar and ¼ cup flour in mixer bowl; mix well with electric mixer. Add lemon juice. Pour over crust. Bake 25 minutes longer or until light golden color. Sprinkle with additional confectioners' sugar. Cool before cutting.

Ethel Wertenberger, C.W.A.
Brimfield Grange, No. 2166
Kent, Ohio

VELMA'S LEMON COOKIES

Flour
½ c. margarine, softened
Confectioners' sugar
⅓ c. lemon juice
1 tbsp. lemon rind
2 eggs, slightly beaten
1 c. sugar

Combine 1 cup flour, margarine and ½ cup confectioners' sugar. Pat into 8 x 10-inch baking pan. Bake at 350 degrees for 15 minutes or until lightly browned. Mix remaining ingredients with 2 tablespoons flour. Pour over crust. Bake at 350 degrees for 25 minutes. Sprinkle with additional confectioners' sugar. Cut into squares. Yield: 15 cookies.

Velma Hockett
Cimarron Grange, No. 1932
Ulysses, Kansas

LEMON-HONEY SNAPS

2 c. sifted all-purpose flour
1½ tsp. soda
1 tsp. salt
½ tsp. cinnamon
½ tsp. ginger
¼ tsp. cloves
¾ c. shortening
1 c. (firmly packed) brown sugar
1 egg, slightly beaten
⅓ c. honey
1 tsp. grated lemon peel
1 c. walnuts, finely chopped

Resift flour with soda, salt and spices. Combine next 5 ingredients; cream until well blended. Blend in flour mixture to form moderately stiff dough. Stir in half the walnuts. Chill dough for 30 minutes for easier handling. Shape into small balls, using about 1 level teaspoon dough for each. Dip tops in remaining ½ cup walnuts. Place on lightly greased cookie sheets 2 inches apart. Place above oven center. Bake at 350 degrees for 12 to 13 minutes or just until edges are lightly browned. Cookies will seem soft in centers. Allow to stand for 3 or 4 minutes. Remove carefully to wire racks with broad spatula. Cool. Yield: 40 cookies.

Photograph for this recipe on page 164.

MAPLE-PECAN BARS

Sifted flour
Brown sugar
½ c. butter or margarine, softened
1 c. maple syrup
2 eggs, slightly beaten
½ tsp. vanilla extract
¼ tsp. salt
1 c. chopped pecans

Combine 1½ cups flour and ¼ cup firmly packed brown sugar. Cut in butter until mixture is crumbly. Press into greased 9 × 13-inch baking pan. Bake in 350-degree oven for 15 minutes. Combine ⅔ cup firmly packed brown sugar and syrup in small saucepan. Simmer for 5 minutes. Pour over eggs slowly, stirring constantly with a wire whisk to keep smooth. Stir in vanilla, 2 tablespoons flour and salt; mix thoroughly. Pour over baked crust. Sprinkle pecans on top. Bake in 350-degree oven for 20 to 25 minutes or until done. Cool in pan on rack. Cut into bars. I won a Blue-Ribbon for these at our Plumas County Fair last year. Yield: about 2½ dozen bars.

Cheryle Harte,
Indian Valley Grange
Greenville, California

MAPLENUT SNOWBALLS

1 c. margarine
2¼ c. flour
¼ tsp. salt
1½ tsp. maple flavoring
¾ c. walnuts
Confectioners' sugar

Combine all ingredients with ½ cup confectioners' sugar; mix together thoroughly. Roll into small balls. Place on ungreased cookie sheet. Bake at 350 degrees for 12 minutes or until lightly browned. Remove from cookie sheet; roll in additional confectioners' sugar. Cool.

Donna May Miller
Washington Co., Buffalo Grange, No. 1523
Washington, Pennsylvania

MINCEMEAT GOODIES

1 c. Crisco
2 c. sugar
3 eggs, well beaten
Flour
1 c. homemade mincemeat
1 tsp. soda
½ tsp. ginger

1 tsp. cloves
1 tsp. nutmeg
½ tsp. salt
½ c. ground nuts

Cream Crisco and sugar together until light. Add eggs and enough flour to prevent mixture from curdling. Add mincemeat. Sift dry ingredients together. Add dry mixture and nuts. Cookie mixture should be stiff enough to roll. Drop at least 2-inches apart on cookie sheet. Bake at 375 degrees until done. Yield: 4 dozen 3-inch cookies.

Marjorie Furnas
Jamestown Grange, No. 2358
Jamestown, Ohio

HERMITS

1 c. sugar
½ c. shortening
½ c. molasses
1 tsp. soda
3 c. flour
1 tsp. cinnamon
½ tsp. salt
1 c. chopped raisins, dates or walnuts
1 egg

Cream sugar and shortening. Add molasses. Combine soda and ½ cup lukewarm water; add to molasses mixture. Add next 3 ingredients; stir in fruit. Add egg. Fill greased 15 × 18-inch pan with mixture. Bake at 350 degrees for 10 to 12 minutes or until done. Cool. Cut into squares.

Rita Holding
Falmouth Grange, No. 29
Falmouth, Maine

MOLASSES COOKIES

1 c. shortening, melted
1 c. sour milk
4 tsp. soda
1 tsp. (rounded) cinnamon
1 c. sugar
2 c. molasses
1 tsp. salt
1 tsp. ginger
6 or 6½ c. flour
Cinnamon-sugar mixture

Combine all ingredients except cinnamon-sugar mixture using enough flour to make a stiff batter. Roll out ⅜ inch thick on floured board. Cut with cookie cutter. Place on greased cookie sheet;

sprinkle with cinnamon-sugar mixture. Bake in a 350-degree oven for 10 minutes. Yield: 50 cookies.

Louisa O. Williams,
Lake Placid Grange, No. 198
Lake Placid, Florida

MOLASSES HERMITS

½ c. butter, softened
½ c. molasses
Sugar
1 egg
1 tsp. vinegar
2½ c. flour
1 tsp. soda
1 tsp. cream of tartar
Spices to taste
1 c. raisins

Combine first 2 ingredients with ½ cup sugar; blend well. Add egg, 1 tablespoon cold water and vinegar. Sift dry ingredients together. Add to first mixture. Add raisins. Chill overnight. Divide batter into 6 parts. Roll with hands on floured board. Form 6 long thin rolls to fit cookie sheet length. Use 2 cookie sheets placing 3 rolls on each. Sprinkle with additional sugar. Flatten with glass dipped in water. Bake at 350 degrees for about 15 minutes. Remove from oven. Crease with knife; cool. Break on creases when cool. Yield: 24 cookies.

Janet B. Douglas
Tuftonboro Grange, No. 142
Wolfeboro, New Hampshire

MOLASSES ROLL COOKIES

1 c. sugar
1 c. melted lard
1 c. molasses
Flour
1 tsp. cinnamon
1 tsp. (scant) ginger
1 tsp. (scant) salt
1½ tsp. soda

Stir sugar, lard, molasses and ½ cup hot water in large mixer bowl. Add 3 cups flour and remaining ingredients; stir to mix. Add about 2½ cups flour or enough to roll. Cut with any size cookie cutter. Place on lightly greased cookie sheet. Bake at 350 degrees for about 10 minutes.

Mrs. Robert Forsythe, C.W.A.
Livingston Co., Linwood Grange, No. 1084
Pavilion, New York

MOLASSES CRINKLES

2¼ c. all-purpose flour
2 tsp. soda
¼ tsp. salt
1 tsp. cinnamon
1 tsp. ginger
½ tsp. cloves
1 c. (firmly packed) brown sugar
¾ c. shortening
⅓ c. molasses
1 egg
Sugar

Pour flour onto waxed paper. Add soda, salt, and spices; stir well. Combine remaining ingredients. Add to dry ingredients. Mix well. Shape dough into balls; dip top in sugar. Place on ungreased cookie sheet. Bake at 350 degrees for 12 to 15 minutes.

Mrs. Vera Kenville
Guyanoga Valley Grange, No. 1556
Penn Yan, New York

BEST-EVER COOKIES

1 c. shortening
1 c. (firmly packed) brown sugar
1 c. sugar
2 eggs, well beaten
1 tsp. almond extract
1 tsp. vanilla extract
2 c. flour
½ tsp. salt
1 tsp. soda
2 c. quick oats
½ to 1 c. crushed nuts

Cream shortening and sugars. Add eggs and flavorings. Sift flour, salt and soda together. Add oats and nuts. Add to sugar mixture; mix well. Form dough into small balls. Place on greased cookie sheet; flatten with a fork. Bake at 425 degrees for 5 to 8 minutes. Yield: 3 dozen.

Minnie Beard
Cimarron Grange, No. 1932
Satanta, Kansas

BANANA-OATMEAL COOKIES

1 c. sugar
¾ c. Crisco
1 egg, beaten
1 c. mashed bananas
1½ c. flour
1 tsp. soda
¼ tsp. cloves
½ tsp. allspice
¾ tsp. cinnamon
½ tsp. salt
1¾ c. quick oats
¾ c. seedless raisins
¾ c. chocolate chips

Combine first 3 ingredients; blend well. Stir in mashed banana. Sift next 6 ingredients together into banana mixture. Stir in oats. Add raisins and chocolate chips. Drop by heaping spoonfuls onto greased cookie sheet. Bake in 350 degree oven for 10 to 12 minutes. Yield: 25-30 cookies.

Mrs. Bertha L. Burnham
Hollis Grange, No. 132
Hollis Center, Maine

CHEWY OATMEAL COOKIES

1 c. flour
¾ tsp. soda
½ tsp. salt
1 tsp. cinnamon
¼ tsp. nutmeg   butter doesn't work
¾ c. shortening
1½ c. (firmly packed) brown sugar
2 eggs, beaten
1 tsp. vanilla extract
2 c. old-fashioned oatmeal
1 c. raisins

Sift flour, soda, salt and spices together. Add next 4 ingredients. Beat until smooth. Stir in oatmeal and raisins. Drop by spoonfuls on cookie sheet. Bake at 350 degrees for 10 to 12 minutes.

flat + crispy
takes 12 min

Mrs. Merle Boyles
Biglick Center Grange
Alvada, Ohio

GLITTER BARS

2 c. flour
½ tsp. salt
1 lb. brown sugar, firmly packed
1 lb. orange slice candy, chopped
1 c. chopped nuts
1 tsp. vanilla extract
½ tsp. lemon extract
4 eggs, slightly beaten

Mix all ingredients in order given. Spread in greased and floured 9 × 13-inch baking pan. Bake at 350 degrees for 45 minutes. Cut into bars while warm.

Ella Mae Palmer
Garland Grange
Garland, Kansas

ORANGE-COCONUT CRISP

2 eggs
⅔ c. salad oil
Sugar
¼ c. frozen orange juice concentrate, thawed
2½ c. sifted flour
2 tsp. baking powder
½ tsp. salt
1 c. grated coconut

Beat eggs; stir in oil and 1 cup sugar. Beat until mixture thickens. Stir in orange juice. Sift flour with baking powder and salt. Add to egg mixture; mix well. Stir in coconut. Drop from teaspoon 2-inches apart onto ungreased baking sheet. Press each cookie flat with bottom of oiled glass dipped in sugar. Bake in preheated 400-degree oven for 8 minutes or until cookies are delicate brown.

Joyce Keller
Hopewell Grange, No. 1747
Washington, Illinois

ORANGE-DATE SQUARES

⅛ c. shortening
½ c. sugar
1 egg
1 tbsp. grated orange rind
2 tbsp. orange juice
Pinch of salt
1 c. flour
½ tsp. soda
½ c. chopped walnuts
¾ c. cut-up dates

Combine first 3 ingredients in mixer bowl. Mix in remaining ingredients. Spread in greased 8 × 12-inch pan. Bake at 300 degrees for 20 minutes. Cool. Frost with desired frosting substituting orange juice for milk.

Mrs. Edwin Hussey
Progressive Grange, No. 523
Waldoboro, Maine

ORANGE SLICE COOKIES

2 c. (firmly packed) brown sugar
1 c. sugar
2 c. shortening
2 eggs, beaten
1½ tbsp. soda
3 c. flour
1½ tsp. baking powder
20 candy orange slices, diced
1 sm. can Angel Flake coconut
3 c. quick oats
10 oz. nuts, chopped

Cream sugars and shortening until smooth. Add eggs; mix well. Mix soda and 3 tablespoons water. Add to sugar mixture and mix well. Sift flour and baking powder together. Add to sugar mixture; blend well. Add remaining ingredients in order listed mixing well after each addition. Pour mixture on waxed paper. Form into rolls. Chill thoroughly. Slice. Place on cookie sheet. Bake at 350 degrees for 8 to 10 minutes. Let stand 5 minutes before removing from cookie sheet. Yield: 10 dozen cookies.

Marvina Gold, C.W.A.
Big Rock Grange, No. 408
Springfield, Colorado

PEANUT BUTTER COOKIES

1 c. Crisco
1 c. sugar
1 c. (firmly packed) brown sugar
2 eggs, well beaten
1 tsp. vanilla extract
1 c. peanut butter
2⅔ to 3 c. flour
2 tsp. soda
1 tsp. salt
2 tbsp. milk

Combine all ingredients; mix well. Drop from wet spoon onto greased baking sheet. Press ridges across top with fork. Bake at 350 degrees about 10 minutes. Yield: 7-8 dozen.

Hazel Hagen
Oakfield Grange
Batavia, New York
Miss Leona Ogden
Genesco Grange, No. 1221
Mt. Morris, New York

NO-BAKE PEANUT BUTTER COOKIES

2 sticks margarine, melted
2⅛ c. confectioners' sugar
1¾ c. graham cracker crumbs
1 c. chunky peanut butter
2 c. chocolate chips

Combine first 4 ingredients; mix well. Pack firmly into ungreased 9 × 12-inch pan. Melt chocolate chips; spread over mixture on pan. Chill; cut into squares.

Ruth M. Shalbis
Green Mountain Grange, No. 347
Woodstock, Vermont

PEANUT BUTTER ROUND-UPS

1 c. shortening
1 c. (firmly packed) brown sugar
2 eggs
1 c. creamy peanut butter
2 c. flour
2 tsp. soda
½ tsp. salt
1 c. quick oats

Beat shortening and brown sugar together until creamy. Add eggs and peanut butter; beat well. Sift flour, soda and salt together. Add to creamed mixture; mix well. Stir in oats. Shape dough to form 1-inch balls. Place on ungreased cookie sheets. Press crisscrosses on each cookie with fork. Bake in preheated 350-degree oven for 8 to 10 minutes.

Hulda Cole
Friendship Grange, No. 1018
Uniondale, Pennsylvania

REAL-EASY PEANUT BUTTER COOKIES

1 c. sugar
1 c. peanut butter
1 egg, beaten

Combine all ingredients. Shape into balls. Place on cookie sheet. Press with a fork. Bake at 350 degrees for 8 to 12 minutes.

Mrs. John Rorabaugh
Sugar Grove Grange, No. 2044
Colfax, Iowa

OATMEAL-PEANUT BUTTER BARS

1 c. (firmly packed) brown sugar
½ c. shortening or margarine
1 egg
1 tsp. vanilla extract
Peanut butter
1½ c. sifted flour
1 tsp. soda
Salt
½ c. quick oatmeal
2 tbsp. butter
1½ c. confectioners' sugar
2½ tbsp. milk

Cream together first 4 ingredients with ½ cup peanut butter. Add flour, soda and ¼ teaspoon salt; mix well. Add oatmeal; blend. Press into greased 10 × 15-inch baking pan. Bake at 375 degrees for 12 to 15 minutes. Cool. Cream butter and 2 tablespoons peanut butter. Add confectioners'

sugar, salt to taste and milk; mix well. Spread over cookies. Let set. Cut into bars. Yield: 12 servings.

Betty Hal
Centre Co., Half Moon Grange, No. 29(
Port Matilda, Pennsylvani(

TREASURE COOKIES

½ c. shortening
½ c. sugar
½ c. (firmly packed) brown sugar
2 eggs
½ c. peanut butter
½ tsp. vanilla extract
1 c. flour
½ tsp. baking powder
½ tsp. soda
¼ tsp. salt
1 c. quick oats
1 c. corn flakes
½ c. semisweet chocolate chips

Cream together shortening and sugars. Beat in eggs, peanut butter and vanilla. Add flour, baking powder and soda; mix thoroughly. Stir in remaining ingredients. Drop from teaspoon onto ungreased baking sheet. Bake at 375 degrees for 10 minutes. Remove from baking sheet at once. Yield: 3 dozen cookies.

Fannie A. Belcher, C.W.A.
Lincoln Grange, No. 421
Springfield, Vermont

DAISY'S PINEAPPLE COOKIES

½ c. butter
1 c. sugar
1 egg
½ c. crushed pineapple, undrained
¼ tsp. salt
¼ tsp. soda
1 tsp. baking powder
2¼ c. flour
1 tsp. vanilla extract
½ c. nuts

Cream butter with sugar. Add egg; stir in pineapple. Sift dry ingredients. Add to pineapple mixture. Add vanilla and nuts; mix well. Drop from teaspoon onto cookie sheet. Bake at 350 degrees for 15 minutes.

Daisy Shager
Friendship Grange, No. 1018
Uniondale, Pennsylvania

PHYLLIS' PINEAPPLE COOKIES

1 c. shortening
1 c. firmly packed brown sugar
1 c. sugar
2 eggs
1 c. crushed pineapple, undrained
1 tsp. vanilla extract
4 c. sifted flour
1 tsp. baking powder
½ tsp. each salt and soda
1 c. chopped nuts

Cream shortening with sugars. Add eggs; mix well. Add pineapple and vanilla. Sift dry ingredients; add to creamed mixture. Stir in nuts. Drop from teaspoon onto greased cookie sheet. Bake at 375 degrees 10 to 15 minutes. Yield: 6 dozen cookies.

Mrs. Phyllis M. Hemphill,
Cornish Grange, No. 25
Windsor, Vermont

POTATO CHIP COOKIES

1 c. margarine
½ c. sugar
1 tsp. vanilla extract
1 c. crushed potato chips
½ c. chopped nuts
2 c. flour

Cream margarine, sugar and vanilla. Add remaining ingredients. Roll 1 tablespoon dough into ball. Press balls flat with sugared glass. Bake at 350 degrees for 16 to 18 minutes. Remove from pan to rack. Cool. Yield: 30 cookies.

Mildred I. Hawk
Austinburg Grange, No. 2596
Ashtabula, Ohio

PUMPKIN BARS

2 c. flour
2 tsp. soda
½ tsp. salt
2 tsp. pumpkin pie spice or cinnamon
1 tsp. soda
2 c. sugar
2 c. pumpkin
4 eggs
1 c. chopped nuts
1 c. oil
1 stick soft butter or margarine
1 box confectioners' sugar
1 8-oz. package cream cheese
2 tsp. vanilla extract

Combine first 10 ingredients in large mixer bowl. Mix well. Place in shallow greased cookie sheet.

Desserts / 171

Bake at 350 degrees for 25 minutes. Cool. Blend remaining ingredients together with 3 teaspoons warm water until creamy. Frost. Chill 1 hour. Cut into bars.

Marilyn Whittlesey
Wittemburg Grange
Newton, Iowa

GRANDMOTHER'S OVERNIGHT COOKIES

1 c. (firmly packed) brown sugar
1 c. sugar
4½ c. flour
1 tsp. salt
2 tsp. soda
1 tsp. cinnamon
½ tsp. nutmeg
½ tsp. cloves or allspice
1 c. chopped pecans
1 c. dark raisins or dates, chopped (opt.)
3 eggs, well beaten
1½ c. shortening, melted

Sift dry ingredients together. Add pecans and raisins. Add eggs. Add shortening; mix well. Work dough with hands into small 2 × 9-inch rolls. Wrap each roll in waxed paper. Chill overnight. Slice into ⅛-inch slices. Place on greased cookie sheet. Bake at 350 degrees for 10 minutes or until just brown. Yield: 5-6 dozen.

Mrs. Lorena D. Stigers
Potomac Grange, No. 1
Falls Church, Virginia

PHYLLIS' RAISIN COOKIES

1½ c. small raisins
Sugar
1 c. margarine, softened
3 eggs
1 tsp. soda
1 tsp. baking powder
⅛ tsp. salt
1 tsp. vanilla extract
3½ c. flour

Simmer raisins and 1 cup water until liquid evaporates. Cream 1½ cups sugar and margarine. Add eggs one at a time, beating well after each addition. Add next 5 ingredients. Add raisins. Chill dough; roll into balls. Roll balls in additional sugar. Bake at 350 degrees for 12 to 15 minutes. Yield: 60 cookies.

Phyllis Brackley
Aurora Grange, No. 202
Strong, Maine

RAISIN-FILLED COOKIES

1 c. (firmly packed) brown sugar
1 c. sugar
1 c. shortening
3 eggs
5 c. flour
1 tsp. salt
¼ tsp. nutmeg
1½ tsp. cinnamon
2 tsp. vanilla extract
1 tsp. soda
1 tsp. baking powder
6 tbsp. sour milk
1 lb. raisins
Lemon slice
1½ tbsp. cornstarch
1 c. nuts

Cream sugar, shortening and eggs. Add next 8 ingredients. Blend well. Roll out ¼-inch thick. Cut with round cookie cutter. Place raisins and lemon in saucepan. Cover with water. Cook until raisins are plump. Thicken with cornstarch mixed with ¼ cup cold water. Add nuts. Place 1 tablespoon filling on half the cookies. Top with remaining halves. Press edges together. Place on cookie sheet. Bake at 400 degrees for 8 to 10 minutes. Yield: 3 dozen.

Mrs. Harry Deibler
Baileyville Grange, No. 1991
Pennsylvania Furnace, Pennsylvania

POOR MAN'S COOKIES

1 c. raisins
½ c. shortening or margarine
2 c. flour
1 tsp. soda
½ c. nuts (opt.)
½ tsp. nutmeg
1 tsp. cinnamon
1 tsp. salt
1 egg
1 recipe thin confectioners' sugar icing

Simmer raisins, 1½ cups water and shortening for 20 minutes. Cool until lukewarm. Combine remaining ingredients. Add to raisin mixture. Spread on 10 × 13-inch cookie sheet. Bake at 275 degrees for 20 minutes or until lightly browned. Spread with thin icing while warm; cut into squares. Yield: 15 or more cookies.

Mrs. Florence Ward
Columbiana Co., Butler Grange, No. 993
Salem, Ohio

B.J. COOKIES

2 c. raisins
3½ c. all-purpose flour
1 tsp. baking powder
1 tsp. soda
1 tsp. salt
½ tsp. cinnamon
½ tsp. nutmeg
1 c. shortening
1¾ c. sugar
2 eggs, slightly beaten
1 tsp. vanilla extract
½ c. chopped nuts

Boil raisins and 1 cup water together for 3 minutes. Cool; do not drain. Combine next 6 ingredients. Cream shortening. Add sugar gradually, beating well after each addition. Beat in eggs; stir in raisins with liquid and vanilla. Add flour mixture gradually, blending well after each addition. Stir in nuts. Drop onto cookie sheet. Bake at 375 degrees for 12 to 15 minutes.

Mrs. Ruby Stoops
Highland Grange, No. 1771
Norwich, Ohio

RAISIN DROPS

½ c. shortening
½ c. margarine
1¼ c. honey
2 eggs, well beaten
2 1-oz. squares unsweetened chocolate, melted
1½ c. quick-cooking oats
2½ c. sifted cake flour
1 tsp. baking powder
¼ tsp. soda
1 tsp. salt
1 tsp. cinnamon
1½ c. seedless raisins
½ c. chopped nuts, (opt.)

Combine shortening, margarine and honey; blend well. Blend in eggs. Stir in chocolate and oats. Resift flour with baking powder, soda, salt and cinnamon. Add to honey mixture. Blend in raisins and nuts. Drop by teaspoonfuls onto greased baking sheets about 1½ inches apart. Bake at 325 degrees for 20 minutes. Remove to wire racks to cool. Yield: 6 dozen.

Photograph for this recipe on page 172.

RHUBARB BARS

Flour
5 tbsp. confectioners' sugar
½ c. butter
2 c. finely chopped rhubarb
2 eggs, well beaten
1½ c. sugar
¾ tsp. salt

Sift 1 cup flour with confectioners' sugar; cut in butter. Mix as for pie crust. Press into ungreased 9 × 13-inch pan. Bake at 350 degrees for 15 minutes. Set aside. Combine rhubarb, eggs, sugar, 5 tablespoons flour and salt; mix thoroughly. Spoon over crust. Bake at 350 degrees for 35 minutes. Serve warm or cold. Yield: 12 bars.

Eleanor Paine, Home Economics Chm. 1979
Junction City Grange, No. 744
Junction City, Oregon

SOUR CREAM DROP COOKIES

½ c. shortening
½ c. (firmly packed) brown sugar
2 eggs
2½ c. flour
1 tsp. baking powder
1 tsp. soda
½ tsp. salt
1 c. sour cream
2 tsp. vanilla extract
⅔ c. nuts
6 tbsp. butter, melted and browned
1½ c. confectioners' sugar

Cream shortening and brown sugar. Add eggs; mix well. Sift dry ingredients; add to creamed mixture alternately with sour cream. Blend in 1 teaspoon vanilla and nuts. Drop from teaspoon onto greased baking sheet. Bake at 350 degrees for 10 to 12 minutes. Combine remaining ingredients with 1 teaspoon vanilla and enough hot water for spreading consistency. Frost cookies with mixture. Yield: 6 dozen cookies.

Marcella Davis
Huntingdon Co., Shavers Creek Grange, No. 353
Petersburg, Pennsylvania

ALICE'S SUGAR COOKIES

1 c. sugar
1 c. confectioners' sugar
1 c. butter
1 c. cooking oil
2 eggs
1 tsp. salt

1 tsp. baking powder
1 tsp. cream of tartar
1 tsp. vanilla extract
4 c. plus 1 tbsp. flour

Combine all ingredients except flour. Add flour; mix well. Roll in small balls. Place on greased cookie sheet. Press flat. Bake in 375 degree oven for 8 to 10 minutes. Yield: 5 dozen.

Alice Thon
Daggett Brook Grange
Brainerd, Minnesota

GRANDMA GATES' SUGAR COOKIES

1 c. shortening
1 c. buttermilk
2 c. sugar
2 eggs
4 c. flour
½ tsp. salt
2 tsp. baking powder
1½ tsp. soda
½ tsp. nutmeg
1 tsp. vanilla extract

Cream shortening. Add buttermilk, sugar and eggs. Beat until fluffy. Sift 1 cup flour with salt, baking powder and soda. Combine with egg mixture; add nutmeg and vanilla. Add 3 cups flour gradually. Roll out; cut into desired shapes. Bake at 350 degrees about 6 minutes. Yield: 6 dozen.

Mrs. Harland Trumble
Papillion Grange, No. 401
Papillion, Nebraska

MAUDE'S SUGAR COOKIES

1 c. shortening
½ c. (firmly packed) brown sugar
1 lg. egg
1 tsp. vanilla
Sugar
2 c. flour
1 tsp. cream of tartar
1 tsp. soda
½ tsp. salt

Cream first 4 ingredients with ½ cup sugar until fluffy. Sift remaining ingredients together into creamed mixture. Mix until moderately stiff. Roll into small balls. Dip in additional sugar. Place on ungreased cookie sheet; press to flatten. Bake in 350-degree oven for 9 to 10 minutes.

Maude L. Griffith
Lincoln Grange, No. 395
Waldport, Oregon

GRANDMA PITTENGER'S SUGAR COOKIES

2 c. sugar
½ c. lard
½ c. butter
1 c. sour milk
2 eggs
4 c. flour
1 tsp. soda
1 tsp. baking powder
Dash of salt
¼ tsp. nutmeg
½ tsp. vanilla extract

Cream sugar, lard and butter together. Add sour milk and eggs. Sift together flour, soda, baking powder, salt and nutmeg. Add to creamed mixture; mix well. Add vanilla. Drop from teaspoon onto ungreased cookie sheet. Bake at 350-degrees for 15 minutes. Yield: 4 dozen.

Lori Judt
Richland Co., Olivesburg Grange, No. 2641
Mansfield, Ohio

OLD-FASHIONED SUGAR COOKIES

1½ c. shortening
Sugar
1 tsp. salt
3 tsp. vanilla extract
3 eggs
1½ tsp. soda
1½ c. buttermilk
4½ c. (about) flour

Cream shortening and 3 cups sugar; add salt, vanilla and eggs. Dissolve soda in buttermilk. Add to sugar mixture, alternately with enough flour to make stiff dough. Place on floured surface; roll out about ¼-inch thick. Cut cookies. Sprinkle with sugar. Bake in 375-degree oven for 12 to 15 minutes.

Mrs. Lillie Wolfe
Bell Township Grange, No. 2047
Mahaffey, Pennsylvania

OLD-FASHIONED DROP SUGAR COOKIES

½ c. shortening
½ c. margarine
2 c. sugar
3 eggs
1 c. milk
3½ to 4 c. flour
3 tsp. baking powder
Cinnamon-sugar

Cream shortening, margarine and sugar. Add eggs and milk. Blend in flour and baking powder. Drop from rounded teaspoon 2-inches apart onto greased or teflon cookie sheet. Bake at 375 degrees for 10 minutes or until golden brown. Sprinkle with cinnamon-sugar mixture. Yield: 3-4 dozen cookies.

Ruth Wanner
Honeybrook Grange, No. 1688
Narvon, Pennsylvania

STRAWBERRY ISLAND COOKIE

1½ c. sifted flour
½ tsp. soda
½ tsp. salt
¾ c. shortening
1 egg, separated
1 c. sugar
2 tbsp. pineapple juice
1 c. quick oats
⅔ c. strawberry jam
½ c. pineapple wedges

Sift dry ingredients together. Mix shortening, egg yolk, sugar and pineapple juice. Add to dry ingredients; beat until smooth. Stir in oats. Dough will be stiff. Shape into balls; place on baking sheet. Make a hollow in center of each. Glaze with beaten egg white. Place about 1 teaspoon jam in center of each ball. Top with small wedge of pineapple. Bake in 350-degree oven for 12 to 15 minutes. Yield: 4 or 5 dozen cookies.

Frances Goodger
Clearfield Grange, No. 1451
Eudora, Kansas

STRAWBERRY MERINGUE BARS

¾ c. shortening
Sugar
2 eggs, separated
1½ c. sifted flour
Strawberry or apricot preserves

Beat together shortening, ⅓ cup sugar and egg yolks. Add flour. Stir until thoroughly blended. Spread in ungreased 9 × 12-inch pan. Bake at 350 degrees for 20 minutes or until light brown. Spread with preserves. Beat egg whites until stiff. Add ½ cup sugar gradually. Continue beating until stiff peaks form. Spread carefully over preserves. Bake at 350 degrees for 25 minutes longer. Cool; cut into bars. Yield: 14 bars.

Irene M. Eaton
Kent Grange, No. 154
Kent, Connecticut

WALNUT AND DATE COOKIES

1½ c. (firmly packed) brown sugar
1 egg
1 tsp. vanilla extract
1 c. finely chopped walnuts
2 c. flour, sifted
½ c. shortening
½ lb. dates
Juice of 1 orange
1 tbsp. butter
1 tbsp. honey
Whole walnuts

Beat brown sugar and egg together. Add vanilla. Stir in chopped walnuts and flour. Knead in shortening. Form into rolls 1½-inch in diameter. Chill for 7 or 8 hours. Slice thin. Moisten dates with orange juice. Heat in saucepan. Stir in butter and honey. Spread mixture over cookies. Place whole walnut in center of cookie. Bake at 350 degrees until light brown. Yield: 3 dozen cookies.

Marjorie Wilcox, C.W.A.
Blue Mountain Grange, No. 263
Wells River, Vermont

LEFF KUCHEN

2 c. sorghum
1½ c. white sugar
1 c. margarine, melted
⅓ c. lemon juice
½ c. ground black walnuts
1 tsp. each ginger, allspice, nutmeg mace and cinnamon
½ tsp. cloves
1 tsp. soda
1 tsp. cream of tartar
Flour

Combine first 5 ingredients. Sift spices, soda and cream of tartar with 2 cups flour; add to sorghum mixture. Add additional flour gradually until dough is thick enough to roll. Dough is ready when palm of hand does not stick. Chill dough in covered container. Roll dough very thin with floured covered rolling pin on floured pastry cloth. Cut into fancy shapes. Decorate with colored sugars, nuts and candied fruit, if desired. Bake at 350 degrees for about 10 minutes until crisp. Dough can be stored for several weeks in airtight containers.

Jenny Grobusky, Director of Women's Activities
National Grange
Washington, D.C.

MERRY CHRISTMAS ITALIAN COOKIES

⅓ c. soft shortening
⅓ c. sugar
1 egg
⅔ c. honey
1 tsp. lemon or orange flavoring
2¾ c. sifted flour
1 tsp. soda
1 tsp. salt

Mix first 5 ingredients thoroughly. Blend flour, soda and salt together; stir in. Chill dough. Roll out to ¼-inch thickness. Cut into desired shapes. Place 1-inch apart on lightly greased baking sheet. Bake in preheated 375-degree oven for 8 to 10 minutes. Cool. Ice or decorate, as desired.

Mrs. Dorothy J. Caltagarone
Reynoldsville Grange, No. 1825
Reynoldsville, Pennsylvania

SCANDINAVIAN JELLY DROPS

1 c. butter
½ c. sugar
2 eggs, separated
2½ c. flour
½ tsp. salt
2 tsp. vanilla extract
Crushed nuts
Jelly

Cream butter and sugar. Add egg yolks; beat well. Sift flour and salt together. Add to creamed mixture. Add vanilla. Form into 1-inch balls. Dip in beaten egg whites; roll in crushed nuts. Use sugar-dipped thimble to press hole in cookie. Bake at 325 degrees for 20 minutes. Press hole in again when almost done. Fill with red and green jelly while still warm.

Joan Boyle
Millville Grange, No. 443
Palo Cedro, California

SWEDISH HEIRLOOM COOKIES

1 c. softened butter
Confectioner's sugar
½ tsp. salt
1¼ c. ground almonds
2 c. sifted flour
1 tbsp. vanilla extract

Cream butter and 1 cup confectioners' sugar. Add salt and almonds. Blend in flour; mix thoroughly. Add 1 tablespoon water and vanilla. Mix thoroughly with fork. Shape into balls or crescents, using 1 level tablespoon of dough for each cookie. Place on ungreased cookie sheet; flatten slightly. Bake at 325 degrees 12 to 15 minutes. Roll in additional confectioners' sugar while still warm.

> Rose Canning
> Wheat Ridge Grange, No. 155
> Wheat Ridge, Colorado

YUGOSLAVIA KIFLE

2 c. flour
1 pkg. dry yeast
½ c. butter, softened
2 eggs, separated
½ c. sour cream
Confectioners' sugar
1 c. chopped nuts
½ c. sugar
1 tsp. vanilla extract

Place flour in large bowl. Dissolve yeast in ¼ cup of warm water. Mix flour, yeast mixture and butter until crumbly and fine. Add egg yolks and sour cream; mix well. Form into ball; knead 5 to 10 minutes on floured surface. Divide dough into 3 balls. Wrap each in waxed paper or plastic wrap. Chill for 1 hour. Sprinkle confectioners' sugar generously on a flat surface. Roll each ball into 8-inch rounds. Cut in 8 pie-shaped pieces. Fold remaining ingredients into stiffly beaten egg whites. Fill each wedge with 1 teaspoon filling. Roll into crescent shapes. Bake at 375 degrees for about 25 minutes.

> Mrs. Ruby Stoops
> Highland Grange, No. 1771
> Norwich, Ohio

DEEP-DISH APPLE PIE

10 apples, peeled and sliced
½ c. sugar
1 tsp. cinnamon
1 c. sifted flour
½ c. (firmly packed) brown sugar
¼ tsp. salt
½ c. butter

Combine apples, sugar and ⅛ teaspoon cinnamon; stir to coat well. Spoon into buttered 2½-quart casserole. Combine flour, brown sugar, salt and ½ teaspoon cinnamon in bowl. Cut in butter with pastry blender. Sprinkle mixture over apples; pat down. Bake in 350-degree oven about 45 minutes or until juice bubbles around edge and topping is brown. May be served plain or with cream.

> Mrs. Marie Turley,
> Violet Grange, No. 1949
> Pickerington, Ohio

DRIED APPLE PIE

2 c. dried apples
½ c. sugar
1 tsp. allspice
1 tsp. cinnamon
1 recipe 2-crust pie pastry
3 tbsp. butter

Soak dried apples in water to cover overnight. Drain off water. Mix apples with sugar and spices. Line 8-inch pie pan with pastry. Add apple mixture. Dot with butter. Cover with top crust. Slash top in several places for ventilation. Bake in 350-degree oven for 1 hour or until crust is golden brown.

> Rhoda Hooper,
> Rohner Grange, No. 509
> Fortuna, California

NAKED APPLE PIE

1 egg
½ c. (firmly packed) brown sugar
¼ c. sugar
1 tsp. vanilla extract
Pinch of salt
½ c. sifted flour
1 tsp. baking powder
2 med. apples, pared and chopped
¼ c. chopped nuts

Beat egg in medium bowl. Add remaining ingredients. Spread in 9-inch pie pan. Bake at 350 degrees for 30 minutes.

> Lucy S. Briggs
> Huntingdon Co., Shavers Creek Grange, No. 353
> Petersburg, Pennsylvania

NORWEGIAN PIE

¾ c. sugar
½ c. flour
1 egg
1 tsp. baking powder
¼ tsp. salt
½ tsp. vanilla extract
1 c. diced apples
½ c. chopped nuts

Combine first 3 ingredients; mix well. Add next 3 ingredients; stir to mix. Fold in apples and nuts. Pour into greased 8-inch pie pan. Bake at 350 degrees for 30 minutes. Serve with whipped cream, if desired.

> Mildred W. Eames,
> Perry Grange, No. 1163
> Perry, New York

APPLE DUMPLINGS WITH SWEET-SOUR SAUCE

2 c. flour
1 tsp. salt
Margarine
½ c. milk
1½ c. sugar
2 tsp. cinnamon
¼ tsp. nutmeg
6 med. apples, pared and cored
¼ c. vinegar
2 tbsp. cornstarch
¼ tsp. allspice
1 tbsp. red cinnamon candies (opt.)

Combine flour and salt; cut in ⅔ cup margarine. Stir in milk just until flour is moistened. Place on lightly-floured board; roll into 18 × 12-inch rectangle. Cut into six 6-inch squares. Combine ¾ cup sugar, 1 teaspoon cinnamon and nutmeg. Place 1 apple on each pastry square. Fill cavities of apples with sugar mixture. Dot each with margarine. Moisten edges of squares with water. Bring opposite corners of pastry to center; seal edges. Place in ungreased 13 × 9 × 2-inch baking pan. Bake at 375 degrees for 35 minutes or until apples are tender. Combine 1½ cups water, vinegar and ¼ cup margarine in saucepan; heat until margarine is melted. Combine ¾ cup sugar, cornstarch, 1 teaspoon cinnamon and allspice. Stir into hot mixture along with red cinnamon candies. Cook over low heat, stirring until thickened. Serve hot over warm apple dumplings. Yield: 6 servings.

Photograph for this recipe on page 178.

BLENDER PIE

2 c. cold milk
½ c. sugar
4 eggs
2 tsp. vanilla extract
½ tsp. salt
½ c. flour
1 c. coconut
⅔ c. margarine

Put all ingredients in blender container. Blend 30 seconds on high speed. Pour into greased 9-inch pie pan. Bake at 350 degrees for 45 minutes. One fourth cup sugar substitute may be used for ½ the sugar.

Dorothy Harper,
Twanoh Grange, No. 1118
Belfair, Washington

FRESH BLACKBERRY PIE

Flour
½ tsp. salt
¾ c. shortening
3 tbsp. milk
4 c. fresh blackberries
1¼ c. sugar
2 tsp. lemon juice
1 tbsp. melted butter

Mix 2½ cups flour, salt and shortening. Add milk to make a soft dough. Divide in half; roll out ½ for bottom crust. Arrange in 9-inch pie pan. Combine blackberries, 3 tablespoons flour and sugar in bowl; mix. Add lemon juice; stir well. Pour into crust. Drizzle with butter. Roll out remaining half dough. Place over blackberries. Bake at 375 degrees for 40 minutes.

Mrs. Alice Menear
Bell Township Grange, No. 2047
Mahaffey, Pennsylvania

GLADYS' BUTTERSCOTCH PIE

1½ c. (firmly packed) brown sugar
½ c. cornstarch
2 tbsp. butter
3 egg yolks, beaten
⅛ tsp. salt
1 baked 8-in. pie shell

Boil brown sugar, cornstarch and 1½ cups water until thickened. Remove from heat. Add butter, egg yolks and salt. Pour in pie shell. Cover with 1 recipe of meringue. Bake in 350-degree oven for 25 minutes.

Gladys Myers
Murphy Grange, No. 735
Sligo, Pennsylvania

HELEN'S BUTTERSCOTCH PIE

1 c. (firmly packed) brown sugar
3 tbsp. (rounded) flour
Pinch of salt
2 eggs, separated
1½ c. milk
3 tbsp. butter or margarine
1 baked 9-in. pie shell

Combine first 3 ingredients. Mix egg yolks and ½ cup milk. Add to first mixture. Add remaining milk and butter. Cook in double boiler until thickened. Pour into pie shell. Top with 1 recipe of meringue.

Helen Spencer
Flowler Grange, No. 2545
Vienna, Ohio

BUTTERSCOTCH PIE

1 c. (firmly packed) brown sugar
¼ c. butter
2 egg yolks
3 to 5 tbsp. flour
2 c. milk
1 tsp. vanilla extract
1 baked 9-in. pie shell

Combine brown sugar, butter and ¼ cup water in saucepan. Boil until mixture waxes when dropped from spoon. Mix together egg yolks, flour, milk and vanilla. Pour slowly into boiling sugar mixture stirring constantly. Cook until thick. Pour into pie shell. Cover with 1 recipe of meringue.

Josephine C. Bristor, Sec.
Aleppo Township Grange, No 2054
Wind Ridge, Pennsylvania

Mrs. Blanche Montle
Lodi grange, No. 2430
Guysville, Ohio

MELLO-SCOTCH PIE

6 tbsp. flour
1 c. (firmly packed) brown sugar
2 eggs, separated
2 c. milk
¼ tsp. salt
2 tbsp. butter
½ tsp. vanilla extract
1 baked 9-in. pie shell
2 tsp. cornstarch
4 tbsp. sugar

Combine flour and brown sugar in bowl; mix well. Beat egg yolks in saucepan. Add flour mixture, 2 tablespoons water, milk and salt. Cook until thickened. Remove from heat. Add butter and vanilla. Cool. Pour into pie shell. Combine cornstarch with ⅛ cup cold water in small saucepan. Cook until transparent. Cool. Beat egg whites until stiff. Add sugar gradually, beating well after each addition. Add cornstarch mixture. Continue beating until stiff peaks form. Spread over pie filling. Bake at 350 degrees for 10 minutes or until meringue browns lightly.

Mrs. Gay D. Cree,
Carmichaels Grange, No. 1389
Carmichael, Pennsylvania

OPAL'S MELLOWSCOTCH PIE

Brown sugar
2 c. milk

4 tbsp. cornstarch
2 eggs, separated
2 tbsp. butter
1 tsp. vanilla extract
1 baked 9-in. pie shell

Combine 1 cup (firmly packed) brown sugar and 2 tablespoons water in saucepan. Cook over moderate heat to a thick syrup. Blend ¼ cup milk and cornstarch to a thin paste in separate saucepan. Add remaining milk. Add beaten egg yolks. Pour into hot syrup. Cook until thick and smooth, stirring constantly. Add butter and ½ teaspoon vanilla. Cool. Pour into pie shell. Beat egg whites until stiff and dry. Sift 4 tablespoons brown sugar. Add to egg whites, 1 tablespon at a time, beating well after each addition until mixture is stiff. Beat in ½ teaspoon vanilla. Pile meringue on filling. Bake at 325 degrees for 15 minutes or until firm and browned.

Opal Elrod,
Pekin Grange, No. 2378
Salem, Indiana

CANTALOUPE CHIFFON PIE

1½ c. finely crushed graham cracker crumbs
¼ c. butter, softened
1 cup sugar
1 med. cantaloupe, peeled
1 env. unflavored gelatin
3 eggs, separated
½ tsp. salt
¼ c. freshly squeezed lemon juice
1 c. heavy cream, whipped

Combine crumbs, butter and ¼ cup sugar; mix well. Press into 9-inch pie pan. Bake in preheated 375-degree oven for about 8 minutes. Cool. Shred finely or puree in blender half the cantaloupe or enough to make 1 cup pulp. Place in top of double boiler. Soften gelatin in pulp. Add slightly beaten egg yolks, ¼ cup sugar and salt. Cook over boiling water, stirring, until thickened. Add lemon juice; cool. Cut remaining cantaloupe into small cubes; add to cooled mixture. Beat egg whites until foamy. Beat in ½ cup sugar gradually until stiff but not dry. Fold meringue and half of whipped cream into cantaloupe mixture. Pour into crust. Decorate top with remaining whipped cream. Chill until firm.

Ruth Thames
Shive Grange, No. 1629
Hamilton, Texas

CHOCOLATE CREAM PIE

4 tbsp. cornstarch
Sugar
¼ tsp. salt
2 c. milk
2 sq. chocolate
2 eggs, separated
1 tsp. vanilla extract
1 baked 9-in. pie shell

Combine cornstarch, ½ cup sugar and salt. Add milk. Melt chocolate in top of double boiler. Add chocolate and slightly beaten egg yolks to milk mixture. Cook, stirring constantly, until mixture thickens. Add vanilla. Pour into pie shell. Place in 400 degree oven. Beat egg whites until foamy. Add 2 tablespoons sugar slowly, beating constantly until stiff peaks form. Remove pie from oven. Spread meringue on hot filling. Bake until meringue is delicately browned. Remove; cool.

Mrs. Alice H. Morton,
Freeport Grange, No. 2337
Freeport, Ohio

MOM'S CRUMB PIE

2½ c. all-purpose flour
1½ c. (firmly packed) brown sugar
½ c. butter or margarine, softened
½ tsp. nutmeg
Dash of salt
1 c. buttermilk
1 tsp. soda
½ tsp. baking powder

Mix first 5 ingredients into crumbs. Reserve 1 cup crumbs for top. Add remaining ingredients to first mixture. Pour into 2 greased 8-inch pie pans. Sprinkle reserved crumbs over top. Bake at 350 degrees for 25 to 30 minutes. Yield: 8 to 10 servings.

Ethel Peters
Centre Co., Half Moon Grange, No. 290
Port Matilda, Pennsylvania

EMMA'S CUSTARD PIE

6 eggs
⅔ c. sugar
2 tsp. vanilla extract
1 qt. milk
½ tsp. salt
1 unbaked 10-in. pie shell

Beat eggs until foamy. Add sugar and vanilla; beat well. Add milk and salt; mix well. Pour into pie shell. Bake in 425-degree oven for 15 minutes. Reduce heat to 350 degrees. Bake until knife inserted in center comes out clean.

Emma Jordan, C.W.A.
Old Town Grange, No. 522
Old Town, Maine

OLD-FASHIONED CUSTARD PIE

4 eggs, beaten
⅔ c. sugar
½ tsp. salt
¼ tsp. nutmeg
2 c. hot milk
1 tsp. vanilla extract
1 unbaked 9-in. pie shell

Combine first 6 ingredients; beat well. Pour into pie shell. Bake at 450 degrees for 15 minutes. Reduce heat to 350 degrees. Bake for 25 to 30 minutes or until silver knife inserted into pie 1-inch from outside edge comes out clean. Center will set when removed from oven.

Elizabeth Lackie,
Moosilauke Grange, No. 214
North Haverhill, New Hamsphire

LEMON MERINGUE PIE

1 unbaked 9-in. pie shell
Sugar
1 tbsp. flour
4 eggs, separated
Juice and grated rind of 1 lemon
¾ tsp. salt
1 c. milk

Refrigerate pie shell overnight. Combine 1 cup sugar and flour; mix well. Add 4 egg yolks and 2 egg whites; beat well. Stir in lemon juice, rind and salt; mix well. Add milk; mix. Cover. Chill overnight. Place filling in pie shell. Bake at 400 degrees for 10 minutes. Reduce heat to 325 degrees. Bake for 20 to 30 minutes or until knife inserted in center comes out clean. Beat 2 egg whites until stiff peaks form. Add 2 tablespoons sugar gradually. Spread over filling, touching crust. Bake at 350 degrees until lightly browned.

Margaret Wicks
Chinango Co., Coventry Grange, No. 1511
Green, New York

LEMON CAKE PIE

1 c. sugar
3 tbsp. flour
3 tbsp. butter
2 eggs, separated
Juice and grated rind of 1 lemon
1 c. milk
1 unbaked 9-in. pie shell

Cream sugar, flour and butter. Stir in beaten egg yolks. Add lemon juice and grated rind slowly. Add milk. Beat egg whites in separate bowl until stiff peaks form. Fold into lemon mixture. Pour into pie shell. Bake in 350-degree oven for 30 minutes or until custard is set.

Edith Zable
Stevenson Grange, No. 121,
Stevenson, Washington

ERMA'S LEMON PIE

Flour
½ tsp. baking powder
¾ tsp. salt
¼ c. shortening
Sugar
Juice and grated rind of 1 lemon
3 eggs, separated
1 c. milk
1 tbsp. butter

Combine 1½ cups flour, baking powder and ½ teaspoon salt in bowl. Cut in shortening until mixture resembles cornmeal. Add cold water, 1 tablespoon at a time, mixing lightly, until mixture cleans the bowl. Roll out; fit into 9-inch pie pan. Bake at 375 degrees for 15 minutes or until lightly browned. Combine 1 cup sugar, 3 tablespoons flour, ¼ teaspoon salt, lemon juice and rind in bowl. Add a small amount of water, if necessary, to make a paste. Add egg yolks; stir well. Place milk and butter in saucepan. Bring to a boil; add flour mixture. Cook, stirring constantly, until thickened. Turn into pie shell. Beat egg whites until soft peaks form. Add 3 to 6 tablespoons sugar gradually, beating well after each addition until stiff peaks form. Spread on lemon filling. Bake in 325-degree oven for 12 to 18 minutes or until lightly browned.

Erma F. Mason
Warren Pond Grange, No. 47
Alstead, New Hamsphire

MINCEMEAT CHIFFON PIE

1⅛ c. graham cracker crumbs
Sugar

¼ c. butter, melted
⅛ tsp. salt
1 tbsp. unflavored gelatin
2 eggs, separated
1 c. milk
1 c. whipping cream, whipped
1 c. mincemeat
2 tbsp. grated orange rind

Combine crumbs and 2 tablespoons sugar; stir in butter. Press mixture firmly onto bottom and sides of buttered 9-inch pie plate, building up sides slightly. Bake in 350 degree oven for 5 minutes. Cool on wire rack. Combine ¼ cup sugar, salt and gelatin. Beat egg yolks and milk together. Add to gelatin mixture. Heat over low heat, stirring constantly, until gelatin is dissolved. Chill until mixture mounds slightly. Beat egg whites until soft peaks form. Add ¼ cup sugar gradually, beating until stiff peaks form. Fold in gelatin mixture. Fold in whipped cream, mincemeat and orange rind. Turn into pie shell. Chill 4 hours or until set.

Dorothy Willard
Navy Grange, No. 495
Montpelier, Vermont

MOLASSES-COCONUT CUSTARD PIE

1 c. (firmly packed) brown sugar
3 tbsp. flour or cornstarch
1 egg, beaten
½ tsp. soda
½ c. cream
¾ c. milk
1 tbsp. butter
1 c. molasses
1 c. shredded coconut
1 unbaked 9-in. pie shell

Combine first 8 ingredients in large mixer bowl. Beat until smooth. Stir in coconut. Pour into pie shell. Bake at 375 degrees for 30 to 40 minutes.

Jane Teichler
Virginville Grange, No. 1832
Kutytown, Pennsylvania

FRESH PEACH PIE

1 c. sugar
3 tbsp. cornstarch
1 tbsp. butter
6 or 7 fresh peaches, peeled
1 baked 9-in. pie shell
Whipped cream

Combine sugar and cornstarch in saucepan. Add ½ cup water and butter. Bring to a boil. Mash 3 peaches; add to syrup. Reduce heat; simmer until thickened. Cool. Slice remaining peaches into pie shell. Pour syrup mixture over sliced peaches. Chill. Top with whipped cream.

Mrs. Joyce L. Reiner
York Co., Eureka Grange, No. 1915
Dillsburg, Pennsylvania

PEACH COBBLER PIE

¼ c. butter or margarine
Sugar
1 c. flour
2 tsp. baking powder
¼ tsp. salt
½ c. milk
Canned peaches

Cream butter and ½ cup sugar together. Sift flour, baking powder and salt together. Add to sugar mixture. Add milk; mix well. Pour batter into greased pie pan or dish. Drain, reserving juice from fruit. Place fruit on top of batter. Sprinkle ¾ cup sugar over fruit. Pour juice over cobbler. Bake at 375 degrees for 45 minutes. Batter will rise and form crust over fruit. Serve with ice cream or whipped cream.

Jane Ring Eudy
Old Richmond Grange
Pfafftown, North Carolina

PEACH UPSIDE-DOWN PIE

2 tbsp. soft butter
⅔ c. toasted sliced almonds or pecan halves
Brown sugar
1 receipe 2-crust pie pastry
5 c. sliced fresh peaches
2 tbsp. lemon juice
¾ c. sugar
2 tbs. tapioca
⅛ tsp. nutmeg
⅛ tsp. cinnamon
¼ tsp. almond extract

Line 9-inch pie pan with 12-inch square foil, letting excess hang over edge. Spread with 2 tablespoons butter. Press almonds and ⅓ cup (firmly packed) brown sugar into butter. Fit bottom crust into pie pan over nuts and brown sugar. Combine sliced peaches, lemon juice, sugar, ¼ cup (firmly packed) brown sugar, tapioca, nutmeg, cinnamon and almond extract. Pour into pie shell. Cover with top crust. Seal, flute and prick with fork. Brush lightly with milk. Bake in preheated 450-degree oven for 10 minutes. Reduce heat to 375 degrees. Bake 35 to 40 minutes longer. Cool thoroughly. Turn upside down on serving plate. Remove foil.

Dorris Gibson, C.W.A.
Plumas-Sierra Pomona Grange, No. 18
Quincy, California

PEANUT BUTTER PIE

½ c. peanut butter
1 c. confectioners' sugar
2 c. milk, scalded
1 tbsp. butter
⅔ c. sugar
¼ c. cornstarch
2 egg yolks, beaten
2 tsp. vanilla extract
1 baked 9-in. pie shell

Combine peanut butter and confectioners' sugar. Mix until blended. Place half the mixture in bottom of pie shell. Combine milk, butter, sugar and cornstarch in saucepan. Cook until thickened over low heat. Add egg yolks and vanilla slowly, stirring constantly. Pour on peanut butter mixture while still hot. Top with 1 recipe meringue. Sprinkle remaining peanut butter crumbs on top. Cool.

Mrs. Chester W. Hill, C.W.A.
Cosh. Co., Plainfield Grange, No. 1326
West Lafayette, Ohio

PECAN TASSIES

1 3-oz. package cream cheese, softened
Butter or margarine, softened
1 c. sifted all-purpose flour
1 egg
¾ c. (firmly packed) brown sugar
1 tsp. vanilla extract
Dash of salt
⅔ c. coarsely broken pecans

Blend cream cheese and ½ cup butter together. Stir in flour. Chill 1 hour. Shape into 2 dozen 1-inch balls. Place in ungreased 1¾-inch muffin pans. Press dough evenly against bottoms and sides of muffin cups. Beat together egg, brown sugar, 1 tablespoon butter, vanilla and salt just until smooth. Divide half the pecans among pastry-lined pans. Add egg mixture; top with remaining pecans. Bake in 325-degree oven for 25 minutes or until pastry is lightly browned. Cool before removing from pans. Yield: 2 dozen.

Judy McLure
Blue Mt. Grange, No. 263
Wells River, Vermont

PECAN PIE

½ c. melted butter or margarine
1 c. sugar
1 c. light corn syrup
4 eggs, beaten
1 tsp. vanilla extract
¼ tsp. salt
1 unbaked 9-in. pastry shell
1 c. chopped pecans

Combine butter, sugar and corn syrup. Cook over low heat, stirring constantly, until sugar is dissolved. Cool. Add eggs, vanilla and salt; blend well. Pour filling into pastry shell. Top with pecans. Bake at 325 degrees for 50 to 55 minutes.

Mrs. James L. Reeves, Sr.
Leicester Grange, No. 1042
Leicester, North Carolina

MOM'S OLD-FASHIONED PUMPKIN PIE

2 eggs
1 c. (firmly packed) brown sugar
1 tsp. cinnamon
1 tsp. nutmeg
½ tsp. ginger
½ tsp. salt
2 c. milk and cream
1½ c. strained pumpkin
1 unbaked 9-in. pie shell

Beat eggs until light. Continue beating while adding brown sugar. Add next 6 ingredients; mix well. Pour into pie shell. Bake in 350-degree oven until knife inserted in center comes out clean.

Joan Boyle
Millville Grange, No. 443
Palo Cedro, California

PUMPKIN-PECAN PIE

3 eggs, slightly beaten
1 c. pumpkin
1 c. sugar
1 c. dark corn syrup
1 tsp. vanilla extract
½ tsp. cinnamon
½ tsp. salt
2 tbsp. melted butter
1 unbaked 9-in. pie shell
½ c. pecans

Combine first 8 ingredients in bowl; mix well. Pour into pie shell. Top with pecans. Bake at 350 degrees for 40 to 50 minutes.

Mrs. Lowell L. Smith
Greeley Grange, No. 1741
Minerva, Ohio

RASPBERRY PIE

1 recipe 2-crust pie pastry
3 c. fresh raspberries
1 c. sugar
2 tbsp. cornstarch or 4 tbsp. flour
1 tbsp. butter
Dash of salt

Line pie pan with half the pastry. Combine remaining ingredients. Pour into crust. Top with remaining pastry. Bake at 400 degrees for 45 minutes.

Mrs. Carolee J. Kissel
Richland Co., Union Grange, No. 1648
Shelby, Ohio

GOLDEN RHUBARB PIE

2 eggs, slightly beaten
1 c. sugar
2 tbsp. flour
1 tbsp. orange juice
½ tsp. grated orange rind
2 c. rhubarb, cut into ½-in. pieces
1 recipe 2-crust pie pastry
1 tbsp. margarine or butter

Combine first 5 ingredients in bowl; mix well. Add rhubarb; mix. Pour into pastry shell. Dot with margarine. Cover with strips of pastry in crisscross pattern. Bake in preheated 450-degree oven for 10 minutes. Reduce heat to 350 degrees. Bake 30 minutes longer.

Aldena M. Cornella
Kootenai Grange, No. 312
Kootenai, Idaho

RHUBARB AMBROSIA PIE

3 c. finely cut rhubarb
1 c. crushed pineapple, drained
Sugar
4 tbsp. cornstarch
2 eggs, separated
1 unbaked 9-in. pie crust
1 tbsp. brown sugar
1 tsp. cinnamon
¼ c. melted margarine
½ c. coconut

Combine rhubarb, pineapple, 1¼ cups sugar, 3 tablespoons cornstarch and beaten egg yolks. Spoon into crust. Combine brown sugar, cinnamon and 1 tablespoon cornstarch. Sprinkle over rhubarb mixture. Drizzle with margarine. Bake in 375-degree oven for 40 minutes. Remove from oven. Beat egg whites and 3 tablespoons sugar until stiff peaks form. Spread over pie. Sprinkle coconut over meringue. Bake until golden brown.

Ethel Hidy
Madison Goodwill Grange
Bloomingburg, Ohio

RHUBARB-RAISIN PIE

1 egg, well beaten
1 c. sugar
3 tbsp. flour
¼ tsp. salt
½ c. chopped raisins
Pat of butter
3 c. finely cut rhubarb
1 recipe 2-crust pie pastry

Combine first 6 ingredients in heavy saucepan. Cook over low heat, stirring constantly, until butter melts. Add rhubarb; mix well. Pour into unbaked pie shell. Top with crust. Bake at 450 degrees for 10 minutes. Reduce heat to 350 degres. Bake 30 minutes longer.

Carolyn Small
Litchfield Grange, No. 127
Gardiner, Maine

STRAWBERRY WHIPPED CREAM PIE

4 c. strawberries
2 c. sweetened whipped cream
1 9-inch baked pie shell
2 to 3 tbsp. honey
Slivered toasted almonds

Slice 2 cups strawberries; fold into whipped cream. Turn into pie shell; spread evenly. Halve remaining strawberries; arrange, cut side down, on whipped cream filling. Drizzle honey over strawberries. Sprinkle with almonds.

Photograph for this recipe on page 186.

DOROTHY'S STRAWBERRY PIE

1½ c. sugar
¼ c. cornstarch
1 sm. package strawberry gelatin
1 qt. strawberries
1 baked 9-in. pie shell

Combine sugar, cornstarch and 1½ cups water. Cook over low heat until thick and clear. Remove

from heat. Stir in gelatin. Cool. Fold in strawberries. Pour into pastry shell. May add topping.

Mrs. Dorothy DeHoff
Mahoning Co., Dublin Grange, No. 1409
Canfield, Ohio

ESTELLA'S STRAWBERRY PIE

3 tbsp. (rounded) cornstarch
1 c. sugar
2 tbsp. corn syrup
3 tbsp. strawberry gelatin
Red food coloring
1 qt. strawberries
1 baked 9-in. pie shell
Whipped cream

Combine cornstarch and sugar. Blend in corn syrup and 1 cup water. Cook, stirring constantly, until thick and clear. Remove from heat. Stir in gelatin and a few drops of food coloring. Cool. Place strawberries in pie shell. Pour cornstarch mixture over berries. Let pie set overnight. Do not refrigerate as this does something to the glaze. Top with whipped cream.

Mrs. Estella L. Cagg, C.W.A.
Athens Co., York Grange, No. 2436
Nelsonville, Ohio

GLAZED FRESH STRAWBERRY PIE

1 qt. strawberries, washed and hulled
1 c. sugar
3 tbsp. cornstarch
Few drops of red food coloring
1 baked 10-in. pie shell

Select 1 cup small berries. Place in blender with ⅔ cup water. Process until pureed. Pour into 1½-quart saucepan. Stir in ⅓ cup water, sugar and cornstarch. Bring to boiling point over medium heat, stirring constantly. Boil for 2 minutes. Remove from heat; cool. Stir in food coloring. Cool. Arrange whole berries in pie shell with tips up to cover bottom. Pour ¾ of the glaze over berries. Arrange second row of berries, tips up. Pour remaining glaze over berries. Cool; chill. Serve with Cool Whip or ice cream.

Mrs. Frances Ratcliffe
Flora Grange, No. 1762
Oregon, Illinois

STRAWBERRY GLAZED PIE

1⅓ c. sugar
¼ c. cornstarch
⅛ tsp. salt
1 tbsp. lemon juice
Red food coloring
1 qt. strawberries, washed, drained and hulled
1 baked 9-in. pastry shell

Bring sugar and ½ cup water to boiling point in saucepan over medium heat. Dissolve cornstarch in ¾ cup cold water. Add to syrup mixture. Cook, stirring occasionally, about 10 minutes over low heat or until clear. Blend in salt, lemon juice and enough food coloring to produce light red shade. Pour glaze over strawberries; mix gently. Cool. Place in pie shell. Garnish with whipped cream.

Alma Lewis
Washington Grange, No. 521
South Charleston, West Virginia

OLD-TIME SUGAR-CREAM PIE

1 c. sugar
⅔ c. (firmly packed) brown sugar
¼ c. flour
⅛ tsp. salt
1 c. light cream
½ tsp. vanilla extract
1 unbaked 9-in. pie shell
Nutmeg

Combine sugars, flour and salt thoroughly. Stir in 1 cup boiling water slowly. Add cream and vanilla; stir well. Pour mixture into pie shell. Sprinkle top with nutmeg. Bake at 450 degrees for 10 minutes. Reduce heat to 350 degrees. Bake 35 to 40 minutes longer or until bubbly in center.

Mrs. Mary Barnes
Pleasant Grange, No. 2124
DeGraff, Ohio

VINEGAR PIE

2 eggs, separated
½ c. cider vinegar
1 tbsp. melted butter
Sugar
⅓ c. flour
½ tsp. lemon extract
1 baked 9-in. pie shell

Combine egg yolks, 1½ cups water, vinegar and butter in saucepan. Mix 1¼ cups sugar and flour. Stir into egg mixture, mixing well. Cook in double boiler over low heat, stirring constantly, until mixture is thickened. Remove from heat. Add lemon extract; mix well. Pour into cooled pie shell. Beat the 2 egg whites until soft peaks form. Add 4 tablespoons sugar gradually, beating constantly, until stiff peaks form. Spread on pie filling. Bake in 350-degree oven for 12 to 15 minutes or until lightly browned. Cool.

Mrs. Mendal Jordan
Meigs Co., Pomona Grange, No. 46
Albany, Ohio

WALNUT PIE

3 egg whites
½ tsp. baking powder
1 c. sugar
1 c. graham cracker crumbs
1 c. chopped walnuts
1 tsp. vanilla extract
Whipped cream

Beat egg whites with baking powder until stiff. Add sugar gradually while beating. Fold in graham cracker crumbs and walnuts. Stir in vanilla. Pour into greased 9-inch pie pan. Bake in 350 degree oven for 25 minutes. Serve topped with whipped cream.

Arlene R. Anderson
Crescent Grange, No. 1123
Port Angeles, Washington

ZWIEBACK PIE

1 box Zwieback, toasted and ground
½ c. butter, softened
2½ c. sugar
1 tsp. cinnamon
4 c. milk
4 tbsp. flour
6 eggs, separated

Reserve ½ cup Zwieback crumbs for topping. Melt butter and ½ cup sugar together. Add crumbs and cinnamon. Spread in two 9-inch pie pans. Combine milk, flour, egg yolks and 1½ cups sugar in saucepan. Cook until thickened. Pour over crumb mixture. Beat egg whites, adding ½ cup sugar gradually, until stiff peaks form. Spread over filling. Sprinkle with reserved crumbs. Bake at 300 degrees for 20 minutes.

Margaret Thomson
El Camino Grange, No. 462
Gerber, California

PIE CRUST

2 c. flour
1 tsp. salt
⅔ c. salad oil

Combine flour and salt. Add salad oil and 4 tablespoons cold water. Mix lightly until dough holds together. Lay half the dough on 1 piece Saran Wrap. Lay another piece of Saran Wrap directly over dough. Roll out with rolling pin. Remove top piece of Wrap. Turn rolled dough into pie pan. Remove second piece of Wrap; form edge on crust. Repeat process with second half of dough. Yield: 2 pie crusts.

Patricia Fitch, C.W.A.
Olivesburg Grange, No. 2461
Ashland, Ohio

BROWN SUGAR ANGEL FOOD

1½ c. egg whites
2 tsp. vanilla extract
1½ tsp. cream of tartar
1 tsp. salt
2 c. (firmly packed) brown sugar
1¼ c. sifted cake flour

Beat egg whites with vanilla, cream of tartar, and salt until soft peaks form. Sift 1 cup brown sugar over egg whites. Beat until stiff peaks form. Sift remaining brown sugar with flour. Fold into egg whites. Pour into ungreased 10-inch tube pan. Bake at 350 degrees for 45 to 50 minutes.

Mrs. Alice F. Shutts
Clinton Co., Adams Township Grange
Martinsville, Ohio

CARAMEL-NUT ANGEL FOOD CAKE

1½ c. sugar
1 c. cake flour
1 tsp. cream of tartar
12 egg whites
¼ tsp. salt
1 tsp. maple flavoring
⅔ c. English walnuts

Brown ½ cup sugar in heavy frypan until caramelized. Add ½ cup water. Let boil to thin custard consistency. Cool. Sift flour, remaining sugar and cream of tartar together 7 times. Beat egg whites with salt until stiff but not dry. Add flavoring. Fold in flour mixture with 3 tablespoons caramelized syrup and walnuts, a small amount at a time; mix

well. Pour into ungreased tube pan. Bake at 300 degrees for 1 hour. Yield: 12 servings.

Mrs. Alta Van Cleave
Buena Grange, No. 836
Zillah, Washington

CHOCOLATE ANGEL FOOD CAKE

12 egg whites
1 tsp. cream of tartar
1 tsp. baking powder
1½ c. sugar
1½ c. cake flour
5 tbsp. cocoa
¼ tsp. salt
2 tsp. vanilla extract

Beat egg whites until foamy. Add cream of tartar and baking powder. Beat until stiff. Sift sugar 4 times. Sift flour and cocoa 4 times. Add sugar slowly to egg whites, beating well after each addition. Fold flour and cocoa gently into egg whites. Add salt and vanilla. Pour in ungreased tube pan. Bake at 350 degrees for 50 minutes on lowest oven rack. Cool upside down before removing from pan.

Madaline Horman
Huntingdon Co., Shanes Creek Grange, No. 353
Alexandria, Pennsylvania

QUICK-BAKE ANGEL FOOD CAKE

1½ c. egg whites
½ tsp. salt
1½ tsp. desired flavoring
1½ tsp. cream of tartar
1½ c. sugar
1 c. cake flour

Combine first 3 ingredients in large mixer bowl. Sprinkle cream of tartar over all. Beat until soft peaks form. Add 1¼ cups sugar, 1 tablespoon at a time, beating well after each addition. Sift flour and ¼ cup sugar together. Fold into egg whites with a fork, 1 tablespoon at a time. Pour into ungreased tube pan. Bake in a preheated 425-degree oven for 10 to 15 minutes or until brown. Turn off heat. Let stand in oven 20 to 25 minutes longer; do not open oven door. Yield: 12-15 servings.

Mrs. Sam Bry
Friendship Grange, No. 2404
Auburn, Indiana

MY MOTHER'S APPLE-BUTTER CAKE

½ c. butter, softened
1 c. sugar
4 eggs, beaten
2½ c. flour
1 tsp. soda
1 tsp. cinnamon
1 tsp. cloves
4 tbsp. sour milk
1 c. apple butter

Cream butter and sugar. Add eggs; mix thoroughly. Sift flour; measure and sift again with soda and spices. Add to creamed mixture alternately with the sour milk. Add apple butter; blend well. Pour into greased pan. Bake at 350 degrees for 45 minutes.

Mrs. Merle U. Fox
Salem Grange, No. 964
Falls Creek, Pennsylvania

APPLESAUCE FRUITCAKE

2 c. sugar
½ c. shortening, softened
3 eggs, beaten
1½ c. unsweetened applesauce
2½ c. flour
¼ tsp. baking powder
1¼ tsp. soda
1 tsp. salt
¾ tsp. cinnamon
½ tsp. each cloves and allspice
1 c. each walnuts, raisins and candied fruit

Cream sugar and shortening. Add eggs. Stir in applesauce. Combine dry ingredients, add to creamed mixture. Add walnuts, raisins and candied fruit. Pour into 4½ × 8-inch loaf pan. Bake in 350-degree oven for 40 to 45 minutes or until cake tests done. If sweetened canned applesauce is used, cut sugar to 1¼ cups. Yield: 10 servings.

Mrs. W. O. Preston
Melrose Grange, No. 434
Roseburg, Oregon

FRESH APPLE CAKE

2 c. coarsely chopped apples
2 c. sugar
¾ c. butter
1 egg, beaten
1½ c. sifted all-purpose flour
1 tsp. soda
½ tsp. salt
1 tsp. cinnamon

½ tsp. nutmeg
½ tsp. allspice
½ c. chopped nuts
½ c. washed raisins, drained
Orange juice made from concentrate
½ c. evaporated milk
Vanilla to taste

Place apples into large bowl. Pour 1 cup sugar over apples; mix. Let stand 10 minutes. Add ½ cup melted butter; mix well. Add egg. Sift dry ingredients; add to apple mixture. Stir in nuts and raisins. Add enough orange juice to make mixture thin. Pour into an 8 or 9-inch greased pan. Bake at 350 degrees for 55 minutes. Combine 1 cup sugar, ¼ cup butter and evaporated milk in saucepan. Bring to boiling point, stirring constantly. Remove from heat; add vanilla. Spoon over warm or cold cake.

Mrs. Bea Gooden, D.W.A.
Delaware State Grange
Woodside, Delaware

STIR-AND-BAKE-IN-PAN APPLE CAKE

1 c. hot coffee
1 c. raisins
2 c. all-purpose flour
1 c. sugar
1 tsp. cinnamon
1 tsp. salt
½ tsp. cloves
1 tsp. soda
2 tsp. baking powder
1 c. peeled chopped apples
¾ c. chopped nuts
1 tbsp. vanilla extract
2 tbsp. vinegar
6 tbsp. oil
2 eggs

Pour hot coffee over raisins. Let stand until raisins plump. Drain, reserving coffee. Sift dry ingredients into 9 × 13-inch baking pan. Stir apple, nuts and raisins into flour mixture. Make 3 grooves in mixture. Place vanilla in 1 groove, vinegar in the second, oil in the third. Break eggs over this mixture. Pour reserved coffee over cake batter; stir well. Bake at 350 degrees for 35 minutes or until cake tests done.

Agnes Duerfeldt
Tillamook Co., Kilchis Grange, No. 800
Tillamook, Oregon

JANE'S APPLE CAKE

1½ c. vegetable oil
2 c. sugar
3 eggs
1 tsp. soda
1 tsp. salt
3 c. flour
1 tsp. cinnamon
1 tsp. vanilla extract
3 c. apples, chopped
1 c. chopped nuts
1½ c. (firmly packed) brown sugar
½ c. butter or margarine
1 c. evaporated milk

Blend oil, sugar and eggs. Sift together soda, salt, flour and cinnamon. Add to first mixture; mix well. Add vanilla, apples and nuts. Pour into well-greased and floured tube pan. Bake in 325-degree oven for 1 hour and 15 minutes. Combine last 3 ingredients in saucepan. Heat. Pour over cooled cake.

Jane Ring Eudy
Old Richmond Grange
Pfafftown, North Carolina

OHIO FRESH APPLE CAKE

3½ c. peeled apples, coarsely chopped
2 c. sugar
3 c. flour
2 tsp. soda
1 tsp. salt
½ tsp. nutmeg
1 tsp. cinnamon
½ tsp. allspice
1 c. butter, melted
2 eggs, beaten
1 c. raisins
1 c. chopped walnuts
Confectioners' sugar

Place apples in large mixer bowl. Add sugar; let stand 10 minutes. Sift dry ingredients together. Blend butter and eggs into apple mixture. Add dry ingredients. Mix well. Fold in raisins and walnuts. Spread in a well-greased and floured 9 × 13-inch baking pan. Bake in 350-degree oven for 50 to 55 minutes. Cool in pan for 10 minutes. Remove from pan; cool thoroughly on wire rack. Sprinkle with confectioners' sugar. Yield: 16 servings.

Mrs. Dorothy Stewart, C.W.A.
Victory Grange, No. 1592
Jackson, Ohio

AVOCADO LOAF CAKE

¾ c. shortening
2 c. sugar

3 eggs
2 c. sifted all-purpose flour
⅓ c. cocoa
¾ tsp. each allspice, cinnamon and salt
1½ tsp. soda
1½ c. mashed avocado
¾ c. buttermilk
½ c. each chopped dates and walnuts
¾ c. raisins
Corn syrup
Pecans

Cream shortening. Add sugar gradually; beat until light and fluffy. Add eggs one at a time, beating well after each addition. Sift dry ingredients together; reserving ¼ cup mixture. Fold dry ingredients into creamed mixture alternately with avocado and buttermilk. Mix dates, walnuts and raisins with reserved flour; add to batter. Pour into 2 greased brown paper lined loaf pans. Bake at 350 degrees for 1 hour and 5 minutes. Brush top with corn syrup, sprinkle with pecans. Broil until bubbly, if desired. This cake freezes well.

Betty Conroy
Mission Grange, No. 767
Riverside, California

SOUTH SEAS AVOCADO CAKE

2 c. sugar
⅔ c. butter
3 eggs
2 med. avocados, mashed
2⅔ c. cake flour
¾ tsp. each allspice, cinnamon and salt
1½ tsp. soda
¾ c. buttermilk
¾ c. white seedless raisins
½ c. chopped dates
¾ c. chopped nuts

Cream sugar and butter. Add eggs one at a time, beating well after each addition. Add avocado; mix thoroughly. Sift flour, spices and salt together. Dissolve soda in buttermilk. Add buttermilk and dry ingredients alternately to creamed mixture. Mix well; stir in fruits and nuts. Pour into ungreased tube pan. Bake at 300 degrees for 1 hour or until cake tests done. Serve with whipped cream, if desired.

Luella Crandall
Ramona Grange, No. 632
El Cajon, California

BANANA CAKE SUPREME

½ c. shortening
1½ c. sugar
2 eggs, beaten
2 c. flour

½ tsp. salt
1 tsp. baking powder
¾ tsp. soda
¼ c. sour milk
1 tsp. vanilla extract
1 c. mashed bananas

Cream shortening and sugar. Add eggs; beat. Sift dry ingredients together; add to creamed mixture alternately with sour milk, vanilla and bananas. Mix well. Pour into greased and floured 9 × 13-inch pan. Bake at 375 degrees for 30 to 35 minutes. Cool. Frost with peanut butter frosting.

Huena M. Wetmore
Hamden Grange, No. 99
Hamden, Connecticut

BROWN SUGAR CAKE

2 c. flour
2 c. (firmly packed) brown sugar
½ c. shortening
½ c. chopped nuts
1 egg, beaten
1 c. sour milk
1 tsp. soda
½ tsp. salt
1 tsp. vanilla extract

Combine first 4 ingredients; mix until crumbly. Set aside 1 cup of mixture. Place remaining mixture in mixer bowl. Add remaining ingredients. Mix until well blended. Pour into 8 × 8-inch baking pan. Spread reserved mixture on top. Bake at 400 degrees for 35 minutes. Serve with whipped cream.

Marie Bush,
DuBois Grange, No. 808
DuBois, Pennsylvania

BARB'S NUTRITIONAL GOODY CAKE

1½ c. whole wheat flour
½ c. soy flour
2 tsp. cinnamon
½ tsp. salt
2½ tsp. soda
2 c. grated carrots
1 c. crushed pineapple, drained
½ c. chopped nuts
½ c. ground sesame seed
3½ oz. coconut
3 eggs
¾ c. oil
¾ c. buttermilk
3 c. sugar
½ c. butter
1 tsp. corn syrup

Combine flours, cinnamon and salt with 2 teaspoons soda. Mix next 5 ingredients together. Beat

eggs, oil and buttermilk with 2 cups sugar. Combine carrot mixture with egg mixture. Add flour mixture; beat well. Pour into well-greased tube pan. Bake at 350 degrees for 1 hour. Place remaining ingredients in saucepan. Cook for 5 minutes; do not boil. Cool cake 10 minutes. Remove from pan. Punch tiny holes in top. Pour sauce over cake.

Agnes Stewart
Gardner, Kansas

BUTTERMILK WHITE CAKE

¾ c. shortening
1½ c. sugar
2¼ c. sifted cake flour
½ tsp. salt
1 tsp. baking powder
½ tsp. soda
1 c. buttermilk
1 tsp. each vanilla extract and lemon extract
4 egg whites

Cream shortening with sugar. Combine all dry ingredients; add to creamed mixture alternately with buttermilk. Beat until smooth. Stir in egg whites, one at a time, beating well after each addition. Add flavorings. Pour into 2 greased 9-inch layer cake pans. Bake at 350 degrees for 30 minutes. Frost as desired.

Emma Martin
Neighborhood Grange, No. 891
Mica, Wisconsin

CARROT-PINEAPPLE BUNDT CAKE

3 c. sifted cake flour
2 c. sugar
2 tsp. cinnamon
1½ tsp. salt
1 tsp. baking powder
1 8¾ oz. can crushed pineapple
3 eggs, beaten
1½ c. salad oil
2 tsp. vanilla extract
2 c. grated carrots
1½ c. finely chopped nuts

Combine first 5 ingredients in large bowl. Drain pineapple, reserving juice. Add juice to dry mixture; mix well. Add eggs, oil and vanilla. Beat for 3 minutes. Stir in pineapple, carrots and nuts. Pour into greased and lightly floured bundt pan. Bake at 325 degrees for about 1 hour and 30 minutes. Cool in pan 10 minutes. Remove from pan. Good with cream cheese icing.

Mrs. Marion Schilliger, Home Ec. Chm.
Delaware Co., Ashley Grange
Ashley, Ohio

CHARLOTTE'S CARROT CAKE

4 eggs
1⅓ c. salad oil
2 c. grated carrots
2 c. sugar
2 c. flour
3 tsp. cinnamon
1 tsp. salt
2 tsp. soda
1 tsp. baking powder
1 8-oz. package cream cheese, softened
1 stick margarine, softened
1 box confectioners' sugar
2 tsp. vanilla extract
½ c. drained crushed pineapple
½ c. chopped nuts

Mix eggs, oil, carrots and sugar. Beat 1 minute. Add next 5 ingredients. Beat 2 minutes longer. Pour into three 8-inch cake pans. Bake at 350 degrees for 30 minutes or until cake tests done. Cool. Mix cream cheese and margarine. Add confectioners' sugar; mix well. Add vanilla, pineapple and nuts. Frost cake when cool.

Charlotte Marcellus
Petries' Corners Grange, No. 561
Lowille, New York

GOLDEN GATE CARROT CAKE

2 c. all-purpose flour
2 tsp. soda
2 tsp. cinnamon
½ tsp. salt
3 eggs
¾ c. vegetable oil
¾ c. buttermilk
2 c. sugar
2 tsp. vanilla extract
1 8-oz. can crushed pineapple, drained
4 c. grated carrots
1 c. chopped walnuts
1 c. grated coconut
1½ c. golden raisins, coarsely chopped
Buttermilk Glaze

Sift flour, soda, cinnamon and salt together. Beat next 5 ingredients together. Blend well. Add to dry ingredients; mix thoroughly. Stir in pineapple, carrots, walnuts, coconut and raisins. Pour into greased and floured 9 × 13-inch pan. Bake at 350 degrees for 55 minutes or until cake tests done. Pour Buttermilk Glaze over hot cake until it is absorbed.

Buttermilk Glaze

1 c. sugar
½ tsp. soda
½ c. buttermilk
1 tsp. light corn syrup
1 stick butter or margarine
1 tsp. vanilla extract

Mix sugar, soda, buttermilk, corn syrup and butter in saucepan. Bring to a boil; boil for 5 minutes. Remove from heat; add vanilla.

Mrs. Wm. J. McCarthy
Hancock Co., Eagle Grange, No. 2726
Findlay, Ohio

14-CARAT CAKE

2 c. flour
2 tsp. baking powder
1½ tsp. soda
1 tsp. salt
2 tsp. cinnamon
2 c. sugar
1½ c. oil
4 eggs, beaten
2 c. grated carrots
1 8½-oz. can crushed pineapple, drained
1 c. chopped nuts
½ c. butter or margarine, softened
1 8-oz. package cream cheese, softened
1 tsp. vanilla extract
1 box confectioners' sugar

Sift first 5 ingredients in large mixer bowl. Add sugar, oil and eggs; mix well. Add carrots, pineapple and nuts. Pour into 2 greased and floured 9-inch round cake pans. Bake at 350 degrees for 35 to 40 minutes. Cool in pan for a few minutes. Turn out on wire rack. Beat butter and cream cheese until smooth. Add vanilla. Beat in confectioners' sugar; mix well. Frost cake. Yield: 10-12 servings. Iced cake should be kept in the refrigerator. Can be frozen with icing on cake.

Lillie Haeg
Goat Mountain Grange, No. 818
Landers, California

ORANGE-CARROT LAYER CAKE

2 c sifted flour
1 tsp. baking powder
1 tsp. soda
1 tsp. ground cinnamon
½ tsp. salt
¾ c. butter or margarine, softened
1 c. sugar
2 eggs, beaten
1 c. mashed cooked carrots, cooled
¼ c. orange juice
1 tsp. orange rind

½ c. chopped raisins
½ c. chopped walnuts
1 8-oz. package cream cheese, softened
1 tsp. vanilla extract
1 1-lb. box confectioners' sugar

Sift first 5 ingredients together; set aside. Cream ¼ cup butter and sugar until light and fluffy, using electric mixer at medium speed. Add eggs, one at a time, beating well after each addition. Add carrots, orange juice and rind. Add flour mixture; stir with spoon. Stir in raisins and walnuts. Pour into 2 waxed paper-lined 8-inch cake pans. Bake at 350 degrees for 25 to 30 minutes or until cake tests done. Cool in pans on rack for 10 minutes. Remove from pans. Combine ½ cup butter, cream cheese and vanilla in mixer bowl. Beat until smooth and creamy. Add confectioners' sugar gradually. Add a small amount of milk for spreading consistency, if needed. Frost cool cake.

Mrs. Marshall Dean
New Antiock Grange, No. 2695
Wilmington, Ohio

RHODA'S CARROT CAKE

2 c. flour
2 c. sugar
2 tsp. cinnamon
2 tsp. soda
1 tsp. salt
4 eggs, well beaten
1½ c. vegetable oil
3 c. grated carrots
1 3-oz. package cream cheese, softened
½ c. butter or margarine, softened
¾ c. confectioners' sugar
1 tsp. vanilla extract

Sift flour, sugar, cinnamon, soda and salt together 3 or 4 times in a bowl. Add eggs, oil and carrots; mix well. Pour into greased 10 × 13-inch pan. Bake in 350 degree oven for 40 minutes. Blend cream cheese, butter, confectioners' sugar and vanilla until smooth. Spread on cooled cake.

Mrs. Rhoda W. Fennel
Marshall Grange, No. 539
Ford City, Pennsylvania

BLACK MIDNIGHT CAKE

1⅔ c. sugar
⅔ c. shortening or margarine, softened
3 eggs
2¼ c. sifted flour
⅔ c. cocoa
¼ tsp. baking powder
1¼ tsp. soda
1 tsp. salt
1 tsp. vanilla extract

Cream sugar, shortening and eggs in mixer bowl until fluffy. Beat 5 minutes on high speed mixer. Sift dry ingredients together. Add to creamed mixture alternately with 1⅓ cups water. Add vanilla. Pour into two 9-inch cake pans. Bake at 350 degrees for 35 minutes or until cake tests done.

Brown Beauty Icing

1⅓ c. sifted confectioners' sugar
¼ c. shortening
¼ c. milk
3 sq. unsweetened chocolate, melted
1 tsp. vanilla extract
1 egg

Blend all ingredients except eggs. Add egg. Beat with rotary beater just until smooth. Place bowl in ice water. Stir until frosting is of spreading consistency. Frost top, sides and layers of cake. Three egg yolks may be substituted for 1 egg.

Betty Behn
Cromwell Grange, No. 67
Middletown, Connecticut

CHOCOLATE CREAM CAKE

¾ c. grated chocolate
1 c. milk
1⅔ c. (firmly packed) brown sugar
3 eggs
2 c. sifted flour
½ c. butter, softened
1 tsp. soda
1 tsp. vanilla extract
1 c. nuts (opt.)

Combine chocolate, ½ cup milk, ⅔ cup brown sugar and beaten yolk of 1 egg in medium saucepan; mix well. Heat over low heat, stirring occasionally, until of custard consistency. Cool. Combine 1 cup brown sugar, flour, butter, ½ cup milk and 2 beaten eggs in large mixer bowl. Blend well. Stir in the chocolate mixture; mix well. Dissolve soda in small amount of hot water. Add with vanilla to batter. Add nuts, if desired. Pour into two 8-inch layer pans. Bake at 350 degrees for 40 minutes.

Alma H. Lehman
Plainfield Grange, No. 1727
Plainfield, Pennsylvania

CHOCOLATE ECONOMY CAKE

3 c. flour
2 c. sugar
2 tsp. soda
½ tsp. salt
½ c. cocoa
½ c. oil
2 tbsp. vinegar
1 tsp. vanilla extract

Mix ingredients together in order given, adding 2 cups cold water last. Pour into 9 × 13-inch baking pan. Bake at 350 degrees for 30 to 40 minutes.

Mrs. Alice Nason
Crown Point Grange, No. 65
Rochester, New Hampshire

CHOCOLATE-PEANUT CAKE

2 c. flour
2 c. sugar
1 stick margarine
½ c. peanut butter
3½ tbsp. cocoa
½ c. buttermilk
2 eggs
1 tsp. soda
½ tsp. salt
1 tsp. vanilla extract

Stir flour and sugar together in large mixer bowl. Place margarine, peanut butter and cocoa in saucepan. Bring to a boil. Pour over flour-sugar mixture. Mix well. Add remaining ingredients. Beat until well blended. Pour into 9 × 13-inch baking pan. Bake at 400 degres for 20 minutes or until cake tests done.

Frosting:

1 stick margarine
3½ tbsp. cocoa
⅓ c. buttermilk
1 box sifted confectioners' sugar
1 tsp. vanilla extract
1 c. fresh roasted peanuts, chopped

Boil first 3 ingredients together until thickened, stirring constantly. Remove from stove. Add remaining ingredients. Mix well. Spread on hot cake.

Mrs. Philip E. Sloop
Corriher Grange, No. 627
Mooresville, North Carolina

CHOCOLATE-POTATO CAKE

½ lb. potatoes, pared
½ c. milk

2 c. sifted flour
2 tsp. baking powder
½ tsp. salt
1 c. shortening
2 c. sugar
4 eggs
1 tsp. vanilla extract
1½-oz. unsweetened chocolate, melted
Whipped cream

Place potatoes in small amount of boiling water in covered saucepan. Cook until tender; drain well. Shake pan over low heat to dry contents thoroughly. Force hot potatoes through ricer or sieve. Measure 1 cup sieved potatoes. Combine potatoes with milk; set aside to cool. Sift together flour, baking powder and salt. Cream shortening. Add sugar gradually; beat until light and fluffy. Add eggs, one at a time, beating well after each addition. Mix in vanilla and chocolate. Add dry ingredients alternately in 4 parts with potato mixture in 3 parts to creamed mixture. Beat only until smooth after each addition. Spread batter in 2 greased, waxed paper-lined 9-inch layer cake pans. Bake at 350 degrees for 45 minutes or until cake tests done. Remove from oven. Let stand in pans 10 minutes. Remove from pans; cool. Fill with whipped cream; frost with favorite chocolate frosting.

Photograph for this recipe on page 194.

VERA'S CHOCOLATE-POTATO CAKE

2 c. sugar
1 c. melted butter
4 eggs, beaten
1 c. mashed potatoes without salt
2 c. flour
½ c. chocolate or cocoa
2 tsp. baking powder
1 tsp. each cloves, allspice and cinnamon
½ c. milk
1 tsp. vanilla extract
1 c. chopped nuts
1 c. floured raisins

Cream sugar and butter. Add eggs and mashed potatoes. Mix well. Sift dry ingredients together; add to creamed mixture alternately with milk. Mix well. Add vanilla, nuts and raisins. Pour into 9 × 13-inch baking pan. Bake at 350 degrees for 30 to 40 minutes. Frost with favorite icing. This recipe has been a favorite cake recipe in my family for more than fifty years.

Vera R. Coulter
Clackamas Co. Clarkes Grange, No. 261
Oregon City, Oregon

BRIDE'S DEVIL'S FOOD CAKE

3 tbsp. cocoa
1 c. sugar
1¼ c. flour
1 tsp. soda
¼ tsp. salt
1 c. sour cream
2 eggs, beaten
1 tsp. vanilla extract

Sift first 5 ingredients together. Combine sour cream and eggs; mix well. Combine egg mixture and flour mixture. Add vanilla; mix well. Pour into greased 8 × 10-inch pan. Bake at 375 degrees for 30 to 35 minutes.

Mrs. Clifford Wentzler
Capt. John Brady Grange
Muncy, Pennsylvania

DEVIL'S FOOD CAKE

⅔ c. chocolate
Brown sugar
1 c. milk
1 tsp. vanilla extract
½ c. butter, softened
2 eggs, beaten
2 c. flour
1 tsp. soda

Combine chocolate and ⅔ cup (firmly packed) brown sugar in saucepan. Heat slowly, adding ½ cup milk. Stir constantly until smooth. Add vanilla. Remove from stove. Set in pan of cold water to cool. Cream butter with ½ cup (firmly packed) brown sugar. Add eggs. Beat until light and smooth. Add chocolate mixture; beat well. Sift flour and soda together; add to creamed mixture alternately with ½ cup milk. Blend well. Pour into two 9-inch layer pans. Bake at 350 degrees for 30 minutes. Cool. Frost with Seven Minute Frosting.

Margaret Dobbins
Yokima Co., Buena Grange
Zellah, Washington

FRENCH CHOCOLATE CAKE

½ c. butter, softened
1½ c. sugar
2 eggs, beaten
½ c. milk
1¾ c. cake flour
1½ tsp. cream of tartar
2 sq. unsweetened chocolate, melted
1 tsp. soda

Cream butter and sugar. Add eggs and milk. Sift flour and cream of tartar together. Add to liquid mixture. Add chocolate; mix well. Stir soda into ¾ cup boiling water. Mix into cake batter. Pour into two 9-inch cake pans. Bake at 350 degrees for 30 minutes.

Chocolate Frosting

2 sq. unsweetened chocolate
1 tbsp. butter
2½ c. confectioners' sugar
½ c. whipping cream
1 egg, unbeaten
1 tsp. vanilla extract

Melt chocolate and butter together in medium saucepan. Add remaining ingredients in mixer bowl. Place bowl in pan of cold water. Beat mixture until it stands in peaks. Spread between layers and on top of cake.

Florence Cheek
Dos Palos Grange, No. 541
Dos Palos, California

CHOCOLATE FUDGE CAKE

1 c. oatmeal
¼ c. butter
1 c. (firmly packed) brown sugar
1 c. sugar
2 eggs, beaten
1¾ c. flour
1 tsp. vanilla extract
½ tsp. salt
1 tsp. soda
2 tbsp. cocoa
Nuts
Chocolate chips

Add oatmeal to 1¾ cup boiling water; let stand for 10 minutes. Add butter and sugars; stir until butter is melted. Add eggs. Add next 5 ingredients. Add ¾ cup nuts and 1 cup chocolate chips; mix well. Pour in 9 × 13-inch pan. Spread additional chocolate chips and nuts on top. Bake at 350 degrees for 40 minutes or until cake tests done. Can be served with whipped cream. Yield: 18 servings.

Arlene H. Burda
Oak Leaf Grange, No. 569
Harris, Minnesota

COCONUT-FUDGE CAKE

2¼ c. sugar
1 c. oil
3 eggs, beaten

3 c. flour
¾ c. cocoa
2 tsp. soda
2 tsp. baking powder
1 tsp. salt
1 c. hot coffee
1 c. sour milk or buttermilk
2 tsp. vanilla extract
1 8-oz. package cream cheese, softened
½ c. coconut
6 oz. package chocolate morsels

Combine 2 cups sugar, oil and 2 eggs in a large mixer bowl; beat on high speed of electric mixer for 1 minute. Add next 7 ingredients and 1 teaspoon vanilla. Beat 3 minutes at medium speed. Pour half the batter into greased and floured 10-inch tube pan. Beat cream cheese, ¼ cup sugar, 1 teaspoon vanilla and 1 egg together in a small bowl. Add remaining ingredients. Mix well. Spoon filling over batter. Add remaining batter. Bake at 350 degrees for 1 hour and 20 minutes. Cool 15 minutes; remove from pan.

Glaze

½ c. confectioners' sugar
1½ tbsp. cocoa
1 tbsp. butter
1 tsp. vanilla extract

Combine all ingredients with 2 tablespoons hot water. Pour over cooled cake.

Geraldine Watson
Rochester Grange, No. 86
Rochester, New Hampshire

$100 FUDGE CAKE AND MOCHA FROSTING

2½ c. sugar
1 c. butter
5 eggs, separated
3 c. flour
½ tsp. salt
1 tsp. soda
4 tsp. cocoa
5 tbsp. strong coffee
1 c. buttermilk
2 tsp. vanilla extract

Cream sugar and butter together in mixer bowl. Add egg yolks, one at a time, beating well after each addition. Sift dry ingredients together. Mix coffee with buttermilk. Add dry ingredients and liquid ingredients alternately to creamed mixture beating well after each addition. Add vanilla. Beat egg whites until stiff. Fold into batter. Pour into three 9-inch layer pans. Bake at 350 degrees for 40 minutes. Cool.

Mocha Frosting

1 box confectioners' sugar
1 egg, beaten
1 stick butter, softened
1 tsp. vanilla extract
3 tbsp. strong coffee

Combine all ingredients; mix well. Frost cake.

Mrs. Norene G. Cox, D.W.A.
Virginia State Grange
Mouth of Wilson, Virginia

MILK CHOCOLATE CAKE

2¼ c. sugar
2 sq. unsweetened chocolate, melted
¾ c. butter, softened
1 tsp. vanilla extract
4 eggs, separated
2¼ c. sifted cake flour
1 tsp. cream of tartar
½ tsp. soda
½ tsp. salt
1 c. milk

Combine ¼ cup sugar, 3 tablespoons water and chocolate in small bowl. Cream butter well. Add remaining sugar gradually. Beat until light and fluffy. Add vanilla and egg yolks one at a time, beating well after each addition. Add chocolate mixture; blend thoroughly. Sift dry ingredients; add to creamed mixture alternately with milk. Beat until smooth. Beat egg whites until stiff. Fold into batter. Pour into 3 round 9-inch layer pans, lined with paper and greased. Bake at 350 degrees for 50 minutes or until cake tests done. Let stand in pans 5 minutes. Turn onto racks to cool. Remove paper.

Chocolate Cream Cheese Frosting

¼ c. butter, softened
1 8-oz. package cream cheese, softened
3 sq. unsweetened chocolate, melted
Dash of salt
3 c. sifted confectioners' sugar
⅓ c. cream
1 tsp. vanilla extract

Cream butter. Add cream cheese, chocolate and salt. Blend. Add sugar alternately with cream, beating well after each addition. Add vanilla. Frost cake.

Mrs. Stanley Frederes
Lincoln Grange, No. 122
Walworth, New York

CHOCOLATE CAKE WITH BURNT SUGAR ICING

6 tbsp. cocoa
9 tbsp. cooking oil
1½ c. sugar
6 tbsp. sour milk
1 c. plus 6 tbsp. sifted flour
¾ tsp. soda
½ tsp. (scant) salt
2 eggs

Combine cocoa, oil, ¾ cup hot water, sugar and milk; beat well. Add sifted dry ingredients; beat well. Beat in eggs. Bake in 7-inch square pan for 40 minutes at 350 degrees.

Burnt Sugar Icing

2 tbsp. sugar
1 sm. can evaporated milk
1⅓ c. sugar
1⅓ tbsp. butter

Brown 2 tablespoons sugar in heavy skillet; add remaining ingredients. Bring to a boil. Boil to soft-ball stage. Cool slightly; beat until of spreading consistency. Spread on cake. Yield: 6 servings.

From a Grange Friend

VIENNESE PECAN-CHOCOLATE CAKE

6 eggs, separated
½ tsp. salt
1 tsp. vanilla extract
¾ c. sugar
1 c. sifted all-purpose flour
Pecans, chopped
Chocolate Creme Filling
Chocolate Satin Frosting

Combine egg yolks, salt and vanilla in mixer bowl; beat until very light and lemon-colored. Add ½ cup sugar gradually; beat 5 minutes at medium speed or until very light and fluffy. Stir in flour and 1 cup finely chopped pecans. Beat egg whites until soft peaks form. Add remaining sugar gradually; continue beating until glossy. Fold into egg yolk mixture. Divide batter equally between 3 greased and floured 8-inch layer pans. Spread just enough to level. Bake at 300 degrees for 20 to 25 minutes or until cake tests done. Cool in pans on rack 10 minutes. Remove from pans; cool thoroughly on rack. Put layers together with Chocolate Creme Filling using ⅓ of filling on each layer. Sprinkle top with chopped pecans. Chill until filling is firm. Scrape excess filling off cake. Cover sides with Chocolate Satin Frosting. Chill and serve. Yield: 8 to 10 servings.

Chocolate Creme Filling

1 6-oz. package semisweet chocolate bits
¾ c. cold butter or margarine
1¼ c. sifted confectioner's sugar
⅛ tsp. salt
1 egg
3 tsp. rum or 2 tsp. vanilla extract, as desired

Melt chocolate bits. Cool, stirring often during cooling. Chocolate must be cold, but not chilled, when added to butter mixture. Whip butter until fluffy. Add confectioners' sugar and salt; beat for 6 minutes at medium high speed or until very light and fluffy. Add egg; continue beating for two minutes or until mixture is fluffy and smooth. Fold flavoring and chocolate in carefully but quickly. Cool to stiffen slightly before spreading on cake layers.

Chocolate Satin Frosting

1 c. sugar
¼ c. cornstarch
¼ tsp. salt
2 sq. unsweetened chocolate, melted
3 tbsp. butter or margarine

Combine sugar, cornstarch and salt in saucepan; mix well. Add 1 cup boiling water gradually, stirring constantly. Place over low heat; cook until smooth and thickened, stirring constantly. Add chocolate and butter. Cook, stirring until smooth and thick. Chill over ice water until cool and thick enough to spread; stir frequently during cooling. Spread sides of cake with frosting.

Photograph for this recipe on page 199.

SCREWBALL CAKE

1½ c. flour
1 c. sugar
⅓ c. cocoa
1 tsp. soda
1 tsp. salt
1 tsp. vinegar
1 tsp. vanilla extract
⅓ c. salad oil

Combine all ingredients in order listed with ¼ cup hot water; beat well. Pour into 8x8-inch baking pan. Bake at 350 degrees for 25 minutes. Yield: 10 servings.

Mrs. Stephen Markowski
Georgetown Grange, No. 1540
Erieville, New York

DOROTHY'S MISSISSIPPI MUD CAKE

4 sq. unsweetened chocolate
¾ stick butter or margarine
2 c. sugar
2 c. flour
1 tsp. soda
1 tsp. salt
2 eggs, slightly beaten
1 tsp. vanilla extract

Boil 2 cups water in large saucepan. Add chocolate; boil for 1 minute. Remove from heat. Add butter and sugar; mix well. Cool. Sift dry ingredients together. Add to first mixture with eggs and vanilla. Pour into greased large deep baking pan. Bake at 275 to 300 degrees for 1 hour and 15 minutes or until cake tests done.

Dorothy M. Bowers
Potomac Grange, No. 1
Arlington, Virginia

MAUDE'S MISSISSIPPI MUD CAKE

2 c. sugar
1 c. margarine
4 eggs, beaten
1 tsp. vanilla extract
1½ c. flour
3 tsp. cocoa
1 tsp. baking powder
1 c. coconut
1 c. nuts

Cream sugar and margarine. Add eggs and vanilla. Sift flour, cocoa and baking powder together. Add to sugar mixture. Add coconut and nuts; beat well. Pour into 9 × 12-inch pan. Bake in 350-degree oven for 30 to 40 minutes. Spread with marshmallow cream or confectioners' sugar icing while warm.

Mrs. Maude Beatty
Bell Township Grange, No. 2047
Mahaffey, Pennsylvania

MISSISSIPPI MUD CAKE WITH FUDGE ICING

½ lb. butter or margarine, melted
⅓ c. cocoa
1 tsp. vanilla extract
1½ c. flour
2 c. sugar
½ tsp. salt
4 eggs
1 c. chopped nuts
Miniature marshmallows
Fudge Icing

Melt butter in saucepan. Blend in cocoa until smooth. Add vanilla. Sift dry ingredients together. Add with eggs to butter mixture; mix well. Stir in nuts. Pour into greased and floured 9 × 13-inch baking pan. Bake at 350 degrees for 20 minutes. Remove fron oven. Cover with marshmallows. Return to oven to melt marshmallows slightly. Ice with Fudge Icing.

Fudge Icing

¼ c. butter or margarine, melted
⅓ c. cocoa
¼ c. flour
1 1-lb. package confectioners' sugar
1 tsp. light corn syrup
⅓ c. milk

Combine butter and cocoa. Blend well. Add remaining ingredients. Beat until smooth.

Thelma Tost,
Dixie Grange
West Alexandria, Ohio

MYSTERY MOCHA CAKE

1¼ c. sugar
1 c. sifted all-purpose flour
2 tsp. baking powder
⅛ tsp. salt
1 sq. unsweetened chocolate
2 tbsp. butter
½ c. milk
1 tsp. vanilla extract
½ c. chopped nuts (opt.)
½ c. (firmly packed) brown sugar
4 tbsp. cocoa
1 c. cold coffee

Sift ¾ cup sugar, flour, baking powder and salt together in large mixer bowl. Melt chocolate and butter together in double boiler over hot water. Add to first mixture; blend well. Combine milk and vanilla. Add to batter; mix well. Stir in nuts. Pour into greased 9-inch square baking pan. Combine brown sugar, ½ cup sugar and cocoa. Sprinkle over batter. Pour coffee over top. Bake in 350-degree oven for 40 minutes. Serve warm or cold. Garnish with whipped cream, if desired.

Carol V. Shorey
Garrison Hill Grange, No. 497
Sheepscott, Maine

MARGURETE'S CHOCOLATE CAKE

½ c. cocoa
1 c. (firmly packed) brown sugar
¼ c. butter or shortening

1 egg, beaten
¼ c. sour milk
1 c. flour
1 tsp. soda
1 tsp. vanilla extract

Add enough boiling water to cocoa to measure 1 cup. Cream sugar and butter. Add egg, sour milk and cocoa mixture. Beat well. Sift flour and soda together. Add to cocoa mixture; mix well. Add vanilla. Pour into 8-inch baking pan. Bake at 350 degrees for 30 minutes or until cake tests done.

Mrs. Margurete Rinebold
North Cameron Grange
Cameron Mills, New York

NAOMI'S CHOCOLATE CAKE

2 c. sugar
2 c. flour
2 sticks margarine
3 tbsp. cocoa
½ c. buttermilk
1 tsp. vanilla extract
1 tsp. soda
2 eggs, beaten

Sift sugar and flour into large mixer bowl. Combine margarine, cocoa and 1 cup water in saucepan. Bring to a boil. Add to first mixture; mix well. Add remaining ingredients. Mix well. Pour into well greased and floured 10 × 15-inch baking pan. Bake at 400 degrees for 20 minutes.

Cream Chocolate Icing

1 stick margarine
3 tbsp. cocoa
5 tbsp. cream or evaporated milk
1 tsp. vanilla extract
1 lb. confectioners' sugar
Chopped nuts

Place first 4 ingredients in saucepan. Bring to a boil, stirring constantly. Remove from heat. Add sugar; beat well. Spread on cake. Sprinkle with nuts.

M. Naomi Sawn, C.W.A
Mohican Grange, No. 1300
Glens Fall, New York

NORMA'S CHOCOLATE CAKE

1½ c. sugar
½ c. shortening
2 eggs, beaten
1 tsp. salt
1 tsp. baking powder

1 tsp. vanilla extract
3 tbsp. cocoa
1 tsp. soda
2 c. flour
½ c. milk or sour cream

Cream first 3 ingredients together in large mixer bowl. Stir in salt, baking powder and vanilla. Mix cocoa and 1 cup boiling water in small bowl. Stir in soda. Add to creamed mixture. Stir in flour; beat well. Add milk; mix well. Pour into greased and floured 9 × 12-inch cake pan. Bake at 375 degrees for 25 minutes.

Norma Conley
Mt. Allison Grange, No. 308
Ignacio, Colorado

PEARL'S CHOCOLATE CAKE

2 sq. unsweetened chocolate
2 c. sifted cake flour
1 tsp. soda
⅛ c. butter
1½ c. sugar
3 eggs
1 tsp. vanilla extract
1 c. sour cream

Melt chocolate in ½ cup water over low heat; stir. Sift flour and soda together. Cream butter and sugar; add eggs. Beat 2 minutes. Add chocolate mixture and vanilla. Add flour mixture and sour cream alternately, beginning and ending with flour. Pour into 2 greased and floured 9-inch baking pans. Bake at 325 degrees for 35 minutes. Frost as desired when cool.

Pearl Childers
Norton Grange, No. 2566
Norton, Ohio

QUICK CHOCOLATE CAKE

2 c. flour
1¾ c. sugar
1 tsp. soda
1 tsp. baking powder
1 tsp. salt
⅔ c. cocoa
⅔ c. oil
1 tsp. vanilla extract
3 eggs, beaten

Combine all ingredients in large mixer bowl with 1 cup water. Beat at medium speed for 4 minutes. Pour into 9 × 12-inch baking pan. Bake at 350 degrees for 30 to 40 minutes.

Edith Dougherty
Mahoning Valley Grange
Edinburg, Pennsylvania

VIRGINIA'S CHOCOLATE CAKE

2 sq. Hershey's baking chocolate
2 c. sugar
2 c. flour
1½ tsp. salt
1 tsp. soda
½ c. Crisco
2 eggs, beaten
½ c. milk

Combine chocolate and 1 cup boiling water in large saucepan. Cool. Sift dry ingredients together into chocolate mixture. Add Crisco. Beat well. Add eggs and milk; mix well. Pour into 9 × 13-inch paper-lined pan. Bake in 350-degree oven for 40 to 45 minutes.

Virginia Hayes
Rochester Grange, No. 86
East Rochester, New Hamsphire

CINDERELLA CAKE

2 c. sugar
4 eggs, beaten
1 c. oil
2 c. flour
2 tsp. soda
1 tsp. cinnamon
½ tsp. salt
2 c. cooked pumpkin or squash
1 3-oz. package cream cheese, softened
1 stick margarine, softened
1 box confectioners' sugar
2 tsp. vanilla extract

Combine first 3 ingredients. Blend until smooth. Sift dry ingredients. Add dry ingredients to creamed mixture alternately with pumpkin. Mix well. Pour into an 8-inch tube pan. Bake in 350 degree oven for 55 minutes. Combine remaining ingredients; mix well. Frost cake when cool.

Mrs. John Kropp
Albany Co., Hiawatha Grange, No. 1460
Rensselaerville, New York

COMMITTEE CAKE

½ c. butter or margarine
½ c. sugar
1 c. (firmly packed) light brown sugar
3 eggs, beaten
1½ tsp. vanilla extract
1½ c. sifted all-purpose flour
½ c. enriched cornmeal
1 tsp. salt
2 tsp. baking powder

1 c. milk
1 c. semisweet chocolate pieces

Cream butter with sugars until light and fluffy. Add eggs and vanilla; beat well. Sift dry ingredients together. Add to creamed mixture alternately with milk. Stir in chocolate pieces. Pour into well-greased 9 × 13-inch baking pan. Bake at 350 degrees for 40 to 45 minutes. Cool. Frost with any chocolate frosting. Sprinkle with chopped nuts.

Mrs. Nova Killion, C.W.A
Rulerdorx Grange, No. 611
Riverside, California

DATE-NUT CAKE

1 lb. dates, chopped
1 c. sugar
½ tp. soda
1 tsp. butter
1 egg
1½ c. flour
1 tsp. baking powder
Pinch of salt
1 tsp. vanilla extract
1 c. chopped nuts

Pour 1 cup boiling water over dates. Add sugar, soda and butter. Cool. Add remaining ingredients. Place in 6 × 10-inch greased baking pan. Bake in 400-degree oven for 20 minutes. Reduce heat to 350 degrees for 15 minutes longer. Keeps well.

Mrs. George H. Elchert
McCutchen Grange
New Riegel, Ohio

GRANDMA'S FRUITCAKE

1 lb. solid pork fat
4 c. flour
2 c. sugar
1 tsp. nutmeg
2 tsp. cloves
3 tsp. cinnamon
1 tsp. soda
1 c. raisins
1 c. watermelon preserves or 1 c. candied mixed fruit

Grind pork fat to medium fine. Cover with 1 pint boiling water. Cool. Combine remaining ingredients. Add to pork; mix well. Pour into a greased and floured 9 × 13-inch pan. Bake in a 350-degree oven for 1 hour or until cake tests done.

Mrs. Ernest Suesz
Gooding Grange, No. 138
Gooding, Idaho

DORIS' WHITE FRUITCAKE

1 c. sugar
½ lb. butter, softened
5 eggs
1½ tsp. vanilla extract
1 lb. mixed fruit
1 lb. white raisins
3 c. flour
¼ tsp. salt
5 tbsp. baking powder
1 lb. walnuts
¼ c. orange juice

Cream sugar and butter. Add eggs, one at a time, beating well after each addition. Add vanilla. Combine fruit and raisins in large bowl. Dredge with flour, salt and baking powder. Add butter mixture to fruit mixture; mix well. Add walnuts and orange juice; mix well. Pour into 10-inch tube pan lined with greased brown paper. Bake in preheated 350-degree oven for 30 minutes. Reduce heat to 300 degrees. Bake 1 hour and 30 minutes longer. Yield: 6 pounds.

Mrs. Doris T. Shaw
Tunxis Grange, No. 13
Hartford, Connecticut

YELLOW FRUITCAKE

¾ c. butter or margarine, softened
1½ c. sugar
9 eggs, beaten
3 c. flour
1½ tsp. baking powder
¾ tsp. salt
2 lb. candied fruit
1 c. nuts

Combine all ingredients except fruit and nuts in large mixer bowl. Blend for 30 seconds on low speed; scrape sides of bowl. Beat for 3 minutes at high speed. Stir in fruit and nuts. Line two 5 × 9-inch loaf pans with greased aluminum foil. Spread batter in pans evenly. Bake in preheated 275-degree oven for 2 hours and 30 minutes or until cake tests done. Remove from pans; cool. Wrap.

Margaret M. Brite
Gardner Grange, No. 68
Gardner, Kansas

GRANDMA'S DARK FRUITCAKE

2½ c. unsweetened applesauce
4 tsp. soda
2 c. brown sugar, firmly packed
½ c. butter or margarine, softened
½ lb. dried apricots
1 lb. mixed candied fruit
1 sm. package figs
1 lb. dates
1 lb. raisins
¼ lb. candied cherries
Flour
1 tsp. salt
1 tsp. cinnamon
¼ tsp. cloves
½ tsp. allspice
1 c. chopped walnuts

Heat applesauce; add soda. Cream brown sugar and butter together. Add applesauce; mix well. Cut fruits into small pieces in separate bowl. Cover with enough flour to coat. Sift 4 cups flour and spices together; add to applesauce mixture. Stir in mixed fruits and walnuts. Pour into well-greased and floured tube pan and small loaf pan. Decorate with colored cherries, pineapple slices and nuts. Bake in 300-degree oven for 1 hour and 30 minutes. Yield: 15 servings.

Arda M. Stief
Lake Placid Grange, No. 198
Lake Placid, Florida

PAULINE'S FRUITCAKE

1 c. butter
1 c. sugar
5 lg. eggs
¼ c. Brandy or orange juice
¼ c. light corn syrup
2 c. flour
1 tsp. salt
1 tsp. soda
1 tsp. nutmeg
1 tsp. cinnamon
¼ tsp. cloves
1¾ c. chopped walnuts
1½ c. chopped dried figs
1¼ c. chopped dates
1 c. raisins
¾ c. candied cherries
1¼ candied mixed fruit

Cream butter and sugar in large mixer bowl until light and fluffy. Add eggs one at a time, beating well after each addition. Add Brandy and syrup; beating well after each addition. Sift dry ingredients together using only 1 cup of flour. Combine walnuts and fruits in separate bowl; mix with 1 cup flour, coating well. Add dry ingredients to egg mixture. Fold in fruits. Pour into well-greased and floured tube pan. Bake in 300-degree oven for 2 hours and 15 minutes.

Mrs. Pauline Moats
Range Community Grange
Mt. Sterling, Ohio

FRUIT COCKTAIL CAKE

2 c. flour
2 c. sugar
2 pinches of cinnamon
2 tsp. soda
2 tsp. salt
2 eggs, well beaten
1 lg. can fruit cocktail, undrained
1 c. chopped nuts
1 c. (firmly packed) brown sugar

Combine first 5 ingredients. Add eggs and fruit cocktail; mix well. Pour into greased 9×13-inch baking pan. Mix nuts and brown sugar together. Sprinkle on top of batter. Bake in 300-degree oven for 1 hour and 20 minutes. Yield: 12 servings.

Rose Baun
Norton Grange, No. 2566
Norton, Ohio

MILDRED'S FRUIT COCKTAIL CAKE

2 c. flour
3½ c. sugar
2 tsp. soda
½ tsp. salt
2 eggs, beaten
1 No. 2½ can fruit cocktail, undrained
1 c. chopped nuts
1 sm. can evaporated milk
¼ lb. margarine
1 c. crushed pineapple, drained

Combine flour, 2 cups sugar, soda and salt. Add eggs and fruit cocktail. Stir in nuts. Add some of the pineapple juice if mixture is too stiff. Pour into 9×12-inch greased and floured pan. Bake in 325-degree oven for 50 to 55 minutes. Combine milk, 1½ cups sugar and margarine in saucepan. Boil 4 to 5 minutes. Stir in pineapple. Pour over hot cake. Yield: 15-20 servings.

Mildred L. Dalrymple
Warren Grange, No. 1715
Leavittsburg, Ohio

APPLE GINGERBREAD

7 to 8 tart apples, peeled and sliced
1¼ c. (firmly packed) brown sugar
Butter, softened
1 egg, beaten
½ c. milk
½ c. molasses
1¼ c. sifted flour
½ tsp. each salt, soda and baking powder
1 tsp. ginger
¼ tsp. cinnamon

Place apples in buttered 8×13-inch baking dish. Sprinkle with ¾ cup brown sugar; dot with butter. Bake at 350 degrees for 10 minutes. Place ½ cup brown sugar, ¼ cup butter, egg, milk and molasses in mixer bowl. Add dry ingredients all at once; beat well. Pour over hot apples. Bake at 350 degrees for 30 minutes or until cake tests done. Serve plain or with whipped cream, custard sauce, or ice cream.

Florence Wagstaff, C.W.A.
St. Lawrence Co., Winthrop Grange, No. 538
Winthrop, New York

GINGERBREAD

½ c. sugar
½ c. lard
1 egg, beaten
1 c. molasses
2 tsp. each soda and cinnamon
2½ c. flour
1 tsp. ginger
⅛ tsp. salt

Combine all ingredients. Add 1 cup hot water; mix well. Pour into greased 9×13-inch baking pan. Bake in 350-degree oven until gingerbread tests done.

Mrs. Lucille Sweany
Deemston Grange, No. 1372
Fredericktown, Pennsylvania

YANKEE GINGERBREAD

¼ c. butter, softened
½ c. sugar
1 egg, beaten
¼ c. dark molasses
1 c. flour
Dash of salt
1 tsp. soda
¼ tsp. cinnamon
¼ tsp. cloves
¼ tsp. ginger

Cream butter and sugar together. Add egg and molasses; mix well. Sift dry ingredients together. Add to creamed mixture; mix well. Add ½ cup boiling water. Blend well. Pour into greased 8×8-inch pan. Bake at 400 degrees for 35 to 40 minutes. Cool. Sprinkle top with confectioners' sugar, if desired. Yield: 9 servings.

Ella M. Griswold
Westport Grange, No. 181
Westport, Massachusetts

GREEK HONEY CAKE (KARIDOPITA)

3 c. walnuts
6 eggs, separated
½ tsp. salt
½ tsp. cream of tartar
1 c. sugar
1 c. sifted all-purpose flour
2 tsp. baking powder
½ tsp. cinnamon
¼ tsp. cloves
Honey Syrup

Grind walnuts using fine blade of food chopper. Beat egg whites with salt and cream of tartar until stiff. Beat in sugar gradually. Beat egg yolks until light colored with same beater. Fold into egg white mixture. Resift four with baking powder and spices; fold into batter gradually. Fold in walnuts. Spoon into ungreased 10-inch tube pan. Bake at 375 degrees for 35 minutes or until cake tests done. Invert over neck of bottle; allow cake to hang until cold. Invert onto seving plate. Spoon warm Honey Syrup gradually over cake, allowing syrup to absorb before adding more.

Honey Syrup

½ c. sugar
½ c. honey
2 tsp. lemon juice

Combine sugar and honey with ½ cup water in saucepan; simmer 5 minutes. Remove from heat; stir in lemon juice.

Photograph for this recipe on page 208.

ITALIAN CREAM CAKE

2 sticks margarine, softened
½ c. Crisco
2 c. sugar
5 eggs, separated
1 tsp. soda
2 c. flour
1 c. buttermilk
1 c. coconut
2 c. chopped pecans
1 box confectioners' sugar
1 8-oz. package cream cheese, softened
1 tsp. vanilla extract

Combine 1 stick margarine and Crisco; add sugar. Cream. Add eggs yolks, one at a time, beating well after each addition. Add soda to flour; add to creamed mixture alternately with milk. Stir in coconut and 1 cup pecans. Fold in stiffly beaten egg whites. Pour into 3 greased 9-inch layer pans. Bake at 325-degrees for 20 minutes or until cake tests done. Cool. Combine 1 stick margarine, 1 cup

pecans, confectioners' sugar, cream cheese and vanilla. Beat 3 minutes or until thoroughly mixed. Spread on cake.

Mrs. L. W. Carter
Rowan Co., Patterson Grange, No. 616
Salisbury, North Carolina

HERE'S-ALL-YOU-DO CAKE

Flour
2½ tsp. baking powder
1¼ tsp. salt
1 c. shortening
2½ tsp. vanilla extract
Sugar
2 c. milk
2 eggs
½ c. butter

Place 2 cups flour, baking powder, 1 teaspoon salt, ½ cup shortenig, 1½ teaspoon vanilla and 1⅛ cups sugar in large mixer bowl. Add ⅞ cup milk. Beat with electric mixer on low speed for 3 minutes. Add ⅛ cup milk and eggs; beat 3 minutes more. Pour into 2 greased 9-inch round pans. Bake at 375 degrees for 30 minutes. Cook 1 cup milk with 6 tablespoons flour until thick. Cool. Add remaining shortening, salt, vanilla, 1½ cups sugar and butter. Beat until peaks form. Frost cooled cake.

Esther Stoughton
Slippery Rock Grange, No. 1441
Slippery Rock, Pennsylvania

HUMMINGBIRD CAKE

3 c. flour
2 c. sugar
1 tsp. each salt, soda and cinnamon
½ c. chopped nuts
5 lg. eggs, slightly beaten
1½ c. oil
2 c. chopped bananas
1 c. crushed pineapple, undrained
2½ tsp. vanilla extract
1 8-oz. package cream cheese, softened
1 stick margarine, softened
1 lb. box confectioners' sugar

Sift flour, sugar, salt, soda and cinnamon into large bowl. Add next 5 ingredients. Mix with 1½ teaspoon vanilla; do not beat. Pour into greased and floured 10-inch tube pan. Bake at 350 degrees for 1 hour and 15 minutes. Combine remaining ingredients with 1 teaspoon vanilla. Spread on top and sides of cooled cake.

Frances S. Carter
Orange Co., Buckhorn Grange, No. 1167
Mebane, North Carolina

HICKORY-NUT CAKE

2 c. sugar
Margarine
3 eggs, separated
1 c. milk
2 tsp. vanilla extract
2½ c. flour
½ tsp. salt
3 tsp. baking powder
2¼ c. chopped nuts
1½ c. (firmly packed) light brown sugar
1 c. light cream

Cream sugar and ¾ cup margarine. Add egg yolks; mix well. Add milk and 1 teaspoon vanilla. Add flour, salt and baking powder; beat well. Fold in beaten egg whites. Add 1¼ cups nuts. Pour into 2 greased and floured 9-inch cake pans. Bake in preheated 350-degree oven for 30 to 35 minutes. Cool. Boil brown sugar and cream together until mixture reaches spreading consistency. Remove from heat. Add 1 tablespoon margarine and 1 teaspoon vanilla; mix well. Add remaining nuts. Frost cooled cake.

Naomi Lauchnor
Lehigh Co., Washington Grange, No. 1763
Slatington, Pennsylvania

MOLASSES CAKE

1 tsp. soda
⅔ c. molasses
½ c. sugar
½ c. shortening
1 egg
2 c. all purpose flour, sifted
2 tsp. cinnamon
½ tsp. salt

Dissolve soda in ⅔ cup boiling water. Mix remaining ingredients together in order listed. Add water mixture; blend well. Pour into greased 9-inch square pan. Bake at 350 degrees for 40 minutes. Serve warm with whipped cream, if desired.

Mrs. Hope A. Knight
Ulysses Grange, No. 419
Jacksonville, New York

OATMEAL CAKE

1 c. butter or margarine
1 c. old-fashioned oats
1 c. sugar
2 eggs
1⅓ c. flour
½ tsp. salt
1 tsp. soda
½ tsp. nutmeg
1 tsp. cinnamon
1½ c. (firmly packed) brown sugar
1 c. chopped nuts
¼ c. milk or cream
1 c. coconut
1 tsp. vanilla extract

Add ½ cup butter and oatmeal to 1¼ cups boiling water. Bring to a boil. Remove from stove. Allow to stand for 20 minutes. Combine sugar, eggs and 1 cup brown sugar. Blend well. Mix flour with salt, soda and spices. Add flour mixture and oatmeal alternately to sugar mixture. Beat with fork only. Pour into greased 7×11-inch pan. Bake at 350 degrees for 40 to 60 minutes. Combine ½ cup brown sugar and ½ cup butter with remaining ingredients. Spread over hot cake. Broil until topping is bubbly.

Lela Hughes, C.W.A.
Tulare Co., Porterville Grange, No. 718
Porterville, California

ORANGE CANDY CAKE

1 c. butter
2 c. sugar
4 eggs
½ tsp. vanilla extract
1 tsp. soda
1 c. buttermilk
1 lb. orange slice candy, chopped
1 lb. chopped dates
3½ c. flour
1 tsp. salt
1 c. flaked coconut
2 c. chopped nuts

Cream butter; add sugar gradually. Add eggs, one at a time, beating well after each addition. Add vanilla. Dissolve soda in buttermilk; add to creamed mixture. Toss orange candy and dates with flour and salt to coat. Combine two mixtures; add coconut and nuts. Makes a stiff dough. Pour into 2 greased and waxed paper-lined loaf pans. Bake at 250 degrees for 2 hours and 30 minutes or until done. Top hot cake with orange juice and confectioners' sugar glaze, if desired. Remove from pan. Let stand overnight.

From a Grange Friend

ORANGE-RAISIN CAKE

1 c. sugar
1 c. Crisco
2 eggs, well-beaten
1 tsp. soda
¾ c. milk
1 whole orange
1½ c. raisins
2 c. flour

Cream sugar and Crisco. Add eggs. Dissolve soda in 1 tablespoon warm water. Add soda and milk to creamed mixture; blend well. Chop orange and raisins in food chopper. Add chopped fruit and flour to creamed mixture. Beat until smooth. Pour into a tube pan. Bake at 325 degrees for 50 minutes.

Mrs. Thomas Yeo
Stevenson Grange, No. 121
Stevenson, Washington

PEANUT BUTTER CAKE

⅓ c. margarine
1½ c. sugar
2 eggs
⅓ c. peanut butter
1 tsp. vanilla extract
1½ c. milk
1 tsp. salt
3 tsp. baking powder
2¼ c. flour

Cream margarine, sugar and eggs. Blend in peanut butter and vanilla. Add milk alternately with sifted dry ingredients. Beat until smooth. Pour into a greased 9 × 13-inch pan. Bake in 350-degree oven for 35 minutes or until cake tests done.

Evelyn Bierly
Charity Grange, No. 103
Harrisburg, Oregon

PINEAPPLE UPSIDE-DOWN CAKE

8 tbsp. butter
1 c. (firmly packed) brown sugar
5 or 6 slices pineapple
3 eggs, separated
1½ c. sugar
½ c. pineapple juice
1½ c. cake flour
¼ tsp. salt
1½ tsp. baking powder
½ tsp. vanilla extract

Melt butter and brown sugar in 9-inch iron or heavy frypan until bubbly and smooth. Add pineapple to cover bottom of pan. Beat egg yolks until light yellow. Beat egg whites until stiff peaks form. Add remaining ingredients; mix well. Fold in egg whites. Pour batter over pineapple. Bake at 450 degrees for 5 minutes. Reduce temperature to 350 degrees. Bake for about 45 minutes longer or until cake tests done. Turn upside down onto serving plate.

Doris Sawyer
White Mt Grange, No. 50
Littleton, New Hampshire

DEANNA'S PINEAPPLE CAKE

2 c. sugar
2 c. flour
2 tsp. soda
½ tsp. salt
2 eggs, slighty beaten
1 15-oz. can crushed pineapple
½ stick butter, melted
2 3-oz. packages cream cheese, softened
½ box confectioners' sugar

Mix first 6 ingredients. Pour into 9 × 13-inch baking pan. Bake at 350 degrees for 40 to 45 minutes. Mix butter, cream cheese and confectioners' sugar. Spread on cake. Broil until brown.

Deanna Lee Gass
Cross Anchor Grange
Greeneville, Tennessee

PORK CAKE

1 lb. pork sausage
1 lb. raisins
1 lb. currants
1 c. chopped nuts (opt.)
4 c. brown sugar
2 tbsp. cinnamon
1 tbsp. cloves
1 tbsp. soda
6 c. flour

Mix first 7 ingredients in order given. Dissolve soda in 1½ pints boiling water. Add to pork mixture. Add flour 1 cup at a time; stir well. Pour batter into 2 bundt pans. Bake at 275 degrees for 1 hour and 30 minutes.

Mrs. John Wakefield
Charlesville Grange, No. 698
Bedford, Pennsylvania

PORK LOAF

½ pt. strong hot coffee
1 c. finely diced salt pork
2 c. (firmly packed) brown sugar
1 c . molasses
1 tsp. soda

6 c. flour, sifted
2 tsp. cinnamon
1 tsp. each cloves and nutmeg
1 lb. seedless raisins
¼ lb. citron

Pour coffee over salt pork. Add brown sugar, molasses and soda. Combine flour with spices. Add to pork mixture; mix well. Add raisins and citron; mix well. Pour into 4 × 9-inch loaf pans, greased and lined with waxed paper. Bake at 350 degrees for 1 hour or until done. Boiling water may be substituted for coffee. Cake keeps for up to 6 months.

Mrs. Guy Alguire
St. Law Co., DeKalb Grange, No. 1481
DeKalb Junction, New York

BEST-OF-ALL-POUND CAKE

3 c. sugar
1½ c. (scant) Crisco
6 lg. eggs
3½ c. sifted flour
1 tsp. salt
1 c. milk
1 tsp. lemon or vanilla flavoring
1 tsp. imitation butter flavoring
6 to 7 tbsp. whipping cream
1 stick butter or margarine, softened
1 box confectioners' sugar

Cream sugar and Crisco. Add eggs, 2 at a time, beating until smooth after each addition. Sift flour and salt together; add to creamed mixture alternately with milk. Add ½ teaspoon each lemon and butter flavoring; blend well. Pour into greased 10-inch tube pan. Bake at 275 degrees for 1 hour and 30 minutes or until cake tests done. Invert in pan until cool. Heat whipping cream in saucepan. Combine butter, confectioners' sugar and warm cream in bowl of electric mixer. Mix well. Add ½ teaspoon each lemon and butter flavoring, stirring with a spatula. Ice cake when cool.

Miss Floy G. Hunter
Old Richmond Grange, No. 675
Pfafftown, North Carolina

CRISCO POUND CAKE

1 c. Crisco
3 c. sugar
5 eggs
1 tsp. vanilla extract
3 c. all-purpose flour
¼ tsp. soda
1 c. buttermilk

Cream Crisco and sugar; mix well. Add eggs, one at a time, beating well after each addition. Add vanilla; beat well. Sift flour and soda together. Add dry ingredients to creamed mixture with buttermilk alternately, beginning and ending with flour. Pour into a greased and floured 10-inch pan. Bake at 325 degrees for 30 minutes. Reduce temperature to 300 degrees. Bake 1 hour longer or until cake tests done. Cool in pan for 5 minutes.

Mrs. Norman Smith
Seagrove Grange
Asheboro, North Carolina

MARGARET'S POUND CAKE

1 c. Crisco
2 c. sugar
¼ tsp. salt
5 tbsp. fresh orange juice
2 c. cake flour
5 eggs

Cram Crisco and sugar. Add salt, orange juice and flour; mix well. Add eggs, one at a time, beating well after each addition. Pour into greased and floured bundt pan. Bake at 325 degrees for 1 hour or until done. Yield: 16 servings.

Margaret Rhodes
Summitt Co., Union Grange, No. 2380
Akron, Ohio

VELVET POUND CAKE

3 c. cake flour
½ tsp. salt
1 tsp. baking powder
3 c. sugar
1½ c. shortening
5 lg. eggs
1 c. milk
1 tsp. vanilla extract
1 tsp. lemon extract

Sift flour, salt and baking powder together. Cream sugar and shortening. Add eggs one at a time, beating well after each addition. Add milk and flour alternately to creamed mixture; mix well. Add flavorings. Pour into large tube pan. Bake at 350 degrees for 1 hour and 15 minutes to 1 hour and 30 minutes. Do not open oven door while cake is baking. Yield: 15 servings.

Mildred Crawford
Grantham Grange
Goldsboro, North Carolina

LOLA'S JELLY ROLL CAKE

4 eggs, separated
1 c. sugar
1 c. flour
1 tsp. baking powder
Jelly
Confectioners' sugar

Beat egg whites until stiff peaks form. Set aside. Add next 3 ingredients to beaten egg yolks. Fold in egg whites. Pour into jelly roll pan. Bake at 325 to 350 degrees until cake tests done. Turn onto damp towel. Spread with jelly. Roll up. Sprinkle with confectioners' sugar. A 1915 recipe.

Lola Chandler, C.W.A.
Nezperce Grange, No. 295
Nezperce, Idaho

PARTY ROLL

4 eggs
¾ c. sugar
¾ c. flour
¾ tsp. baking powder
¼ tsp. salt
1 tsp. vanilla extract
Confectioners' sugar
Orange Cream Filling

Place eggs in small mixer bowl; beat at high speed until foamy. Add sugar gradually; beat until very thick. Sift together flour, baking powder and salt; fold into egg mixture. Stir in vanilla. Pour into greased, waxed paper-lined 15 × 10 × 1-inch jelly roll pan. Bake at 400 degrees for 13 minutes or until light brown. Lightly dust clean dish towel with confectioners' sugar. Loosen cake; invert onto towel. Roll up cake very gently from narrow end. Cool 10 minutes. Unroll. Spread with Orange Cream Filling. Roll cake up again. Wrap towel tightly around to shape it for 1 hour.

Orange Cream Filling

¼ c. sugar
1½ tbsp. flour
¼ tsp. salt
½ c. orange juice
1 tsp. grated orange rind
1 egg yolk
½ c. heavy cream, whipped
2 tbsp. semisweet chocolate morsels, chopped

Combine sugar, flour and salt in saucepan. Add orange juice, orange rind and egg yolk. Place over medium heat; bring to a boil, stirring constantly. Cook 1 minute. Cool thoroughly. Fold in heavy cream and semisweet chocolate morsels. Refriger-

ate 30 minutes before spreading if needed to thicken filling.

Photograph for this recipe on page 214.

PUMPKIN CAKE ROLL

3 eggs
1 c. sugar
⅔ c. pumpkin
1 tsp. lemon juice
¾ c. flour
1 tsp. each baking powder and ginger
2 tsp. cinnamon
½ tsp. each nutmeg and salt
1 c. finely chopped nuts
Confectioners' sugar
2 3-oz. packages cream cheese, softened
¼ c. butter, softened
½ tsp. vanilla extract

Beat eggs on high speed for 5 minutes, gradually adding sugar. Stir in pumpkin and lemon juice. Sift together flour, baking powder, spices and salt. Fold flour into pumpkin mixture. Spread in well greased and floured jelly roll pan. Top with nuts. Bake at 375 degrees for 15 minutes. Turn out immediately onto towel sprinkled with confectioners' sugar. Roll towel and cake together. Cool. Combine 1 cup confectioners' sugar, cream cheese, butter and vanilla. Beat until smooth. Add milk, if needed, to make spreading consistency. Unroll cake. Spread with cream cheese mixture. Reroll. Chill.

Mrs. Lucille M. Pfister
Shelby Co., Unity Grange, No. 2105
Quincy, Ohio

STRAWBERRY ROLL

4 eggs
1¼ c. sugar
1 c. flour
2 tsp. baking powder
1 tsp. vanilla extract
Confectioners' sugar
1 tbsp. unflavored gelatin
2 c. sliced strawberries
½ tbsp. lemon juice
½ pt. whipping cream, whipped

Beat eggs on high speed until light and fluffy. Add 1 cup sugar 1 spoonful at a time, while beating at medium speed. Sift flour and baking powder together. Add to egg mixture alternately with ¼ cup water and vanilla; beat at low speed. Pour into greased jelly roll pan lined with waxed paper. Bake at 375 degrees for 14 to 18 minutes. Turn cake out at once onto cloth dusted with confectioners' sugar. Roll. Soften gelatin in ¼ cup cold water. Dissolve by setting bowl over hot water. Add berries, lemon juice, and ¼ cup sugar. Chill until partially set. Fold in whipped cream. Chill until almost set. Unroll cake; spread with strawberry mixture. Re-roll. Package in moisture proof material. May be frozen.

Mrs. Sarah Cross
Slippery Rock Grange, No. 1441
Slippery Rock, Pennsylvania

EMMA'S RHUBARB CAKE

1½ c. (firmly packed) brown sugar
½ c. margarine, softened
1 egg
2 c. flour
1 tsp. soda
¼ tsp. salt
1 c. milk
1 tsp. vanilla extract
2½ c. diced rhubarb
½ c. sugar
2 tsp. cinnamon

Cream brown sugar and margarine. Add egg; beat well. Add next 4 ingredients. Beat until smooth. Fold in vanilla and rhubarb. Pour into greased and floured 9 × 13-inch baking pan. Combine sugar and cinnamon. Sprinkle over batter. Bake at 350 degrees for 40 minutes.

Mrs. Emma Smith, C.W.A.
Mahapac Grange, No. 840
Carmel, New York

MARY'S RHUBARB CAKE

½ c. shortening
2 c. sugar
1 egg, beaten
2 c. flour
¼ tsp. salt
1 tsp. soda
1 c. buttermilk
1½ c. diced rhubarb
1½ tsp. cinnamon

Cream shortening and 1½ cups sugar. Add egg. Sift flour, salt and soda together; add to creamed mixture. Add buttermilk slowly; mix well. Add rhubarb. Mix. Pour into 9 × 12-inch pan. Combine ½ cup sugar and cinnamon. Sprinkle over cake. Bake at 350 degrees for 35 minutes.

Mary Perkins
Mt. Valley Grange
Amboy, Washington

MITZI'S RHUBARB CAKE

½ c. shortening
1¾ c. sugar

1 egg, slightly beaten
1 tsp. vanilla extract
1 c. sour milk or buttermilk
1 tsp. soda
2 c. flour
1 tsp. salt
2 c. cut up rhubarb
1 tsp. cinnamon

Cream shortening and 1½ cup sugar. Add next 4 ingredients; mix well. Add flour and salt. Fold in rhubarb. Pour into greased 9 × 13-inch baking pan. Mix ¼ cup sugar and cinnamon. Sprinkle over cake. Bake at 350 degrees for 30 to 40 minutes.

Mitzi Furst
Hopewell Grange, No. 1747
Washington, Illinois

SHOOFLY CUPCAKES

1 c. molasses
1 tsp. soda
3 c. flour
1 c. sugar
½ tsp. salt
½ c. shortening

Combine molasses and soda with 1½ cups boiling water. Mix flour, sugar and salt; cut in shortening. Mix until crumbly. Reserve 1 cup of crumb mixture for topping. Mix remaining flour mixture with molasses mixture. Pour into cupcake containers; top with reserved crumbs. Bake in 350-degree oven for 25 minutes. Yield: 2 dozen cupcakes.

Mrs. Nevin Hill
Berks Co., Virginville Grange, No. 1832
Kutztown, Pennsylvania

POOR MAN'S SPICE CAKE

1 c. sugar
1 tbsp. Crisco
2 c. flour
1 tsp. soda
2 tsp. cinnamon
½ tsp. cloves
½ tsp. salt
1 c. buttermilk
1 c. raisins
1 c. chopped pecans (opt.)

Cream sugar and Crisco. Combine dry ingredients; add to creamed mixture alternately with buttermilk. Add small amount of water if dough appears heavy. Add raisins and pecans. Pour into 9 × 13-inch baking pan. Bake at 350 degrees for 1 hour and 30 minutes.

Mrs. Edrie Dodson
Leon Valley Grange, No. 1581
San Antonio, Texas

SPICE CAKE

2⅛ c. all-purpose flour
1 c. sugar
1 tsp. soda
1½ tsp. cinnamon
¾ tsp. nutmeg
¾ tsp. cloves
1 tsp. salt
1 c. (firmly packed) light brown sugar
⅔ c. shortening
1 c. buttermilk
3 eggs

Sift together first 7 ingredients. Add next 3 ingredients; beat for 2 minutes. Add eggs; beat 2 minutes longer. Pour into 2 greased and floured 9-inch cake pans. Bake at 350 degrees for 30 to 35 minutes. Frost with desired frosting.

Mrs. Gladys Wisner
Glade Valley Grange, No. 417
Walkersville, Maryland

GLORIOUS SPONGE CAKE

7 eggs, separated
1 c. sugar
1 tsp. lemon flavoring
1 tsp. grated lemon rind
1 c. flour
½ tsp. cream of tartar
¼ tsp. salt

Beat egg yolks until thick and lemon colored. Beat in sugar gradually. Add ¼ cup cold water, flavoring and rind. Mix well. Sift flour once before measuring. Beat in flour. Beat egg whites until frothy. Add cream of tartar and salt. Continue beating until stiff. Fold into egg yolk mixture. Pour into ungreased tube pan. Bake at 325 degrees for 60 minutes.

Frances Hoover
Saluskin Grange, No. 793
Harrah, Washington

GRAND CHAMPION SPONGE CAKE

1¼ c. cake flour
1½ c. sugar
½ tsp. baking powder
½ tsp. salt
6 eggs, separated
1 tsp. cream of tartar
1 tsp. vanilla extract

Sift together flour, 1 cup sugar, baking powder and salt. Beat egg whites until foamy in large mixer bowl. Add cream of tartar. Beat in ½ cup sugar gradually until whites form stiff peaks. Combine egg yolks, ¼ cup water, vanilla and sifted dry ingredients in small bowl. Beat at medium high speed for 4 minutes. Fold yolk mixture gently into beaten egg whites. Pour into ungreased 10-inch tube pan. Bake at 350 degrees for 45 minutes. Invert to cool.

Jean Myers
Thurmont Grange, No. 409
Thurmont, Maryland

WALNUT CAKE

1 c. butter
1 c. sugar
3 eggs
1½ c. flour
2 tsp. baking powder
½ c. milk
½ c. chopped walnuts

Cream butter and sugar together. Add eggs; blend well. Combine flour and baking powder; add to creamed mixture alternately with milk. Add walnuts. Pour into greased 9-inch tube pan. Bake at 350 degrees for 45 minutes or until cake tests done.

Mrs. Wm. F. Sheppard
Westcaln Grange, No. 1365
Coatesville, Pennsylvania

WINTERGREEN LOZENGE CAKE

1 c. of wintergreen lozenges
1 c. milk
1 c. sugar
½ c. shortening
3 eggs, separated
2 c. flour
3 tsp. baking powder
Pinch of salt

Soak lozenges in milk overnight. Stir until dissolved. Cream sugar and shortening together. Beat egg yolks. Add to creamed mixture. Beat well. Sift dry ingredients together 2 or 3 times. Add to creamed mixture alternately with milk. Beat egg whites until stiff. Fold into batter. Pour into 9-inch baking pan. Bake at 350 degrees for 30 to 35 minutes.

Mrs. Paul Blanchard
Fairmount Grange, No. 1428
Minerva, Ohio

YUM YUM CAKE

1 c. raisins
1 c. sugar
½ c. melted shortening
1 tsp. cinnamon
Pinch of salt
2 tbsp. cocoa or 1 sq. chocolate
2 c. flour
1 tsp. soda
½ c. nuts

Combine first 6 ingredients in saucepan with 1½ cups hot water. Boil for 8 minutes. Cool. Sift flour and soda together into large bowl. Stir in liquid until well blended. Pour into 7 × 12-inch baking pan. Bake 375 degrees for 45 minutes. Cool. Frost with confectioners' sugar frosting.

Betty-Jane Gardine, C.W.A.
Connecticut State Grange
West Simsbury, Connecticut

ORANGE-ZUCCHINI CAKE

1 c. butter or margarine, softened
1 tbsp. grated orange rind
1 tsp. cinnamon
½ tsp. nutmeg
¼ tsp. cloves
2 c. (firmly packed) light brown sugar
4 eggs
3 c. sifted all-purpose flour
3 tsp. baking powder
½ tsp. salt
⅓ c. orange juice
1 c. shredded unpared zucchini
White Glaze

Combine butter, orange rind, cinnamon, nutmeg, cloves and brown sugar in large mixing bowl; blend until light and fluffy. Add eggs one at a time, beating after each addition. Sift together flour, baking powder and salt; blend into creamed mixture alternately with orange juice. Stir in zucchini. Spoon into greased 10-inch tube pan. Bake at 350 degrees for 55 to 65 minutes or until cake tests done. Cool 10 minutes. Remove from pan; cool completely. Spread top with White Glaze. Garnish with slivered orange rind and shredded zucchini, if desired. Yield: 12-16 servings.

White Glaze

1½ c. sifted confectioners' sugar
1 tbsp. butter or margarine, softened
½ tsp. vanilla extract
2 to 3 tbsp. milk

Beat all ingredients in bowl until smooth.

Photograph for this recipe on page 217.

ENDSLEY'S ZUCCHINI CAKE

3 c. grated unpeeled zucchini
2½ c. sugar
1½ c. salad oil
4 eggs
3 c. flour
2 tsp. baking powder
1 tsp. soda
2 tsp. cinnamon
½ tsp. salt
1 c. chopped nuts
Orange Sauce

Beat together zucchini, sugar, oil and eggs. Combine dry ingredients. Add to zucchini mixture. Mix well. Stir in nuts. Pour into greased and floured 9 × 13-inch pan. Bake in 325-degree oven for 45 to 60 minutes, or until done. Cool and top with Orange Sauce.

Orange Sauce

¾ c. sugar
¼ c. cornstarch
1 c. orange juice
1 tsp. lemon juice
2 tbsp. butter
2 tbsp. grated orange peel
¼ tsp. salt

Combine sugar and cornstarch in saucepan. Add juices slowly; stir until smooth. Add remaining ingredients. Cook over low heat until thick and glossy. Pour hot sauce over cake.

Mrs. Lister Endsley
Keene Hill Grange, No. 1602
Coshocton, Ohio

KNARR ZUCCHINI CAKE

3 eggs
2 c. sugar
1 c. oil
3 c. flour
1 tsp. salt
1 tsp. cinnamon
1 tsp. baking powder
1 tsp. soda
½ c. Angel Flake coconut
3 c. grated zucchini
2 tsp. vanilla extract
½ c. chopped nuts

Blend eggs and sugar; add oil. Combine dry ingredients. Add to creamed mixture; mix well. Stir in remaining ingredients. Pour into 9 × 12-inch baking pan. Bake at 325 degrees for 1 hour and 15 minutes.

Mrs. Burnette Knarr
Clearfield Co. Brady Grange, No. 1218
Puntsutawney, Pennsylvania

CHOCOLATE-ZUCCHINI CAKE

2½ c. all-purpose flour
½ c. cocoa
2½ tsp. baking powder
1½ tsp. soda
1 tsp. each salt and cinnamon
¾ c. butter or margarine, softened
2 c. sugar
3 eggs
2 tsp. vanilla extract
2 tsp. grated orange peel
2 c. coarsely shredded zucchini
½ c. mik
1 c. chopped pecans or walnuts

Combine first 5 ingredients set aside. Cream butter and sugar. Add eggs, one at a time, beating well after each addition. Stir in with a spoon vanilla, orange peel and zucchini. Add dry ingredients alternately with milk. Stir in pecans. Pour into greased and floured 10-inch tube pan. Bake in 350-degree oven for about 1 hour. Cool in pan 15 minutes. Turn out on wire rack to cool.

Glaze

2 c. confectioners' sugar
3 tbsp. milk
1 tsp. vanilla extract

Combine all ingredients; beat until smooth. Drizzle over cake.

Mrs. Monroe Detwiler
Fairfield Grange, No. 1534
Baltimore, Ohio

CREAMY FROSTING

2½ tsp. flour
½ c. milk
½ c. sugar
Pinch of salt
1 tsp. vanilla extract
¼ c. shortening
¼ c. butter

Mix flour with enough milk to make a paste in saucepan. Cook over low heat. Add remaining milk, stirring constantly, to thicken. Remove from heat; cool. Combine remaining ingredients; beat well. Add to milk mixture. Beat until fluffy. Frosts a 3-layer cake.

Daisy Shager
Friendship Grange, No. 1018
Uniondale, Pennsylvania

THE PERFECT ICING

2½ tbsp. flour
½ c. milk
½ c. sugar
½ c. butter or shortening, softened
Dash of salt
1 c. confectioners' sugar

Combine flour and milk in saucepan. Heat until thickened. Cool. Cream sugar and butter. Add salt and milk mixture. Beat well. Add confectioners' sugar. Mix. If chocolate icing is desired; reduce flour to 1 tablespoon flour and add ¼ cup cocoa and increase milk by a tablespoon.

Dixie Pfeiffer
Boerne Grange 1545
Boerne, Texas

MAPLE-WALNUT FROSTING

¼ c. butter
1 1-lb. box confectioners' sugar
⅛ c. condensed milk
½ tsp. maple flavoring
1½ c. chopped walnuts

Cream butter. Gradually add half of the sugar; cream until light and fluffy. Add milk and remaining sugar until frosting is of spreading consistency. Stir in maple flavoring. Spread on cake. While still moist, cover with walnuts. Frosting is good on pumpkin cake.

From a Grange Friend

BROWN SUGAR FROSTING

5 egg whites
3 tsp. sugar
2 c. (firmly packed) brown sugar
¼ tsp. salt

Beat egg whites until soft peaks form; add granulated sugar. Combine remaining ingredients with 1 cup hot water; cook until it forms a hard ball in cold water. Pour slowly over egg whites, beating constantly.

From a Grange Friend

FLUFFY UNCOOKED FROSTING

1 egg white
1 c. sugar

¼ tsp. cream of tartar
½ tsp. vanilla, lemon or orange flavoring

Combine egg white, sugar and cream of tartar. Add ½ cup boiling water; beat at high speed until very thick and fluffy. Add flavoring. Spread on cake. Yield: 2 layer cake.

From a Grange Friend

BUTTERSCOTCH CREAM FROSTING

1 c. (firmly packed) brown sugar
⅓ c. butter or margarine
¼ c. sweet or sour cream or evaporated milk
2 c. sifted confectioners' sugar

Combine sugar and butter; cook over medium-high heat for 2 minutes, stirring constantly. Add cream; bring to a boil, stirring. Remove from heat; add confectioners' sugar gradually, beating until smooth. Spread on cake.

From a Grange Friend

DEVIL'S DELIGHT

1½ c. sugar
4½ tbsp. cornstarch
3 1-oz. squares unsweetened chocolate
¼ tsp. salt
3 tbsp. butter
1½ tsp. vanilla extract
¾ c. chopped walnuts

Mix sugar and cornstarch; add chocolate and salt. Add 1½ cups boiling water; cook until mixture thickens. Remove from heat; add butter, vanilla and walnuts. Spread on cake while warm.

From a Grange Friend

BEVILLE FILLING

1 c. sugar
1 tbsp. cornstarch
Milk from 1 coconut
1 tbsp. lemon juice
1 fresh grated coconut
1 c. chopped nuts

Mix sugar and cornstarch; add gradually to coconut milk. Cook over low heat until thick, stirring constantly. Add lemon juice, coconut and nuts;

cool. Spread between cake layers. Yield: 3 layer cake.

From a Grange Friend

BROILER COCONUT FROSTING

6 tbsp. butter, melted
½ c. (firmly packed) brown sugar
¼ c. cream
½ tsp. vanilla extract
1 c. shredded coconut
¾ c. pecans, broken

Combine all ingredients; spread over warm cake. Brown under broiler. Yield: 9 x 12-inch cake.

From a Grange Friend

STRAWBERRY CREAM FROSTING

1 10-oz. package frozen strawberries, thawed
2 envelopes unflavored gelatin
1 pt. heavy cream
¼ c. sugar
Red food coloring

Drain strawberries, reserving liquid. Dissolve gelatin in small amount of strawberry juice. Heat remaining juice; add to gelatin. Whip cream; fold in sugar and berries. Add drop of red food coloring. Drip cool gelatin mixture into cream. Frost and fill center of cake. Refrigerate several hours before serving. Yield: 10-12 servings.

From a Grange Friend

DIVINE DIVINITY FROSTING

3 tbsp. light corn syrup
1½ c. sugar
3 egg whites
1 tsp. baking powder
¼ tsp. salt

Combine syrup, sugar and ½ cup water; bring to a boil. Beat egg whites, baking powder and salt. Add 1 tablespoon syrup mixture to egg whites until 5 tablespoons of hot mixture have been added, beating constantly. Cook remaining syrup mixture until it spins an 8-inch thread. Pour slowly over egg whites, beating constantly. Continue beating until frosting is of spreading consistency.

From a Grange Friend

Family Recipes
From Young Folks

The enjoyment of cooking to please family members knows no age limit. Young people love to cook and for many very good reasons. First of all, they love to imitate and impress their parents, and then they enjoy the praise they receive for a job well done. But, most of all, young people love to eat! Moreover, as children learn to cook, they gain self-confidence, an appreciation for menu planning and good nutrition, and a sense of responsibility in the home at the same time.

Most young people's cookbooks concentrate on simple recipes that rely on prepackaged foods. Uncomplicated recipes may be helpful for children just learning to cook, but even better are uncomplicated "from scratch" recipes. There's no better way than that to learn one of the basic rules of truly delicious cooking: the fresher your ingredients, the tastier and more nutritious the results will be.

Most important of all for a child to learn about cooking are the safety and good sense rules to follow in the kitchen, as well as how to set a pleasing table. Teaching a child these first makes cooking easy and successful from then on.

Young people are known to be imaginative and innovative, especially when it comes to food! So, whether you are young or young-at-heart, these recipes are definitely for you. You might learn a new trick and you will surely enjoy them all!

CRANBERRY FUN SALAD

It's quick and easy, fun to eat,
Yet no other salad can quite compete.
One bag of cranberries, chop 'em or grind,
Then, add little marshmallows—
Half a bag will do fine.
Mix in one cup of sugar,
Add ½ pint of whipped cream.
Chill for two hours,
Then you'll see what I mean!

Jennifer Nelson, Youth Chairman
Blue Mountain Grange, No. 263
Ryegate, Vermont

CANDLESTICK SALAD

1 lettuce leaf
1 canned pineapple slice
1 sm. banana
1 maraschino cherry

Wash lettuce leaf well. Place lettuce leaf on salad plate. Place pineapple slice on lettuce. Cut banana flat on bottom to stand straight. Stand banana in pineapple hole. Place cherry on top of banana to make the flame, using toothpick to keep it in place. Yield: 1 serving.

From a Young Grange Friend.

TOMATO FLOWER SALAD

4 tomatoes
Lettuce
Cottage cheese
Paprika
French dressing

Cut away core of tomato. Cut each tomato into 8 wedges. Place on lettuce leaf. Fill tomato with cottage cheese. Sprinkle with paprika. Serve with French dressing. Yield: 4 servings.

Sherry Adams
Blue Mountain Grange, No. 263
Wells River, Vermont

TOMATO AND PEPPER SALAD

Tomatoes, peeled and quartered
Green peppers, sliced thin
Onion, sliced thin
¼ c. oil
¼ c. vinegar

¼ c. sugar
Salt and pepper to taste

Combine all ingredients in serving bowl; mix well. Let stand for 2 hours or longer for flavors to blend.

Heather L. Maple
Hamilton Junior Grange, No. 44
Lawrenceville, New Jersey

TABOULI

1½ c. bulgur
2 c. chopped parsley
1 c. chopped scallions
¾ c. chopped fresh mint leaves
¾ c. olive oil
½ c. lemon juice
Salt and pepper to taste
Carrots, chopped
Celery, chopped
Cucumbers, chopped
Egg, chopped
Tomatoes, chopped
Grated cheese
Green pepper, chopped

Soak bulgur in cold water to cover for 1 hour. Squeeze out water thoroughly. Mix with next 6 ingredients. Add remaining ingredients. Toss well. This is a Middle Eastern salad.

Meg Witey
Potomac Grange, No. 1
Arlington, Virginia

FRENCH DRESSING

½ tsp. salt
½ tsp. onion or celery salt
¼ tsp. paprika
1 tbsp. sugar
½ c. oil
2 tbsp. lemon juice
1 tbsp. vinegar

Place all ingredients in bowl. Mix well. Store in airtight container.

Linda Penn
Locktown Junior Grange, No. 48
Flemington, New Jersey

LONG BURGERS

1 lb. ground beef
Salt and pepper to taste
4 sweet gherkins, quartered lengthwise

2 oz. grated American cheese
4 toasted frankfurter rolls
Catsup, mustard or choice of pickle relishes

Season ground beef with salt and pepper to taste. Shape hamburger into 5×6-inch patties. Place gherkins in center of each hamburger lengthwise. Sprinkle with cheese. Roll up each burger to frankfurter shape. Broil or panfry. Serve on rolls with choice of accompaniment. Yield: 4 servings.

Photograph for this recipe on page 223.

KATHY'S PIZZABURGERS

1 sm. onion, chopped
1 lb. ground beef
½ tsp. salt
⅛ tsp. pepper
¼ tsp. oregano
¾ c. catsup
4 hamburger buns
Cheese slices

Saute onion until soft in small amount of oil. Add ground beef. Cook, stirring until pink is gone. Add seasonings and catsup. Spread evenly all the way to edge on 8 hamburger bun halves. Top with slice of cheese. Broil until cheese melts.

Kathy Boomgarden
Leaf River Junior Grange, No. 15
Ogle County, Illinois

PIZZABURGERS

1 lb. ground beef, browned
¾ lb. bologna, ground
¾ lb. process cheese, cubed
1 tsp. oregano
1 16-oz. can spaghetti sauce
Hamburger buns

Combine all ingredients except buns. Spread on hamburger buns. Place on cookie sheet. Bake at 400 degrees for 15 to 20 minutes.

Donna Lingbeck
Leaf River Junior Grange, No. 15
Ogle County, Illinois

OVEN CHICKEN

Chicken parts
1 c. crushed soda crackers

1 c. grated Parmesan cheese
1 stick butter or margarine, melted

Wash, drain and pat chicken with paper towel. Combine crackers and Parmesan cheese. Place cracker mixture in double paper bag. Melt butter in saucepan. Roll each chicken piece in butter. Place in bag; shake well. Place cracker-coated chicken in foil-lined baking pan. Bake at 350 degrees for 1 hour or until brown.

Angela Joseph
Turkey Hill Junior Grange
Belleville, Illinois

CRUMBY CHICKEN

1 med. chicken, cut in pieces
1½ sticks margarine, melted
1 c. bread crumbs
1 c. grated Parmesan cheese
1 tsp. garlic salt
Salt and pepper to taste

Dip each chicken piece into melted margarine. Combine remaining ingredients; mix well. Roll chicken in crumb mixture. Place in shallow baking dish. Bake at 350 degrees for 1 hour. Yield: 4-6 servings.

Carolyn Sipos
Reliance Grange, No. 58
Seaford, Delaware

CONNIE'S POTATOES

8 med. unpeeled potatoes
½ c. butter, melted
Salt, pepper and garlic salt to taste
1 tbsp. chopped parsley

Scrub potatoes well. Slice potatoes ¼-inch thick. Place in buttered 9 × 13-inch baking pan. Drizzle butter over potatoes. Season with salt, pepper and garlic salt. Sprinkle on parsley. Bake, uncovered in preheated 350-degree oven for 1 hour or until potatoes test done.

Donna Lingbeck
Leaf River Junior Grange, No. 15
Ogle County, Illinois

WHITE BREAD

1 tsp. sugar
2 tsp. yeast
Flour
1 tsp. salt

Mix ½ cup warm water, sugar and yeast in glass. Place 2 cups flour and salt in large bowl. Make a hole in center. Pour yeast mixture into hole. Sprinkle with a small amount of flour. Wait for yeast to bubble. Add ½ cup warm water; mix well. Cover bowl with a cloth. Wait 45 minutes. Dump dough onto floured board or table. Knead for 10 minutes. Add more flour if sticky. Place in greased loaf pan.

Wait 45 minutes for bread to double in bulk. Bake at 400 degrees for about 50 minutes. Take out of pan to cool. Slice. Eat with butter and jelly.

Adam Steel
Great Falls Junior Grange, No. 9
Arlington, Virginia

IRISH OATMEAL BREAD

3 c. flour
1¼ c. quick oats
1½ tsp. baking powder
1 tbsp. salt
1 egg, beaten
¼ c. honey
1½ c. milk
1 tbsp. butter

Combine all ingredients in a large bowl; mix well. Pour into well-greased loaf pan. Bake at 350 degrees for 20 to 30 minutes.

Threasa Penn
Locktown Junior Grange
Flemington, New Jersey

ZUCCHINI BREAD

3 eggs, beaten
1 c. oil
2 c. sugar
2 c. grated zucchini

2 tsp. vanilla extract
3 c. flour
1 tsp. salt
1 tsp. soda
½ tsp. baking powder
2 tsp. cinnamon
½ c. raisins

Combine all ingredients in a large bowl; mix well. Pour into 2 greased loaf pans. Bake at 325 degrees for 1 hour and 10 minutes.

Kathy O'Day
Reliance Grange, No. 58
Seaford, Delaware

EASY-DO DONUTS

Sugar
½ c. milk
1 egg
2 tbsp. shortening, melted
1½ c. sifted all-purpose flour
2 tsp. baking powder
½ tsp. salt
½ c. seedless raisins
Oil for deep frying
½ tsp. nutmeg or cinnamon

Blend together ⅓ cup sugar, milk, egg and 2 tablespoons melted shortening. Sift together flour, baking powder and salt. Add to liquid mixture; stir lightly. Mix in raisins. Drop from heaping teaspoon into oil heated to 365 degrees. Fry 2 to 3 minutes or until golden brown. Drain on paper towels. Mix ¼ cup sugar and nutmeg in a bag. Shake warm donuts in bag with sugar. For ease in spooning batter, dip teaspoon into hot shortening before dipping into batter. Yield: 2½ dozen.

Photograph for this recipe on page 224.

SPICE DOUGHNUTS

4 tbsp. butter or margarine
¼ tsp. cinnamon
¼ tsp. nutmeg
⅛ tsp. mace
1 c. sugar
2 eggs, beaten
4 c. sifted flour
4 tsp. baking powder
1 tsp. salt
1 c. milk
Shortening for frying

Blend butter and spices in large bowl. Add sugar, ¼ cup at a time, creaming after each addition until fluffy. Add eggs; blend well. Sift flour, baking powder and salt together; add to creamed mixture alternately with milk. Blend well. Chill dough for 5 minutes. Use enough shortening to fill a deep heavy pan ½ to ⅔ full when melted. Heat to 370 degrees. Place dough on lightly floured board. Shape into a ball. Roll dough ⅓-inch thick; cut with floured cutter. Lift doughnuts with wide spatula. Place 3 or 4 doughnuts at a time in hot oil. Cook to golden brown, turning once. Drain on absorbent paper.

Caron Green,
Green Valley Grange, No. 441
Brighton, Colorado

BLUEBERRY MUFFINS

1½ c. flour
2 tsp. baking powder
½ tsp. salt
½ c. sugar
¼ c. shortening
1 egg, beaten
½ c. milk
1 c. blueberries, drained

Combine dry ingredients in a large bowl. Cut in shortening until crumbly. Add egg and milk. Stir until just blended. Fold in blueberries gently. Fill greased muffin cups ⅔ full. Bake at 400 degrees for 20 to 25 minutes or until golden brown.

Donna Brauer
Turkey Hill Junior Grange, No. 7
Belleville, Illinois

BEST-EVER BLUEBERRY MUFFINS

1¾ c. flour
4 tbsp. sugar
2½ tsp. baking powder
¾ tsp. salt
1 egg, well beaten
½ c. milk
⅓ c. salad oil
1 c. fresh or frozen blueberries, drained

Sift flour, 2 tablespoons sugar, baking powder and salt into mixer bowl. Make well in center. Combine egg, milk and salad oil. Add all at once to dry ingredients. Stir quickly only until dry ingredients are moistened. Add 2 tablespoons sugar to blueberries. Toss lightly. Stir berries into batter. Spoon muffin tins or paper bake cups ⅔ full. Bake at 400 degrees about 25 minutes. Yield: 12 servings.

Carol Ann Robinson
Elmer Junior Grange, No. 67
New Jersey

PEANUT BUTTER AND JELLY FRENCH TOAST

1 egg, beaten
¼ c. milk
4 slices white bread
Peanut butter
Jelly

Break egg into large shallow bowl. Beat egg with a fork; stir in milk. Spread 2 slices of bread with peanut butter; spread jelly on top of peanut butter. Top each with another slice of bread. Dip sandwiches into egg-milk mixture. Cook on buttered griddle until brown on one side. Turn over; brown on second side. Serve hot with spoonful jelly on top of each sandwich. Eat with a knife and fork.

From a Young Grange Friend

SOFT PRETZELS

2 pkg. dry yeast
5 to 6 c. all-purpose flour
1 ½ c. cornmeal
3 eggs, beaten
⅓ c. sugar
2 tsp. salt
Coarse salt (opt).
Parmesan cheese (opt.)
Caraway, poppy or sesame seed (opt.)

Dissolve yeast in 2 cups warm water in large mixer bowl. Add 2 cups flour, cornmeal, 2 eggs, sugar and salt. Beat at medium speed of electric mixer for 2 minutes. Stir in enough additional flour to make a stiff dough. Shape to form a ball. Place in large greased bowl, turning once to coat surface of dough; cover. Let rise in warm place for 1 hour to 1 hour and 30 minutes or until doubled in bulk. Punch down dough. Divide dough in half on lightly floured surface. Shape each half into a ball. Flatten. Cut each flattened ball into 16 wedges. Roll each wedge to form 18-inch long rope. Shape to form pretzel. Place on lightly greased baking sheet. Beat 1 egg with 1 tablespoon water. Brush over pretzels. Sprinkle with coarse salt, grated Parmesan cheese, caraway, poppy or toasted sesame seed. Let rise in warm place for 30 to 45 minutes or until doubled in bulk. Bake at 425 degrees for 12 to 13 minutes or until golden brown. Serve hot or cool on wire rack. Dip in prepared mustard, or spread with softened butter or margarine.

Angela Joseph
Turkey Hill Junior Grange
Bellerville, Illinois

SOPAIPILLAS

2 eggs
1 c. milk
4 c. flour
¾ tsp. salt
1 tsp. baking powder
Oil for frying

Beat eggs. Add milk; mix well. Stir in dry ingredients adding as much flour as it will absorb. Roll as thin as possible. Cut in small squares. Fry in deep oil until golden brown and puffed like little pillows.

Caron Green
Green Valley Grange, No. 441
Brighton, Colorado

SOUR CREAM-PECAN COFFEE CAKE

½ c. butter, softened
1 c. sugar
3 eggs, beaten
2 c. sifted all-purpose flour
1 tsp. baking powder
½ tsp. salt
½ tsp. soda
1 c. sour cream
½ c. white raisins
1 c. candied fruit (opt.)
¾ c. (firmly packed) brown sugar
1 tbsp. flour
1 tsp. cinnamon
2 tbsp. butter
1 c. chopped pecans

Cream butter and sugar until light. Add eggs one at a time, beating thoroughly after each addition. Sift dry ingredients together. Add to creamed mixture alternately with sour cream. Beat until smooth. Stir in raisins and candied fruit. Spread in greased 9 × 13-inch baking pan. Combine remaining ingredients. Sprinkle over batter. Bake at 350 degrees for 40 to 45 minutes. Serve warm or cold.

April Adams
Arlington, Virginia

WHOLE WHEAT PANCAKES

1 c. flour
1 c. whole wheat flour
2 eggs
¾ tsp. salt
1 tbsp. plus ½ tsp. baking powder
¼ c. vegetable oil
⅛ c. liquid brown sugar
1½ c. milk

Combine all ingredients; beat until smooth. Refrigerate overnight. Cook as for pancakes. May be stored in covered container for several days. Yield: 6 servings.

John W. Alderson
White Lake Grange
Colville, Washington

SPICED TEA AND CIDER DRINK

3 tea bags
¼ c. sugar
2 c. cider or apple juice
Cinnamon sticks

Bring 1 quart of water to a boil in medium saucepan. Cover pan; steep 5 minutes. Remove tea bags. Stir in sugar until dissolved. Add cider; reheat. Pour into mugs. Add cinnamon stick stirrers. Garnish with apple cartwheels, if desired. Yield: 1½ quarts.

Photograph for this recipe on page 234.

THICK CHOCOLATE MALT

½ c. milk
2 scoops chocolate ice cream
3 tbsp. chocolate-flavored malted milk

Pour milk into small mixing bowl. Add 1 scoop ice cream. Beat until ice cream is well-mixed. Add remaining ice cream and malted milk. Beat until foamy. Yield: 1 serving.

Michael Joseph
Turkey Hill Junior Grange
Belleville, Illinois

SUNNY ORANGE SIPPER

2 c. orange juice
1 c. ginger ale
½ pt. vanilla ice cream
Orange slices
Maraschino cherries

Put first 3 ingredients in blender container. Blend for 15 seconds. Pour into tall glasses. Garnish with orange slice and cherry. Yield: 3½ cups.

Krista Arnold
Westminster Junior Grange, No. 59
Westminster, Colorado

DATE CANDY ROLL

3 c. sugar
1 c. thin cream
1 c. chopped dates
1 c. chopped walnuts
1 tsp. vanilla extract
1 tbsp. butter

Combine sugar and cream in saucepan. Stir over low heat until blended. Increase heat; cook to soft-ball stage. Add dates. Cook, stirring constantly, until dates are dissolved. Remove from heat. Add remaining ingredients. Beat until thick. Pour onto cold wet cloth. Shape into 2-inch roll. Chill. Slice.

Wanda Peterson
Weissert Grange, No. 419
Berwyn, Nebraska

CHOCOLATE-COCONUT CANDY

2 sq. unsweetened chocolate
1 15-oz. can condensed milk
2½ c. flaked coconut
½ c. Bran Buds

Melt chocolate in microwave oven or double boiler. Stir in remaining ingredients. Drop by teaspoon onto greased baking sheet. Place in preheated 350-degree oven. Turn off heat immediately. Leave in oven 15 to 20 minutes or until candy has a glazed appearance. Remove from baking sheet while warm. This was first place winner in State Womens' Activities Junior "Cereal Candy" contest in 1977. She was 6 at the time and used the microwave to melt chocolate. Yield: 48 candies.

Gail Schlueter
Turkey Hill Junior Grange, No. 7
Belleville, Illinois

O HENRY BARS

1 c. sugar
1 c. corn syrup
1 pkg. milk chocolate chips
1¼ c. chunky peanut butter
6 c. Special K. cereal

Combine sugar and corn syrup in saucepan. Bring to a boil; add peanut butter. Place cereal in large bowl. Add peanut butter mixture; mix well. Press into greased jelly roll pan. Melt chocolate chips in top of double boiler. Pour over cereal mixture. Cool; cut into bars.

Faye Zimmerman
Glade Valley Grange
Walkersville, Maryland

CARAMEL POPCORN

6 qt. popped popcorn
1 c. (firmly packed) brown sugar
½ c. molasses
¼ c. light corn syrup
¼ c. sugar
½ c. butter
1 tbsp. vinegar
1½ tsp. soda

Keep popcorn warm in roasting pan in 150 degree oven. Combine brown sugar, molasses, corn syrup, sugar, butter, 2 tablespoons water and vinegar in heavy 4-quart saucepan. Cook over medium heat, stirring constantly, until sugar dissolves and mixture boils. Continue cooking without stirring until mixture reaches hard-ball stage or to 260 degrees on candy thermometer. Remove from heat. Stir in soda, mixture will foam up. Pour hot syrup over popcorn, stirring while pouring. Cool well. Store in covered container. Tastes like cracker jacks. Will keep several weeks, if you can keep it that long!!!

Beth Sherow
Pleasant Valley Grange, No. 838
Pleasant Valley, New York

PEANUT BUTTER BITES

1 egg
⅓ c. peanut butter
1 tbsp. butter, softened
½ tsp. vanilla extract
⅛ tsp. salt
2 c. confectioners' sugar
¾ c. salted nuts, finely chopped

Beat egg with rotary egg beater in bowl. Add remaining ingredients except nuts; beat until smooth. Shape mixture into tiny balls. Add more sugar if necessary to make candy firm enough to handle. Roll each ball in nuts. Place on waxed paper. Refrigerate until firm.

Eric Smith
Norton Junior Grange
Norton, Ohio

PEANUT BUTTER BONBONS

1 lb. confectioners' sugar
1 c. graham cracker crumbs
1 c. finely chopped nuts
1 c. flaked coconut
1 c. peanut butter
1 c. margarine, softened
1 lg. package chocolate chips
½ bar paraffin wax

Combine first 6 ingredients: mix well. Form into small balls. Place on cookie sheet. Cover with waxed paper. Chill until firm. Mix chocolate chips and paraffin in top of double boiler; melt. Dip balls in mixture. Place on waxed paper to cool. Store in airtight container in cool place. Yield: 100 bonbons.

Darcy Andrews
Pony Express Grange, No. 815
Camino, California

PEANUT BUTTER CREAMS

1 egg, slightly beaten
⅛ tsp. salt
½ tsp. vanilla extract
⅓ c. peanut butter
1 tbsp. butter or margarine, softened
2 c. confectioners' sugar
¾ c. finely chopped salted peanuts

Combine first 5 ingredients and 1 cup confectioners' sugar in mixer bowl. Mix well. Add remaining sugar. Shape into 1-inch balls. Roll in peanuts. Refrigerate.

Jacqueline Marie Stanton
Elmer Junior Grange, No. 67
Elmer, New Jersey

PEANUT BUTTER CUPS

⅓ lb. graham cracker crumbs
½ lb. butter, melted
1 c. peanut butter
1 lb. confectioners' sugar
2 c. chocolate chips

Combine crumbs, butter, peanut butter and sugar in mixer bowl. Mix until smooth and well-blended. Pat into buttered 9×9-inch pan. Melt chocolate chips in saucepan over low heat. Spread over candy mixture. Cool. Cut into 1½-inch squares. Yield: 36 pieces.

Marjorie Zelenski, Delavan Lake Grange
Elkhorn, Wisconsin
Caron Green; Green Valley Grange, No. 441
Brighton, Colorado

PEANUT BUTTER DROPS

1 c. sugar
½ c. (firmly packed) brown sugar
1 c. white corn syrup
2 tsp. vanilla extract
½ tsp. salt

1 12-oz. jar crunchy peanut butter
6 c. (heaping) Captain Crunch cereal

Mix first 3 ingredients in a saucepan. Bring just to a boil. Remove from heat. Add next 3 ingredients; mix well. Pour over cereal. Drop by teaspoons onto waxed paper. Cool.

Brooke Dunn
Mossyrock Grange, No. 355
Ethel, Washington

PEANUT BUTTER FUDGE

1 c. peanut butter
1 c. butter, softened
1 1-lb. box confectioners' sugar

Combine peanut butter and butter in saucepan. Cook over medium heat until mixture comes to a boil. Remove from heat. Stir in confectioners' sugar; blend well. Place in buttered 8-inch square pan. Cool. Cut into 2-inch squares. Yield: 16 squares.

Pamela List
Bergen Junior Grange, No. 88
Bergen, New York

IRISH POTATOES

1 med. potato, cooked and mashed
1½ to 2 lb. confectioners' sugar
⅛ tsp. vanilla extract
⅛ tsp. salt
½ lb. coconut
1 tsp. cinnamon
¼ c. cocoa

Mix first 4 ingredients with wooden spoon until stiff. Knead with hands. Add coconut. Chill overnight. Mix cinnamon and cocoa. Shape potato mixture into potato shapes. Roll in cinnamon-cocoa mixture.

Mark Counsellor
Elmer Junior Grange, No. 67
Sewell, New Jersey

ICE CREAM TREATS FOR THE YOUNG

Cones
—Fill ice cream cones (flat bottom or cone-shaped) with ice cream; garnish in one of these ways.
1. Make a flower on top of cone using jellied fruit slices for petals and center of flower.
2. Make a ring of small spicy or fruit-flavored

gelatin candies around center top of ice cream. Plunge a tiny birthday candle in center of candy ring. Light candle if a flat bottom cone has been used.
3. Dip ice cream into chopped peanuts, chopped hard candy, chocolate sprinkles.

Flower Pot
—Fill a heavy paper cup with handle with scoops of ice cream and plunge a flowered or plain candy sucker in center of top scoop of ice cream. Stand candy leaves upright on either side of sucker.

Ice Cream Nosegay
—Fill a double thickness of fluted baking cup with a scoop of ice cream. Stand round peppermint candies up around edge of ice cream and sprinkle tiny candies over top. To serve, place on plate on a small lace paper doily.

Candy Topped Cups
—Fill paper cups wth ice cream. Plunge a stick of candy of favorite flavor in center and sprinkle chopped candy of same flavor on ice cream as desired.

Ice Cream Cart
—Cut a pint brick of ice cream into quarters or thirds. Arrange each slice on a chilled plate to one side of center. Freeze. Just before serving stand 2 animal cookies up in front of each ice cream slice and make "wheels" along either side of ice cream slices using hard chocolate candy wafers or small round flat cookies along either side of ice cream slice to resemble wheels of a cart. Serve plain or top with a toy.

Ice Cream—Graham Cracker Sandwich
—Put 2 graham crackers together sandwich-fashion using a thick slice of ice cream as the filling. Dip sandwich sides into chocolate shot or small candies, if desired. Serve plain or top with favorite sundae sauce.

Photograph for this recipe on page 230.

FINGER JELL-O

9-oz. flavored Jell-O
4 env. Knox gelatin

Dissolve Jell-O in 3 cups boiling water. Dissolve gelatin in 1 cup cold water in 9 × 13-inch pan. Add Jell-O mixture to gelatin. Stir to mix. Chill until set. Cut in blocks. Good "finger food" for snack or school party.

Jodi and Ann Thompson
Lewis Co., Logan Hill Grange
Chehalis, Washington

ALL NATURAL GRANOLA

6 c. oatmeal
1 12-oz. jar wheat germ
½ c. whole wheat flour
1 to 2 tbsp. cinnamon (opt.)
1½ c. (firmly packed) brown sugar
1 tsp. salt
2 tsp. vanilla extract
1 c. oil

Combine first 4 ingredients in large bowl. Combine brown sugar, salt and ⅛ cup water in saucepan. Bring to a boil, stirring often. Boil 1 minute. Cool slightly. Add vanilla and oil. Combine liquid and dry ingredients; mix well. Spread into two 9 × 13-inch baking pans. Bake at 200 degrees for 2 hours stirring every 30 minutes. Cool. Add raisins, chopped dried fruit, nuts or coconut, if desired. Yield: 9 cups.

Tina Lundgren
Potomac Grange, No. 1
Arlington, Virginia

CHERRY JUMBLE

2 c. sour red cherries
1 tbsp. butter or margarine
1 c. sugar
⅛ tsp. cinnamon
1 c. sifted all-purpose flour
1 tsp. baking powder

½ tsp. salt
2 tbsp. shortening

Pour cherries and juice into small saucepan. Add butter, ½ cup sugar and cinnamon. Bring to a boil. Place flour in a bowl with ½ cup sugar, baking powder and salt. Stir together. Add shortening. Mix with a fork. Add ½ cup water to flour mixture. Stir only until lightly blended. Spread dough evenly in greased 8 × 8-inch pan. Spoon hot cherry mixture over top. Bake at 375-degrees for 20 to 30 minutes. Yield: 9 servings.

Jill Eckert
Turkey Hill Junior Grange, No. 7
Belleville, Illinois

KNOX BLOX

4 env. unflavored gelatin
3 3-oz. packages flavored gelatin

Mix unflavored and flavored gelatin in a bowl. Pour in 4 cups boiling water; stir until gelatin dissolves. Pour into 9 × 13-inch pan. Chill until firm. Cut into squares; serve.

Donna Furst
Hopewell Grange, No. 1747
Washington, Illinois

FRENCH CHOCOLATE ICE CREAM

3 c. sugar
6 tbsp. all-purpose flour
½ tsp. salt
4 1-oz. squares unsweetened chocolate
6 c. milk
6 eggs, beaten
3 c. heavy cream
4½ tbsp. vanilla extract
3 c. half and half

Combine first 4 ingredients in saucepan; stir milk in gradually. Cook over low heat, stirring until thick. Add small amount of hot mixture to eggs; mix well. Return to hot mixture. Cook 1 minute. Chill. Add cream, vanilla and half and half. Pour into 1 gallon freezer container. Freeze according to manufacturer's directions. Churn for 20 to 30 minutes. Yield: 1 gallon.

Mike Peterson
Weissert Grange, No. 419
Berwyn, Nebraska

CHOCOLATE BROWNIES

1 stick butter or margarine
2 sq. baking chocolate
1 c. sugar
2 eggs
1 tsp. vanilla extract
½ c. chopped nuts (opt.)
¾ c. sifted flour
½ tsp. baking powder
½ tsp. salt

Place butter and chocolate in a saucepan over low heat until melted. Remove from heat; add sugar. Be careful of hot pan! Add 1 unbeaten egg; mix well with a fork. Add remaining egg; mix until combined. Add vanilla and nuts. Sift flour, baking powder and salt together on a piece of waxed paper. Add flour mixture to chocolate mixture; mix thoroughly. Pour into 8-inch square baking pan. Bake in preheated 350-degree oven for 25 to 30 minutes. Remove from oven. Set on rack to cool slightly. Cut in squares while still warm. Remove from pan when completely cool.

Nancy N. Perkins
Blue Mountain Grange, No. 263
Wells River, Vermont

FROSTED BROWNIES

¾ c. butter, softened
1 c. sugar
2 eggs
2 tsp. vanilla extract
¾ c. all-purpose flour
Unsweetened cocoa
½ tsp. baking powder
Salt
½ c. chopped nuts
Miniature marshmallows
2 c. confectioners' sugar
2 tbsp. milk

Cream ½ cup butter and sugar in large bowl. Beat in eggs and 1 teaspoon vanilla. Sift together flour, ⅓ cup cocoa, baking powder and ¼ teaspoon salt. Add to creamed mixture, blending thoroughly. Stir in nuts. Pour into well-greased 6½ × 10½-inch pan. Bake at 350 degrees for 25 to 30 minutes or until brownies test done. Do not overbake. Remove from oven. Cover entire top immediately with marshmallows. Return to oven; bake additional 2 to 3 minutes. Cool completely in pan. Cream ¼ cup butter. Blend in ¼ cup cocoa, 1 teaspoon vanilla and pinch of salt. Add confectioners' sugar alternately with milk. Beat until light and fluffy. Frost brownies. Yield: 2 dozen.

The Graper Children
Locktown Junior Grange
Hemington, New Jersey

QUICK BROWNIES

½ c. margarine
1 c. sugar
1 tsp. vanilla
1 lb. can chocolate syrup
½ tsp. salt
1 c. flour
1 c. chopped nuts

Combine all ingredients; mix together. Spread in a greased sheet pan. Bake at 350 degrees for 30 minutes.

Pam Craven
Leaf River Junior Grange, No. 15
Ogle County, Illinois

YUMMY BROWNIES

3 sq. unsweetened chocolate
⅓ c. shortening
1 c. sugar
2 eggs
¾ c. flour
½ tsp. baking powder
½ tsp. salt
½ c. chopped nuts (opt.)

Melt chocolate and shortening in double boiler over hot water. Beat in sugar and eggs. Blend flour, baking powder and salt. Stir into egg mixture. Add nuts. Spread into 8 × 8-inch pan. Bake in preheated 350-degree oven for 30 to 35 minutes. Cool; cut into squares. Yield: 16 2-inch squares.

Ann Piano
Locktown Junior Grange
Flemington, New Jersey

CONGO BARS

⅔ c. salad oil
1 1-lb. package brown sugar
3 eggs, beaten
1 tsp. vanilla extract
2¾ c. flour
2½ tsp. baking powder
1 c. nuts
1 sm. package chocolate chips

Combine oil, brown sugar and eggs. Add vanilla, flour and baking powder; mix well. Stir in nuts and chocolate chips. Drop by spoonfuls onto greased cookie sheet. Bake at 350 degrees for 25 to 30 minutes.

Sharon Gantz
Elmer Junior Grange, No. 67
Elmer, New Jersey

FUDGIE SCOTCH SQUARES

1½ c. graham cracker crumbs
1 can sweetened condensed milk
1 6-oz. package semisweet chocolate morsels
1 6-oz. package butterscotch morsels
1 c. coarsely chopped walnuts

Blend together all ingredients; mix well. Press mixture into very well-greased 9-inch square pan. Bake at 350 degrees for 30 to 35 minutes. Cool for 45 minutes. Cut into 1½-inch squares. Yield: 36.

Todd Stuller
Hamilton Junior Grange, No. 44
Lawrenceville, New Jersey

GENIE BARS

1 c. sugar
1 c. light corn syrup
1½ c. peanut butter
7 c. Rice Crispies
1 sm. package butterscotch chips
1 sm. package chocolate chips

Place sugar and syrup in saucepan. Bring to a boil. Remove from heat. Add peanut butter; mix well. Place cereal in large well-greased bowl. Pour syrup over cereal; mix well. Spread on 10 × 15½-inch cookie sheet. Melt butterscotch and chocolate chips over boiling water in a double boiler. Spread over cereal mixture. Cut into bars before completely cool.

Kathy Boomgarden
Leaf River Junior Grange, No. 15
Ogle County, Illinois

CHOCOLATE COOKIES

2 c. sugar
½ c. butter
½ c. milk
4 tbsp. Hershey's cocoa
¼ c. salt
½ c. peanut butter
3 c. oatmeal

Mix sugar, butter, milk, cocoa and salt in saucepan. Bring to a boil; boil for 1 minute only. Add peanut butter and oatmeal. Drop from teaspoon onto waxed paper. Cool.

John Robinson
Elmer Junior Grange, No. 67
Elmer, New Jersey

CHOCOLATE DROP QUICKIES

2 c. sugar
½ c. cocoa
½ c. milk
½ c. butter
½ c. peanut butter or ½ c. nuts
1 tsp. vanilla extract
3 c. quick oats

Mix sugar and cocoa in saucepan. Add milk and butter. Boil 1 minute. Add peanut butter, vanilla and oats. Spoon onto waxed paper. Let harden. Remove with spatula. Yield: 3 dozen.

Michele Haudrich
Floraville Community Junior Grange, No. 71
St. Clair County, Illinois

CHOCOLATE-OATMEAL COOKIES

¼ c. butter
¼ c. shortening
½ c. (firmly packed) brown sugar
½ c. sugar
¾ c. sifted all-purpose flour
½ tsp. soda
½ tsp. salt
1 egg
½ tsp. vanilla extract
1½ c. quick oats
¼ c. chopped pecans
Chocolate bars
Pecan halves

Cream butter and shortening. Add sugars; cream together. Sift flour, soda and salt; add to creamed mixture. Add egg and vanilla. Beat thoroughly for 2 minutes. Stir in oats and pecans. Shape dough into one 12-inch roll. Wrap in waxed paper; chill thoroughly. Slice; place on ungreased cookie sheets. Bake in preheated 375-degree oven for 10 to 12 minutes. Remove from oven; place small square of milk chocolate bar immediately on each. Remove from cookie sheets. Press a pecan half into chocolate.

Tammy Lynn Walker
Winona Grange, No. 1038
Endicott, Washington

NO-BAKE CHOCOLATE-OATMEAL COOKIES

2 c. sugar
½ c. cocoa
½ c. shortening
½ c. milk
1 tsp. vanilla extract

½ c. peanut butter
3 c. oatmeal
½ c. coconut or nuts (opt.)

Boil sugar, cocoa, shortening and milk for 2 to 3 minutes or until desired hardness. Remove from heat. Add vanilla, peanut butter, oatmeal and coconut. Mix quickly. Drop on greased cookie sheets. Let set for 10 to 15 minutes. Yield: 4-6 dozen.

Becky Lucas
Oakfield Grange
Oakfield, New York

CHOCOLATE NO-BAKE COOKIES

½ c. butter
½ c. cocoa
1½ c. sugar
½ c. milk
1 tsp. vanilla extract
3 c. quick oats
¼ to ½ c. coconut (opt.)

Combine first 4 ingredients in saucepan. Cook 3 minutes. Add vanilla. Pour over oats. Add coconut if desired. Shape quickly into balls. Place on waxed paper. Cool.

Renee Koenig
Central Junior Grange, No. 519
Slatington, Pennsylvania

TEENAGER'S DELIGHT

2 c. sugar
3 c. flour
1 tsp. salt
½ c. cocoa
2 tsp. soda
3 tbsp. vinegar
2 tsp. vanilla extract
⅔ c. salad oil

Pour all ingredients into mixer bowl. Add 2 cups cold water. Beat until smooth. Pour into ungreased 11 × 13-inch baking pan. Bake at 375 degrees for 35 minutes.

Judith E. Williams
South Sangerville Grange, No. 335
Sangerville, Maine

GUMDROP BARS

2 c. sifted flour
½ tsp. salt

2 c. (firmly packed) light brown sugar
½ c. nuts
1 c. orange gumdrops, chopped
4 eggs, separated

Combine dry ingredients in a bowl. Mix in gum-drops. Beat egg yolks well. Add to dry mixture with 2 tablespoons water. Beat egg whites until stiff. Fold into batter. Spread thin layer in 2 shallow 8 × 10-inch pans. Bake at 400 degrees for 15 to 18 minutes. Cool. Cut into squares or bars.

Kathy Boomgarden
Leaf River Junior Grange, No. 15
Ogle County, Illinois

HAYSTACK COOKIES

1 12-oz. package butterscotch chips
½ c. peanut butter
4 c. corn flakes
1 c. coconut

Melt butterscotch chips and peanut butter until smooth in top of double boiler, stirring frequently. Mix corn flakes and coconut in large bowl. Pour peanut butter mixture over dry mixture; stir until cereal is coated. Drop from teaspoon onto a lightly greased cookie sheet. Put in cool place to harden.

Donna Lingbeck
Leaf River Junior Grange, No. 15
Ogle County, Illinois

LEMON SQUARES

1 c. flour
½ c. margarine
¼ c. confectioners' sugar
2 eggs
1 c. sugar
½ tsp. baking powder
¼ tsp. salt
2 tbsp. lemon juice

Mix flour, margarine and confectioners' sugar. Press evenly into bottom of ungreased 8 × 8-inch pan. Bake in preheated 350-degree oven for 20 minutes. Beat remaining ingredients 3 minutes. Pour over hot crust. Bake at 350 degrees for 25 minutes longer or until tests done. Cool; cut into squares. Yield: 16 squares.

Craig Lee
Turkey Hill Junior Grange, No. 7
Belleville, Illinois

¾ tsp. soda
½ tsp. baking powder
¼ tsp. salt
5 doz. candy-coated chocolates

Cream together peanut butter and butter. Add sugars gradually; cream together until light and fluffy. Add vanilla and egg; beat well. Stir dry ingredients together; add to creamed mixture. Mix thoroughly. Chill dough if necessary. Shape into balls, using 1 heaping teaspoonful for each ball. Place on cookie sheets. Bake in 375-degree oven for 10 to 12 minutes or until cookies are golden brown. Remove from oven. Top each cookie with a candy-coated chocolate. Cool on racks.

Photograph for this recipe on page 234.

PEANUT BUTTER COOKIES

½ c. shortening
½ c. peanut butter
½ c. sugar
½ c. (firmly packed) brown sugar
1 egg
1¼ c. flour
½ tsp. baking powder
¾ tsp. soda
¼ tsp. salt

Mix first 5 ingredients thoroughly. Add remaining ingredients. Mix well. Place on greased cookie sheet. Bake at 375 degrees for 10 to 12 minutes.

Beth Crum
Glade Valley Junior Grange, No. 36
Walkersville, Maryland

MOLASSES CRINKLIES

¾ c. lard, softened
1 c. (firmly packed) brown sugar
1 egg
¼ c. molasses
2¼ c. all-purpose flour
2 tsp. soda
1 tsp. cinnamon
1 tsp. ginger
¼ tsp. cloves
¼ tsp. salt
Sugar

Mix first 4 ingredients thoroughly in bowl. Sift flour, soda, spices and salt together; add to lard mixture. Stir until well-blended. Chill dough at least 2 hours. Roll teaspoonful soft dough into balls. Dip in sugar. Place on greased baking sheet 2-inches apart. Bake in preheated 375-degree oven for 10 to 12 minutes. Cook on wire rack.

Wendy Watson
Delrio Grange, No. 828
Mansfield, Washington

PETER PANIC BUTTONS

1 c. crunchy peanut butter
½ c. butter, softened
½ c. sugar
½ c. (firmly packed) brown sugar
½ tsp. vanilla
1 egg
1½ c. sifted all-purpose flour

SEVEN-LAYER BARS

1 stick margarine
1½ c. graham cracker crumbs
1 sm. package chocolate bits
1 c. chopped nuts
1 3½-oz. can flaked coconut
1 can sweetened condensed milk

Melt margarine in 9 × 13-inch pan. Spread evenly over pan. Sprinkle graham cracker crumbs, chocolate bits, nuts and coconut evenly into the pan. Drizzle milk over mixture. Bake in 350-degree oven for 25 minutes or until mixture begins to brown. Let cool in the pan about 15 minutes. Cut into small bars.

Diane Lingbeck
Leaf River Junior Grange, No. 15
Ogle County, Illinois

FROSTED PUMPKIN BARS

4 eggs, beaten
1 c. salad oil
2 c. sugar
1 c. pumpkin
2 tsp. salt
2 tsp. cinnamon
1 tsp. soda
1 tsp. baking powder
2 c. flour
1 c. nuts
3 oz. package cream cheese, softened
6 tbsp. butter, softened
¼ lb. confectioners' sugar
1 tsp. vanilla extract
1 tsp. milk

Combine first 10 ingredients. Pour onto greased and floured cookie sheet. Bake at 350 degrees for 20 to 25 minutes. Cool. Combine remaining ingredients. Add additional milk if needed for desired consistency. Spread on warm pumpkin bars.

Diane Lingbeck
Leaf River Junior Grange, No. 15
Ogle County, Illinois

MOTHER'S SUGAR COOKIES

3 c. sugar
1 c. shortening
2 eggs
½ tsp. salt
4 c. sifted flour
2 tbsp. cornstarch
1 tsp. soda
2 tsp. baking powder
1 c. sour milk or buttermilk
1 tsp. vanilla or lemon extract

Cream sugar, shortening, eggs and salt until light and fluffy. Sift dry ingredients; add to creamed mixture alternately with sour milk and vanilla. Drop from teaspoon onto greased and floured cookie sheet. Bake at 350 degrees about 10 to 15 minutes.

Carol Robinson
Elmer Junior Grange, No. 67
Elmer, New Jersey

WHITE SUGAR COOKIES

Sugar
¾ c. shortening
3 eggs, beaten
1 tsp. salt
1 tbsp. vanilla extract
1 c. milk
Flour
½ tsp. soda

3 tsp. baking powder
1 pkg. raisins

Cream 2 cups sugar and shortening. Add eggs, salt, vanilla and milk; mix well. Combine 4½ cups flour, soda and baking powder. Mix well. Drop by spoonfuls on cookie sheet. Place raisins in saucepan. Add enough water to cover. Add 4 tablespoons each flour and sugar. Cook until thick. Fill cookies before baking if desired. Bake at 350 degrees for 12 minutes. Yield: 5 dozen.

Joyce Reaser
Spring Garden Grange, No. 32
Allenwood, Pennsylvania

TOFFEE-NUT BARS

¼ c. butter, softened
¼ c. shortening
1½ c. (firmly packed) brown sugar
Flour
2 eggs, beaten
1 tsp. vanilla extract
1 tsp. baking powder
½ tsp. salt
1 c. moist shredded coconut
1 c. almonds

Cream together butter, shortening and ½ cup brown sugar. Stir in 1 cup sifted flour. Press into 9 × 13-inch pan. Bake at 350 degrees for 10 minutes. Combine eggs, 1 cup brown sugar and vanilla. Mix together 2 tablespoons flour, baking powder and salt. Add to egg mixture. Stir in coconut and almonds. Pour over baked mixture. Bake 25 minutes longer or until topping is golden brown. Cool. Cut into bars. Yield: 30 bars.

Judy Avara
Floraville Community Junior Grange, No. 71
St. Clair County, Illinois

IMPOSSIBLE PIE

1 stick margarine or butter, softened
1 c. coconut
2 c. milk
4 eggs
1 c. sugar
2 tsp. vanilla extract
1 tsp. nutmeg
½ c. flour

Combine all ingredients in blender container. Blend on high speed for 30 seconds. Pour into a 9-inch well-buttered pie pan. Bake in a preheated 350-degree oven for 50 minutes.

Mary Alice Trew
Riverside Junior Grange, No. 10
Buffalo Gap, South Dakota

CHEESE TARTS

½ c. sugar
¼ tsp. lemon juice
2 eggs, beaten
2 8-oz. packages cream cheese, softened
20 vanilla wafers
Fruit pie filling

Add sugar and lemon juice to eggs gradually. Add ceam cheese; mix well. Place cupcake papers in muffin pan. Place 1 vanilla wafer in bottom of each cup. Pour cheese mixture over wafer. Bake in 350-degree oven for 15 minutes. Cool. Top each with about 1 tablespoon of fruit pie filling.

Jann Heberer
Turkey Hill Junior Grange, No. 7
Belleville, Illinois

FRESH STRAWBERRY PIE

¾ to 1 c. sugar
1 tbsp. cornstarch
¼ c. strawberry flavor gelatin
Few drops of red food coloring (opt.)
1 qt. fresh, sweet strawberries
1 baked 9-in. pie shell
Lightly sweetened whipped cream

Combine 1 cup water and first 3 ingredients in small saucepan. Cook until thick. Add food coloring. Cool. Combine strawberries and sauce gently. Pour into pie shell. Chill. Top with whipped cream. Add a few additional strawberries as a garnish.

Lisa G. Young
Goodwill Grange, No. 959
Troutdale, Virginia

CHOCOLATE CHIP CAKE

2 c. (firmly packed) brown sugar
2 c. flour
½ c. butter or margarine, softened
1 tsp. soda
½ tsp. salt
1 egg, beaten
1 c. milk
1 tsp. vanilla extract
½ c. nuts (opt.)
¾ c. chocolate chips

Combine first 3 ingredients in a mixing bowl; mix well. Reserve 1 cup mixture. Add next 6 ingredients to remaining mixture; mix well. Pour into greased and floured 9 × 13-inch pan. Sprinkle on reserved mixture. Scatter chocolate chips over top. Press into batter. Bake at 350 degrees for 35 minutes.

Trea Hegge
Flora Junior Grange, No. 10
Capron, Illinois

CRAZY CHOCOLATE QUICK CAKE

3 c. flour
6 tsp. cocoa
2 c. sugar
2 tsp. soda
1 tsp. salt
2 tsp. vinegar
2 tsp. vanilla extract
10 tsp. Wesson oil
½ c. chopped pecans

Sift dry ingredients together into a greased 9 × 13-inch pan. Make 3 indentions in dry ingredients. Pour vinegar into one, vanilla into the second and oil into the third. Pour 2 cups water over all; mix until smooth. Place pecans on top. Bake at 350 degrees for 1 hour. Cool; cut in squares. Serve with ice cream or whipped cream.

Diane Lingbeck
Leaf River Junior Grange, No. 15
Ogle County, Illinois

FRUITCAKE

2 eggs
2 c. sugar
2 tsp. soda
1 16-oz. can crushed pineapple
2 c. flour
1 c. nuts
1 8-oz. package cream cheese, softened
1 stick margarine
2 c. confectioners' sugar

Combine first 6 ingredients; beat well. Pour into 9 × 12-inch pan. Bake at 350 degrees for 30 minutes or until done. Combine cream cheese, margarine and confectioners' sugar. Beat until fluffy. Frost cake. Nuts may be added if desired.

Nancy Armstrong
Pittsford Grange, No. 13?
Pittsford, Michigan

ANGEL GINGERBREAD

½ c. sugar
¼ c. butter or margarine, softened
1 egg, beaten
1¼ c. molasses
Pinch of salt
½ tsp. cinnamon
¼ tsp. cloves
1 c. sifted flour
1 tsp. soda

Cream sugar and butter. Add egg, molasses, salt, cinnamon, cloves and flour; mix well. Dissolve soda in ½ cup boiling water. Add to mixture; beat well. Pour in greased cake pan. Bake at 350 degrees for 20 to 25 minutes. Yield: 12 servings.

Mary Ann Pullen
Plieades Junior Grange, No. 328
Glenburn, Maine

SCOTCH SHORTBREAD

2 sticks butter, softened
1 egg yolk
1 c. confectioners' sugar
2¾ to 3 c. flour

Cream butter. Add egg yolk. Add confectioners' sugar; mix well. Add flour, working with hands. Roll or press 1-inch thick on ungreased cookie sheet. Make thumbprints around edge; fork pricks on surface. Bake in 325-degree oven for 30 to 35 minutes. Yield: 20 to 24 servings.

Meg Wiley
Potomac Grange, No. 1
Arlington, Virginia

BANANA-ORANGE FROST

1 banana
⅛ c. orange juice
½ c. cold milk
1 pt. orange sherbet

Peel and slice banana; place in bowl or blender. Mash. Add orange juice; beat until smooth. Add milk and half the sherbet; beat until smooth. Pour into 2 tall glasses; top each with scoop of sherbet. Decorate each glass with orange slice and banana slice, if desired. Yield: 2 servings.

From a Young Grange Friend

SHERBET PUNCH

1 qt. vanilla ice cream
5 pt. sherbet
1 6-oz. can frozen orange juice, thawed
2 sm. cans frozen lemonade, thawed

Combine all ingredients with 9 cups cold water in large punch bowl. Mix well.

From a Young Grange Friend

SWEDISH GLUG

4 tsp. tea
2 sticks cinnamon
1 46-oz. can grapefruit-pineapple juice
1 pt. apple juice

Steep the tea and 1 quart boiling water with cinnamon for 3 minutes. Heat juices with strained tea. Bring all ingredients to a boil. Serve hot. Store in refrigerator. Yield: 20 servings.

From a Young Grange Friend

FRUIT FIZZ

⅛ c. lemon juice
1 c. orange juice
¾ c. sugar
1 c. strawberries, halved
1 pt. ginger ale

Do not strain lemon and orange juice. Mix juices. Add sugar; shake or beat thoroughly. Add strawberries and ginger ale; serve with an ice cube. Yield: 6 cups.

From a Young Grange Friend

BANANA SHAKE

1 c. cold milk
1 banana, chopped
2 tsp. sugar
1 egg

Blend all ingredients in blender or mix at high speed in mixer. May be served as breakfast in a glass or with cinnamon toast. Yield: 1 serving.

From a Young Grange Friend.

Men's
Family Favorites

Although they may pretend to feel otherwise, men are really very much at home in the kitchen. In fact, until recent generations, it was exclusively the men who were the world-famous chefs and cookbook authors, not women. Somewhere along the way, of course, women have taken over in the kitchen—but it would be a definite mistake to keep the men out of it!

One probable reason why men succeed so easily in the kitchen is that they take cooking less seriously than the homemaker whose job it is to be in the kitchen every day, several times per day, to prepare the family's meals and stick to the budget. For a man who has worked all day outside the home, it is like a hobby to come into the kitchen and work "over a hot stove"—and he probably approaches it with all the creativity he would a hobby. For that reason, men are as much at home with a seafood casserole, a chocolate souffle or zesty appetizers as they are with their golf clubs, tools, or in the garden.

Today, when people think of a man doing the cooking, they actually picture him over the charcoal grill. But, as the following recipes prove, Grange men—like most men—are capable of creating a great variety of tasty dishes. Let the man in your house cook for a change and treat you and the rest of the family to a delicious meal!

CIBOLO CREEK CHOWDER

1 lb. fish fillets, fresh or frozen
½ c. chopped onion
2 tbsp. shortening, melted
2 c. chopped potatoes
1 c. chopped celery
1 bay leaf, crumbled
¾ tsp. salt
2 oz. salt pork or crisp bacon, diced
Pepper to taste
2 c. milk
1 8-oz. can cream-style corn

Cut fish into 1-inch squares. Saute onion in shortening until soft. Add 1 cup boiling water, fish and next 5 ingredients; cover. Simmer 15 minutes or until potatoes are tender. Add milk and corn; heat thoroughly. Serve immediately.

Col. (Ret) Henry Luther
Boerne Grange, No. 1545
Boerne, Texas

OYSTER STEW

1 pt. oysters
Salt and pepper to taste
1 can evaporated milk
1 evaporated milk can of whole milk
1½ to 2 tbsp. butter
Paprika to taste

Drain oysters through strainer reserving liquor. Wash oysters. Place in pan; cover oysters. Cook until the edges of oysters curl. Add salt and pepper. Heat milk. Add to oysters. Add butter. Sprinkle with paprika.

Robert G. Proctor, National Grange Secretary
Potomac Grange, No. 1
Falls Church, Virginia

BROWN POTATO SOUP

2 med. potatoes, diced
1 tsp. salt
2 tbsp. pastry flour
1½ tbsp. bacon grease or butter

Place potatoes and salt into large saucepan; add 4 quarts water. Cook until potatoes are tender. Place flour and bacon grease in skillet. Brown flour. Add potato soup. Stir until thickened.

Edward Kniecly
Muskingum Co., New Concord Grange, No. 2416
Norwich, Ohio

RANCH-STYLE POTATO SOUP

3 med. potatoes, peeled and cut up
1 sm. onion, diced
2 eggs
2 c. milk
¼ tsp. celery salt

Combine potatoes and onion in saucepan with enough water to cover. Boil until tender. Mash potatoes coarsely in the water. Break eggs into the simmering potatoes. Stir in. Add milk; simmer. Stir frequently until desired thickness. Stir in celery salt.

Francis Guthrie, Master
Colorado State Grange
Denver, Colorado

SEVEN-LAYER SALAD

1 to 1½ c. frozen peas, thawed
½ head lettuce, shredded
1 to 2 stalks celery, diced
1 med. green pepper, diced
8 thinly sliced green onions, with some tops
1½ c. mayonnaise
Parmesan cheese

Run water over peas to thaw; do not cook. Layer lettuce, celery, pepper, onion and peas in 2-quart glass dish. Cover peas with mayonnaise, sealing to edge of bowl. Sprinkle Parmesan cheese over top. Decorate top with finely shredded carrot, if desired. Cover. Chill. Prepare a day ahead for best results.

Bill Steel
Potomac Grange
Arlington, Virginia

SPAGHETTI SALAD

1 1-lb box spaghetti, cooked
1 head cabbage, chopped fine
2 onions, chopped fine
1 bunch celery, chopped fine
1 c. sugar
Salt and pepper to taste
1 c. vinegar
2 tbsp. prepared mustard
1 tbsp. (heaping) flour
1 sm. jar pimentos
2 hard-boiled eggs, chopped

Chop cooked spaghetti fine. Add cabbage, onions and celery. Add sugar, salt and pepper; mix well. Heat vinegar, mustard and flour in saucepan. Stir constantly until thick. Cool. Add to spaghetti mixture. Add pimentos and eggs. Chill.

Kenneth Smith
Norton Grange, No. 2566
Norton, Ohio

ARDEN'S CREAMY SALAD DRESSING

1¼ c. sugar
½ tsp. paprika
½ tsp. salt
½ tsp. celery seed
½ c. catsup
½ c. vinegar
1 to 1¼ c. salad oil

Put all ingredients in blender container. Process several seconds until well-blended. Store in refrigerator in airtight container.

Arden Fitch, Master
Olivesburg Grange, No. 2641
Ashland, Ohio

SMOKEY CHILI BEANS

1½ c. dried pinto beans
1¼ tsp. salt
1 tsp. sugar
1 tsp. chili powder
1 tsp. liquid smoke
Pieces of smoked pork, bacon or ham hocks

Place all ingredients with 4½ cups water in pressure cooker. Reduce heat to medium low when gauge jiggles. Cook for 1 hour. Release pressure. Boil in open cooker for 25 minutes; stir well. Add water if more juice is needed.

Lynn Kees
LaPlata Co., Animas Valley Grange, No. 194
Durango, Colorado

ZUCCHINI BOATS

Zucchini squash
Sausage and hamburger
Bread crumbs

Scoop pulp from squash. Combine with ground sausage and hamburger. Season to taste. Pack into squash. Sprinkle with bread crumbs. Place in baking pan. Bake at 350 degrees until tender.

Joe Peters, Master
Arkansas State Grange
Rogers, Arkansas

NO-CLEAN-UP VEGETABLES

4 peeled potatoes, diced
4 peeled carrots, cut into ½-inch pieces

1 onion, sliced
Salt and pepper to taste
½ stick butter
6 to 8 slices crisp-cooked bacon, crumbled (opt.)
½ cup Cheddar cheese, cubed (opt.)

Place potatoes and carrots in greased 18-inch length of heavy-duty aluminum foil. Place onion over potatoes. Season with salt and pepper. Slice butter into thin pats. Scatter over vegetables. Add bacon and cheese. Seal foil securely. Grill over hot coals about 20 to 25 minutes, turning every 5 minutes. May be cooked in a 350-degree oven for 45 to 50 minutes. Yield: 3-5 servings.

Bill Steel
Potomac Grange, No. 1
Arlington, Virginia

SUPREME TOMATO SAUCE

6 lb. fresh tomatoes, skinned
⅛ c. oil
1 c. finely diced onions
⅛ c. flour
½ tsp. sugar
5 garlic cloves, mashed
3 1-in. pieces orange peel
1 lg. bouquet garni
½ tsp. fennel seeds
½ tsp. dried basil
¼ tsp. coriander
1 tsp. salt
½ tsp. pepper
½ tsp. celery salt
Pinch of saffron
Tomato paste

Cut tomatoes in half; squeeze out seeds and juice. Chop coarsely. Heat oil in heavy kettle. Add onions; cook slowly, covered for 15 minutes until soft and transparent. Add flour; cook 2 or 3 minutes. Add tomatoes and seasonings. Cover. Simmer for 15 minutes. Add 2 tablespoons tomato paste. Simmer slowly, partially covered, for 1 hour to 1 hour and 30 minutes. Stir occasionally, adding small amount of tomato juice, if needed. Sauce should be very thick. Remove herb bouquet. Add more tomato paste if needed for color. Check seasoning. Add salt, if needed. Cool. Spoon into 1 cup plastic containers. Freeze.

Art Du Lac, Master
Virginia State Grange
Great Falls, Virginia

CHEESE OMELET

Eggs
Milk
Salt and pepper to taste
Butter
Cheese slices

Beat eggs until fluffy. Beat in 1 tablespoon milk, salt and pepper for each egg. Pour into sizzling butter in skillet over low heat. Cook slowly, keeping heat low. Start lifting slightly with spatula as under surface becomes set to let uncooked portion flow underneath and cook. Place slices of cheese on half the egg mixture when mixture is almost set. Fold gently over the other half to cover.

Frank H. Warner, Master
Connecticut State Grange, Hamden Grange No. 99
Hamden, Connecticut

MACARONI AND CHEESE ELEGANTE

1 7-oz. package elbow macaroni
1 egg, slightly beaten
1 pt. small curd cottage cheese
½ pt. sour cream
¾ tsp. salt
Dash of pepper
2 c. shredded sharp Cheddar cheese
Paprika

Cook macaroni according to package directions. Combine egg, cottage cheese, sour cream, salt and pepper. Add cheese; mix well. Stir in macaroni. Pour into a buttered 2-quart casserole. Sprinkle with paprika. Bake in preheated 350-degree oven about 45 minutes. Yield: 6-8 servings.

Robert Granger
Rexville Grange, No. 815
Anacortes, Washington

QUICHE LORRAINE

1½ c. half and half
4 eggs, slightly beaten
½ tsp. salt
Dash of pepper
2 c. shredded Swiss cheese
2 tsp. flour
8 slices crisply cooked bacon, crumbled
1 unbaked 9-in. pastry shell

Combine first 4 ingredients; beat well. Toss cheese with flour; add cheese mixture and bacon to egg mixture. Pour into pastry shell. Bake at 350 degrees for 40 to 45 minutes. Add onions, green pepper or mushrooms, if desired. Yield: 6 servings.

George C. Grobusky, Master
South Carolina State Grange
Walhalla, South Carolina

OLD-FASHIONED POT ROAST WITH EGG NOODLES

    4 lb. eye-of-round or beef rump roast
    2 tbsp. salad oil
    ¼ lb. mushrooms, sliced
    2 med. onions, sliced
    1 lg. carrot, halved
    1 rib of celery, halved
    2 cloves of garlic, minced
    Salt
    2 beef bouillon cubes
    ¼ tsp. pepper
    2 bay leaves
    ⅓ c. tomato paste
    2 tbsp. flour
    2 tbsp. chopped parsley (opt.)
    1 lb. wide egg noodles

Brown meat on all sides in oil in Dutch oven. Remove meat; drain fat. Combine vegetables, garlic, 1¼ teaspoons salt, bouillon cubes, pepper, bay leaves, tomato paste and 1 cup water in pan; heat to boiling. Return roast. Cover; simmer 4 hours. Discard carrot, celery and bay leaves. Remove meat to platter; keep warm. Blend flour and 3 tablespoons water; stir into cooking liquid. Cook, stirring, until gravy boils for 1 minute. Stir in parsley. Add 2 tablespoons salt to rapidly boiling water. Add noodles gradually so that water continues to boil. Cook, uncovered, stirring occasionally, until tender. Drain in colander. Toss noodles with small amount of gravy. Serve with pot roast and remaining gravy. Yield: 8 servings.

Photograph for this recipe on page 244.

SMOKEY BARBECUE RIBS

    4 lb. beef short ribs
    ¼ c. Morton's Seasoning Salt
    1½ tsp. pepper
    1 tsp. garlic powder
    1 tsp. onion powder
    1 pt. dry white wine

Mix all ingredients together. Cover. Chill for 24 hours. Drain. Cook in barbecue oven, using hot smoke. Cook for 1 hour and 30 minutes at 300 degrees. Yield: 4 servings.

                    Adrian B. Locke
    La Plata Co., Animas Valley Grange, No. 194
                    Durango, Colorado

BEEF RAREBIT

    ½ lb. ground round steak
    Salt and pepper to taste

    4 fresh tomatoes, peeled and sliced
    7 thick slices Velveeta cheese
    2 c. milk
    3 tbsp. (heaping) flour
    10 to 12 slices toast

Place ground steak in 2 tablespoons shortening in large skillet. Season. Brown. Spread tomatoes over meat. Cover with cheese slices. Place milk and flour in a jar; cover tightly. Shake until mixed well. Add to skillet; cook until thickened. Add more milk, if desired. Serve over toast. Yield: 4 servings.

                    Jack M. Cook
            Hilltop Grange, No. 225
            Ree Heights, South Dakota

GRILLED FLANK STEAK

    1 flank steak
    1 c. salad oil
    ¾ c. soy sauce
    ½ c. lemon juice
    ¼ c. Worcestershire sauce
    ¼ c. prepared mustard
    1½ tbsp. salt
    1 tsp. pepper
    1 clove of garlic, sliced

Place steak in double plastic bags. Blend remaining ingredients; pour over steak. Marinate 3 to 4 hours or overnight, turning occasionally. Grill over hot coals for 10 to 15 minutes per side. Baste with sauce. Slice thin across grain of steak to serve. Sauce may be stored in airtight jar in refrigerator 3 to 4 weeks. Yield: 3-5 servings.

                    Bill Steel
            Potomac Grange, No. 1
            Arlington, Virginia

HUNTER'S STEW

    1 lb. ground beef
    1 med. onion, diced
    1 med. potato, diced
    1 10-oz. can vegetable soup
    1 15-oz. can kidney beans
    ½ tsp. salt
    ¼ tsp. pepper

Brown ground beef in skillet. Add remaining ingredients with 1 soup can of water. Simmer for 30 minutes. Yield: 4 servings.

                    Clarence Kronenbitter
        Pleasant Grove Grange, No. 1681
                    Zanesville, Ohio

HAM BARBECUE SANDWICHES

1 c. catsup
2 tbsp. vinegar
2 tbsp. (firmly packed) brown sugar
1 tbsp. Worcestershire sauce
1½ lb. chipped ham, shredded
Hamburger buns

Mix first 4 ingredients in skillet. Bring to a boil. Add ham. Stir until ham is well-coated, cook until heated through. Serve warm on split hamburger buns.

John W. Scott
Unionville Grange, No. 197
Mechanicsburg, Pennsylvania

PORK CHOPS WITH DILL

6 pork chops, 1½-inches thick
Salt and freshly ground pepper to taste
½ c. Dusseldorf or Dijon mustard
2 tbsp. butter
1½ c. thinly sliced onions
3 tbsp. flour
1½ c. chicken broth
¾ c. heavy cream
1 tsp. finely chopped dill or ½ tsp. dillseed

Sprinkle chops with salt and pepper. Brush both sides with mustard. Heat butter; brown chops on all sides. Remove chops from pan. Keep warm. Add onions to skillet. Cook, stirring for 5 minutes or until they start to brown. Pour off most of fat from skillet. Sprinkle onions with flour, stirring constantly with a whisk. Stir in broth and cream; simmer until smooth. Add chops; spoon sauce over them. Sprinkle with dill. Cover. Simmer about hour. Yield: 6 servings.

Art Du Lac, Master
Virginia State Grange
Great Falls, Virginia

CHICKEN CASSEROLE

4 chicken breasts, stewed
Salt and pepper to taste
¼ stick butter, melted
1 can cream of chicken soup
1 c. broth
1½ to 2 c. seasoned stuffing mix

Bone chicken breasts; add salt and pepper. Combine chicken, butter and soup. Combine broth and stuffing mix. Combine mixtures. Place in 9 × 14-inch casserole. Bake at 350 degrees for 30 minutes.

Joe B. Cox
Cox's Chapel Grange, No. 954
Mouth of Wilson, Virginia

BARBECUED RABBIT

1 rabbit
1 med. onion
¼ c. chopped celery
Flour
Butter
½ c. catsup
1 tbsp. brown sugar
1 tbsp. vinegar
1 tbsp. prepared mustard

Cook rabbit, onion, and celery in water to cover for about 1 hour or until rabbit is tender; drain. Roll rabbit in flour; brown in butter in skillet. Mix remaining ingredients and ½ cup water together. Place rabbit in casserole. Pour sauce over rabbit. Bake, uncovered, at 325 degrees until sauce is baked into rabbit. Yield: 4 servings.

Doug Moffit
Fichville Grange, No. 2356
Huron Co., Ohio

SPICED SHRIMP

3 bay leaves
1 tbsp. whole allspice
1½ tsp. crushed red peppers
2 tbsp. peppercorns
2 med. onions, sliced
6 garlic cloves
2 lemons, sliced
½ c. salt
2 lb. shrimp

Tie first 4 ingredients in a cheesecloth bag; place in 2 quarts water. Add onions, garlic, lemon and salt. Bring to a boil; add shrimp. Cover; return to a boil. Simmer 3 to 5 minutes, depending on size of shrimp. Remove from heat. Let stand 3 minutes. Drain; chill. Empty contents of seasoning bag onto shrimp.

J. C. Stigers
Potomac Grange, No. 1
Falls Church, Virginia

CRAB CAKES

1 lb. crab meat
6 slices white bread, trimmed and cubed
1 tsp. parsley flakes
½ green pepper, chopped
1 tsp. dry mustard
Salt to taste
2 eggs, beaten
2 tbsp. mayonnaise
Cracker crumbs
Oil for frying

Combine first 8 ingredients in bowl. Mix well. Form into cakes. Roll in cracker crumbs. Fry until lightly browned.

J. C. Stigers
Potomac Grange, No. 1
Falls Church, Virginia

FRIED CATFISH

2 lb. fresh catfish
½ lemon
¾ c. cornmeal
1 tsp. salt
⅛ tsp. pepper
Oil for frying

Rub prepared catfish on both sides with lemon. Combine cornmeal and seasonings. Roll fish in mixture. Pour ⅛-inch oil in heavy skillet over medium heat. Fry fish 8 to 9 minutes or until golden brown on both sides. Serve with hot hush puppies.

Marc Spivey
Round Valley Grange, No. 805
Covelo, California

WESTERN BARBECUE SAUCE

1 c. Spanish tomato sauce
⅓ c. cider vinegar
2 tbsp. lemon juice
2 tbsp. sugar
1 tsp. pepper
2½ tsp. salt
⅛ tsp. garlic salt
1 tsp. chili powder
¼ tsp. cayenne pepper
1 tbsp. instant minced onion
1 tsp. dry mustard

Combine first 10 ingredients and ½ cup water in saucepan. Simmer 5 minutes. Blend mustard with 1 tablespoon water; let stand 10 minutes. Add; mix well. Baste chicken, beef or pork while cooking over hot coals.

Leo E. Choate, Master
Potomac Grange, No. 1
Arlington, Virginia

APPLESAUCE-BRAN MUFFINS

2 c. Bran Buds
½ c. milk
2 c. sweetened applesauce
2 eggs, beaten
½ c. vegetable oil
2 c. sifted all-purpose flour
4 tsp. baking powder
½ tsp. soda
1 tsp. salt
1½ tsp. cinnamon
½ tsp. nutmeg
½ c. sugar

Combine Bran Buds and milk; let stand until soggy. Add applesauce, eggs and vegetable oil; beat well. Sift dry ingredients. Add to first mixture stirring lightly. Fill greased muffin pans ⅔ full. Bake in 400-degree oven about 30 minutes.

Arthur H. Hary
Glastonbury Grange, No. 26
Rockville, Connecticut

BLUEBERRY MUFFINS

2 eggs, beaten
1¼ c. milk
1 tsp. salt
2 tbsp. melted shortening
1 c. blueberries
2 tsp. baking powder
¼ c. sugar
1½ c. flour

Combine all ingredients in a bowl; mix well. Pour into hot well-greased muffin tins. Bake at 350 degrees for 20 to 25 minutes. Yield: 18 muffins.

B. Franklin Hayes, Master
New Hampshire State Grange
Lebanon, Maine

CINNAMON GEMS

⅓ c. shortening
1 c. sugar
1 egg, beaten
1½ c. all-purpose flour
1½ tsp. baking powder
½ tsp. salt
¼ tsp. nutmeg
½ c. milk
1 tsp. cinnamon
½ c. butter, melted

Cream shortening and ½ cup sugar; blend well. Add egg; mix until light and fluffy. Sift next 4 ingredients together; add to creamed mixture alternately with milk. Mix well. Fill greased muffin pan ⅔ full. Bake in preheated 350-degree oven for 20 to 25 minutes. Combine ½ cup sugar and cinnamon. Roll hot muffins in melted butter; roll in sugar-cinnamon mixture. Serve warm. Yield: 12 muffins.

Morris J. Halladay, Master
New York State Grange
Groton, New York

DANISH PUFFS

1 c. butter
2 c. flour
1¼ tsp. almond extract
3 eggs
1 c. confectioners' sugar
½ tsp. vanilla extract
1 to 2 tbsp. milk

Cut ½ cup butter into 1 cup flour until it resembles coarse meal. Stir in 2 tablespoons cold water; shape into a ball. Divide dough. Pat each half into a 3 × 12-inch strip. Place on a 10 × 15-inch sheet. Measure 1 cup water and ½ cup butter into a saucepan. Bring to a boil. Remove from heat. Add almond extract. Stir in 1 cup flour quickly. Add eggs one at a time, beating well with a spoon after each addition. Spread mixture over strips. Bake at 400 degrees for about 40 minutes or until puffed and golden. Combine confectioners' sugar, vanilla and milk. Frost while hot. Yield: 12-16 servings.

Jack Barker
Mt. Wheeler Grange, No. 696
Arlington, Washington

JOHNNYCAKE

1 c. sour milk
1 tbsp. sugar
2 tbsp. cream
¾ c. flour
¾ c. cornmeal
1 tbsp. soda
1 tbsp. salt

Combine all ingredients; mix well. Pour into 8 × 8-inch pan. Bake at 425 degrees for 20 to 25 minutes. Butter may be substituted for cream.

Walter Wilcox
Blue Mountain Grange, No. 263
Wells River, Vermont

BOILED APPLE DUMPLINGS

1 recipe baking powder biscuits, made with
  extra shortening
Apples, peeled and halved
Sugar
Cinnamon

Roll out biscuit dough as thin as pie crust. Cut into squares large enough to cover apple. Place 2 apple halves in center of each square. Sprinkle with 1 spoonful sugar and pinch of cinnamon. Turn ends of dough over apple; pinch to seal edges. Dip small coarse cloth into hot water; dust with floor. Tie cloth around apples securely, leaving room for dumpling to swell. Place in saucepan of boiling water. Boil for 45 minutes. Serve with sweet sauce.

James H. Kiles, Master
Texas State Grange
Fredricksburg, Texas

GRANDMA JEFFERS' CRACKER JACK

3 tbsp. sorghum
1 tbsp. butter
½ c. sugar
¼ tsp. salt
2 tbsp. vinegar
¼ tsp. soda
1 gal. popped popcorn

Combine first 5 ingredients in saucepan. Cook over medium-low heat to hard-crack stage or 290 degrees. Remove from heat. Add soda; stir thoroughly. Pour over popped corn; mix well. Shape in 10 balls.

Robert Jeffers
Hopewell Grange, No. 1747
Washington, Illinois

CORNSTARCH PUDDING

3 tbsp. cornstarch
5 tbsp. sugar
¼ tsp. salt
3 eggs, well beaten
2½ c. milk
2 tbsp. butter
1 tsp. vanilla extract

Combine dry ingredients with eggs in saucepan; blend until smooth. Add milk and butter. Cook, stirring constantly, for 15 minutes or until mixture starts to thicken. Beat with beater until mixture is smooth. Bring to a boil. Remove from heat. Add milk if mixture is too thick. Add vanilla. Serve warm or cold. Yield: 4-5 servings.

John W. Scott
Unionville Grange, No. 1971
Mechanicsburg, Pennsylvania

BANANA-OATMEAL COOKIES

½ c. (firmly packed) brown sugar
¾ c. salad oil
4 c. uncooked regular oats
1¾ c. mashed bananas
½ tsp. salt
½ c. chopped nuts
½ c. raisins

Beat brown sugar and oil until well-blended. Add oats, bananas and salt. Stir in nuts and raisins. Drop from teaspoon onto greased baking sheet. Bake in 350-degree oven for 25 minutes. Cool on baking sheet for 10 minutes. Yield: 4 dozen.

Raymond Crum
Glade Valley Grange, No. 417
Walkersville, Maryland

JACK'S GOOD BROWNIES

Butter
2 c. sugar
4 eggs, beaten
1 1-lb. can chocolate syrup
1 c. plus 1 tsp. flour
Pinch of salt
½ c. chopped nuts
4 tbsp. milk
⅓ c. chocolate chips

Cream 1 stick softened butter and 1 cup sugar. Add next 4 ingredients. Mix well. Pour into 9 × 13-inch pan. Bake at 350 degrees for 30 minutes. Combine 4 tablespoons buttermilk and 1 cup sugar in a saucepan. Bring to a boil. Boil for 30 seconds. Add chocolate chips. Cool. Beat until thick enough to spread. Ice brownies.

John U. Maple, Master
New Jersey State Grange
Lawrenceville, New Jersey

CHOCOLATE BROWNIES

1 stick butter or margarine
2 sq. baking chocolate
1 c. sugar
2 eggs
1 tsp. vanilla extract
½ c. chopped nuts (opt.)
¾ c. sifted flour
½ tsp. baking powder
½ tsp. salt

Melt butter and chocolate in saucepan over low heat. Remove from heat. Add sugar. Add eggs one at a time beating well after each addition. Add vanilla and nuts. Sift flour, baking powder and salt together. Add to creamed mixture; mix thoroughly. Pour into 8-inch square baking pan. Bake in preheated 350-degree oven for 25 to 30 minutes. Cut into squares while still warm. Yield: 16 2-inch squares.

David Newhard
Lehigh Co., Washington Grange, No. 1763
Slatington, Pennsylvania

RAYMOND'S BROWNIES

2 sq. unsweetened chocolate
⅓ c. butter or shortening
⅔ c. flour
½ tsp. baking powder
¼ tsp. salt
1 c. sugar
2 eggs, well beaten
1 tsp. vanilla extract
½ c. chopped nuts

Melt chocolate and butter in saucepan. Mix flour, baking powder and salt. Add sugar to eggs gradually, beating well. Blend in chocolate and vanilla. Add flour mixture. Add nuts. Spread in greased 8-inch square pan. Bake at 350 degrees for 25 minutes.

Raymond Crum
Glade Valley Grange, No. 417
Walkersville, Maryland

CHOCOLATE CHIP BLOND BROWNIES

2 c. flour
1 tsp. baking powder
½ tsp. soda
1 tsp. salt
1 c. chopped nuts
⅔ c. butter or margarine
2 c. (firmly packed) brown sugar
2 eggs, beaten
2 tsp. vanilla extract
1 c. chocolate chips

Mix first 5 ingredients in bowl. Set aside. Melt butter in a saucepan; remove from heat. Add brown sugar; mix well. Add eggs and vanilla to sugar mixture. Blend well with mixer. Add flour mixture; blend well. Spread in a cake pan or cookie sheet. Sprinkle chocolate chips over top. Bake at 350 degrees for 20 to 25 minutes.

D. Vincent Andrews, Master
Florida State Grange
Sarasota, Florida

PANOCHA

1 lb. light brown sugar
½ c. milk
3 tbsp. margarine, softened
1 tsp. vanilla extract
½ c. chopped walnuts (opt.)

Mix sugar, milk and butter. Boil slowly to soft-ball stage, stirring often. Remove from heat; add vanilla and walnuts. Beat until creamy. Pour into buttered pan. Cut into squares when firm.

Alfred Barringer
Oakfield Grange
Byron, New York

KEN'S CHEESECAKE

1½ c. graham cracker crumbs
Sugar
⅓ c. butter or margarine, melted
1½ pkg. cream cheese, softened
1 tsp. vanilla extract
½ c. whipping cream, whipped
Fresh fruit thickened with cornstarch

Combine crumbs and 3 tablespoons sugar in
medium bowl. Stir in butter; blend well. Pack
mixture firmly into 9-inch pie pan. Press evenly on
bottom and sides. Chill for 1 hour. Blend cream
cheese, ½ cup sugar and vanilla. Fold in whipped
cream. Pour mixture into crust. Spread cherries
evenly on top. Chill for 1 hour or longer.

Kenneth Conklin
Evening Star Grange, No. 183
Washington, Maine

LIME PIE

1 14-oz. can sweetened condensed milk
¼ tsp. salt
¼ c. lime juice
1 No. 2¼ can crushed pineapple, drained
1 baked pie shell
Whipped cream

Beat milk, salt, and lime juice until thick. Add
pineapple. Pour into pie shell. Top with whipped
cream.

W. C. Harris, Master
Oregon State Grange
Portland, Oregon

PUMPKIN PIE

2 c. pumpkin
¾ c. (firmly packed) light brown sugar
2 tsp. cinnamon
¾ tsp. salt
¾ tsp. ginger
½ tsp. nutmeg
¼ tsp. mace
⅛ tsp. ground cloves
4 eggs, slightly beaten
1½ c. light cream or half and half
1 unbaked 9-inch pie shell
Sweetened whipped cream

Combine pumpkin and brown sugar in large bowl.
Blend in next 6 ingredients. Add eggs; gradually stir
in cream. Pour into pie shell. Bake in preheated
400 degree oven for 40 to 45 minutes or until knife
inserted off center comes out clean. Cool on wire
rack. Top with whipped cream.

Photograph for this recipe on page 250.

FRESH APPLE CAKE

¼ c. milk
¾ c. oil
1½ c. sugar
2 eggs, beaten
2 tsp. baking powder
1 tsp. salt
1 tsp. soda
3 c. sifted flour
1 tsp. vanilla extract
3 c. chopped apples

Combine first 4 ingredients; mix well. Sift dry
ingredients together. Add to first mixture. Add
chopped apples and vanilla. Pour into greased and
floured 9 × 13-inch pan. Bake at 350 degrees for 35
minutes. Chopped nuts may be added to batter.
Serve with confectioners' sugar or whipped cream.

John Schanbacker
Spencer Grange, No. 1110
Van Etten, New York

COUNTRY GINGERBREAD

1 c. molasses
1 c. sour milk
2¼ c. sifted flour
1¾ tsp. baking powder
2 tsp. ginger
½ tsp. salt
1 egg, beaten
½ c. oil

Mix molasses and milk. Sift dry ingredients together. Add to milk mixture. Add egg and oil. Beat until smooth and creamy. Pour into greased 9×9-inch pan. Bake at 350 degrees about 30 minutes.

Roland H. Hamel
Mt. Etna Grange, No. 147
North Baldwin, Maine

GINGERBREAD

¼ c. shortening
¼ c. sugar
1 egg, beaten
½ c. molasses
½ tsp. salt
1¼ c. flour
½ tsp. (heaping) soda

Cream shortening and sugar. Add egg. Add remaining ingredients; beat well. Add ½ cup boiling water; mix well. Pour into greased and floured 8×8-inch pan. Bake at 350 degrees for 30 minutes or until cake tests done. Won second prize in 1979 baking contest sponsored by Maine State Grange.

Almon F. Harmon, Sr.
Norway Grange, No. 45
Norway, Maine

PINEAPPLE CAKE

2 c. flour
2 c. sugar
2 tsp. soda
2 eggs
1 No. 2 can crushed pineapple, undrained
4 tsp. vanilla extract
1¾ c. confectioners' sugar
1 8-oz. package cream cheese, softened
½ c. butter, softened
½ c. chopped nuts

Combine first 5 ingredients and 3 teaspoons vanilla; mix well. Pour into oblong cake pan. Bake at 350 degrees for 35 to 40 minutes. Cool. Combine remaining ingredients. Add 1 teaspoon vanilla; mix well. Add nuts. Spread on cake.

Arden Fitch
Olivesburg Grange, No. 2641
Ashland, Ohio

COCONUT POUND CAKE

½ lb. butter, softened
1 lb. confectioners' sugar
6 eggs

2 c. sifted flour
1 pkg. frozen coconut, thawed

Cream butter and sugar. Add eggs one at a time, beating well after each addition. Add flour and coconut. Pour into a tube pan. Bake at 325 degrees for 1 hour.

Raymond Crum
Glade Valley Grange, No. 417
Walkersville, Maryland

ONE-STEP POUND CAKE

2¼ c. sifted flour
2 c. sugar
½ tsp. salt
½ tsp. soda
1 tsp. vanilla extract
1 c. butter or margarine
1 c. sour cream
3 eggs
1 c. confectioners' sugar (opt.)
2 tbsp. lemon juice (opt.)

Combine first 8 ingredients in large mixer bowl. Beat at medium speed until well blended. Pour into well greased bundt pan. Bake at 325 degrees for 60 to 70 minutes. Cool in pan for 15 minutes. Remove from pan. Combine confectioners' sugar and lemon juice. Glaze cake with mixture if desired.

Richard J. Massabny
Potomac Grange, No. 1
Arlington, Virginia

GREEN TOMATO CHOWCHOW

5 c. coarsely chopped cabbage
1 c. canning salt
4 c. coarsely chopped cucumbers
3 c. chopped red and green sweet peppers
5 to 6 c. chopped green tomatoes
3 c. chopped sweet onions
6 c. cider vinegar
6 c. sugar
2 tsp. turmeric
1 tsp. allspice

Soak cabbage for 1 to 2 hours in water with canning salt added. Rinse. Drain. Combine all ingredients in large kettle. Bring to a boil. Simmer for 2 to 3 minutes. Pour into hot sterilized pint jars leaving ½-inch head space. Seal. Process in boiling water bath for 10 minutes. Yield: 11 pints.

George Elliott, Grange Friend
Falls Church, Virginia

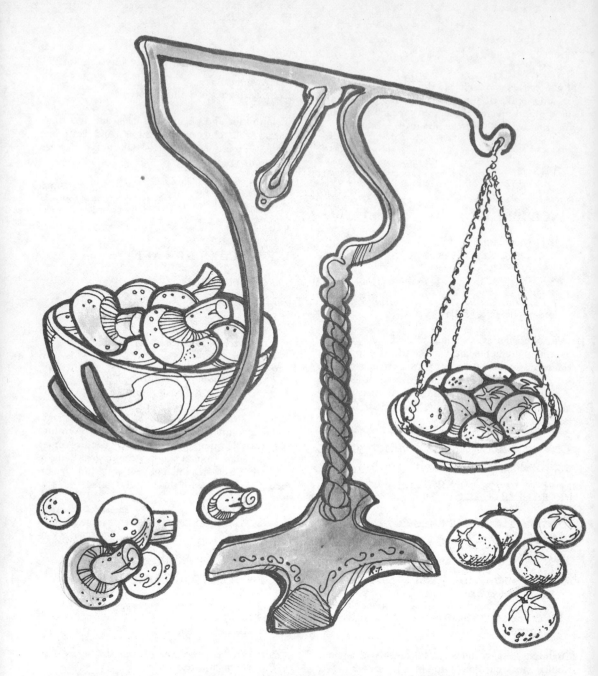

Special Diabetic
Recipes

Wholesome, delicious, and appetizing are the words to describe a diabetic diet because it allows such a variety of favorite foods. A balanced diabetic menu can include lean meats, fish, poultry, eggs, cheese and milk products, plus a wide range of vegetables and many fruits.

A list like that makes it hard to believe that once a person is diagnosed as having diabetes, their eating habits have to change. Protein, fat and calorie intake must be watched, but carbohydrate intake must be monitored carefully so the body receives only what it is able to handle.

The recipes in this section have been submitted by Mrs. Melvin Stepon of Quincy Grange No. 990 in Quincy, Washington, and all Grange members truly appreciate her thoughtful cooperation. Helpful Hints for these Special Diabetic/Dietetic Recipes include: 1. Measure ingredients carefully. 2. Always soften gelatin in at least 1 tablespoon cold water before using. 3. Where recipes call for lightly oiled or greased dishes, it is suggested that you use vegetable cooking spray according to directions on the container. Mrs. Stepon suggests the use of Fru-Tex from the Crescent Company as a thickening agent in whipped toppings, egg whites, fruit pies and syrups, and other syrups. It is low in calories and therefore preferable to cornstarch.

It is strongly recommended that you check with your doctor before using any sweetener, artificial or natural, if you are on a diabetic diet.

COTTAGE CHEESE LUNCHEON LOAF

1 tbsp. unflavored gelatin
1 carton cottage cheese, sieved
1 oz. blue cheese, crumbled
6 stuffed olives, sliced
¼ c. lemon juice
½ c. skim milk
1 tsp. liquid sweetener
2 tbsp. chopped parsley
½ tsp. salt
1 egg white, stiffly beaten

Soak gelatin in ¼ cup cold water for 5 minutes. Dissolve in double boiler over hot water. Combine next 8 ingredients; mix well. Fold in egg white. Turn into 8-inch mold; chill until firm. Serve on lettuce or endive. Yield: 6 servings.

SALMON MOUSSE

1 env. gelatin
¼ c. vinegar
1 tbsp. Sugartwin
1¼ tsp. salt
1 tsp. dry mustard
2 c. flaked cooked salmon
1 c. finely diced celery
1 tbsp. capers (opt.)
½ c. ice cold evaporated milk, whipped

Soften gelatin in ¼ cup cold water and vinegar. Place over boiling water. Stir until dissolved. Add Sugartwin, salt and mustard. Stir until blended. Cool. Stir in salmon, celery and capers. Fold in milk. Pour into large or individual molds. Chill until firm.

SHRIMP ASPIC

2 c. tomato juice
1 tsp. liquid sweetener
1 tsp. salt
⅛ tsp. pepper
1 tbsp. minced onion
1 sm. bay leaf
1 tsp. lemon juice
1 tbsp. unflavored gelatin
1 5-oz. can shrimp, cleaned and diced
1 c. chopped celery
¼ c. chopped green pepper

Combine first 7 ingredients in saucepan. Bring to a boil; strain. Soften gelatin in ¼ cup cold water. Dissolve in hot mixture. Cool until it begins to thicken. Fold in remaining ingredients. Pour into 1-quart ring mold. Chill until firm. Yield: 6 servings/75 calories each.

TUNA MOLD

1 env. gelatin
2 c. milk
2 egg yolks, slightly beaten
1 tsp. salt
¼ tsp. paprika
1⅓ c. drained flaked tuna
1 tsp. prepared mustard
1 tbsp. lemon juice or vinegar

Soften gelatin in ½ cup cold milk. Dissolve thoroughly in 1½ cups scalded milk. Stir in egg yolks, salt and paprika slowly. Cook over hot, not boiling, water. Stir constantly until mixture thickens and coats a spoon. Chill. Stir in tuna, mustard and lemon juice. Pour into mold. Chill until firm.

APPLE AND CELERY SALAD

1 c. diced unpared apples
1 c. diced celery
½ c. grated American low-calorie cheese
½ c. diced pineapple
1 tsp. Sugartwin
Juice of 1 lemon
2 tbsp. diet mayonnaise
Salt to taste

Combine all ingredients. Chill in serving dish. Serve on salad greens. Yield: 4 to 6 servings.

CHERRY MOLD SALAD

1 1-lb. can diet Bing or Royal Anne cherries
1 pkg. cherry-flavored diet Jell-O
½ c. sliced stuffed olives
½ c. chopped nuts
¾ c. chopped celery

Drain juice from cherries, reserving juice. Add enough water to cherry juice to make 1¾ cups liquid. Heat 1 cup to boiling point; dissolve Jell-O in hot liquid. Add remaining juice. Chill until slightly thickened. Add remaining ingredients. Pour into 1½-quart mold. Chill until firm.

FRUIT MEDLEY SALAD

1 env. unflavored gelatin
½ c. unsweetened orange juice
½ tsp. salt
1¼ tsp. liquid sweetener
Food coloring if desired
1 med. pear or apple, diced
½ c. Tokay grapes, halved and seeded

Soften gelatin in orange juice in medium mixing bowl. Stir in 1¼ cups boiling water, salt and sweetener. Chill until partly thickened. Stir in food coloring and fruit gently. Pour into 3 or 4-cup mold or 6 individual molds. Chill until firm.

MELON BALL COOLER

1 env. gelatin
2 c. canned orange or grapefruit juice
¼ c. Sugartwin
15 lg. fresh mint leaves
1½ c. melon balls

Soften gelatin in ¼ cup juice. Combine remaining juice and Sugartwin in small saucepan; bring to a boil. Remove from heat. Add softened gelatin mixture; stir until dissolved. Pour 2 tablespoons boiling water over mint leaves in small bowl; press leaves with back of spoon to extract flavor. Strain. Add to gelatin mixture. Chill until just thickened. Fold in melon balls. Pour into 6 individual molds or into 1-quart mold. Chill until firm.

GLORIFIED RICE

2 lg. packages diet Jell-O or 4 env. Knox gelatin
1½ pkg. raspberry Kool-Aid
2 tbsp. liquid sweetener
1 lg. can unsweetened pineapple
3 c. cooked rice
Canned milk, whipped to make 1 pt.

Dissolve Jell-O in 6 cups boiling water. Chill until partially set. Fold in remaining ingredients. Chill until firm.

DUTCH BEAN SALAD

3 slices bacon
2 tsp. Sugartwin
2 tbsp. vinegar
Dash of salt
1 1-lb. can green beans
6 tomatoes, cored
Lettuce

Fry bacon crisp; add Sugartwin, vinegar, salt and beans incuding liquid. Stir until beans are well seasoned. Remove from heat. Chill; drain. Place mixture into tomatoes. Serve on lettuce. Can be served as a hot vegetable with meat or poultry.

ICEBOX SALAD

1 head lettuce, finely shredded
6 carrots, thinly sliced

1 bunch celery, thinly sliced
6 tomatoes, thinly sliced
2 c. shredded cabbage
3 cucumbers, thinly sliced
3 onions, thinly sliced
1 tbsp. Sugartwin
1 tbsp. diet mayonnaise
2 slices bacon, cooked and crumbled

Layer first 7 ingredients in deep bowl. Sprinkle with Sugartwin, mayonnaise and bacon. Cover; chill for 45 minutes. Do not toss.

MOLDED CABBAGE SALAD

1 pkg. diet lemon gelatin
½ tsp. salt
1 tbsp. chopped pimento
1½ c. finely shredded cabbage
2 tbsp. diced green pepper
1 tsp. grated onion
½ c. carrot slices
Lettuce

Dissolve gelatin and salt in 1 cup hot water. Add 8 ice cubes; stir 2 to 3 minutes. Remove ice cubes. Fold in remaining ingredients. Pour into 1-quart mold or individual molds. Chill until firm. Unmold on lettuce. Serve with dash of diet mayonnaise.

PUMPKIN ASPIC

1 pkg. diet orange-flavored gelatin
1 tbsp. brown Sugartwin
1 tbsp. grated orange rind
¼ tsp. ginger
1 c. canned pumpkin

Dissolve gelatin in 1½ cups water, stir in remaining ingredients. Chill until firm. Stir occasionally, until thick. Yield: 4 servings/45 calories each.

TOMATO-CUCUMBER MARINADE

1 pt. cherry tomatoes
1 med. cucumber, thinly sliced
1 sm. mild onion, thinly sliced
1 tsp. salt
¼ tsp. celery salt
2 tsp. sweetener
1 tbsp. unsweetened lemon juice
½ c. cider vinegar
¼ c. cooking oil

Combine tomatoes, cucumbers and onion in bowl. Place in pint containers. Combine remaining ingredients with 1 cup cold water. Pour ⅓ of the mixture into each pint. Cover. Store in refrigerator.

RUBY RED RING WITH DIET DRESSING

1½ tbsp. gelatin
⅔ c. Sugartwin
½ c. lemon juice
1 tbsp. vinegar
1½ tbsp. horseradish
Dash of celery salt
½ tsp. salt
1 c. diced celery
¾ c. finely chopped cabbage
¾ c. shoestring beets
½ pt. yogurt
½ cucumber, grated
Paprika, salt and pepper to taste

Soften gelatin in ¼ cup cold water. Combine next 6 ingredients with 1¾ cups boiling water. Chill until partially set; fold in vegetables. Pour into 1-quart mold or 6 to 8 individual molds. Chill until firm. Combine ingredients. Serve with molded salad.

TOMATO FRENCH DRESSING

2 tbsp. Sugartwin
1 tbsp. lemon juice
1½ tsp. dry mustard
1 tsp. paprika
1 tsp. grated onion
¼ tsp. celery salt
¼ tsp. pepper
1 can condensed tomato soup
½ c. salad oil
⅓ c. vinegar

Combine Sugartwin, lemon juice, and seasonings in bottle or jar. Add soup, salad oil and vinegar. Cover tightly; shake well. Chill several hours.

LOW-CAL DRESSING

1 to 2 tbsp. Sugartwin
1 tbsp. flour
1 tsp. salt
½ tsp. dry mustard
Dash of cayenne
½ c. vinegar
2 eggs, sightly beaten
1 tbsp. lemon juice

Combine first 5 ingredients in top of double boiler. Add vinegar and ½ cup water. Cook over boiling water, stirring constantly until thickened. Pour a small amount over eggs. Add eggs to hot mixture. Cook 2 minutes. Beat with wire whisk. Remove from heat; stir in lemon juice. Cool; chill.

GRILLED TURKEY CAKES

1 c. flour
2 tsp. baking powder
½ tsp. salt
¼ tsp. nutmeg
⅛ tsp. thyme
Dash of pepper
1 c. thin chicken or turkey gravy
3 tbsp. butter or maragarine, melted
1 sm. onion, grated
2 c. finely chopped cooked turkey

Sift first 6 ingredients together. Stir in remaining ingredients. Shape with large spoon into cakes. Bake on a moderately hot, lightly greased griddle. Note: 1 cup milk or diluted cream of chicken soup may be used instead of gravy. Yield: 5 servings.

BARBECUE SAUCE

½ c. tomato catsup
½ tsp. liquid sweetener
½ tsp. salt
½ tsp. dry mustard
Dash of hot pepper sauce
Dash of chili powder
¼ c. finely chopped dill pickle

Combine all ingredients; gradually stir in 1 cup water. Use as a sauce for meat. Yield: 1½ cups.

NATURAL FRUIT JUICE JELLY OR SAUCE

1 c. grape or other juice
1 to 2 tbsp. cornstarch
Dash of salt

Mix all ingredients together with wire whisk. Cook in saucepan until thickened, stirring constantly. Use on waffles or refrigerate and use on toast.

ORANGE SAUCE

1 tbsp. cornstarch
Dah of salt
⅛ tsp. cinnamon
1 c. orange juice
½ tsp. liquid sweetener
1 tsp. lemon juice

Mix cornstarch, salt and cinnamon in saucepan. Add orange juice gradually; add sweetener. Bring to a boil. Cook 5 minutes. Add lemon juice; cool. May be served hot or cold on desserts.

TANGY SEAFOOD COCKTAIL SAUCE

½ c. tomato juice
¼ tsp. liquid sweetener
1 tsp. horseradish
½ tsp. Worcestershire sauce

1 tsp. finely chopped parsley
1 tsp. lemon juice
½ tsp. salt

Combine all ingredients. Chill to blend flavors. Spoon over seafood cocktails. Yield: ½ cup.

LOW-CALORIE PANCAKES

1 c. cottage cheese
3 eggs
1 c. skim milk
½ tsp. salt
¼ tsp. liquid sweetener
½ c. flour

Force cheese through fine strainer. Add remaining ingredients; mix well. Preheat griddle. Brush with ¼ teaspoon fat. Pour pancake mixture on griddle. Brown on both sides. Yield: 40 3-inch pancakes.

COTTAGE CHEESE-APPLESAUCE PANCAKES

3 eggs
1 c. sieved cottage cheese
2 tbsp. salad oil
¼ c. flour
¼ tsp. salt
Dash of cinnamon
1 c. applesauce

Beat eggs until light in color; blend in cottage cheese and oil. Sift flour, salt and cinnamon into mixture; stir until just blended. Pour on hot griddle. Cook each pancake until brown on each side. Spoon applesauce onto each pan; roll up.

BAKED CUSTARD

2 eggs
1¼ tsp. liquid sweetener
¼ tsp. salt
1 tsp. vanilla extract
2 c. skim milk, scalded
Nutmeg

Beat eggs until frothy; add remaining ingredients. Pour into 5 custard cups. Sprinkle tops with nutmeg. Place in shallow pan of water. Bake at 300 degrees for 1 hour or until knife inserted in center comes out clean. Chill.

SPANISH CREAM

1 env. gelatin
2 c. cold milk

⅓ c. Sugartwin
⅛ tsp. salt
2 eggs, separated
1 tsp. vanilla extract

Soften gelatin in cold milk in top of double boiler. Place over boiling water. Add Sugartwin and salt; stir until dissolved. Pour small amount of the hot mixture over slightly beaten egg yolks slowly. Return to double boiler. Cook over hot, not boiling, water. Stir constantly until mixture coats spoon. Remove from heat. Add vanilla. Fold in stiffly beaten egg whites. Pour into 1 large or individual molds. Chill. Serve with sliced oranges.

KNOX BLOX

4 env. unflavored gelatin
3 pkg. diet Jell-O

Combine gelatin and Jell-O in large bowl. Add 4 cups boiling water; stir until well-dissolved. Pour into shallow 9 × 13-inch baking pan. Chill. Cut into squares. May also use 7 envelopes of unflavored gelatin and 1 pkg. diet Kool-Aid for flavoring, or use fruit juice instead of boiling water.

APPLE SNOW SPONGE

1 env. gelatin
1 8-oz. can dietetic applesauce
¼ tsp. grated lemon rind
2 tbsp. lemon juice
⅛ tsp. nutmeg
Non-caloric sweetener to taste
2 egg whites

Soften gelatin in ¼ cup cold water; add ½ cup boiling water. Stir well to dissolve. Add next 5 ingredients. Chill until mixture begins to thicken. Beat egg whites until stiff but not dry. Fold into gelatin mixture. Spoon into 1 cup molds. Chill 3 to 4 hours or until set. Yield: 4 servings.

FRUIT CHARLOTTE

1 env. gelatin
½ c. cold fruit juice
1 c. hot fruit juice
⅓ c. Sugartwin
⅛ tsp. salt
⅔ c. canned milk, whipped

Soften gelatin in cold juice. Add hot juice, Sugartwin and salt. Stir until dissolved. Chill until slightly thicker than unbeaten egg whites. Fold gelatin mixture into milk. Pour into mold. Chill.

STRAWBERRY CROWN

1 c. diced diet canned pears
1 pkg. strawberry diet gelatin
½ tsp. salt
½ tsp. ground ginger
1 3 oz. package cream cheese

Drain pears, reserve liquid. Add water to liquid to make 1¾ cup. Add gelatin and salt. Pour enough of the liquid into 1½-quart mold to make a crown. Chill until firm. Chill remaining mixture until slightly thickened or syrupy. Pour into mixer bowl. Beat at medium speed until doubled in volume and is fluffy and thick. Add ginger to cream cheese. Mix well. Fold into whipped gelatin. Add pears; pour over firm gelatin in mold. Chill. Garnish with whipped topping, or fresh strawberries if desired.

LOW-CAL ANGEL DELIGHT

4 env. diet strawberry Jell-O
1 16-oz. package unsweetened strawberries
1 9-oz. carton Cool Whip
1 lg. angel food cake, broken into pieces

Dissolve Jell-O in 2½ cups boiling water. Add 2 cups cold water. Chill until partially set. Add strawberries and Cool Whip. Place half the cake pieces into large angel cake pan. Add half the Jell-O mixture. Blend well. Repeat. Chill at least 4 hours. Slice. Whipped canned milk may be used in place of Cool Whip. Yield: 14 servings.

SPEEDY STRAWBERRY FLUFF

1 pkg. diet strawberry instant pudding mix
1 10-oz. frozen package strawberries
3 egg whites

Sprinkle dry pudding mix over chopped strawberries in bowl. Mix only until combined. Let stand 5 minutes. Beat egg whites until stiff but not dry. Fold into strawberries. Note: strawberries may be sweetened with no-cal sweetener. Yield: 4 servings.

HAWAIIAN DELIGHT CHEESECAKE

4 tbsp. graham cracker crumbs
2 env. or 2 tbsp. unflavored gelatin
¾ c. pineapple juice
1½ c. creamed cottage cheese
3 eggs, separated
¼ tsp. salt
2 tbsp. unsweetened lemon juice
1 tbsp. liquid sweetener
1 tsp. vanilla extract
¼ c. skim milk
1 c. unsweetened pineapple chunks, drained

Sprinkle 3 tablespoons crumbs in 8 or 9-inch square pan; set aside. Soften gelatin in ½ cup cold water. Bring pineapple juice to a boil; stir in softened gelatin. Beat cottage cheese at high speed until almost smooth in large bowl. Blend egg yolks in with cottage cheese. Add salt, lemon juice, sweetener, and vanilla to cottage cheese mixture. Beat well. Add milk. Blend in dissolved gelatin; chill. Stir occasionally until partially thickened but not set. Beat egg whites in small mixer bowl at high speed until soft peaks form. Fold gently into gelatin mixture. Pour carefully over crumbs in pan; sprinkle remaining crumbs over filling. Top with pineapple chunks. Chill 4 hours or until firm. Top with fresh strawberries, if desired. Yield: 9 servings.

PHILADELPHIA VANILLA ICE CREAM

1 env. gelatin
¼ c. cold milk
1¾ c. scalded milk
1 pt. light cream
¼ tsp. salt
2 tsp. vanilla extract
¾ c. Sugartwin

Soften gelatin in cold milk; dissolve in scalded milk. Combine with cream, salt, vanilla and Sugartwin. Pour into refrigerator trays. Freeze at coldest position until mixture has frozen about 1-inch from edge. Place in chilled bowl. Beat until smooth. Return to trays; freeze until firm.

VANILLA ICE CREAM

6 rennet tablets
2⅔ c. Sugartwin
2 qt. milk
2⅔ c. heavy cream
8 tsp. vanilla

Dissolve rennet tablets in ¼ cup cold water. Combine remaining ingredients in a large saucepan. Heat to lukewarm. Stir in dissolved tablets. Pour into 1 gallon ice cream freezer container. Let stand 10 minutes. Freeze according to manufacturer's directions. Yield: 1 gallon.

APPLESAUCE TEACAKES

½ c. shortening
1 egg
2½ teaspoons Sugartwin
1¾ c. sifted cake flour
1 tsp. soda
¼ tsp. salt
1 tsp. cinnnamon
½ tsp. nutmeg
¼ tsp. each cloves, ginger and allspice

1 c. unsweetened applesauce
2 tsp. vanilla extract
⅓ c. raisins
⅓ c. chopped walnuts

Cream shortenng until fluffy. Beat egg and Sugartwin until lemon-colored; add to shortening. Blend well. Sift together all dry ingredients. Add to creamed mixture alternately with applesauce, blending well after each addition. Add vanilla; stir in raisins and walnuts. Line 2 small tea-sized cupcake pans with paper baking cups. Fill ⅔ full. Bake in preheated 375-degree oven for 15 to 20 minutes.

CHOCOLATE CHIP COOKIES

¼ c. margarine, softened
4 tsp. liquid sweetener
1½ tsp. vanilla extract
1 egg
1 c. plus 2 tbsp. flour
½ tsp. salt
2 tsp. baking powder
¼ tsp. soda
½ c. semisweet chocolate chips
¼ c. chopped nuts

Combine first 4 ingredients in small mixer bowl. Beat at high speed for 1 to 2 minutes or until light and fluffy. Add next 4 ingredients with ½ cup water. Blend at low speed 2 minutes or until well combined. Stir in chocolate chips and nuts. Dough will be soft. Drop from well-rounded teaspoon 2-inches apart onto ungreased cookie sheet. Bake at 425 degrees for 10 to 12 minutes or until lightly brown.

FRESH APPLE CAKE

1 tsp. cocoa
½ c. hot coffee
1 c. Sugartwin
½ c. vegetable shortening
1 egg
½ c. raisins or nuts
1 tsp. soda
1 c. grated raw apple
1½ c. sifted flour
1 tsp. cinnamon
¼ tsp. nutmeg
½ tsp. cloves

Dissolve cocoa in coffee. Combine next 4 ingredients. Dissolve soda in cocoa. Add to nut mixture. Add remaining ingredients. Pour into greased loaf or square baking pan. Bake in preheated 350-degree oven for 40 to 45 minutes or until done. Use Pam or Cooking-Ease to grease pan.

CHOCOLATE CAKE

⅓ c. margarine, softened
¼ c. (firmly packed) brown sugar
1 egg
2 tbsp. liquid sweetener
1⅓ c. flour
3 tsp. cocoa
2 tsp. baking powder
½ tsp. soda
1 tsp. vanilla extract
½ c. skim milk
2 tbsp. finely chopped nuts

Combine first 4 ingredients in large mixer bowl. Beat 2 minutes at high speed. Add next 6 ingredients. Blend 2 minutes at low speed. Spread batter into greased 8-inch pan. Sprinkle with nuts. Bake in 350 degree preheated oven for 25 to 30 minutes.

SPONGE CAKE

6 eggs, separated
½ tsp. cream of tartar
¼ c. sugar
2 tbsp. unsweetened lemon juice
2 tbsp. liquid sweetener
1 tbsp. vanilla extract
1⅓ c. all-purpose flour
1 tsp. baking powder
½ tsp. salt

Beat egg whites and cream of tartar at high speed until foamy; gradually add sugar. Continue beating until stiff peaks form. Beat egg yolks in small mixer bowl until thick and lemon-colored. Add remaining ingredients. Blend at low speed until moistened; beat 2 minutes at medium speed, scraping bowl occasionally. Pour over egg whites. Fold carefully by hand just until well-blended. Pour batter into ungreased 9 or 10-inch tube pan. Bake in preheated 325-degree oven for 55 to 60 minutes. Invert. Cool completely; remove from pan. Store in refrigerator.

CREAM TOPPING

½ c. evaporated milk
¼ tsp. gelatin
1 tbsp. Sugartwin
1 tsp. vanilla extract

Pour milk into top part of double boiler. Heat uncovered. Soften gelatin in 1 teaspoon cold water. Add to hot milk; stir until dissolved. Chill; whip until stiff. Fold in Sugartwin and vanilla.

FROZEN BLUEBERRIES

1 tbsp. liquid sweetener
2 pt. blueberries

Mix sweetener with 2 cups cold water. Fill freezer containers about ⅓ full of sweetener solution. Add fruit to ½ inch of top. Be sure liquid covers fruit. If necessary put a crumpled piece of waxed paper on top to hold fruit in liquid. Store in freezer.

FROZEN DARK CHERRIES

2 tsp. sweetener
¼ tsp. ascorbic acid
2 to 3 lb. cherries

Mix sweetener, ascorbic acid and 2 cups water. Fill freezer containers about ⅓ full of sweetener solution. Add fruit to ½ inch of top. Be sure liquid covers fruit. If necessary put a crumpled piece of waxed paper on top to hold fruit in liquid. Store in freezer.

FROZEN PEACHES

1 tbsp. sweetener
½ tsp. ascorbic acid
2 lb. peeled peaches, chopped.

Mix sweetener, ascorbic acid and 2 cups water. Fill freezer containers about ⅓ full of sweetener solution. Add fruit to ½ inch of top. Be sure liquid covers fruit. If necessary put a crumpled piece of waxed paper on top to hold fruit in liquid. Store in freezer.

FROZEN STRAWBERRIES

2 tsp. sweetener
3 pt. strawberries

Mix sweetener with ½ cup cold water. Toss strawberries with liquid until mixed. You may also freeze cleaned berries whole. Quick freeze on cookie sheet; store in bags.

CANNED APRICOTS

1 tbsp. lemon juice
1 tbsp. liquid sweetener
2 to 3 lb. apricots

Prepare fruit for canning. Combine in saucepan 2 cups water, lemon juce and sweetener. Bring to a boil. Pack fruit in hot, sterilized pint jars. Fill to within ½-inch of top with hot liquid. Seal. Process 15 to 20 minutes in boiling water bath.

CANNED DARK SWEET CHERRIES

1 tbsp. lemon juice
2 tbsp. liquid sweetener
2 to 3 lb. dark sweet cherries

Prepare fruit for canning. Combine in saucepan 2 cups water, lemon juice and sweetener. Bring to a boil. Pack fruit in hot, sterilized pint jars. Fill to within ½-inch of top with hot liquid. Seal. Process 15 to 20 minutes in boiling water bath.

CANNED PEACHES

1 tbsp. lemon juice
1 tbsp. liquid sweetener
2 to 3 lb. peaches

Prepare fruit for canning. Combine in saucepan 2 cups water, lemon juice and sweetener. Bring to a boil. Pack fruit in hot, sterilized pint jars. Fill to within ½-inch of top with hot liquid. Seal. Process 15 to 20 minutes in boiling water bath.

CANNED PEARS

1 tbsp. lemon juice
1 tbsp. liquid sweetener
2 to 3 lb. pears

Prepare fruit for canning. Combine in saucepan 2 cups water, lemon juice and sweetener. Bring to a boil. Pack fruit in hot, sterilized pint jars. Fill to within ½-inch of top with hot liquid. Seal. Process 15 to 20 minutes in boiling water bath.

CANNED PLUMS

1 tbsp. lemon juice
1 tbsp. liquid sweetener
2 to 3 lb. plums

Prepare fruit for canning. Combine in saucepan 2 cups water, lemon juice and sweetener. Bring to a boil. Pack fruit in hot, sterilized pint jars. Fill to within ½-inch of top with hot liquid. Seal. Process 15 to 20 minutes in boiling water bath.

APPLE-DATE SPREAD

2 c. finely chopped apples
2 c. dates, diced
¾ cup fruit juice or water
Pinch of salt
1 can unsweetened crushed pineapple

Combine all ingredients in saucepan. Boil gently until consistency of jam. Add more water if necessary.

MARMALADE AMBROSIA

1 lb. dried apricots
1 lb. dried prunes
1 lb. dried peaches or pears
1 No. 2 can crushed pineapple
Pure honey or sweetener to taste

Wash and soak dried fruit overnight. Use only enough water to soften fruit. Lift out all but prunes. Cook prunes in same water. Cool. Remove pits. Put all fruit except pineapple through food grinder. Add crushed pineapple and sweetener. Mix thoroughly. Note: This mixture may be brought to a boil and canned.

CANNED FRUIT JAM

1 qt. home-canned diet fruit
Lemon or orange rind to taste

Process diet fruit in blender. Place in flat baking dish. Add lemon rind. Bake at 150 degrees until consistency desired. Add lemon or orange grated rind as desired.

FROZEN FRUIT JAM

1 pkg. frozen unsweetened blueberries
4 tbsp. cornstarch, tapioca or arrowroot
Pure honey or sweetener to taste.

Combine all ingredients in saucepan. Cook until thickened.

FRENCH DRESSING WITHOUT SUGAR

½ c. salad oil
⅔ c. red taco sauce
⅛ tsp. salt
½ tsp. onion salt
¼ tsp. garlic salt
¼ tsp. pepper
1 tbsp. prepared mustard
¼ c. white vinegar

Combine all ingredients in a quart jar; shake well. Chill.

Velma Fellows
Coquille Grange
Coquille, Oregon

RAISED MUFFINS

2 eggs, beaten
Dash of salt
1 tbsp. butter, melted

½ cake compressed yeast
1 pt. milk, warmed
4 c. flour

Combine first 5 ingredients. Stir flour in gradually. Beat until batter is light and smooth. Let rise for 4 hours in a warm place. Fill greased muffin tins ⅔ full. Let stand until batter rises to top of muffin tin. Bake at 350 degrees for 20 to 30 minutes or until muffins test done.

Cheryle Harte
Indian Valley Grange
Greenville, California

SOUR CREAM MUFFINS FOR DIABETICS

¼ c. diet margarine
¾ c. imitation sour cream
1⅛ c. sifted all-purpose flour
½ tsp. soda
¼ tsp. salt
$1/16$ tsp. nutmeg
Non-nutritive sweetener equivalent to ½ c. sugar
1 med. egg, beaten

Cream margarine; add sour cream. Mix well. Sift dry ingredients; add to creamed mixture alternately with egg. Spoon into greased muffin tins. Bake in preheated 450-degree oven for 15 minutes. Yield: 8 muffins.

Mrs Pauline Moats
Range Community Grange
Mt. Sterling, Ohio

STRAWBERRY JAM WITH PECTIN

1 qt. cleaned strawberries
4 to 5 tsp. liquid artifical sweetener
1¾ oz. package powdered fruit pectin
1 tbsp. lemon juice

Crush strawberries in 1½-quart saucepan. Stir in sweetener, fruit pectin and lemon juice. Bring to a boil. Boil 1 minute. Remove from heat. Continue to stir for 2 mintues. Pour into freezer containers. Cover; freeze. Thaw before serving. Store in refrigerator after opening. Yield: 2⅔ cups.

Kholetta Downard, C.W.A
Michigan State Grange
Adrian, Michigan

Canning and
Preserving Recipes

No good family cookbook is complete without a food preservation section. In fact, with the trend toward the use of fresh and natural foods in family diets, a canning and preserving section might well be the most important in this cookbook.

You don't have to tend an acre garden of fruits and vegetables in the summer to have a pantry full of gleaming jars of food "put up" for the winter. Reasonably priced fresh produce is available all through the spring and summer in most areas. And, it is just as rewarding to put up someone else's market-fresh produce as it is your own garden-fresh fruits and vegetables.

In home canning, there are two USDA-approved methods considered safe. These are the water bath method and the steam pressure canning method. The water bath is safe to use with high-acid foods such as tomatoes, fruits, rhubarb, relishes and pickles, preserves, fruit butters and marmalades. Low acid foods such as peas, beans, carrots, corn, asparagus, okra, squash, meats, and fish MUST BE processed by the steam pressure canning method.

Low-acid foods require a temperature higher than 212 degrees to kill dangerous bacteria. If you live at an altitude of 1,000 feet or more above sea level, add 1 minute to the processing time per thousand feet if the processing time is 20 minutes or less. For more than 20 minutes, add 2 minutes to the processing time per thousand feet. Some recipes in this section have been altered slightly to conform to USDA canning standards.

3 oranges
3 pt. sugar
1 c. chopped walnuts

Remove grapes from skins, reserve skins. Put pulp through colander; add enough to skins to measure 3 pints. Add raisins, grated rind and pulp of oranges. Add sugar and 1 pint water. Bring to a boil. Boil for about 30 minutes or until thick, stirring constantly, to prevent burning. Add walnuts just before removing from heat. Pour in hot sterilized jars; seal. Process in boiling water bath for 10 minutes.

Mrs. Maude Sayers
Litchfield Grange, No. 1860
Grafton, Ohio

BANANA BUTTER

3 c. mashed bananas
¼ c. lemon juice
¼ c. finely chopped maraschino cherries
6½ c. sugar
1 6-oz. bottle of liquid pectin

Place bananas in large saucepan. Add lemon juice, cherries and sugar; mix well. Bring to a hard rolling boil. Boil hard for 1 minute, stirring constantly. Remove from heat; quickly stir in pectin. Ladle into hot sterilized jars. Seal. Process in boiling water bath for 10 minutes. Yield: 8-9 half pints

Mrs. John Farquhar, Master
Bangor Grange, No. 967
North Bangor, New York

APPLE BUTTER

4 c. canned applesauce
2 tbsp. lemon juice
½ tsp. grated orange rind
½ tsp. ground cloves
1 tsp. cinnamon
1 c. (firmly packed) brown sugar
¼ tsp. allspice

Combine all ingredients in saucepan. Simmer, stirring occasionally, for 1 hour. Cool. Pour into hot sterilized glass jars. Seal with paraffin at once. Yield: 4 cups.

Photograph for this recipe on page 264.

GRAPE CONSERVE

3 pt. grapes
1 lb. raisins

PEAR CONSERVE

2 oranges
1 lemon
2 c. chopped pears or peaches
4 c. crushed pineapple
Sugar

Grind oranges and lemon with peeling. Mix all fruit. Measure. Add 1 cup sugar to each cup fruit. Mix thoroughly. Let stand overnight. Stir occasionally. Cook 15 minutes or until syrupy. Pour into hot sterilized jars; seal. Process in boiling water bath for 10 minutes.

Alta Van Cleave
Buena Grange, No. 836
Zillah, Washington

APRICOT-PINEAPPLE JAM

1 qt. peeled, chopped fresh California apricots
4 c. sugar
2 c. pared fresh pineapple, diced
Rind of 1 orange, cut in thin slivers
2 tbsp. lemon juice

Dip apricots into boiling water for 30 to 60 seconds or until skins are loosened. Remove skins and pits from apricots; discard. Chop enough apricots to measure 1 quart. Combine all ingredients in 4-quart saucepan. Stir constantly over medium heat until sugar dissolves. Boil rapidly for 25 minutes or until thickened. Stir frequently. Pour jam into hot sterilized jam jars. Seal with paraffin at once. Yield: 6 8-oz. glasses.

Photograph for this recipe on page 266.

JUNE JAM

3 c. shredded fresh pineapple
2 c. fresh rhubarb, cut in pieces

4 c. hulled strawberries
Pinch of salt
4½ c. sugar

Cook pineapple in large saucepan for 10 minutes; do not add additional liquid. Add rhubarb, strawberries and salt. Cook for 20 minutes. Add sugar. Bring to a boil. Boil rapidly for 20 to 30 minutes or until thick, stirring frequently. Skim off foam. Pour into hot, sterilized jars. Seal. Process in boiling water bath for 10 minutes. Store in cool place.

Mrs. Gladys Hauenstein, C.W.A.
Wayne Co., Sugar Creek Grange, No. 2555
Dalton, Ohio

RUTH'S RHUBARB JAM

6 c. chopped rhubarb
4 c. sugar
1 20-oz. can crushed pineapple and juice
1 lg. package apricot Jell-O

Place rhubarb, sugar, pineapple and juice in saucepan. Bring to a boil; simmer about 25 minutes. Remove from heat; stir in Jell-O. Stir until well dissolved. Pour into hot sterilized containers; seal. Store in freezer or refrigerator.

Mrs. Ruth Adams
Golden Rod Grange, No. 114
Keene, New Hampshire

RHUBARB JAM

3 c. rhubarb, cut in small pieces
2½ c. sugar
1 pkg. strawberry or raspberry Jell-O

Cook rhubarb and ½ cup water as for sauce. Add sugar; stir until dissolved. Remove from heat; add Jell-O. Stir until Jell-O is dissolved. Pour into hot sterilized glasses; add paraffin. Seal.

Mrs. G. H. Brooke
Amboy Grange
Newton, Iowa

SQUASH JAM

3½ c. zucchini, ground
4 c. sugar
2 oranges, juice
½ orange rind, grated
1 lemon, juice

Place all ingredients except lemon juice in refrigerator container. Chill overnight. Place in saucepan. Add lemon juice to zucchini. Bring mixture to a boil; heat for 15 minutes. Do not allow sugar

crystals to form around edge of saucepan while cooking. Ladle hot jam into hot sterilized jars, leaving ¼-inch head space. Adjust caps to seal. Process jars in boiling water bath for 10 minutes.

Photograph for this recipe on page 269.

STRAWBERRY JAM

4 c. crushed or sliced strawberries
5 c. sugar

Bring strawberries to a boil in a 4 or 6 quart kettle with a broad flat bottom. Add 3 cups sugar; boil 3 minutes. Add 2 cups sugar; boil 2 minutes. Let stand for 4 days, stirring each day. Fill hot sterilized containers; seal. Process in boiling water bath for 10 minutes. Yeild: 2 pints

Mercedes Kiles, Past Lecturer
Texas State Grange
Fredricksburg, Texas

SPICED APPLE JELLY

2½ c. apple juice
1 tsp. lemon juice
¼ tsp. lemon rind, grated
3½ c. sugar
¼ c. cinnamon candies
⅛ tsp. allspice
⅛ tsp. ground cloves
½ c. liquid pectin

Combine all ingredients except pectin in a saucepan. Bring to a boil, stirring constantly. Boil for 10 minutes. Stir in pectin quickly. Boil for 1 minute, stirring constantly. Remove from heat. Skim; pour into hot sterilized jelly glasses. Seal with paraffin at once. Yield: 4 jelly glasses.

Photograph for this recipe on page 264.

CORN COB JELLY

12 bright red corn cobs
1 pkg. pectin
3 c. sugar
1 drop of red food coloring

Break corn cobs; place in saucepan. Cover with 3 or more pints of water. Boil for 30 or more minutes. Strain; reserving liquid. Add enough water to measure 3 cups. Add pectin. Bring to a rolling boil. Add sugar. Boil until mixture reaches jelly stage. Add 1 drop of red food coloring if desired. Pour into hot sterilized jars. Cover with paraffin; seal.

Rosa E. Shultz
Harrison Co., Mt. Hope Grange
Scio, Ohio

NEW MEXICO SUNSHINE JELLY

1 c. chopped bell pepper
1 c. chopped Jalapeno chili pepper
2 c. cider vinegar
5½ c. sugar
1 bottle of Certo

Combine first 4 ingredients in saucepan. Bring to a rolling boil. Add Certo. Boil for 5 minutes. Pour into hot sterilized jars. Seal. Process in boiling water bath for 10 minutes.

Sarah Swanson
Welcome Grange, No. 791
Napa, California

PYRACANTHA JELLY

2 pt. Pyracantha Berries, red or yellow
Juice of 1 grapefruit
Juice of 1 lime
1 pkg. Sure-Jel
5½ c. sugar

Wash berries well. Add 3 pints water. Boil for 20 minutes. Add juices. Drain, reserving juice. Do not squeeze! Measure juice adding additional grapefruit juice to measure 4½ cups. Add Sure-Jel; bring to a boil. Add sugar. Boil hard for 2 minutes, or until jelly drops in sheets from spoon. Pour into hot sterilized glasses; seal. Process in boiling water bath for 10 minutes. Jelly is a delicate pink. May add food coloring to make a Christmas red.

Mercedes Kiles
Wife of Past Master
Texas State Grange
Fredricksburg, Texas

PEPPER JELLY

1 c. chopped sweet pepper, seeds removed
¼ c. chopped hot pepper, seeds removed
5 c. sugar
1 c. vinegar
1 bottle of Certo

Mix first 4 ingredients in saucepan. Bring to rolling boil; boil for 30 seconds. Add Certo; bring to rolling boil. Boil for 1 minute. Skim foam. Pour into hot sterilized jars. Seal with paraffin. Excellent with cream cheese and crackers.

Mrs. Francis Webster
Bell Township Grange, No. 2047
Mahaffey, Pennsylvania

MARY'S PEPPER JELLY

¾ c. bell pepper
1½ c. hot peppers
1½ c. distilled vinegar
6 c. sugar
1 6-oz. package Sure-Jel
Green food coloring

Boil first 4 ingredients until pepper is tender. Add Sure-Jel. Boil for 1 minute. Set aside and skim or strain. Add enough coloring to tint light green. Pour into 6 hot sterilized jelly glasses; seal. Process in boiling water bath for 10 minutes. Yield: 6 jelly glasses.

Mrs. Mary Maskew
Leon Valley Grange, No. 1581
San Antonio, Texas

CARROT AND PINEAPPLE MARMALADE

4 c. sugar
4 c. carrots, chopped
2 c. crushed pineapple, drained
⅓ c. lemon juice
2 lemon rinds, grated
½ tsp. allspice
½ tsp. cinnamon
¼ tsp. nutmeg
⅛ tsp. cloves
½ bottle of liquid pectin

Combine all ingredients except pectin in large saucepan; mix well. Bring to a boil. Boil for 1 minute, stirring constantly. Remove from heat. Add pectin at once. Allow marmalade to rest for 2 minutes. Skim foam from marmalade. Pour hot marmalade into hot sterilized jars, leaving ¼-inch head space. Adjust caps to seal. Process jars in boiling water bath for 10 minutes. Yield: about 6 half pints.

Photograph for this recipe on page 269.

CARROT MARMALADE

> 4 c. ground or finely grated carrots
> 2 ground or finely grated orange rinds
> 2 ground or finely grated lemon rinds
> Juice of 2 lemons
> 3 c. sugar

Mix all ingredients in glass or pottery bowl; Cover. Let stand overnight. Transfer to saucepan; simmer slowly about 1 hour or until jells. Check occasionally while simmering, adding a little water if needed. Ladle into hot sterilized glasses. Cover with melted paraffin to seal. Yield: 5-6 cups.

Mrs. Judy Streeter
Templeton Grange, No. 122
Baldwinville, Massachusetts

GOLDEN GLOW

> 3 lb. pumpkin, peeled
> 3 lb. sugar
> 6 oranges
> 3 lemons

Chop the pumpkin coarsely; cover with sugar. Let stand overnight. Add juice and grated rind of oranges and lemons; cook slowly until thick. Pour into hot sterilized jars. Seal. Process in boiling water bath for 10 minutes. Original name was Pumpkin Marmalade but it seemed too common when the early settler was complimented by the minister so she said, Golden Glow.

Mrs. Ruby Emery
Franklin Grange, No. 124
Bryant Pond, Maine

RHUBARB MARMALADE

> 5 c. sugar
> 2 qt. rhubarb, sliced
> ½ lb. raisins
> 2 oranges, chopped
> 1 c. walnuts

Combine sugar and sliced rhubarb; let stand overnight. Cook with raisins, oranges, and walnuts until thick, about 15 minutes. Pour into hot

sterilized jars. Seal. Process in boiling water bath for 10 minutes.

Mrs. Herman Reuter
Charity Grange, No. 294
Fenn, Idaho

THREE-FRUIT MARMALADE

> 3 peeled, cored apples
> 12 peeled, pitted peaches
> 6 peeled, seeded oranges
> Sugar

Grind all fruit together. Measure pulp and juice. Add 1½ times as much sugar as fruit and juice. Stir thoroughly. Cook very slowly, stirring to keep from burning. Cook until bubbles snap or when cooled in refrigerator it is the consistency of honey. Pour into hot sterilized jars. Seal with paraffin. May be used as ice cream topping, on toast or sandwiches. Mix with mustard and cloves as glaze for ham.

Mary C. Irwin
Camas Valley Grange
Springdale, Washington

RED BEET PRESERVES

> 6 c. peeled red beets cut into thin strips
> 7 c. sugar
> 3 lemons, thinly sliced
> 1 1-inch piece crystallized ginger, chopped

Mix first 3 ingredients together in saucepan with ½ cup water. Allow mixture to stand for about 10 minutes. Cook mixture slowly, stirring frequently. Add chopped ginger when syrup begins to thicken. Cook until mixture is thickened. Pour hot preserves into hot sterilized jars, leaving ¼-inch head space. Adjust caps to seal. Process jars in a boiling water bath for 10 minutes. Yield: about 5 half pints.

Photograph for this recipe on page 269.

PEACH JUBILEE

> 1 c. crushed fresh peaches
> 1 c. sugar

Place peaches and sugar in heavy saucepan. Boil for 20 minutes. Pour into a hot sterilized pint jar. Seal. Process in boiling water bath for 10 minutes. Good on bread or ice cream. Yield: 1 pint.

Mrs. W. Paul McCullough
Big Beaver Grange, No. 1578
New Galilee, Pennsylvania

ROSY STRAWBERRY PRESERVES

1 qt. halved strawberries
4 c. sugar
1 tbsp. vinegar or lemon juice

Combine strawberries and sugar; stir lightly. Let stand 1 hour in flat bottom shallow pan, preferably Pyrex. Bring to a boil. Cook 10 minutes, stirring constantly. Add vinegar. Boil for 3 minutes longer. Remove from heat; cover. Let stand 24 hours. Bring to a boil. Ladle into hot sterilized jars. Seal. Process in boiling water bath for 10 minutes.

Mrs. Emory J. Robb
LaPrairie Grange, No. 79
Whitewater, Wisconsin

STRAWBERRY PRESERVES

2 qt. firm ripe strawberries
6 c. sugar

Scald strawberries in boiling water to cover for 2 minutes. Drain. Add 4 cups sugar. Bring to a boil; boil for 2 minutes. Remove from heat. Add 2 additional cups of sugar when boiling stops. Boil for 5 minutes longer. Pour into shallow pan only 1½ to 2 inches deep. Let stand overnight. Pack preserves in sterilized jars. Seal. Process in boiling water bath for 10 minutes.

Betty B. Hoskorec, C.W.A.
Hagerman Valley Grange, No. 218
Hagerman, Idaho

CRAB APPLE PICKLES

1 gal. crab apples
6 to 8 c. sugar
4 c. vinegar
1 stick cinnamon
1 tbsp. pickling spice

Combine all ingredients with 3 cups water. Cook until tender. Let stand overnight. Reheat. Pour into hot sterilized jars. Seal. Process in boiling water bath for 10 minutes. Yield: 8 pints.

Edith Connely
Custer Center Grange, No. 103
Broken Bow, Nebraska

PICKLED FIGS

1 tbsp. soda
7 lb. figs
3 lb. sugar
1 pt. vinegar
1 tbsp. cinnamon
3 lemons, sliced
1 tsp. cloves

Combine 1 gallon boiling water with soda. Pour over figs. Let stand for a few minutes. Drain; rinse well. Dissolve sugar in vinegar. Add remaining ingredients. Bring to a boil. Add figs. Cook until figs are clear. Remove figs. Pack in hot sterilized jars. Continue to boil syrup until thick. Pour over figs. Seal. Process in boiling water bath for 10 minutes.

Alexine Pouls
Vacaville Grange, No. 575
Vacaville, California

SPICED PEARS

7 lb. winter pears, peeled
3 tbsp. vinegar
2 c. sugar
¾ c. light corn syrup
1 c. distilled white vinegar
½ tsp. whole ginger
2 tsp. whole cloves
1 cinnamon stick, broken

Combine vinegar and 3 quarts water. Cover pears with solution to prevent browning. Mix remaining ingredients; cover. Bring to boiling point. Add drained pears. Cover; simmer for 3 minutes. Fill hot sterilized jars with fruit. Cover with boiling liquid, leaving 1 inch head space. Seal. Process for 15 minutes in boiling water bath.

Mrs. Ruth Payne
New Concord Grange, No. 2416
New Concord, Ohio

EXCELLENT MINCEMEAT

4 lb. lean boiled beef, chopped fine
8 lb. green tart apples
1 lb. chopped suet
3 lb. seeded raisins
2 lb. currants, washed and dried
½ lb. citron, cut up fine
1 lb. brown sugar
1 qt. molasses
2 qt. sweet cider
1 pt. boiled cider
1 tbsp. each pepper, mace, allspice, cloves
4 tbsp. cinnamon
2 grated nutmegs
Juice and rind of 2 lemons
1 tbsp. salt
1 pt Brandy
1 pt. Madeira

Combine all ingredients except Brandy and Madeira in large saucepan. Cook until heated through. Stir in Brandy and Madeira. Pack in a crock; cover closely. Set in cold place. Do not freeze. Keep strictly cold. Will keep all winter.

Dorothy E. Whitehill
Clairion Co., Prosperity Grange, No. 1985
Shippenville, Pennsylvania

TOMATO PRESERVES

4 lb. tomatoes
Juice of 4 lemons or reconstituted lemon juice
8 c. sugar

Wash and prepare tomatoes. Cut out stems and any blemishes. Grind tomatoes and lemons. Place in a 6 to 8-quart pan with sugar and 3 cups water. Bring to a boil. Boil gently until mixture is clear and slightly thickened. Pour into hot sterilized jelly glasses. Cool. Seal with paraffin.

June D. Lull
Westbrook Grange, No. 123
Westbrook, Connecticut

ELIZABETH'S DILL PICKLES

1 peck cucumbers, cut into ¼-inch slices or
* lengths*
2 qt. vinegar
1⅛ c. salt
1 lg. sprig fresh dill
Alum
1 clove of garlic per jar

Pack cucumbers into sterilized jars. Combine vinegar, salt and 4 quarts water in large saucepan. Bring to boiling point. Pour over cucumbers in jars. Place dill, small amount of alum and garlic into each jar. Seal jars. Let set at least 4 weeks.

Elizabeth C. Abbott, Master
Moosilauke Grange, No. 214
Pike, New Hampshire

THELMA'S KOSHER DILLS

Grape leaves
Sm. red peppers
Garlic cloves
Dillseed
Whole cucumbers
1 qt. vinegar
1 c. salt

Place 1 grape leaf, 1 pepper, 1 garlic clove and 1 teaspoon dillseed in hot sterilized 1-quart jars. Pack in cucumbers. Combine vinegar, salt and 3 quarts water in large saucepan. Bring to a boil. Pour over cucumbers, leaving ¼-inch head space. Place grape leaf in top of each jar. Seal. Process in boiling water bath for 10 minutes. Store in cold place for 4 weeks before using.

Thelma Buhler, C.W.A.
Monterey Co., Pomona Grange, No. 17
Salinas, California

MARGARET'S BREAD AND BUTTER PICKLES

12 lg. cucumbers, peeled and sliced
12 onions, peeled and sliced
2 c. vinegar
1½ c. sugar
1 tsp. ground mustard
1 tsp. turmeric
1 tsp. celery seed
1 tsp. ginger

Soak cucumbers and onions in salted water for several hours; drain. Wash; drain well. Combine remaining ingredients in saucepan. Add vegetables. Cook until clear. Pour into sterilized jars. Seal. Process in boiling water bath for 10 minutes.

Margaret Schwarz
Bethel Grange, No. 129
Blackwell, Oklahoma

SPICY BREAD AND BUTTER PICKLES

1 gal. cucumbers, thinly sliced
8 lg. white onions, ground
2 green peppers, ground
½ c. salt
5 c. sugar
5 c. vinegar
1½ tsp. turmeric
½ tsp. ground cloves
2 tbsp. white mustard seed
1 tsp. celery seed

Combine first 4 ingredients. Let stand 3 hours. Drain. Heat remaining ingredients to boiling point, stirring to dissolve sugar. Add cucumber mixture. Heat. Do not boil. Pour into hot sterilized jars. Seal. Process in water bath for 5 minutes.

Catherine Edgerly, C.W.A.
Kennebec Valley Grange, No. 128
Skowhegan, Maine

SWEET SPICY GINGER PICKLES

8 lb. cucumbers, sliced thin
1 c. salt
2 tbsp. alum
2 tbsp. ginger
2 qt. vinegar
6 lb. sugar
½ oz. whole pickling spice, tied in cloth bag

Soak cucumbers in 1 gallon water and salt for 8 days. Place a weighted plate on top to hold slices under brine. Drain. Boil cucumbers in 1 gallon water and 2 tablespoons alum for 30 minutes. Drain. Boil cucumbers in 1 gallon water and 2 tablespoons ginger for 30 minutes. Drain. Combine remaining ingredients with 1 pint water. Boil until clear. Pack in hot sterilized jars. Seal. Process in boiling water bath for 10 minutes.

Mrs. W.C. Harris, Wife of Master
Oregon State Grange
Portland, Oregon

CRISP-AS-ICE CUCUMBER SLICES

½ c. salt
4 qt. thinly sliced cucumbers
8 onions, thinly sliced
2 green peppers, seeded and cut into strips
4 c. sugar
1½ tsp. turmeric
½ tsp. cloves
3½ tsp. mustard seed
4½ c. vinegar

Sprinkle salt over vegetables; mix. Empty tray of ice cubes into center of vegetables. Let stand 3 hours. Combine remaining ingredients; heat to boiling. Drain vegetables. Pour hot syrup over them. Heat over low temperature to scalding, stirring frequently. Do not boil. Ladle into hot, sterilized jars. Seal. Process in boiling water bath for 5 minutes.

Rachel L. Sturman
Newcastle Grange, No. 1100
Renton, Washington

CROSSCUT PICKLE SLICES

1 gal. medium-sized cucumbers, cut into ⅛ to ¼-inch slices
1 lb. onions, sliced
2 lg. garlic cloves
⅓ c. salt
4½ c. sugar
1½ tsp. turmeric
1½ tsp. celery seed
2 tbsp. mustard seed
3 c. white vinegar

Combine cucumbers, onions and garlic. Add salt; mix thoroughly. Cover with crushed ice. Let stand for 3 hours. Drain thoroughly. Remove garlic cloves. Combine next 5 ingredients in saucepan. Bring to boiling point. Add cucumbers and onions. Heat for 5 minutes. Pack loosely into hot sterilized jars, leaving ½-inch head space. Seal. Process in boiling water bath for 5 minutes. Set jars upright to cool.

Betty M. Richard
Temple Grange, No. 66
Marydel, Maryland

MARY'S CUCUMBER PICKLES

3 qt. cucumbers, cut up
4 lg. onions, cut up
6 tbsp. salt
3 tsp. celery seed
3 tsp. mustard seed
1 tsp. turmeric
½ c. flour
4 c. sugar
4 c. vinegar

Combine first 3 ingredients in large bowl. Cover with water. Let set for 3 hours. Drain thoroughly. Mix remaining ingredients in saucepan. Cook until thick. Add vegetables. Heat to boiling point. Fill hot sterilized jars. Seal. Process in boiling water bath for 10 minutes.

Mrs. Mary E. Carter, C.W.A.
Holden Grange, No. 544
East Holden, Maine

DILL-ONION PICKLES

1 gal. medium-sized cucumbers, sliced
Onion slices
Lg. dill head
Alum
1 qt. vinegar
3 c. sugar
½ c. pickling salt

Pack cucumbers in hot sterilized jars. Top each jar with a few onion slices and a few sprigs of dill. Add ⅛ teaspoon alum to each jar. Boil remaining ingredients 2 to 3 minutes. Pour over cucumbers. Seal. Process in boiling water bath for 10 minutes.

Mrs. LeRoy R. Rahn
Rock Creek Grange, No. 1908
Polo, Illinois

ELIZABETH'S MUSTARD PICKLE

Salt
12 cucumbers
3 lb. onions
6 tbsp. flour
2 tsp. turmeric
2 tsp. dry mustard
4 c. sugar
1½ qt. vinegar
Sm. can pimento

Make brine of 1 gallon water to 1 cup salt. Soak cucumbers and onions in brine overnight. Cook in brine next morning until tender. Drain. Combine remaining ingredients. Heat to boiling point. Pour over vegetables. Pour into hot sterilized jars. Seal. Process in boiling water bath for 10 minutes.

Elizabeth Parks
Tucson Grange, No. 6
Tucson, Arizona

PICKLE CHUNKS

1 c. salt
6 qt. sliced cucumbers
1 qt. sliced onions
6 c. sugar
5 c. vinegar
1 tbsp. turmeric
1 tsp. mustard seed
1 tsp. celery seed

Combine 9 cups water and salt in large bowl. Add vegetables. Soak for 3 hours. Drain. Combine remaining ingredients in large saucepan. Heat to boiling point. Add vegetables. Heat thoroughly. Pour into hot sterilized jars; seal. Process in boiling water bath for 10 minutes.

Ruth Metzger
Central Grange, No. 1650
Germansville, Pennsylvania

FROZEN SLICED SWEET DILLS

1 lb. 3-inch cucumbers
¾ lb. yellow onions
4 tsp. salt
¾ to 1 c. sugar
½ c. cider vinegar
1 tsp. dried dillweed

Slice cucumbers and onions ⅛-inch thick. Mix with salt and 2 tablespoons water in 2-quart bowl. Let stand 2 hours. Drain. Do not rinse. Add remaining ingredients to drained vegetables. Let stand until sugar dissolves and liquid covers vegetables. Pack in glass or plastic freezer containers, leaving 1 inch head space. Freeze. Defrost in refrigerator or at room temperature. Yield: 4 cups.

Mrs. Gertrude Gilman
Rocksburg Grange, No. 116
Elkton, Maryland

FREEZER PICKLES

2 c. sugar
1 c. vinegar
1½ tsp. salt
1⅛ tsp. celery seed
7 c. sliced cucumbers
1 c. sliced onions
1 c. chopped mango peppers (opt.)

Mix sugar, vinegar, salt and celery seed in saucepan. Cook until sugar is dissolved; cool. Pour over cucumbers, onions and mangos. Place in airtight freezer containers. Freeze.

Mrs. Arlie Baucher
Mercer Co., Hopewell Grange
Celina, Ohio

REFRIGERATOR PICKLES

4 c. sugar
4 c. vinegar
¼ c. salt
1½ tsp. turmeric
1⅛ tsp. celery seed
1⅛ tsp. mustard seed
Cucumbers, sliced thin
Onions, sliced thin

Combine first 6 ingredients in large bowl. Stir to blend. DO NOT HEAT. Pack cucumbers and onions in sterilized jars. Fill with syrup. Refrigerate for at least 5 days before using. Keep refrigerated.

Mrs. Louis Yunker
Perry Grange, No. 1163
Leicester, New York

SWEET CUCUMBER PICKLE

2 c. lime
8 lb. cucumbers, cut into ¼-inch slices
2 qt. vinegar
2 tbsp. salt
11 c. sugar
¼ c. pickling spices

Combine lime and 2 gallons water. Pour over cucumbers. Soak 24 hours. Drain. Wash in cold water 3 or 4 times. Combine remaining ingredients. Add cucumbers. Let stand for 3 hours. Bring to a boil. Boil for 30 minutes. Pack into hot sterilized jars to within 1-inch of top. Process in boiling water bath for 10 minutes. Yield: 10 pints.

Mrs. Jean Bottoms
Beach Community Grange, No. 958
Chesterfield, Virginia

BETTY'S SWEET PICKLES

1 c. salt
2 gal. cucumbers
3 tbsp. alum
8 c. vinegar
¼ c. whole cloves
¾ box stick cinnamon
1 tbsp. celery seed
10 c. sugar

Combine 1 gallon water and salt. Soak cucumbers for 7 days in brine. Remove from brine; wipe dry. Soak 24 hours in solution of alum and 1 gallon water. Drain. Split each pickle or prick with fork. Heat remaining ingredients. Pour over pickles. Repeat process for 3 days. Place drained pickles in hot sterilized jar on fourth day. Heat syrup. Pour over pickles. Seal. Process in boiling water bath for 5 minutes. This was first place winner at State Grange 1979.

Betty L. Farm
Oak Grove Grange, No. 198
Salem, Oregon

MARIE'S SWEET PICKLES

2 c. salt
7 lb. cucumbers, sliced
2 tbsp. alum
6 lb. sugar
3 pt. vinegar
1-oz. cinnamon stick
4 tsp. celery seed

Make brine of 1 gallon water and salt. Add cucumbers. Soak 5 days. Stir everyday. Drain. Soak in fresh cold water for 1 day; drain. Cover with boiling water and alum. Let stand 1 or 2 days;

drain. Cover with boiling water. Let stand for 1 day; drain. Boil remaining ingredients. Pour over pickles. Pour into hot sterilized jars; seal. Process in boiling water bath for 10 minutes.

Mrs. Marie Turley
Violet Grange, No. 1949
Pickerington, Ohio

DILLED ZUCCHINI SLICES

2 lb. fresh firm zucchini, cut into thin horizontal slices
½ c. salt
2½ c. cider vinegar
1 c. sugar
2 tsp. celery seed
2 tsp. mustard seed
4 heads dill
4 cloves of garlic
1 tsp. cayenne

Cover zucchini with 1 inch water and ¼ cup salt. Let stand for 2 hours. Drain thoroughly. Combine 2½ cups water, vinegar, sugar and remaining salt in a saucepan. Place celery seed and mustard seed in a spice bag. Add bag to vinegar mixture. Bring to a boil. Pour hot brine over zucchini slices. Allow to stand for 2 hours. Bring all ingredients to boiling point; heat 5 minutes. Place zucchini mixture into hot sterilized jars, leaving ¼-inch head space. Add 1 head of dill, 1 garlic clove and ¼ teaspoon cayenne to each jar. Adjust caps to seal. Process in boiling water bath for 10 minutes.

Photograph for this recipe on page 269.

ASPARAGUS PICKLES

Asparagus, cut into 1-inch pieces
2 qt. white vinegar
10 tbsp. pickling salt
1 tbsp. whole pickling spices

Blanch asparagus for 3 minutes; cool. Pack into hot sterilized 1-pint jars. Combine remaining ingredients with 3 quarts water in saucepan. Bring to a boil; boil for 15 minutes. Strain. Pour hot solution over asparagus. Seal. Process in boiling water bath for 10 minutes.

Mrs. Clinton Dougherty
Filer Grange, No. 215
Filer, Idaho

PICKLED BEANS

3 qt. wax beans
Juice of 1 lemon

2½ c. sugar
1 qt. vinegar
1 tbsp. salt

Remove ends from beans. Wash beans. Cook in 1 quart boiling water until tender. Drain. Pack hot beans into hot sterilized jars. Boil remaining ingredients with 1 quart water in large saucepan for 5 minutes. Pour over beans, filling jars ⅔ full. Seal. Process in boiling water bath for 10 minutes.

Ruth Hull
Potter Hollow Grange, No. 1555
Durham, New York

PICKLED BEETS

8 qt. small beets
4 c. sugar
4 c. vinegar
2 tsp. whole cloves
2 tsp. whole allspice
3 sticks cinnamon
2 lemons, thinly sliced

Cook well-scrubbed beets until tender. Dip in cold water. Slip off skins; cut into uniform pieces. Make syrup of sugar, 4 cups water and vinegar. Tie spices in cheesecloth bag. Place in syrup. Add beets and lemon slices. Simmer 15 minutes, stirring occasionally. Small amount of red food coloring may be added to retain bright appearance, if desired. Pack into hot sterilized jars. Seal. Process in boiling water bath for 10 minutes. Yield: 6 quarts.

Mrs. Fern Coffman
Greenwich Grange, No. 2576
Greenwich, Ohio

CORN SALAD

24 ears of corn
¼ c. flour
1 tsp. turmeric
1 head cabbage, finely chopped
2 sweet red peppers, finely chopped
6 onions, finely chopped
1 qt. vinegar
1 c. sugar
1 tsp. dry mustard
1 tsp. celery seed

Scrape corn from cobs. Mix flour and turmeric with corn. Add vegetables; mix well. Add remaining ingredients; mix. Boil 15 minutes. Pour into hot sterilized jars. Seal. Process in boiling water bath for 10 minutes. This recipe is over 75 years old

Hazel G. Huling
Shavers Creek Grange, No. 353
Petersburg, Pennsylvania

TOMATO FLIP

7 lb. ripe tomatoes, sliced
Vinegar
4 lb. sugar
1 tsp. ground cloves
Lemon juice (opt.)

Cover tomatoes with vinegar. Let stand overnight. Drain for 1 hour. Add sugar. Cook 1 hour and 30 minutes over medium heat. Stir carefully to prevent scorching. Bring to boiling point. Let boil until tomatoes are clear and syrup is thick. Add cloves and lemon juice. Pour into hot sterilized half pint jars. Seal. Process in boiling water bath for 10 minutes. Very good served with meat. Yield: 7 half pints.

Roselyn Teelin
South Trenton Grange, No. 1559
Holland Patent, New York

BREAD AND BUTTER GREEN TOMATO PICKLES

8 c. thinly sliced green tomatoes
2 c. thinly sliced onions
4 med. peppers, thinly sliced
Salt
3 c. vinegar
3 c. (firmly packed) light brown sugar
1 tsp. celery seed
2 tsp. turmeric
1 tsp. broken cinnamon stick

Place first 3 ingredients in large bowl. Sprinkle with salt. Let stand for 1 hour. Drain. Combine remaining ingredients in large saucepan. Stir to mix. Add vegetables. Bring to a boil; boil for 20 minutes. Pour into hot sterilized jars; seal. Process in boiling water bath for 10 minutes. Yield: 5 pints.

Loretta Guillemette, C.W.A.
Norwich Grange, No. 172
Norwich, Connecticut

SPIKED APPLE RELISH

4 c. canned apple slices, undrained
1 c. maple-flavored syrup
2 sm. lemons, thinly sliced

Combine all ingredients. Simmer, uncovered, for 30 minutes. Cool. Spoon into hot sterilized glass jars. Seal with paraffin at once. Yield: 4 cups.

Photograph for this recipe on page 264.

BEET RELISH

1 qt. cooked beets, peeled and chopped fine
1 qt. chopped cabbage
1 c. horseradish
2 c. sugar
1 tsp. pepper
1 tsp. celery seed
Vinegar

Combine all ingredients except vinegar in mixing bowl. Cover with vinegar; mix well. Pour into hot sterilized jars. Seal. Process in boiling water bath for 10 minutes.

Mrs. Maude Stiverson
Wheatland Grange, No. 273,
Hudson, Michigan

CARROT RELISH

2 med. heads cabbage
8 med. onions
4 red bell peppers
4 green bell peppers
12 carrots
½ c. salt
2 pt. vinegar
6 c. sugar
1 tsp. celery seed
1 tsp. mustard seed

Grind vegetables together. Add salt. Let stand 2 hours; drain. Mix with remaining ingredients. No cooking required. Pour into hot sterilized jars. Seal. Process in boiling water bath for 10 minutes.

May Pringle
Sacramento Grange, No. 12
Sacramento, California

CHRISTMAS RELISH

10 lg. green tomatoes
9 med. carrots
9 med. onions
Few stalks celery
9 lg. red bell peppers
½ c. salt
1 tsp. celery seed
1 tsp. mustard seed
3 c. vinegar
6 c. sugar

Grind first 5 ingredients together finely; mix thoroughly. Cover with salt. Let stand several hours. Drain. Combine remaining ingredients. Pour over vegetables. Seal in jars. Store in refrigerator.

Mrs. JoAnne Calhoun, D.W.A.
Illinois State Grange
Alexis, Illinois

HARVEST MIX

6 diced green peppers
4 c. diced celery with leaves
4 c. diced onions
4 c. finely diced carrots
16 ripe tomatoes, cut up
3 tbsp. non-iodized salt
2 tbsp. sugar

Combine first 4 ingredients with 4 cups water in large saucepan. Boil for 20 minutes. Combine last 3 ingredients in separate saucepan. Bring to a boil. Add to first mixture. Pour into hot sterilized pint jars; seal. Process in hot water bath for 20 minutes. This can be used in any main dish where tomato sauce is used. I have even used it as a vegetable soup by adding meat broth or water and beef bouillon cubes. Yield: 12 pints.

Vera Penington
Mikkalo Grange
Condon, Oregon

RAW RELISH

2 heads cabbage
12 onions
8 green peppers
10 carrots
½ c. salt
3 pt. vinegar
6 c. sugar
1 tsp. celery seeds

Grind vegetables in food chopper. Add salt. Let stand 2 hours. Drain thoroughly. Add vinegar, sugar and celery seeds. Mix well. Pour into hot sterilized jars. Seal. Process in boiling water bath for 10 minutes. Yield: 10 pints.

Mrs. Kathy Hoad
Mt. Wheeler Grange,
Oso, Washington

GOOD UNCOOKED RELISH

2 lg. heads cabbage, chopped fine
4 red peppers, chopped fine
4 green peppers, chopped fine
12 med. onions, chopped fine
8 carrots, chopped fine
½ c. salt
2 pt. vinegar
6 c. sugar
1 tsp. mustard seed
1 tsp. celery seed

Combine all vegetables in large bowl. Add salt; mix well. Let stand 4 hours. Drain. Add remaining ingredients. Mix well. Let stand a few minutes. Do not cook. Pour into hot sterilized pint jars. Seal. Process in boiling water bath for 10 minutes.

Inez Kruger
Middleton Grange, No. 6
Caldwell, Idaho

FROZEN CUCUMBER RELISH

1 c. vinegar
2 c. sugar
1 tsp. celery seed
1 tsp. mustard seed
1 tbsp. (rounded) non-iodized salt
6 c. cucumbers, sliced thin
1 c. sliced onions
1 c. diced peppers

Heat first 5 ingredients until sugar is dissolved. Cool completely. Pour over vegetables. Refrigerate for 4 days. Stir occasionally. Pour into freezer containers; freeze.

Marcella Wilson
Pittsford Grange, No. 133
Pittsford, Michigan

HAMBURGER RELISH

¾ c. non iodized salt
5 c. large unpeeled cucumbers, ground
3 c. white vinegar
3 c. sugar
2 tsp. mustard seed
1 tbsp. celery seed
3½ c. diced celery
2 green or red peppers, ground
3 onions, ground

Dissolve salt in 6 cups cold water. Cover cucumbers. Let stand overnight. Drain well. Combine vinegar, sugar and spices in large saucepan. Bring to a boil. Add vegetables. Bring to a boil. Simmer 10 minutes. Fill sterilized pint jars. Seal. Process in boiling water bath for 10 minutes. Yield: 5-6 pints.

Marion Jaquet
Rock River Grange,
Franklin Grove, Illinois

PRETTY RELISH STUFF

12 mango peppers, mixed colors
1 lg. bunch celery, chopped
2 qt. shelled lima beans
3 tsp. salt

3 c. sugar
2 c. vinegar

Cut peppers into small pieces. Place peppers, celery and lima beans in separate saucepans in water to cover. Add 1 teaspoon salt to each saucepan. Cook until tender. Drain vegetables. Combine vegetables in saucepan. Add sugar and vinegar. Bring to a boil. Place in hot sterilized jars; seal. Process in hot water bath for 10 minutes. Yield: 4-5 pints.

Mrs. Joseph L. Murray
California Grange, No. 941
Danville, Pennsylvania

ONION RELISH

14 onions, peeled and quartered
6 green peppers, seeded and quartered
6 fresh hot red peppers, seeded and quartered
4 c. white vinegar
3 c. sugar
2 tbsp. salt

Blender-chop onions and peppers in water. Strain. Place vegetables into bowl. Repeat process until all vegetables are chopped. Heat remaining ingredients to boiling point in a large kettle. Add vegetables; simmer 15 minutes. Pour into hot sterilized jars. Seal. Process in boiling water bath for 10 minutes. Yield: 3 pints.

Karen Gorby
Encinitas Grange, No. 634
Encinitas, California

POTTEFIELD PICKLE RELISH

3 pt. chopped green tomatoes
3 pt. chopped ripe tomatoes
6 red peppers, ground or chopped
1 qt. onions, ground or chopped
2 bunches celery, chopped
½ c. salt
2 pt. vinegar
3 pt. sugar
½ tsp. cloves
½ c. white mustard seed

Combine first 6 ingredients. Let stand overnight; drain. Combine remaining ingredients. Add to vegetables. Cook 30 minutes. Pour into hot sterilized jars. Seal. Process in boiling water for 10 minutes. Yield: 9 pints.

Marsha Nelson
Blue Mountain Grange, No. 263
Ryegate, Vermont

THREE PEPPER RELISH

12 green peppers, ground
12 red peppers, ground
1 hot pepper, ground
1 qt. vinegar
2 c. sugar
1½ tsp. salt
5 lg. onions, ground

Cover peppers with boiling water. Let stand 5 minutes. Drain. Cover with boiling water. Let stand 10 minutes. Drain. Boil remaining ingredients 5 minutes. Add onion and peppers. Cook 10 minutes after it comes to a boil. Pour into hot sterilized jars. Seal. Process in boiling water bath for 10 minutes. Yield: 6 pints.

Florence A. Goldthwaite,
Fidelity Grange
South Hampton, New Hampshire

PICCALILLI

½ c. salt
8 qt. green tomatoes, sliced
2 c. sugar
2 c. vinegar
2 tbsp. pickling spice
1 sweet red pepper, chopped
1 green pepper, chopped
3 onions, sliced

Combine salt with tomatoes. Let set for 3 hours. Drain well. Mix sugar, 2 cups water and vinegar in a large kettle until sugar is dissolved. Tie spices in a cloth bag. Add with vegetables. Cook until tender. Pour into hot sterilized pint jars. Seal. Process in boiling water bath for 10 minutes. Yield: 5-6 pints.

Mrs. B.H. McCandless
Unionville Grange, No. 1971
Butler, Pennsylvania

TOMATO RELISH

30 ripe tomatoes, chopped
5 peaches, diced
5 pears, diced
5 apples, diced
5 onions, chopped
2 c. celery, chopped
1 green pepper, chopped
3 c. vinegar
4 c. sugar
4 tbsp. mixed pickling spices

Combine all fruits and vegetables in large kettle. Add vinegar and sugar. Tie spices in cloth bag. Add to kettle. Bring to a boil over low heat. Cook, stirring frequently, for 2 hours and 30 minutes. Remove spice bag. Pour into hot sterilized pint jars. Seal. Process in boiling water bath for 10 minutes. Yield: 8 pints.

Mrs. Doris Savage, C.W.A.
Holland Grange, No. 1023
Holland, New York

ZUCCHINI SQUASH RELISH

10 c. ground zucchini squash, seeds removed
4 c. ground onion
5 tsp. salt
2½ c. vinegar
6 c. sugar
2 tsp. celery seed
1 lg. green pepper, chopped
1 red pepper, chopped
1 tsp. turmeric
4 tsp. cornstarch

Combine first 3 ingredients in large bowl. Let stand overnight. Rinse; drain well. Add remaining ingredients except cornstarch. Cook for 15 minutes. Mix cornstarch with small amount of water. Add to cooked mixture. Pour into hot sterilized pint jars. Seal. Process in boiling water bath for 10 minutes. Be sure to use young tender squash.

Mrs. Frances De Scipio
Binghamton Grange, No. 1072
Binghamton, New York

ZUCCHINI PICKLE RELISH

10 c. coarsely ground zucchini, seeds removed
4 sm. onions, ground
3 green peppers, ground
3 tbsp. salt
2½ c. vinegar
4 c. sugar
1 tbsp. celery seed
1 tsp. pepper
1 tsp. turmeric
1 tbsp. nutmeg

Combine first 4 ingredients. Let stand overnight. Rinse; add remaining ingredients. Bring to a boil. Pour into hot sterilized jars. Seal. Process in boiling water bath for 10 minutes. May add a few drops of green food coloring. Yield: 4-5 pints.

Mary Huck, A Grange Friend
Kansas City, Kansas

FRESH PARSNIP SLAW

½ c. sour cream
1 tbsp. fresh lemon juice
2 tbsp. finely chopped onion
2 tbsp. finely chopped fresh parsley
1 tsp. sugar
1 tsp. salt
⅛ tsp. pepper
8 parsnips, pared
2 apples, cored and diced

Mix first 7 ingredients in medium bowl. Shred parsnips on coarse shredder. Add to sour cream mixture; mix well. Cover; chill several hours. Add apples when ready to serve; mix well. Yield: 6-8 servings.

Photograph for this recipe on page 33.

GLAZED ACORN SQUASH

2 med. acorn squash, quartered
6 tbsp. butter or margarine, melted
⅓ c. fresh orange juice
3 tbsp. honey
⅛ tsp. ground cinnamon
⅛ tsp. ground ginger
¼ tsp. salt

Place squash in shallow baking dish. Combine remaining ingredients. Pour over squash; cover. Bake in 350-degree oven for 30 minutes until almost tender. Baste several times with pan juices during baking. Uncover; baste. Bake for 10 to 15 minutes longer until squash is tender. Yield: 4 servings.

Photograph for this recipe on page 33.

WINTER VEGETABLE MELANGE

½ lb. white turnips, pared
¾ lb. rutabagas, pared
¾ lb. carrots, pared
¼ c. butter or margarine, melted
1 tbsp. chopped fresh parsley
2 tsp. fresh lemon juice
¼ tsp. salt

Cut vegetables into julienne strips. Place in large saucepan. Add 2 inches salted water. Bring to a boil. Cover; reduce heat. Simmer 15 to 20 minutes or until vegetables are tender. Drain; turn into serving dish. Combine remaining ingredients; mix well. Pour over vegetables; stir gently. Yield: 6 servings.

Photograph for this recipe on page 33.

TUNA CASSEROLE

2 6½-oz. cans tuna in oil
1 tsp. salt
4 c. broad egg noodles, cooked
1 10-oz. package frozen chopped spinach, thawed
1 10½-oz. can mushroom soup
¼ c. shredded Swiss cheese

Combine all ingredients in large bowl. Pour into 2-quart casserole. Bake, covered, at 350 degrees for 50 to 60 minutes. Yield: 6 servings.

Photograph for this recipe on page 34.

IRISH MEAT LOAF

1½ lb. ground beef
½ lb. ground pork
3 c. soft bread crumbs
1 egg
½ c. minced onion
¾ c. milk
2 tsp. salt
1¼ tsp. ginger
2 c. peeled chopped apples
1½ c. mashed potato
1 10-oz. package frozen chopped broccoli, cooked and drained
½ c. shredded Cheddar cheese

Blend beef and pork in a bowl. Add next 6 ingredients; mix to blend. Stir in apples. Shape into loaf on jelly roll pan. Bake in preheated 350-degree oven for 45 minutes. Drain off excess fat. Combine potatoes and broccoli; frost loaf with potato mixture. Sprinkle top with Cheddar cheese. Bake 15 minutes longer. Let stand about 5 minutes before removing to warmed platter.

Photograph for this recipe on page 67.

SOUR CREAM DRESSING

1 tbsp. vinegar
1 tsp. sugar
½ tsp. dry mustard
½ tsp. salt
1 c. sour cream
2 tbsp. toasted sesame seed

Blend first 4 ingredients together in a bowl. Stir in sour cream and sesame seed. Cover; chill.

Photograph for this recipe on page 67.

POT ROAST WITH FRESH WINTER VEGETABLES

¼ c. flour
1 clove of garlic, finely minced
2 tbsp. chopped fresh parsley
1½ tsp. salt
½ tsp. celery salt
¼ tsp. paprika
⅛ tsp. pepper
1 6 to 8-lb. chuck roast, rolled and tied
2 tbsp. vegetable oil
6 c. sliced onions
4 med. carrots, cut in 2-inch pieces
4 white turnips, peeled and cubed
3 med. potatoes, peeled and cubed
2 ribs celery, cut in 1-in. pieces

Combine first 7 ingredients in shallow plate. Roll meat in flour mixture until evenly coated. Heat oil in Dutch oven or heavy kettle. Brown meat well on all sides. Remove meat; arrange onions on bottom of Dutch oven. Return meat to Dutch oven. Add 1 cup water; cover. Simmer 3 hours. Add carrots, turnips, potatoes and celery; cover. Simmer 30 minutes longer or until meat and vegetables are tender. Place meat and vegetables on heated platter; sprinkle with parsley, if desired. Yield: 6-8 servings.

Photograph for this recipe on page 68.

FRESH FRUIT BETTY

1⅓ c. graham cracker crumbs
¼ c. butter or margarine, melted
¼ c. sugar
1 tsp. grated fresh lemon rind
½ tsp. ground cinnamon
¼ tsp. ground nutmeg
1 lg. apple, peeled and cored
1 lg. pear, peeled and cored
1 banana, sliced
⅔ c. coarsely chopped nuts
1¼ c. fresh orange juice
2 tbsp. fresh lemon juice

Combine first 6 ingredients in medium bowl. Slice and combine apples, pears, bananas and nuts. Turn half this mixture into buttered 1½-quart casserole. Sprinkle with half the crumb mixture. Repeat. Combine orange and lemon juices; pour over casserole. Bake in 350-degree oven for 1 hour. Serve warm with cream or ice cream. Yield: 8 servings.

Photograph for this recipe on page 68.

SALTED RYE BRAIDS

5 c. unsifted white flour
2 c. unsifted rye flour
1 tbsp. salt
Caraway seed
2 pkg. dry yeast
1 tbsp. margarine, softened
Cornmeal
1 egg white, beaten
1 tsp. coarse salt

Combine flours. Mix thoroughly 3 cups flour mixture, salt, 1 tablespoon caraway seed and yeast in a large bowl. Add margarine. Add 2½ cups very hot water to dry ingredients. Beat 2 minutes at medium speed of electric mixer, scraping bowl occasionally. Add ½ cup flour mixture or enough to make a thick batter. Beat at high speed 2 minutes, scraping bowl occasionally. Stir in enough additional flour mixture to make a soft dough. Turn out onto lightly floured board; knead 8 to 10 minutes or until smooth and elastic. Place in greased bowl, turning to grease top. Cover. Let rise in warm place, free from draft, for 45 minutes or until doubled in bulk. Punch dough down. Turn out onto lightly floured board. Divide dough in half; divide each half into 3 equal pieces. Roll each piece into a rope 18 inches long. Braid 3 ropes together. Seal ends; tuck underneath. Place on greased baking sheet which has been sprinkled with cornmeal. Repeat with remaining ropes. Cover. Let rise in warm place, free from draft, for 30 minutes or until doubled in bulk. Bake in a 450-degree oven for 20 minutes. Remove braids from oven. Combine egg white and 1 tablespoon cold water. Brush braids with egg white mixture. Sprinkle with caraway seed and coarse salt. Return braids to oven. Bake for 5 minutes longer. Remove from baking sheets. Cool on wire racks. Yield: 2 braids.

Photograph for this recipe on page 101.

OLD-FASHIONED WHOLE WHEAT LOAVES

4½ c. unsifted whole wheat flour
2¾ c. unsifted white flour
3 tbsp. sugar
4 tsp. salt
2 pkg. yeast
¾ c. milk
⅓ c. molasses
⅓ c. margarine

Combine flours. Mix thoroughly 2½ cups flour mixture, sugar, salt and yeast in a large bowl. Combine 1½ cups water, milk, molasses and margarine in a saucepan. Heat over low heat until liquids are warm. Margarine does not need to melt. Add gradually to dry ingredients. Beat for 2 minutes at medium speed of electric mixer, scraping sides of bowl occasionally. Add ½ cup flour mixture or enough to make a thick batter. Beat at high speed for 2 minutes, scraping bowl occasionally. Stir in enough additional flour mixture to make a soft dough. If necessary, add additional white flour to obtain desired dough. Turn out onto lightly floured board. Knead 8 to 10 minutes or until smooth and elastic. Place in greased bowl, turning to grease top. Cover. Let rise in warm place, free from draft, about 1 hour or until doubled in bulk. Punch dough down; turn out onto lightly floured board. Divide into 4 equal pieces. Form each piece of dough into a round ball. Place on greased baking sheets. Cover. Let rise in warm place, free from draft, about 1 hour or until doubled in bulk. Bake in 400-degree oven for about 25 minutes or until done. Remove from baking sheets. Cool on wire racks. Yield: 4 small round loaves.

Photograph for this recipe on page 101.

SEEDED WHITE BREAD

3 tbsp. sugar
2 tsp. salt
1 pkg. dry yeast
5½ to 6½ c. unsifted flour
½ c. milk
3 tbsp. margarine
1 egg white, beaten
1 tbsp. poppy seed

Mix first 3 ingredients thoroughly in a large bowl with 2 cups flour. Combine 1½ cups water, milk and margarine in saucepan. Heat over low heat until liquids are warm. Margarine does not need to melt. Add to dry ingredients gradually. Beat 2 minutes at medium speed of electric mixer, scraping bowl occasionally. Add ¾ cup flour, or enough flour to make thick batter. Beat at high speed 2 minutes, scraping bowl occasionally. Stir in enough additional flour to make soft dough. Turn out onto lightly floured board. Knead for 8 to 10 minutes or until smooth and elastic. Place in greased bowl, turning to grease top. Cover; let rise in warm place, free from draft, about 1 hour or until doubled in bulk. Punch dough down. Turn out onto lightly floured board. Cover; let rest 15 minutes. Roll dough into 9 × 16-inch rectangle. Roll up dough; starting from 16-inch side as for jelly roll. Pinch seam to seal. Place dough into greased 10-inch tube pan, sealed edge down. Seal ends together firmly.

Press dough down to fully cover bottom of pan. Cover; let rise in warm place, free from draft, about 1 hour or until doubled in bulk. Brush ring lightly with egg white. Sprinkle with poppy seed. Bake in 400-degree oven for about 40 minutes or until done. Remove from pan. Cool on wire rack.

Photograph for this recipe on page 101.

BANANA MUFFIN SURPRISE

½ c. uncooked oats, quick or regular
½ c. milk
1 c. unsifted all-purpose flour
¼ c. sugar
2½ tsp. baking powder
½ tsp. soda
½ tsp. salt
½ tsp. cinnamon
¼ tsp. nutmeg
¼ c. butter or margarine, melted
1 egg
1 c. mashed ripe bananas
½ c. sunflower seed

Combine oats and milk in medium bowl. Set aside until milk is absorbed. Mix next 7 ingredients in medium bowl. Add butter, egg and bananas to oat mixture. Add to dry ingredients. Stir just until moistened. Stir in sunflower seed. Fill greased 2½-inch muffin cups ⅔ full. Bake in 425-degree oven for 15 minutes or until muffins test done. Yield: 12-14 muffins.

Photograph for this recipe on page 102.

YANKEE BANANA BREAD

2 c. unsifted whole wheat flour
1 c. yellow cornmeal
¾ tsp. salt
1 tsp. soda
1 c. mashed ripe bananas
1 c. buttermilk
¾ c. molasses
¾ c. snipped pitted dates

Mix flour, cornmeal, salt and soda in large bowl. Stir in remaining ingredients. Turn into 3 greased and floured 1-pound cans. Bake in 350-degree oven for 45 minutes or until cake tests done. Cool for 10 minutes. Turn out of cans. Serve warm with butter. Loaves may be frozen. Wrap in foil. Yield: 3 loaves.

Photograph for this recipe on page 102.

APRICOT-BANANA TEA BREAD

⅔ c. shortening
1 c. sugar
2 eggs
1½ c. mashed ripe bananas
1 tbsp. lemon juice
1¾ c. unsifted all-purpose flour
1 tsp. soda
1 tsp. salt
½ c. chopped dried apricots
1 tbsp. flour
Confectioners' sugar

Cream shortening and sugar in a large bowl. Add eggs one at a time, beating well after each addition. Blend in bananas and lemon juice. Mix together flour, soda and salt. Blend into banana mixture; stir in apricots mixed with 1 tablespoon flour. Turn into greased and floured 9 × 5 × 3-inch loaf pan. Bake at 325 degrees for 1 hour and 10 to 20 minutes, or until bread tests done. Remove from pan; cool. Sift confectioners' sugar over top, if desired, before serving. Yield: 1 loaf.

Photograph for this recipe on page 102.

HONEY TWIST

1 recipe Basic Sweet Dough
Melted butter
¼ c. butter, softened
2 tbsp. honey
1 egg white
1 c. confectioners' sugar

Divide dough in half. Roll each half into a long rope 1-inch in diameter. Coil into 8-inch buttered cake pans beginning at outer edge, covering bottom. Press down to level. Brush with butter. Allow to stand in warm place until doubled in bulk. Bake in a preheated 350-degree oven for 30 to 35 minutes. Remove from pans onto wire rack to cool. Cream butter in small mixer bowl. Add honey gradually. Beat in egg white and sugar. Spread on warm coffeecakes.

BASIC SWEET DOUGH

2 pkg. dry yeast
4 c. all-purpose flour
½ c. sugar
1 tsp. salt
¾ c. butter
½ c. scalded milk, cooled

2 eggs, slightly beaten
Butter, melted

Sprinkle yeast over ½ cup warm water to dissolve. Combine flour, sugar and salt in large mixer bowl. Cut in butter on low speed of mixer until it resembles coarse meal. Combine milk, eggs and dissolved yeast. Add to dry ingredients, mixing thoroughly. Brush with melted butter. Cover; chill overnight.

Photograph for this recipe on page 135.

PECAN ROLLS

¼ c. butter
1 c. (firmly packed) light brown sugar
¼ c. light corn syrup
Pecan halves
1 recipe Basic Sweet Dough
Butter, melted
1 tsp. cinnamon

Combine butter, ½ cup sugar and corn syrup in a small saucepan. Bring to a boil. Place about 1½ teaspoons sugar mixture in each muffin cup of three 12-cup buttered muffin pans. Add 2 or 3 pecan halves. Divide dough in half. Roll each half to measure 12 × 18-inches on lightly floured surface. Brush with butter. Combine ½ cup sugar and cinnamon. Sprinkle ¼ cup over each. Roll from large side. Cut into 1-inch slices. Place, cut side up, in muffin cups. Brush with melted butter. Allow to stand in warm place until doubled in bulk. Bake in preheated 375-degree oven for 15 to 20 minutes. Invert immediately onto wire rack to cool. Yield: 36 rolls.

Photograph for this recipe on page 135.

APPLE KUCHEN

1 recipe Basic Sweet Dough
4 apples, peeled and sliced
½ c. sugar
½ tsp. cinnamon
¼ c. butter, melted

Divide dough in half. Press evenly into two 8-inch buttered square pans. Press apple slices into dough, rounded edges up. Combine sugar and cinnamon; sprinkle over apples. Drizzle 2 tablespoons butter over top of each. Allow to stand in warm place until doubled in bulk. Bake in preheated 350-degree oven for 40 to 50 minutes or until apples are tender and the top well-browned. Remove from pan onto wire rack to cool.

Photograph for this recipe on page 135.

ORANGE-SWEET POTATO CAKE

    ¾ c. margarine or butter
    2 c. (firmly packed) light brown sugar
    4 eggs
    ½ c. Florida frozen concentrated orange juice,
      thawed
    ½ tsp. vanilla extract
    2½ c. unsifted all-purpose flour
    1 tsp. soda
    1 tsp. baking powder
    1 tsp. salt
    1 tsp. ground cinnamon
    1 tsp. ground nutmeg
    1 c. mashed sweet potatoes
    1 c. chopped walnuts

Cream margarine with brown sugar in large bowl until light and fluffy. Beat in eggs one at a time, beating well after each addition. Stir in undiluted orange juice and vanilla. Stir together next 6 ingredients in medium bowl. Beat into creamed mixture alternately with mashed sweet potatoes; blend thoroughly. Stir in chopped walnuts. Turn batter into 10 × 4 inch tube cake pan. Bake at 300 degrees for 1 hour to 1 hour 10 minutes or until cake tests done. Cool on wire rack for 30 minutes; remove cake from pan. Cool completely.

Orange Glaze

    2 tbsp. margarine or butter
    ¼ c. Florida frozen concentrated orange juice,
      thawed
    ½ c. confectioners' sugar

Melt margarine in medium saucepan. Beat in undiluted orange juice and confectioners' sugar. Beat until sugar dissolves. Remove from heat, cool. Spoon over cake. Garnish with walnuts, if desired. Yield: 12-16 servings.

Photograph for this recipe on page 136.

HOLIDAY CITRUS COMPOTE

    2¼ c. Florida orange juice
    1 11-oz. package mixed dried fruit
    1½ c. Florida grapefruit sections
    1½ c. Florida orange sections

Combine orange juice and dried fruit in medium saucepan. Simmer for 20 minutes; remove from heat. Add grapefruit sections and orange sections. Serve hot or cold. Yield: 4 servings.

Photograph for this recipe on page 136.

FRESH PEACH SOUFFLE

    6 c. sliced fresh peaches
    2 env. unflavored gelatin
    ¾ c. sugar
    4 eggs, separated
    1⅓ c. milk
    1 c. heavy cream, whipped

Pare and slice peaches. Puree 3 cups peach slices in 5-cup blender container. Mix unflavored gelatin with ½ cup sugar in medium saucepan. Beat egg yolks with milk; blend into gelatin mixture. Stir over low heat until gelatin is completely dissolved. Turn gelatin mixture into large bowl. Stir in pureed peaches. Chill, stirring occasionally, until mixture mounds slightly when dropped from spoon. Beat egg whites in medium bowl until soft peaks form. Add remaining ¼ cup sugar gradually. Beat until stiff. Fold in gelatin mixture and whipped cream. Chop remaining fruit slices; fold in. Make collar for 1½-quart souffle dish. Fold aluminum foil strip, long enough to go around souffle dish with generous overlap, into 4 thicknesses, to make strip 3 inches wide. Wrap around outside of souffle dish so that strip extends 2 inches above rim of dish; attach securely with tape. Pour peach mixture into souffle dish. Chill until firm. Yield: 10-12 servings.

Photograph for this recipe on page 169.

FRESH PLUM SAUCE

    3 c. plums, sliced
    ⅓ c. sugar
    1 tbsp. cornstarch
    ⅛ tsp. salt

Combine plums, sugar and ¼ cup water in medium saucepan. Cover. Bring to a boil; reduce heat. Simmer 5 minutes. Press mixture through a sieve with back of spoon, or process with a food mill. Return sauce to pan. Mix cornstarch and ¼ cup water; stir into plum mixture. Add salt. Bring to a boil, stirring constantly. Cook 2 minutes. Chill. Serve with Fresh Peach Soufflé. Yield: 2 cups sauce.

Photograph for this recipe on page 169.

BLUEBERRY-PEACH SHORTCAKE

2 c. sifted all-purpose flour
3 tsp. baking powder
½ tsp. salt
⅓ c. sugar
½ c. butter or margarine
⅓ c. milk
1 egg, slightly beaten
¼ tsp. grated fresh lemon rind
1 c. fresh blueberries

Sift flour, baking powder, salt and sugar into large bowl. Cut in butter with pastry blender or 2 knives until resembles coarse meal. Add milk, egg and lemon rind. Mix lightly but thoroughly with fork. Stir in blueberries. Form into 2 balls; press gently into 2 greased 8-inch layer cake pans. Bake at 450 degrees for 12 to 15 minutes or until golden brown. Turn cake out of pans. Cool for 5 to 10 minutes.

Fruit and Cream

6 c. sliced fresh peaches
1 c. sugar
1 c. fresh blueberries
1 c. heavy cream
1 tsp. vanilla extract

Peel and slice peaches into large bowl. Sprinkle with sugar; add blueberries. Let stand at room temperature. Whip cream with vanilla until soft peaks form; chill. Place bottom cake layer on plate. Spread with ⅓ of the whipped cream; top with ⅔ of the peaches and blueberries. Pour syrup from sugared fruit on top; top with ⅓ of the whipped cream. Add top layer of shortcake; spread with remaining whipped cream. Top with remaining peaches and blueberries. Yield: 8 servings.

Photograph for this recipe on page 170.

STRAWBERRY DESSERT TART

1 recipe for 2-crust pastry
⅓ c. minced blanched almonds
1¾ c. milk
3 egg yolks
Sugar
½ cup unsifted all-purpose flour
Dash of salt
2 tbsp. Kirsch or orange juice
1 tbsp. butter or margarine
½ c. red currant or apple jelly
2 pt. California strawberries

Add almonds to pie pastry. Roll out pastry on lightly floured surface into 15-inch circle. Place pastry in 14-inch pizza pan; flute edge. Prick bottom and sides of pastry with fork. Bake in 425-degree oven for 10 to 12 minutes or until crust is golden brown. Cool. Heat milk in medium saucepan until tiny bubbles form around edge. Beat egg yolks in small mixer bowl. Add ½ cup sugar, flour and salt. Beat until well mixed. Add milk to egg yolk mixture in slow continuous stream, scraping sides of bowl occasionally. Mix at medium speed. Pour egg yolk mixture into heavy saucepan. Cook over low heat, stirring constantly, until mixture is thick and begins to boil. Boil 2 to 3 minutes, stirring constantly. Remove from heat. Stir in Kirsch and butter until butter is melted. Place waxed paper or plastic wrap directly on custard to prevent skin from forming on top. Chill for 2 hours. Heat jelly in small saucepan over medium-low heat. Add 1 tablespoon sugar. Bring to a boil. Boil 1 minute, stirring constantly. Brush thin layer of jelly mixture on cooled crust. Let stand 5 minutes. Spread chilled custard mixture on glazed crust. Place 1 whole strawberry in center of custard. Halve remaining berries; arrange on custard mixture. Brush strawberries with remaining glaze. Return glaze to heat to melt if glaze becomes too stiff. Chill tart until serving time. Cut tart into wedges. Yield: 12 servings.

Photograph for this recipe on page 203.

CALIFORNIA-STYLE CHICKEN SCALLOPINE

1 17-oz. can apricot halves
2 whole chicken breasts, boned, skinned and flattened
Salt and pepper to taste
¼ c. flour
2 tbsp. butter or margarine
½ c. sliced celery
1 sm. onion, sliced
1 tbsp. soy sauce
¼ tsp. ground ginger

Drain apricots, reserving ½ cup syrup. Sprinkle chicken with salt and pepper; dust with flour. Brown chicken in butter in large skillet on both sides. Place in shallow baking dish. Saute celery and onion in pan drippings until tender but crisp. Place apricots and vegetables in dish with chicken. Combine reserved syrup, soy sauce and ginger in skillet. Bring to boiling point. Pour over chicken and vegetables. Bake in 350-degree oven for 20 minutes. Yield: 4 servings.

Photograph for this recipe on page 204.

PEACHY BLUEBERRY BARS

½ c. soft butter or margarine
¼ c. shortening
1 c. (firmly packed) brown sugar
1 tsp. grated fresh lemon rind
2 c. sifted all-purpose flour
1½ c. uncooked oats
1 tsp. salt
½ tsp. soda

Cream first 4 ingredients together in large mixer bowl. Blend in remaining ingredients. Pat half the dough in bottom of greased 9 × 13 × 2-inch baking pan. Crumble remaining dough; reserve.

Fruit Filling

3 c. sliced fresh peaches, peeled
1 c. fresh blueberries
2 tbsp. flour
¼ c. sugar
2 tsp. fresh lemon juice

Combine peaches and blueberries in medium bowl. Toss with flour, sugar and lemon juice. Spoon on top of dough in pan. Sprinkle with remaining dough. Bake in 400-degree oven for 25 to 30 minutes or until golden brown. Cool. Cut into squares to serve. Yield: 24 bars.

Photograph for this recipe on page 237.

HEARTY POTATO SALAD

6 med. potatoes
1¾ tsp. salt
2 tbsp. salad oil
2 tbsp. fresh lemon juice
½ c. chopped fresh onion
¼ tsp. dried dillweed
⅛ tsp. liquid pepper sauce
1 2½-oz. jar dried beef, shredded
2 c. diagonally sliced celery
½ c. sour cream
2 tbsp. milk

Place potatoes in large saucepan; sprinkle with 1 teaspoon salt. Cover with water. Place over high heat; bring to a boil. Reduce heat. Simmer 20 minutes or until potatoes are tender. Drain; cool 10 minutes. Peel potatoes; cut into slices. Place in large bowl. Toss gently with next 6 ingredients and ¾ teaspoon salt. Cover. Chill. Combine remaining ingredients; mix well. Pour over salad; cover. Chill several hours. Yield: 4 servings.

Photograph for this recipe on page 237.

BARBECUED POT ROAST

½ c. butter
¼ c. chopped onion
3 tbsp. hickory-flavored catsup
1 tbsp. Worcestershire sauce
1 tbsp. vinegar
1 tsp. prepared mustard
1 tsp. salt
2 2 to 2½-lb. round bone pot roasts, 2-inches thick
Salt
Pepper
Carrot sticks
Green pepper strips
Tomato wedges

Combine first 7 ingredients in small saucepan. Stir over low heat until butter is melted; set aside. Trim excess fat from pot roasts. Brown meat about 5 minutes per side over hot coals. Season each side with salt and pepper after brown. Tear off two 5-foot lengths of aluminum foil. Fold each length double. Center 1 roast on each foil strip. Cover with vegetables. Sprinkle with salt and pepper. Pour ½ cup sauce over each pot roast. Bring up sides of foil. Fold down onto meat in tight double folds. Fold ends over and over up close to meat. Place over slow coals for 1 hour and 30 minutes to 2 hours or until tender. Yield: 8 servings.

Photograph for this recipe on page 238.

BLUE CHEESE SLAW

6 c. red and white shredded cabbage
2 tbsp. chopped green onion
1 c. crumbled blue cheese
½ c. sour cream
2 tbsp. light cream or half and half
1 tbsp. lemon juice
½ tsp. sugar
Dash of salt

Combine cabbage and onion in a large bowl. Chill thoroughly. Combine remaining ingredients in small mixer bowl. Beat well. Add dressing to cabbage just before serving. Toss lightly. Yield: 8 servings.

Photograph for this recipe on page 238.

JAM OF FOUR BERRIES

1 qt strawberries
1 qt. raspberries
1 qt. red currants
1 qt. morello cherries
6½ c. sugar

Rinse strawberries carefully; drain. Remove stems. Pick over raspberries; do not rinse. Rinse currants; remove stems. Rinse cherries; remove stones. Place cherries in large saucepan. Cook over low heat for about 10 minutes. Add strawberries, currants and raspberries. Bring to a simmer. Simmer for 5 minutes. Shake pan occasionally, but do not stir with spoon. Add sugar. Simmer for about 30 minutes or until syrup is thick. Pour jam into hot sterilized jars. Seal. Process in boiling water bath for 10 minutes.

Photograph for this recipe on page 271.

BAYERISHCHES SAUERKRAUT MIT WARMER KARTOFFELSALAT (BAVARIAN SAUKERKRAUT WITH HOT POTATO SALAD)

½ lb. sliced bacon, diced
1 lb. frankfurters, cut in halves lengthwise
½ c. chopped onion
1 c. grated carrots
1 c. diced celery
½ c. dry white wine
1¼ tsp. salt
⅛ tsp. pepper

3¼ c. drained sauerkraut
Hot Potato Salad

Fry bacon until crisp. Remove with slotted spoon to paper towels. Reserve for use in Hot Potato Salad. Reserve 3 tablespoons of bacon drippings in skillet. Set remainder aside for Hot Potato Salad. Fry frankfurters in drippings until browned. Remove; set aside. Add onion, carrots and celery to skillet. Saute until vegetables are crisp-tender. Add next 5 ingredients to skillet. Toss ingredients until combined. Cook kraut mixture until hot. Serve with Hot Potato Salad.

Hot Potato Salad

3 lb. peeled potatoes, cut into ¼-inch slices
½ c. onion
1 beef bouillon cube
⅓ c. cider vinegar
2 tsp. sugar
2 tbsp. chopped parsley
Salt and pepper to taste

Cook potatoes in boiling salted water in saucepan just until tender. Drain. Saute onion until tender in reserved bacon drippings. Dissolve bouillon cube in ⅓ cup boiling water. Add to onion in skillet. Add vinegar and sugar. Stir until mixture comes to a boil. Toss with potato slices, parsley and reserved bacon. Season to taste with salt and pepper. Yield: 6 servings.

Photograph for this recipe on page 272.

CAN SIZE CHART

8 oz. can or jar . . . . .1 c.
10 1/2 oz. can (picnic can) . . . . .1 1/4 c.
12 oz. can (vacuum) . . . . .1 1/2 c.
14-16 oz. or No. 300 can . . . . .1 1/4 c.
16-17 oz. can or jar
   or No. 303 can or jar . . . . .2 c.
1 lb. 4 oz. or 1 pt. 2 fl. oz.
   or No. 2 can or jar . . . . .2 1/2 c.

1 lb. 13 oz. can or jar
   or No. 2 1/2 can or jar . . . . .3 1/2 c.
1 qt. 14 fl. oz. or 3 lb. 3 oz.
   or 46 oz. can . . . . .5 3/4 c.
6 1/2 to 7 1/2 lb.
   or No. 10 can . . . . .12-13 c.

EQUIVALENT CHART

3 tsp. . . . . 1 tbsp.
2 tbsp. . . . . 1/8 c.
4 tbsp. . . . . 1/4 c.
8 tbsp. . . . . 1/2 c.
16 tbsp. . . . . .1 c.
5 tbsp. + 1 tsp. . . . . 1/3 c.
12 tbsp. . . . . .3/4 c.
4 oz. . . . . 1/2 c.
8 oz. . . . . .1 c.
16 oz. . . . . .1 lb.
1 oz. . . . . 2 tbsp. fat or liquid
2 c. . . . . .1 pt.

2 pt. . . . . .1 qt.
1 qt. . . . . .4 c.
5/8 c. . . . . .1/2 c. + 2 tbsp.
7/8 c. . . . . .3/4 c. + 2 tbsp.
1 jigger . . . . .1 1/2 fl. oz.(3 tbsp.)
2 c. fat . . . . .1 lb.
1 lb. butter . . . . 2 c. or 4 sticks
2 c. sugar .1 lb.
2 2/3 c. powdered sugar . . . . .1 lb.
2 2/3 c. brown sugar . . . . .1 lb.
4 c. sifted flour . . . . .1 lb.
4 1/2 c. cake flour . . . . .1 lb.

3 1/2 c. unsifted whole wheat flour .1 lb.
8 to 10 egg whites . . . . .1 c.
12 to 14 egg yolks . . . . .1 c.
1 c. unwhipped cream .2 c. whipped
1 lb. shredded American cheese .4 c.
1/4 lb. crumbled blue cheese . . . . .1 c.
1 chopped med. onion . . . . .1/2 c. pieces
1 lemon . . . . 3 tbsp. juice
1 lemon . . . . 1 tsp. grated peel
1 orange . . . . .1/3 c. juice
I orange . . . . about 2 tsp. grated peel
1 lb. unshelled walnuts . . . . .1 1/2 to 1 3/4 c. shelled
1 lb. unshelled almonds . . . . .3/4 to 1 c. shelled
4 oz. (1 to 1 1/4 c.) uncooked macaroni . . . . 2 1/4 c. cooked
7 oz. spaghetti . . . . .4 c. cooked
4 oz. (1 1/2 to 2 c.) uncooked noodles . . . . .2 c. cooked
28 saltine crackers . . . . .1 c. crumbs
4 slices bread . . . . .1 c. crumbs
14 square graham crackers . . . . .1 c. crumbs
22 vanilla wafers . . . . .1 c. crumbs

SUBSTITUTIONS FOR A MISSING INGREDIENT

1 square *chocolate* (1 ounce) = 3 or 4 tablespoons cocoa plus 1/2 tablespoon fat.
1 tablespoon *cornstarch* (for thickening) = 2 tablespoons flour.
1 cup sifted *all-purpose flour* = 1 cup plus 2 tablespoons sifted cake flour.
1 cup sifted *cake flour* = 1 cup minus 2 tablespoons sifted all-purpose flour.
1 teaspoon *baking powder* = 1/4 teaspoon baking soda plus 1/2 teaspoon cream of tartar.
1 cup *sour milk* — 1 cup sweet milk into which 1 tablespoon vinegar or lemon juice has been stirred; or
     1 cup buttermilk (let stand for 5 minutes).

SUBSTITUTIONS FOR A MISSING INGREDIENT

1 cup *sweet milk* = 1 cup sour milk or buttermilk plus 1/2 teaspoon baking soda.

1 cup *canned tomatoes* = about 1 1/3 cups cut-up fresh tomatoes, simmered 10 minutes.

3/4 cup *cracker crumbs* = 1 cup bread crumbs.

1 cup *cream, sour, heavy* = 1/3 cup butter and 2/3 cups milk in any sour milk recipe.

1 cup *cream, sour, thin* = 3 tablespoons butter and 3/4 cup milk in sour milk recipe.

1 cup *molasses* = 1 cup honey.

1 teaspoon *dried herbs* = 1 tablespoon fresh herbs.

1 *whole egg* = 2 egg yolks for custards.

1/2 cup *evaporated milk* and 1/2 cup *water* or 1 cup *reconstituted nonfat dry milk* and 1 tablespoon *butter* = 1 cup whole milk.

1 package *active dry yeast* = 1 cake compressed yeast.

1 tablespoon *instant minced onion, rehydrated* = 1 small fresh onion.

1 tablespoon *prepared mustard* = 1 teaspoon dry mustard.

1/8 teaspoon *garlic powder* = 1 small pressed clove of garlic

METRIC CONVERSION CHARTS FOR THE KITCHEN

VOLUME

1 tsp.	4.9 cc	2 c.	473.4 cc
1 tbsp.	14.7 cc	1 fl. oz.	29.5 cc
1/3 c.	28.9 cc	4 oz.	118.3 cc
1/8 c.	29.5 cc	8 oz.	236.7 cc
1/4 c.	59.1 cc	1 pt.	473.4 cc
1/2 c.	118.3 cc	1 qt.	.946 liters
3/4 c.	177.5 cc	1 gal.	3.7 liters
1 c.	236.7 cc		

CONVERSION FACTORS:

Liters	X	1.056	=	Liquid Quarts
Quarts	X	0.946	=	Liters
Liters	X	0.264	=	Gallons
Gallons	X	3.785	=	Liters
Fluid Ounces	X	29.563	=	Cubic Centimeters
Cubic Centimeters	X	0.034	=	Fluid Ounces
Cups	X	236.575	=	Cubic Centimeters
Tablespoons	X	14.797	=	Cubic Centimeters
Teaspoons	X	4.932	=	Cubic Centimeters
Bushels	X	0.352	=	Hectoliters
Hectoliters	X	2.837	=	Bushels
Ounces (Avoir.)	X	28.349	=	Grams
Grams	X	0.035	=	Ounces
Pounds	X	0.454	=	Kilograms
Kilograms	X	2.205	=	Pounds

WEIGHT

1 dry oz. ....28.3 Grams

1 lb. ....454 Kilograms

LIQUID MEASURE AND METRIC EQUIVALENT

(NEAREST CONVENIENT EQUIVALENTS)

CUPS SPOONS	QUARTS OUNCES	METRIC EQUIVALENTS
1 teaspoon	1/6 ounce	.5 milliliters / 5 grams
2 teaspoons	1/3 ounce	10 milliliters / 10 grams
1 tablespoon	1/2 ounce	15 milliliters / 15 grams
3 1/3 tablespoons	1 3/4 ounces	.50 milliliters
1/4 cup (4 tablespoons)	2 ounces	.60 milliliters
1/3 cup (5 1/3 tablespoons)	2 2/3 ounces	.79 milliliters
1/3 cup plus 1 tablespoon	3 1/2 ounces	100 milliliters
1/2 cup (8 tablespoons)	4 ounces	118 milliliters
1 cup (16 tablespoons)	8 ounces	1/4 liter / 236 milliliters
2 cups	1 pint / 16 ounces	1/2 liter less 1 1/2 tablespoons / 473 milliliters
2 cups plus 2 1/2 tablespoons	17 ounces	1/2 liter
4 cups	1 quart / 32 ounces	.946 milliliters
4 1/3 cups	1 quart, 2 ounces	1 liter / 1000 milliliters

CONVERSION FORMULAS:

To convert Centigrade to Fahrenheit: multiply by 9, divide by 5, add 32.

To convert Fahrenheit to Centigrade: subtract 32, multiply by 5, divide by 9.

DRY MEASURE AND METRIC EQUIVALENT

(MOST CONVENIENT APPROXIMATION)

POUNDS AND OUNCES	METRIC	POUNDS AND OUNCES	METRIC
1/6 ounce	.5 grams	1/4 pound (4 ounces)	114 grams
1/3 ounce	10 grams	4 1/8 ounces	125 grams
1/2 ounce	15 grams	1/2 pound (8 ounces)	227 grams
1 ounce	30 grams (28.35)	3/4 pound (12 ounces)	250 grams
		1 pound (16 ounces)	454 grams
1 3/4 ounces	50 grams	1.1 pounds	500 grams
2 2/3 ounces	75 grams	2.2 pounds	1 kilogram / 1000 grams
3 1/2 ounces	100 grams		

Index

PHOTOGRAPHY CREDITS: Cover, Art, and Book Design—Rose Teasley; United Fresh Fruit and Vegetable Association; Tuna Research Foundation; California Apricot Advisory Board; National Kraut Packers Association; American Dairy Association; Florida Department of Citrus; The Banana Bunch; Fleischmann's Margarine; California Avocado Advisory; United Dairy Industry Association; Rice Council; Best Foods, Division of Corn Products, Inc.; Pineapple Growers Association; National Macaroni Institute; Louisiana Yam Commission; Chiffon Margarine; Planter's Cocktail Peanuts; The Quaker Oats Company; Evaporated Milk Association; Ruth Lundren, Ltd.; Diamond Walnut Kitchen; California Strawberry Advisory Board; C and H Sugar Company; California Raisin Advisory Board; National Pecan Shellers and Processors Association; Pickle Packers International; R. C. Bigelow's Teas; Processed Apple Institute, Inc.; Ball Corporation; Peter Pan Peanut Butter; Florida Citrus Commission; Granny Smith Apple.

NOTES

For Your Convenience . . .
Additional copies of NATIONAL GRANGE FAMILY COOKBOOK FROM COUNTRY
KITCHENS may be ordered, for $6.00 each copy, from: National Grange Cookbook
1616 H Street N. W.
Washington, D. C. 20006

NOTES

NOTES